LONGMAN LINGUISTICS LIBRARY
Title no 26

INTRODUCTION TO TEXT LINGUISTICS

LONGMAN LINGUISTICS LIBRARY

General editors
R. H. Robins, University of London
Martin Harris, University of Salford

TITLE NO

2 **General Linguistics**
An introductory Survey
Third Edition
R. H. ROBINS

6 **A Short History of Linguistics**
Second Edition
R. H. ROBINS

13 **Structural Aspects of Language Change**
JAMES M. ANDERSON

18 **The English Verb**
F. R. PALMER

21 **Text and Context**
Explorations in Semantics and Pragmatics of Discourse
TEUN A. VAN DIJK

22 **The Evolution of French Syntax**
A Comparative Approach
MARTIN HARRIS

23 **Modality and the English Modals**
F. R. PALMER

24 **Grimm's Grandchildren**
Current Topics in German Linguistics
THOMAS HERBST,
DAVID HEATH
HANS-MARTIN DEDERDING

25 **Explanation in Linguistics**
The logical problem of language acquisition
EDITED BY NORBERT HORNSTEIN AND DAVID LIGHTFOOT

26 **Introduction to Text Linguistics**
ROBERT-ALAIN DE BEAUGRANDE AND WOLFGANG ULRICH DRESSLER

27 **Spoken Discourse**
A model for analysis
WILLIS EDMONDSON

28 **Psycholinguistics**
Language, mind, and world
DANNY D. STEINBERG

29 **Dialectology**
W. N. FRANCIS

30 **Principles of Pragmatics**
G. N. LEECH

Introduction to Text Linguistics

Robert-Alain de Beaugrande

University of Florida

Wolfgang Ulrich Dressler

University of Vienna

LONGMAN
London and New York

Longman Group Limited
*Longman House, Burnt Mill, Harlow,
Essex CM20 2JE, England.
Associated companies throughout the world.*

Published in the United States of America by Longman Inc., New York

First published 1981
Second impression 1983
Third impression 1986
ISBN 0 582 55486 1 Cased
ISBN 0 582 55485 3 Paper

Beaugrande, Robert-Alain de
Introduction to text linguistics - (Longman linguistics library; no. 26).
1. Discourse analysis
I. Title II. Dressler, Wolfgang Ulrich
410 P302 80-40581
ISBN 0-582-55486-1
ISBN 0-582-55485-3 Pbk

ISBN 0-582-55485-3

Produced by Longman Singapore Publishers Pte Ltd
Printed in Singapore

Contents

Demonstration texts

Acknowledgements

This book is the outcome of an attempt to introduce the general public to a newly emerging science of text and discourse. Its basic outlines were laid in Robert-Alain de Beaugrande's *Text, Discourse, and Process* (Norwood, New Jersey: Ablex; London: Longman, 1980), a more exhaustive and specialized presentation. We have undertaken to synthesize traditional beyond-the-sentence linguistics with a wide range of interdisciplinary research on the production, reception, and utilization of texts in human interaction. Our personal consultations with many of the researchers whose work we cite frequently were of the greatest value and assistance.

Brad Schultz and Zofia Solczak-Roberts read the manuscript. Peggy Drinkwater patiently negotiated the conditions for creating the book. To all of these, and to all of those whose ideas have left their imprint here, our heartfelt thanks.

RdB WUD

The publishers are grateful to the following for permission to reproduce copyright material:
Jonathan Cape Ltd on behalf of the Executors of the Estate of C. Day Lewis, Hogarth Press and Harper and Row Publishers Inc for 'Come Live With Me and Be My Love' from *Two Songs* from *Collected Poems* 1954 by C. Day Lewis Copyright ©1967 by C. Day Lewis Reprinted by permission of Harper and Row Publishers Inc; the author's agent for the poem 'Ghosts' by

Elizabeth Jennings in *Poems 1976* published by Macmillan; Teachers College Press for an extract from *p 8 McCall-Crabbs Standard Test Lessons in Reading* Book C, New York Teachers College Press © 1926, 1950, 1961 by Teachers College, Columbia University.

O. Foreword

1. At the 1976 summer meeting of the *Societas linguistica Europaea,* we agreed to prepare an updated translation of Prof. Dressler's *Einführung in die Textlinguistik* (1972*a*) which has been well received. During the task of surveying and integrating new research since 1972, we came to realize that our plan was not realistic. In their quest for new theories and methods, recent trends have led to fundamentally changed conditions for a science of texts, rather than to a mere extension of old methods to a new object of inquiry. This evolution has been marked by interdisciplinary co-operation far more than traditional linguistics had been.

2. We accordingly developed a completely new plan and format for our introductory survey.[1] We stress here at the outset that we have by no means been exhaustive or definitive in our treatment of the issues. We were often dealing with newly emerging questions whose resolution will demand many years of concerted research. Still, we thought it would be useful to mention such questions and to suggest some reasonable answers. We will be quite content if our book proves serviceable as a guide in a period of rapid transition and change.

3. Any transitional study of multi-disciplinary issues is bound to evoke controversy. Some partisans may deny the value of text linguistics altogether and insist that sentence linguistics is the proper domain of investigation.[2] Others may wish to admit texts without altering the established methods.[3]

Even those who will accept profound alterations may disagree about the best new directions to pursue.[4] In our view, the nature of texts as communicative occurrences should decide what methods are used, irrespective of personal or institutional commitments made in the past. In practice, our approach is intended more to complement traditional ones than to compete with them. We often address issues which older approaches made no claims to encompass.

4. Thomas Kuhn (1970) has contributed enormously to public awareness of the extent to which activities in "normal science" are controlled by conventions among the scientists rather than the manifest nature of the objects of inquiry. That predicament is egregiously acute in linguistics, where the object is so diversified and flexible. Hardly an aspect of human thought, action, and interaction is not permeated to some degree by language. We cannot escape being reductive in our theories and models. Yet we must bear in mind that reductions are temporary, undesirable conditions to be removed as soon as it is feasible. We may even find that an integrated, comprehensive approach actually leads to a simpler account of language overall than a fragmented, restricted one: preoccupation with exactness of detail in isolated domains can block our vision for sweeping correlations across the whole spectrum (cf.X.29).

5. A young science like linguistics would understandably seek to align itself with older sciences like physics, mathematics, and formal logic. But communication, like any human activity, has its own special physical, mathematic, and logical properties that must not be overlooked. An unduly rigid application of notions from the "exact" sciences could dehumanize the object to the point where the inquiry becomes irrelevant. A formalism is a representation, not an explanation, and a means, not an end. The analysis of formal structures might well fail to uncover the nature and function of an entity in its wider context.

6. The terms and notions of linguistics often attest to ambitions of scientific, logical, and mathematical rigor. Yet their uncritical acceptance on those grounds alone could be dangerous. A science of texts demands its own terms and notions because of the nature of its object. *Probabilistic* models are more adequate and realistic than *deterministic* ones.

Dynamic accounts of *structure-building operations* will be more productive than static descriptions of the structures themselves. We should work to discover *regularities, strategies, motivations, preferences,* and *defaults* rather than *rules* and *laws*. *Dominances* can offer more realistic classifications than can *strict categories*. *Acceptability* and *appropriateness* are more crucial standards for texts than *grammaticality* and *well-formedness*. *Human reasoning processes* are more essential to using and conveying knowledge in texts than are *logical proofs*. It is the task of science to systemize the *fuzziness* of its objects of inquiry, not to ignore it or argue it away.[5]

7. As remarked by Thomas Kuhn (1970: 136–43), textbooks generally create the impression that all discovery and research in a science has been leading up to the constellation of theories and issues we consider important today. Any other mode of presentation would confuse the learner with a disunified array of quarrels, many of which are not relevant in our modern perspective. In the present book, we devote some space to comparing the "paradigm" of text linguistics with older paradigms; yet we too are compelled to maintain a reasonable degree of unity and consistency, even where the community of text linguists is still engaged in lively debate. We try to point out some major areas of dissension, but we will inevitably have overlooked or attenuated some individual claims and viewpoints. Such shortcomings may, we hope, be excused in a textbook on a new domain caught up in rapid evolution.

ROBERT-ALAIN DE BEAUGRANDE
University of Florida

WOLFGANG ULRICH DRESSLER
University of Vienna

Notes

1 In our new division of labour, topics emerging since 1972 were mostly treated by Prof. Beaugrande; Prof. Dressler's contributions were largely in the areas he covered in the 1972 volume, especially cohesion.

2 e.g., Dascal & Margalit (1974).

3 e.g., Ballmer (1975).

4 For an impressive diversity of viewpoints, see papers in Petöfi (ed.) (1979), and surveys in Dressler (ed.) (1978).

5 The scientific status of text studies is explored in Beaugrande (1981*b*).

Orthographic conventions

Linguistic samples are enclosed in *single* quotes, with all punctuation excluded if not part of the sample; other quotations are in double quotes. Main terms are introduced in SMALL CAPITALS. We use **bold** type for terms where we wish to stress their usage according to our approach. We have striven to use our terms for other people's research wherever they were compatible, to save confusion. The paragraphs are numbered throughout for greatest ease in indexing and cross-referencing. We provide a table of demonstration texts according to salient content, in case a sample should be remembered and looked for. We have seen fit to use many well-known texts in order that their contexts can be widely accessible, for example, excerpts from famous dramas rather than recorded conversations in Chapter IX.

Chapter I

Basic notions

1. Here are six language samples that appear to be alike in some ways and different in others:[1]

[1] SLOW
CHILDREN
AT PLAY

[2] The King was in the counting house, counting all his money;
The Queen was in the parlour, eating bread and honey;
The Maid was in the garden, hanging out the clothes;
Along came a blackbird and pecked off her nose.

[3] Twenty-year-old Willie B. is a diehard TV addict. He hates news and talk shows, but he loves football and gets so excited over food commercials that he sometimes charges at the set, waving a fist. Says a friend: "He's like a little child."

Willie B. is a 450-lb gorilla at the Atlanta Zoo. In December a Tennessee TV dealer heard about Willie B.'s lonely life as the zoo's only gorilla and gave him a TV set.

[4] A great black and yellow V-2 rocket 46 feet long stood in a New Mexico desert. Empty it weighed five tons. For fuel it carried eight tons of alcohol and liquid oxygen.

Everything was ready. Scientists and generals withdrew to some distance and crouched behind earth mounds. Two red flares rose as a signal to fire the rocket.

With a great roar and burst of flame the giant rocket rose slowly and then faster and faster. Behind it trailed sixty feet of yellow flame. Soon the flame looked like a yellow star. In a few seconds it was too high to be seen, but radar tracked it as it sped upward to 3,000 mph.

A few minutes after it was fired, the pilot of a watching plane saw it return at a speed of 2,400 mph and plunge into earth forty miles from the starting point.

[5] HEFFALUMP: (*gloatingly*): Ho-ho!

PIGLET (*carelessly*): Tra-la-la, tra-la-la.

HEFFALUMP (*surprised, and not quite so sure of himself*): Ho-ho!

PIGLET (*more carelessly still*): Tiddle-um-tum, tiddle-um-tum.

HEFFALUMP (*beginning to say 'Ho-ho' and turning it awkwardly into a cough*): H'r'm! What's all this?

PIGLET (*surprised*): Hallo! This is a trap I've made, and I'm waiting for the Heffalump to fall into it.

HEFFALUMP (*greatly disappointed*): Oh! (*After a long silence*): Are you sure?

PIGLET: Yes.

HEFFALUMP: Oh! (*nervously*): I – I thought it was a trap *I'd* made to catch piglets.

PIGLET (*surprised*): Oh. no!

HEFFALUMP: Oh! (*apologetically*): I – I must have got it wrong, then.

PIGLET: I'm afraid so. (*politely*): I'm sorry. (*He goes on humming.*)

HEFFALUMP: Well – well – I – well. I suppose I'd better be getting back?

PIGLET: (*looking up carelessly*): Must you? Well, if you see Christopher Robin anywhere, you might tell him I want him.

HEFFALUMP (*eager to please*): Certainly! Certainly! (*He hurries off*).

[6] GHOSTS

Those houses haunt in which we leave
Something undone. It is not those
Great words or silences of love

That spread their echoes through a place
And fill the locked-up unbreathed gloom.
Ghosts do not haunt with any face

That we have known; they only come
With arrogance to thrust at us
Our own omissions in a room.

The words we would not speak they use,
The deeds we dared not act they flaunt,
Our nervous silences they bruise;

It is our helplessness they choose
And our refusals that they haunt.

2. These are all instances of English TEXTS being used in DISCOURSE. The different ways these texts can be used indicates that they belong to different TEXT TYPES: [1] road sign, [2] nursery rhyme, [3] news article, [4] science textbook, [5] conversation between two participants taking turns, and [6] poem. It seems reasonable to require that a science of texts should be able to describe or explain both the shared features and the distinctions among these texts or text types. We ought to find out what standards texts must fulfil, how they might be produced or received, what people are using them for in a given setting of occurrence, and so forth. The words and sentences on the page are reliable clues, but they cannot be the total picture. The more pressing question is how the texts FUNCTION in HUMAN INTERACTION.

3. A TEXT will be defined as a COMMUNICATIVE OCCURRENCE which meets seven standards of TEXTUALITY. If any of these standards is not considered to have been satisfied, the text will not be communicative. Hence, non-communicative texts are treated as non-texts (cf. III.8). We shall outline the seven standards informally in this chapter and then devote individual chapters to them later on.

4. The first standard will be called COHESION and concerns the ways in which the components of the SURFACE TEXT, i.e. the actual words we hear or see,[2] are *mutually connected within a sequence*. The surface components **depend** upon each other according to grammatical forms and conventions, such that cohesion rests upon GRAMMATICAL DEPENDENCIES. As linguists have often pointed out, surface sequences of English cannot be radically rearranged without causing disturbances. We would not, for instance, get very far by converting sample [1] into this order:

[1]*a* Children play slow at

and requesting the traffic authorities to use it on road signs. The series is so disjointed that drivers could hardly tell what goes with what. Obviously, the grammatical dependencies in the surface text are major signals for sorting out meanings and uses. All of the functions which can be used to signal relations among surface elements are included under our notion of COHESION.[3]

5. Notice that our original sample

[1] SLOW
CHILDREN
AT PLAY

might be divided up into various dependencies. Someone might conceivably construe it as a notice about 'slow children' who are 'at play',[4] so that unflattering conclusions could be drawn about the children's intelligence or physical fitness. But the more likely reaction would be to divide the text into 'slow' and 'children at play', and suppose that drivers should reduce speed to avoid endangering the playing children. A science of texts should explain how AMBIGUITIES like this one are possible on the surface, but also how people preclude or resolve most ambiguities without difficulty. The surface is, as we see, not decisive by itself; there must be INTERACTION between cohesion and the other standards of textuality to make communication efficient (cf. III.4).

6. The second standard will be called COHERENCE and concerns the ways in which the components of the TEXTUAL WORLD, i.e. the configuration of CONCEPTS and RELATIONS which *underlie* the surface text, are *mutually accessible* and *relevant*.[5] A CONCEPT is definable as a configuration of knowledge (cognitive content) which can be recovered or activated with more or less unity and consistency in the mind (cf. V.4ff.). RELATIONS are the LINKS between concepts which appear together in a textual world: each link would bear a designation of the concept it connects to. For example, in 'children at play', 'children' is an *object* concept and 'play' an *action* concept, and the relation "agent-of" obtains, because the children are the agents of the action (cf. V.26(*b*)). Sometimes, though not always, the relations are not made EXPLICIT in the text, that is, they are not ACTIVATED directly by expressions of the surface (cf. V.4). People will supply as many relations as are needed to make sense out of the text as it stands. In the road sign [1], 'slow' makes better sense as the "quantity of motion" which a text receiver should assume than as an "attribute" of the children themselves.

7. Coherence can be illustrated particularly well by a group of relations subsumed under CAUSALITY.[6] These relations concern the ways in which one situation or event affects the conditions for some other one. In a sample such as:

[7] Jack fell down and broke his crown.

the event of 'falling down' is the CAUSE of the event of 'breaking', since it created the *necessary* conditions for the latter. A weaker type of causality applies to this sample:

[8] The Queen of Hearts, she made some tarts, all on a summer day.
The Knave of Hearts, he stole those tarts, and took them quite away.

Here, the Queen's action created the *sufficient, but not necessary* conditions for the Knave's action (made it possible, but not obligatory); this relation can be termed ENABLEMENT.

8. These conceptual relations do not cover all kinds of causality. In a sample such as:

[9] Jack shall have but a penny a day
Because he can't work any faster

the low pay is not actually *caused* or *enabled* by the slow working, but is nonetheless a reasonable and predictable outcome. The term REASON can be used for the relation where an action follows as a rational response to some previous event. In contrast, Jack's 'breaking his crown' was independently necessary (we could not ask: "What made him feel like doing that?") (cf. Wilks 1977b: 235f.).

9. Cause, enablement, and reason cannot capture the relation at stake here:

[10] Old Mother Hubbard went to the cupboard to get her poor dog a bone.

Mother Hubbard's first action does enable the second, but there is an important difference between samples [8] and [10]: the agent's PLAN is involved in [10], while the Queen did not do her baking for the sake of allowing a theft. The term PURPOSE can be used for an event or situation which is planned to become possible via a previous event or situation.

10. Another way of looking at events or situations is their arrangement in TIME. Cause, enablement, and reason have forward directionality, that is, the earlier event or situation causes, enables, or provides the reason for the later one. Purpose has backward directionality, that is, the later event or situation is the purpose for the earlier one. Time relations can

be very intricate, depending on the organization of the particular events or situations mentioned. Where sample [10] goes on to say:

[11] When she got there, the cupboard was bare.

our knowledge of the world tells us that the 'getting there' action was later than that of 'going to the cupboard' (being the terminal boundary of the latter), but happened at the same time as the situation of the 'cupboard being bare'. The relation of TEMPORAL PROXIMITY can be specified in many ways, according to the boundaries of events.[7]

11. We reserve the discussion of other coherence relations for section V.25ff. We would only point out here that we have already moved somewhat beyond the text as it is actually made manifest in sound or print. Coherence is clearly not a mere feature of texts, but rather the outcome of cognitive processes among text users. The simple juxtaposition of events and situations in a text will activate operations which recover or create coherence relations. We can notice that effect in this sample:

[2] The King was in the counting house, counting all his money;
The Queen was in the parlour, eating bread and honey;
The Maid was in the garden, hanging out the clothes;

In the explicit text, there is a set of ACTIONS ('counting', 'eating', 'hanging out'); the only relations presented are the LOCATION, the AGENT, and the AFFECTED ENTITY of each action (on these terms, cf. V.26ff.). Yet simply by virtue of the textual configuration, a text receiver is likely to assume that the action is in each case the PURPOSE of being at that location; that the locations are PROXIMATE to each other, probably in or near the royal palace; and even that the actions are proximate in TIME. One might well go on to assume that the actions are intended to signal the ATTRIBUTES of the agents (e.g. the King being avaricious, the Queen gluttonous, the Maid industrious). The adding of one's own knowledge to bring a textual world together is called INFERENCING (cf. V.32ff.).

12. Coherence already illustrates the nature of a science of texts as human activities. A text does not make sense by itself, but rather by the interaction of TEXT-PRESENTED KNOWLEDGE with people's STORED KNOWLEDGE OF THE WORLD (cf. Petöfi

1974; IX.24-40). It follows that text linguists must co-operate with cognitive psychologists to explore even such a basic matter as the sense[8] of a text. We also see that theories and methods will have to be PROBABILISTIC rather than DETERMINISTIC, that is, they will state what is *usually* the case rather than *always*. Different users might set up slightly different senses; yet there will be a common core of probable operations and content consistently found among most users, so that the notion "sense of a text" is not unduly unstable (cf. V.1).

13. Cohesion and coherence are **text**-centred notions, designating operations directed at the text materials. In addition, we shall require **user**-centred notions which are brought to bear on the activity of textual communication at large, both by producers and by receivers. The third standard of textuality could then be called INTENTIONALITY, concerning the text **producer**'s attitude that the set of occurrences should constitute a cohesive and coherent text instrumental in fulfilling the producer's intentions, e.g. to distribute knowledge or to attain a GOAL specified in a PLAN.[9] To some degree, cohesion and coherence could themselves be regarded as operational goals without whose attainment other discourse goals may be blocked. However, text users normally exercise TOLERANCE towards products whose conditions of occurrence make it hard to uphold cohesion and coherence altogether (cf. VI.2ff.), notably in casual conversation. A hybrid structure such as this (documented in Coulthard 1977: 72):

[12] Well where do – which part of town do you live?

did not disturb communication because it still served the superior goal of finding out someone's address, although the subordinate goal of maintaining cohesion did not fully succeed. But if a text producer intended to defy cohesion and coherence, communication would be slowed down for negotiation (cf. IX.15ff.) and could break down altogether.

14. The fourth standard of textuality would be ACCEPTABILITY, concerning the text **receiver**'s attitude that the set of occurrences should constitute a cohesive and coherent text having some use or relevance for the receiver, e.g. to acquire knowledge or provide co-operation in a plan.[10] This attitude is responsive to such factors as text type, social or cultural setting, and the desirability of goals. Here also, we could view

the maintenance of cohesion and coherence by the text receiver as a goal of its own, such that material would be supplied or disturbances **tolerated** as required. The operation of INFERENCING mentioned in I.11 strikingly illustrates how receivers support coherence by making their own contributions to the sense of the text.

15. If acceptability is restricted, communication can be diverted. It is accordingly taken as a signal of non-cooperation if a text receiver raises questions about acceptability when the text producer's intentionality is obviously in effect (Dickens 1947: 774):[11]

[13] "What we require, sir, is a probe of this here."
"Probate, my dear sir, probate," said Pell.
"Well, sir," replied Mr. Weller sharply, "probe and probe it is very much the same; if you don't understand what I mean, sir, I daresay I can find them as does."
"No offence, I hope, Mr. Weller," said Pell meekly.

16. Text producers often speculate on the receivers' attitude of acceptability and present texts that require important contributions in order to make sense. The Bell Telephone Company warns people:

[14] Call us before you dig. You may not be able to afterwards.

People are left to infer that digging without asking might lead to cutting off a ground cable and hence to losing the wiring needed in order to call; or even, to sustaining bodily injury and being incapacitated. It is intriguing that [14] is more **effective** than a version would be that made everything more **explicit** (in the sense of I.6), such as:

[14]*a* Call us before you dig. There might be an underground cable. If you break the cable, you won't have phone service, and you may get a severe electric shock. Then you won't be able to call us.

Apparently, text receivers are readily persuaded by content they must supply on their own: it is as if they were making the assertion themselves (cf. VII.28, 42; VIII.20). Sample [14] is more **informative** than sample [14]*a* – a factor which constitutes the next standard of textuality.

17. The fifth standard of textuality is called INFORMATIVITY and concerns the extent to which the occurrences of the

presented text are expected vs. unexpected or known vs. unknown/certain.[12] In sample [14], the assertion that 'you' will not 'be able to call' is much more unexpected than it is in [14]*a*. The processing of highly informative occurrences is more demanding than otherwise, but correspondingly more interesting as well. Caution must be exercised lest the receivers' processing become overloaded to the point of endangering communication.

18. Every text is at least somewhat informative: no matter how predictable form and content may be, there will always be a few variable occurrences that cannot be entirely foreseen. Particularly low informativity is likely to be disturbing, causing boredom or even rejection of the text. The opening stretch of a science textbook runs like this:[13]

[15] The sea is water

The fact asserted here is so well known to everyone that there seems to be no point in saying it here. The stretch of text is clearly cohesive and coherent, and undoubtedly intended to be acceptable as such. But it is nonetheless a marginal text because it is so uninformative. Not until we look at the continuation does the text's status seem more sound:

[15]*a* The sea is water only in the sense that water is the dominant substance present. Actually, it is a solution of gases and salts in addition to vast numbers of living organisms . . .

The assertion of the obvious fact in [15] functions as a starting point for asserting something more informative. The surface cue 'actually' signals that the well-known "substance-of" relation (cf. V.26(*l*)) is not strictly accurate. The ensuing correction of a common view is less expected, so that the informativity of the whole passage is *upgraded* (cf. VII.16).

19. The sixth standard of textuality can be designated SITUATIONALITY and concerns the factors which make a text RELEVANT to a SITUATION of occurrence.[14] We saw in I.5 that one might treat the road sign

[1] SLOW
CHILDREN
AT PLAY

in different ways, but that the most probable intended use was obvious. The ease with which people can decide such an issue is due to the influence of the situation where the text is presented. In the case of sample [1], the sign is placed in a location where a certain class of receivers, namely motorists, are likely to be asked for a particular action. It is far more reasonable to assume that 'slow' is a request to reduce speed rather than an announcement of the children's mental or physical capacities. Pedestrians can tell that the text is not relevant for themselves because their speeds would not endanger anyone. In this manner, the sense and use of the text are decided via the situation.

20. Situationality even affects the means of cohesion. On the one hand, a text version such as:

[1]*b* Motorists should proceed slowly, because children are playing in the vicinity and might run out into the street. Vehicles can stop more readily if they are moving slowly.

would remove every possible doubt about sense, use, and group of intended receivers. On the other hand, it would not be appropriate to a situation where receivers have only limited time and attention to devote to signs among the other occurrences of moving traffic. That consideration forces the text producer toward a maximum of economy; situationality works so strongly that the minimal version [1] is more **appropriate** than the clearer [1]*b* (cf. I.23).

21. The seventh standard of textuality is to be called INTERTEXTUALITY and concerns the factors which make the utilization of one text dependent upon knowledge of one or more previously encountered texts.[15] A driver who has seen road sign [1] is likely to see another sign further down the road, such as:

[16] RESUME SPEED

One cannot 'resume' something unless one was doing it at an earlier time and then stopped it for some reason. The 'speed' at stake here can only be the one maintained until [1] was encountered and a reduction was made. Clearly, the sense and relevance of [16] depend upon knowing about [1] and applying the content to the evolving situation.

22. Intertextuality is, in a general fashion, responsible for the evolution of TEXT TYPES as classes of texts with typical patterns of characteristics (cf. IX.1ff.). Within a particular

type, reliance on intertextuality may be more or less prominent. In types like parodies, critical reviews, rebuttals, or reports, the text producer must consult the prior text continually, and text receivers will usually need some familiarity with the latter. An advertisement appeared in magazines some years ago showing a petulant young man saying to someone outside the picture:

[17] As long as you're up, get me a Grant's.

A professor working on a research project cut the text out of a magazine, altered it slightly, and displayed it on his office door as:

[17]*a* As long as you're up, get me a Grant.

In the original setting, [17] was a request to be given a beverage of a particular brand. In the new setting, [17]*a* seems to be pointless: research grants are awarded only after extensive preparation and certainly can't be gotten while casually walking across a room. The discrepancy is resolvable via one's knowledge of the originally presented text and its intention, while the unexpectedness of the new version renders it informative and interesting (cf. I.17). This interest effect offsets the lack of immediate situational relevance and the non-serious intention of the new text presenter.

23. We have now glanced at all seven standards of textuality: cohesion (I.4–5), coherence (I.6–12), intentionality (I.13), acceptability (I.14–16), informativity (I.17–18), situationality (I.19–20), and intertextuality (I.21–2). These standards function as CONSTITUTIVE PRINCIPLES (after Searle 1969: 33f.) of textual communication: they define and create the form of behaviour identifiable as textual communicating, and if they are defied, that form of behaviour will break down. There must also exist REGULATIVE PRINCIPLES (again following Searle) that control textual communication rather than define it. We envision at least three regulative principles. The EFFICIENCY of a text depends on its use in communicating with a minimum expenditure of effort by the participants. The EFFECTIVENESS of a text depends on its leaving a strong impression and creating favourable conditions for attaining a goal. The APPROPRIATENESS of a text is the agreement between its setting and the ways in which the standards of textuality are upheld.[16]

24. It will be our task in this book to pursue both the constitutive and the regulative principles of textual communication. We shall present some topics loosely grouped under each of the seven standards in turn. At the same time, we shall be concerned with illustrating how the constitution and use of texts are controlled by the principles of efficiency, effectiveness, and appropriateness. Not surprisingly, our discussion will lead us into some domains outside the confines of usual linguistics, simply because of the different concerns we raise. In particular, we shall be obliged to rely on considerable research in other disciplines, notably COGNITIVE SCIENCE, a new field at the crossroads of linguistics, psychology, and computer science (cf. X.3 and, on artificial intelligence, X.26ff.). The standards of textuality alone entail, as we have seen, factors of cognition, planning, and social environment merely to distinguish what constitutes a text. Still, it is perhaps not unduly optimistic to hope that the broad outlines we shall undertake to sketch are gradually being filled in by the concerted interaction of researchers sharing a commitment to the study of language use as a crucial human activity.

Notes

1 Samples [1] and [2] are public domain. Sample [3] is taken from *TIME* magazine, 22 Jan. 1979. Sample [4] is a selection from Booklet D of McCall & Crabbs (1961); after being used in diverse studies (see note 10 to Chapter V), it formed the basis for a specifically text-linguistic inquiry (see Beaugrande 1980*a*, 1980*c*, 1981*b*). Simmons and Chester (1979) was in turn inspired by the latter's studies. Sample [5] is taken from A. A. Milne's *House at Pooh Corner* (1928: 44f.) Sample [6] is from Elisabeth Jennings' *Poems 1967* (1967: 55). These samples are all treated in the course of the book: [1] in I.4–6 and 19–21; [2] in I.11; [3] in VII.21–8 and 42; [4] in III.26, IV.7–10, 24, 29, V.29–39, and IX.25–39; [5] in VI.29–31; and [6] in VII.29–42.

2 The "surface" is not of course the *raw material* of sounds or printed marks; it already presupposes that language expressions are presented and identified. How this identification is actually done is of course a valid issue for the procedural approach, even though we cannot treat it here. See Selfridge & Neisser (1960); Sperling (1960); Neisser (1967); Crowder & Morton (1969); Woods et al. (1976); Rumelhart (1977*a*); and Walker (ed.) (1978).

3 The term "cohesion" was made current by Halliday and later by his wife Hasan (cf. Halliday 1964; Hasan 1968; Halliday & Hasan 1976). Compare

also Crymes (1968); Harweg (1968); Palek (1968); Hobbs (1976); Webber (1978). Note that our use of the term is extremely broad, including *all* means of signalling surface dependencies (cf. Halliday 1964: 303).

4 We enclose linguistic samples in single quotes, excluding all punctuation not part of the sample. We use double quotes with conventional punctuation for all other purposes.

5 On coherence, see Harweg (1968); Karttunen (1968); Bellert (1970); van Dijk (1972*a*, 1977*a*); Kintsch (1974); Beaugrande (1980*a*). "Coherence" has often been confused or conflated with "cohesion"; but the distinction between connectivity of the surface and connectivity of underlying content is indispensable (cf. Widdowson 1973; Coulthard 1977; Beaugrande, 1980*a*).

6 For different but largely compatible discussions of causality, cf. Schank (1975); Wilks (1977*b*). We mention some typical "junctives" that signal causality later on (IV.46).

7 Some "junctives" for temporal proximity are given in IV.47. On event boundaries, cf. III.24.

8 In V.1, we distinguish between "meaning" as the potential of language expressions (or other signs) for being significant, and "sense" as the knowledge actually conveyed by expressions in occurring texts.

9 "Intentionality" has been much discussed under various conditions, but with inconclusive results. For more directly applicable work, see Wunderlich (1971); Hörmann (1976); Bruce (1977); van Dijk (1977*a*); Schlesinger (1977); Cohen (1978); McCalla (1978); Wilensky (1978*a*); Allen (1979); Beaugrande (1979*a*, 1979*b*, 1980*a*) (compare also VI.6). Note that the *producer* of the text is not always identical with the *presenter*, e.g. in the case of text allusion (IX.12); this factor falls under the notion of **intertextuality** (cf. I.22 on parody).

10 On acceptability, see Quirk & Svartvik (1966); Greenbaum (ed.) (1977). On acceptance of other participants' discourse goals, see Cohen (1978); McCalla (1978); Allen (1979).

11 This excerpt from *The Pickwick Papers* (Dickens 1947: 774) is slightly altered to make dialect features less difficult for non-native readers of English. We adopt the compromise policy throughout of keeping the words, but normalizing idiosyncratic spellings that might be unclear.

12 On informativity, see Shannon (1951); Weltner (1964); Grimes (1975); Loftus & Loftus (1976); Groeben (1978); Beaugrande (1978*b*, 1980*a*). Our use of the term is broader and less formal than in early work (cf. Chapter VII).

13 This excerpt is the first passage of Chanslor (1967: 9). For a full discussion, see Beaugrande (1978*b*).

14 Situationality has been treated less in linguistics proper than in sociolinguistics and ethnomethodology; consult the papers in Gumperz & Hymes (eds.) (1972); Bauman & Scherzer (eds.) (1974). A survey of sociolinguistics overall is given in Dittmar (1976).

15 A narrower use of "intertextuality" is found in Kristeva (1968); for an outlook closer to ours, consult Quirk (1978).

16 We appeal to these notions below in II.6, III.9, IV.11, 28, 37, VII.28, VIII.11, IX.11, and X.16.

Chapter II

The evolution of text linguistics

1. Whereas only ten years ago the notion of "text linguistics" was familiar to few researchers, we can now look back on a substantial expanse of work. Surveys and readers are widely available (see for instance Stempel (ed.) 1971; Dressler 1972*a*; Fries 1972; Schmidt 1973; Dressler & Schmidt (eds.) 1973; Sitta & Brinker (eds.) 1973; Jelitte 1973–4, 1976; Petöfi & Rieser (eds.) 1974; Kallmeyer et al. 1974; Harweg 1974, 1978; Hartmann 1975; Schecker & Wunderli (eds.) 1975; Daneš & Viehweger (eds.) 1976; Coulthard 1977; Gülich & Raible 1977; Jones 1977; Dressler 1978; Gindin 1978; Grosse 1978; Kuno 1978; Nöth 1978; Rieser 1978; Beaugrande (ed.) 1980). The picture that emerges from these works is diffuse and diversified, because there was no established methodology that would apply to texts in any way comparable to the unified approaches for conventional linguistic objects like the sentence.

2. Teun van Dijk (1979*a*) stresses that "text linguistics" cannot in fact be a designation for a single theory or method. Instead, it designates any work in language science devoted to the text as the primary object of inquiry. Our brief overview in this chapter will be centred on a few exemplary studies which demarcate the gradual evolution of theory and method toward an independent, specially tailored foundation for the study of texts. But first, we should glance at some historical roots with important implications.

3. The oldest form of preoccupation with texts can be found

in RHETORIC, dating from Ancient Greece and Rome through the Middle Ages right up to the present (on the current resurgence of classical rhetoric, see for example Corbett 1971; Winterowd (ed.) 1975; Plett (ed.) 1977; Brown & Steinmann (eds.) 1979). The traditional outlook of rhetoricians was influenced by their major task of training public orators. The main areas were usually the following: *invention,* the discovery of ideas; *disposition,* the arrangement of ideas; *elocution,* the discovery of appropriate expressions for ideas; and *memorization* prior to *delivery* on the actual occasion of speaking. In the Middle Ages, rhetoric belonged to the "trivium" (three studies) alongside *grammar* (formal language patterns, usually Latin and Greek) and *logic* (construction of arguments and proofs).

4. Rhetoric shares several concerns with the kind of text linguistics we are exploring here (cf. Spillner 1977), notably the assumptions that:[1]

(*a*) the accessing and arranging of ideas is open to systematic control;
(*b*) the transition between ideas and expressions can be subjected to conscious training;
(*c*) among the various texts which express a given configuration of ideas, some are of higher quality than others;
(*d*) judgements of texts can be made in terms of their effects upon the audience of receivers;
(*e*) texts are vehicles of purposeful interaction.

5. Within limits, researchers can study units of sound and form, or formal patterns of sentences, from a relatively abstract standpoint. But many aspects of texts only appear systematic in view of how texts are produced, presented, and received. Whereas the conventional linguistic question might be: "What structures can analysis uncover in a language?", our question (cf. III.6) would be rather: "How are discoverable structures built through operations of decision and selection, and what are the implications of those operations for communicative interaction?" It is plain that classical rhetoric, despite its different terms and methods, was vitally involved in seeking the answer to the second question.

6. A similar conclusion can be drawn about the traditional domain of STYLISTICS. Quintilian, an early theoretician (1st century A.D.), named four qualities of style: *correctness, clarity,*

elegance, and *appropriateness*. While correctness depends on conformity with prestigious usage, and appropriateness is presumably definable in terms similar to our own notion (cf. I.23), the notions of clarity and elegance seem at first too vague and subjective to be reliably defined and quantified. They are akin to our notions of efficiency and effectiveness, respectively, without being identical. Still, Quintilian's categories reflect the assumption that texts differ in quality because of the extent of processing resources expended on their production (cf. III.28).

7. The range of stylistic studies in modern times has been rather multifarious (cf. surveys in Sebeok (ed.) 1960; Spillner 1974). Recently, linguistics has been employed as a tool for discovering and describing **styles** (cf. survey in Enkvist 1973). Despite the diversity of approaches, nearly all work reflects the conviction that style results from the characteristic *selection of options* for producing a text or set of texts. Hence, we might look into the style of a single text; of all texts by one author; of a group of texts by similar authors; of representative texts for an entire historical period; and even of texts typical of an overall culture and its prevailing language.[2] Obviously, the methodological difficulties increase as we move along toward larger and larger domains.

8. The most neutral means for uncovering the selections made in a text or set of texts is direct statistical tabulation of occurrences (cf. Doležel & Bailey (eds.) 1969). This method, however, obscures some significant considerations. The relative frequency of an occurrence is often less decisive than the immediate likelihood of finding it in the specific context *currently evolving* (cf. VII.5f.). What is expected within the norms of the language overall may be unexpected within a given context, and vice versa (cf. Riffaterre 1959, 1960; Beaugrande 1978*a*: 39f.). In addition, there are variations in the degree to which any option influences the identification of a style, e.g. by being more or less conspicuous. From considerations like the above, it follows that style is really only definable in terms of the operations carried out by the producers and receivers of texts – a major issue of concern in the present volume.

9. When modern linguistics began to emerge, it was customary to limit investigation to the framework of the

sentence as the largest unit with an inherent structure (cf. Bloomfield 1933: 170). Whatever structures might obtain beyond the sentence were assigned to the domain of stylistics. This division does reflect a fundamental property of language. It is much more straightforward to decide what constitutes a grammatical or acceptable sentence[3] than what constitutes a grammatical or acceptable sentence sequence, paragraph, text, or discourse.[4] When we move beyond the sentence boundary, we enter a domain characterized by greater freedom of selection or variation and lesser conformity with established rules. For instance, we can state that an English declarative sentence must contain at least a noun phrase and an agreeing verb phrase, as in that perennial favourite of linguists:

[18] The man hit the ball.

But if we ask how [18] might fit into a text, e.g.:

[19]*a* The man hit the ball. The crowd cheered him on.
[19]*b* The man hit the ball. He was cheered on by the crowd.
[19]*c* The man hit the ball. The crowd cheered the promising rookie on.

it is much harder to decide what expression for the 'man' should be used in a follow-up sentence (e.g. 'him' vs. 'this promising rookie'), and in what format (e.g. active vs. passive). Certainly, we have no hard and fast rules which would force us to prefer just one continuation.

10. For a science of texts as human activities, the distinction we have just raised is not so crucial. If we assume that structures are *always* the outcome of intentional operations (cf. II.5), then even single sentences must evolve through selection rather than being derived from abstract rules alone. Moreover, there are many surface relationships, such as noun followed up by pronoun, which can occur both within one sentence and among an extensive sequence of sentences. Thus, there are good motives for merging sentence linguistics with stylistics when building up a science of texts.

11. Texts have been a long-standing object of LITERARY STUDIES, though emphasis was limited to certain text types (cf. X.13–18). Scholars have at various times embarked on tasks such as these:
(*a*) describing the text production processes and results of an

author, or a group of authors in some time period or setting;

(*b*) discovering some problematic or contestable senses for texts;

(*c*) assigning values to texts.

The attempt to make these tasks more systematic and objective has spurred an application of linguistic methods to literary studies (cf. Spitzer 1948; Levin 1962; Chatman & Levin (eds.) 1967; Jakobson & Jones 1970; Ihwe (ed.) 1971; Koch (ed.) 1972; van Dijk 1972*a*, 1972*b*; Ihwe 1972; Spillner 1974; Kloepfer 1975). Quite possibly, the expanded scope of text linguistics renders it still more useful in this kind of application than the conventional methodology of describing structures as such: we try to go beyond the structures and ask how and why texts are built and utilized (cf. 0.6; X.16ff.).

12. Texts have also come under the scrutiny of ANTHROPOLOGY in its explorations of cultural artifacts (cf. X.8). Bronislaw Malinowski (1923) expounded the importance of viewing language as human activity in order to study meaning. Special attention was devoted to myths and folktales by Vladimir Propp (1928) and later by Claude Lévi-Strauss (1960) and his followers. Anthropologists like these borrowed from linguistics various methods of structural analysis and description (cf. also Dundes 1962; Bremond 1964, Greimas 1967; Žolkovskij & Ščeglov 1967; Colby 1973*a*, 1973*b*). The operational approach of the kind we are following has been adopted more and more in the last few years (cf. Beaugrande & Colby 1979).

13. Anthropological investigation of little-known cultures was massively supported by a linguistic method known as TAGMEMICS (developed largely by Kenneth Pike 1967; see also Longacre 1964, 1970, 1976). The method called for gathering and analyzing data in terms of "slots" and "fillers", i.e. according to the positions open within a stretch of text and to the units that can occupy those positions. Tagmemics looks beyond the boundaries of both sentences and texts toward such large complexes of human interaction as a football game or a church service. The slot-and-filler method, a basic technique of code-breaking, is eminently useful for describing languages about which the investigator knows nothing in advance. The investigator uses means of *language elicitation*

which impel native speakers to produce utterances of particular types.

14. The integration of anthropology and linguistics in the tagmemic approach has provided invaluable documentation of many rapidly disappearing languages in remote regions. The major contribution to a science of texts lies in the systematic recognition of relationships between language and the settings of communication. However, a slot-and-filler approach is too rigid to encompass textuality as depicted in this volume; there must be operational processes before there can be any configurations of slots to fill in the first place. Again, we face the distinction between the discovery or analysis of the structures, and the procedures which select and build structures (cf. 0.6; II.5; III.6).

15. SOCIOLOGY has developed an interest in the analysis of CONVERSATION as a mode of social organization and interaction (cf. X.8). For example, studies have been conducted on how people take turns in speaking (Sacks, Schegloff & Jefferson 1974). The field entitled ETHNOMETHODOLOGY inquires into correlations between patterns of speaking and social roles or groups (cf. Gumperz & Hymes (eds.) 1972; Bauman & Scherzer (eds.) 1974): how people adapt their language behaviour in certain group encounters; how speaking conventions are established or changed; how social dominances emerge in speaking; and so forth.

16. The study of conversation – sometimes also called DISCOURSE ANALYSIS (cf. Sinclair & Coulthard 1975; Coulthard 1977) – is of vital import to a science of texts. The mechanisms which combine TEXTS as single contributions into DISCOURSES as sets of mutually relevant texts directed to each other, reveal major factors about the standards of textuality.[5] **Cohesion** is affected when surface structures are shared or borrowed among separate texts (cf. IV.33; VI.26). **Coherence** of a single text may be evident only in view of the overall discourse (cf. IX.22f.). **Intentionality** is shown in the goal-directed use of conversation (cf. VI.16ff.; VIII.13ff.), and **acceptability** in the immediate feedback (cf. I.15; VI.4). The role of **situationality** is particularly direct (cf. VIII.13), and the whole organization illustrates **intertextuality** in operation (cf. IX 13ff.). The selection of contributions to conversation can be controlled by the demands of **informativity** (cf. IX.14).

17. We have rapidly reviewed some disciplines which, for various motives, share many concerns with a science of texts. Indeed, the regrettable lack of co-operation among these disciplines in past times might well be due to the absence of a pivotal text science. We shall now glance at some previous work in the field of linguistics proper, where the text was generally considered a marginal entity until it became hard to ignore any longer.

18. An early milestone emerged from PHILOLOGY, a forerunner of modern linguistics, dealing with the organization and evolution of language sounds and forms in historical time. Comparing word order in ancient and modern languages, Henri Weil (1844, 1887) detected another principle besides grammar: the relations of "thoughts" to each other evidently affects the arrangement of words in sentences. His investigations were renewed by Czech linguists (many of them in the "Prague School") under the designation of FUNCTIONAL SENTENCE PERSPECTIVE (cf. IV.51–3; VII.18.4). This designation suggests that sentence elements can "function" by setting the knowledge they activate into a "perspective" of importance or newness. In many languages, for instance, elements conveying important, new, or unexpected material are reserved for the latter part of the sentence (cf. IV.52f.).

19. The emergence of modern linguistics in the present century (particularly in the USA) was associated with methods which came to be termed DESCRIPTIVE or STRUCTURALIST.[6] Language samples were gathered and analyzed according to SYSTEMS of MINIMAL UNITS. Minimal units of sound were called "phonemes"; those of form, "morphemes"; those of word order, "syntagmemes"; those of meaning, "semes" or "sememes"; and so on. Each system of minimal units constitutes a LEVEL[7] organized by the OPPOSITION of units and their distinctive features, so that each unit was in some way distinct from all others. Hence, if a "system" is defined as "a set of elements in which each element has a particular function" (cf. III.2), then these systems were upheld by the function of *distinctiveness*. When the several systems of a language had been identified and their units classified, the language would have been completely described.

20. Even this brief outline of the descriptive structural method should indicate that it has no obvious provisions for

the study of texts. Of course, one can analyze a text into levels of minimal units as depicted, but there is no guarantee that we will have uncovered the nature of the text by doing so. On the contrary, the extraction of tiny components diverts consideration away from the important unities which bind a text together.

21. Not surprisingly, early work on texts in this tradition was diverse. Zellig S. Harris (1952, reprinted 1963) proposed to analyze the distribution of morphemes in texts according to "equivalences": relationships in which elements were the same or had the same environments. To increase the number of equivalences and thus to make analysis more exhaustive, Harris applied the notion of "transformation" that was later adopted and modified by his pupil Noam Chomsky. A "transform" of the text gradually emerged with a maximum of equivalences. For example, to obtain a pattern equivalent to 'you will be satisfied', Harris transforms an earlier stretch of text from 'satisfied customers' to 'customers are satisfied' – a familiar operation to sentence grammarians nowadays.

22. Despite the enormous impact of the concept of "transformation" (employed here for the first time in linguistics, as far as we know), Harris's proposal for "discourse analysis" on distributional principles seems to have received little notice (see now Prince 1978). It is not fully clear what Harris's method is supposed to discover. Whereas descriptive linguistics was centred on classification of units, the operation of "representing the order of successive occurrences of members of a class" had never been applied before (Harris 1952: 8). Harris himself admits (1952: 493) that the equivalences of structure among sentences tell us nothing about relationships of meaning (indeed, he is anxious to avoid appealing to meaning in any way); at most, "we can say what criteria a new sentence must satisfy to be formally identical with the sentences of the text". As Bierwisch (1965*a*) shows in his critique of Harris, a very doubtful text can be set up which all the same satisfies the equivalence criteria being used. Still, Harris's paper is an interesting proof that the cohesion of texts entails a certain degree of recurrence and parallelism of syntactic patterns from sentence to sentence (cf. IV.12ff.).

23. Eugenio Coseriu's (1955–6, reprinted 1967) study of "determination and setting" is based on entirely different con-

siderations. He asserts that research on language demands the investigation not only of speakers' knowledge of a language, but also of techniques for converting linguistic knowledge into linguistic activity. He employs the notion of "determination" to show how word meanings can be applied, e.g. via "discrimination" (picking among possible referents of an expression), "delimitation" (singling out certain aspects of meaning), and "actualization" (making potential knowledge currently active, cf. III.12), each of these having subtypes dealing with identities, individualities, quantities, class inclusions, specifications, distinctions, and specializations. He then presents an elaborate classification of "settings" ("entornos") based on such factors as cultural, social, cognitive, and historical surroundings, degree of mediation between text and situation (cf. VIII.1), and range of content being addressed.

24. It is indeed lamentable that Coseriu's proposals went unheeded at the time. The issues he raised are only now being recognized as significant for the empirical study of meaningful communication. Units of content are not fixed particles with a stable identity, but rather fuzzy agglomerates sensitive to the conditions of their usage (cf. V.4). Some of the bizarre side-effects of subsequent attempts to describe language isolated from its uses and functions might have been averted if Coseriu's ideas had been accorded the attention they merited.

25. The first large-scale inquiry into text organization was contributed by Roland Harweg (1968).[8] He postulated that texts are held together by the mechanism of "substitution" (one expression following up another one of the same sense or reference and thus forming a cohesive or coherent relationship). As his chapter on "the phenomenology of pronominal chaining" (1968: 178–260) reveals, his notion of "substitution" is extraordinarily broad and complex, subsuming relationships such as recurrence (cf. IV.12ff.), synonymy (cf. IV.18), class/instance (cf. V.17), subclass/superclass (cf. V.17), cause/effect, part/whole, and much more.[9] He stresses the DIRECTIONALITY of substitution, i.e. the order in which something follows up whatever it is being substituted for. Although our own model has a different organization and terminology from Harweg's, we will be concerned with many of the same textual relationships as those he described.

26. There were a number of other text studies based more or less on the descriptive structural approach,[10] but the main tendencies should now be evident. The text was defined as a unit larger than the sentence (cf. Pike 1967; Koch 1971; Heger 1976). Research proceeded by discovering types of text structures and classifying them in some sort of scheme. Occasionally, the framework of investigation was expanded to include sequences of texts or situations of occurrence (e.g. in Coseriu 1955–6; Pike 1967; Harweg 1968; Koch 1971). But in general, structures were construed as something given and manifest, rather than something being created via operational procedures of human interactants. We end up having classifications with various numbers of categories and degrees of elaboration, but no clear picture of how texts are utilized in social activity.

27. Even within its own boundaries, the descriptive method eventually breaks down in the face of COMPLEXITY (when a language aspect is too intricate, and its constitutents too numerous and diversified, for full classification) and OPEN SYSTEMS (when a language aspect entails sets of unlimited membership). For instance, we can classify endless numbers of English sentences as distributions of morphemes and still not have exhausted the patterns of all possible sentences. The language model usually called "transformational grammar" was well received when it offered a means of handling complexity and open systems: the infinite set of possible data – in the standard model, sentences of a language – is seen as derivable from a small set of basic patterns plus a set of rules for manipulating and creating more elaborate patterns.

28. This new approach leads to a different outlook on texts. Instead of viewing the text as a unit above the sentence, we would see it as a string composed of well-formed sentences in sequence. At first, Katz and Fodor (1963) argued that the text might as well be treated as one super-long sentence that happened to be joined by periods rather than conjunctions. This option is left open by the standard grammar, since there is no limit on sentence length. But there are some structures which are less typical in sequences of separate sentences than within a single long sentence.[11] And the empirically given texts have doubtless assumed the format of separate sentences for potent motives anchored somewhere in speakers'

knowledge of their language. There is no way in which the Katz-Fodor proposal could account for textuality in the sense we are using that notion.

29. Karl-Erich Heidolph (1966) notes that the factors of accent, intonation, and word-order within a sentence depend on the organization of other sentences in the vicinity. He suggested that a feature of "mentioned" vs. "not mentioned" could be inserted in the grammar to regulate these factors. Horst Isenberg (1968, 1971) follows Heidolph with a further enumeration of factors which cannot be solved within the bounds of the isolated sentence, such as pronouns, articles, and sequence of tenses. He adds features intended to capture the status of noun phrases, e.g. knownness, identity, identifiability, generality, and contrastivity. He also appeals to coherence relations like cause, purpose, specification, and temporal proximity.

30. Some time after these scholars had argued in support of text linguistics, a group of researchers convened at the University of Konstanz, Germany, to participate in a federally funded project on the notion of "text grammar". This group, centred around Hannes Rieser, Peter Hartmann, János Petöfi, Teun van Dijk, Jens Ihwe, Wolfram Köck, and others, undertook to formulate an abstract grammar and lexicon that would "generate" a text by Brecht entitled 'Mr K's Favourite Animal', i.e. that would assign structural descriptions to the sentences of the text. The results of the project (some of them set forth in van Dijk, Ihwe, Petöfi, & Rieser 1972) indicate that the differences between sentence grammar and text grammar proved more significant than had been supposed. Despite a huge apparatus of rules, there emerged no criteria for judging the text "grammatical" or "well-formed":[12] why might the sentences not be in some other order or format? The problem of common reference was not solved, but simply incorporated into the "lexicon" for the text.[13] A debate ensued between Werner Kummer (1972*a*, 1972*b*) and members of the project (Ihwe & Rieser 1972), in which he questioned the basic assumptions of the whole undertaking.

31. The Konstanz project is in some ways reminiscent of Harris's (1952) "discourse analysis" (cf. II.21f.). Again, a grammatical method was applied to an unintended task, and again, nothing seems to have been proven except that

sentences share structural properties within a text just as much as within the grammar of a language overall. No standards for distinguishing between texts and non-texts were found. The rules certainly do not reflect the processes that would operate in producing or receiving a text. Indeed, as Kummer (1972*a*: 54) notes, the "generating" of the text is presupposed by the investigators rather than performed by the grammar.

32. Janos Petöfi (1971) had already foreseen the difficulties of using transformational grammar for a theory of texts. He reviewed the "standard" theory (after Chomsky 1965) in which the syntactic structure is generated first and then a "semantic interpretation" is performed, as compared to the "generative semantic" theory (cf. papers in Steinberg & Jakobovits (eds.) 1971) in which the basic structure is a representation of the meaning and the syntactic form is imposed later on. Petöfi asks whether it might not be expedient to construct a grammar with separate components for the speaker and for the hearer. While the speaker would start with meaning and create a sequential pattern, a hearer would begin with the completed sequence and work back to the meaning.[14]

33. Petöfi's 1971 volume ushered in the development of a vastly elaborate theory of texts, often called the "text-structure/world-structure theory" ("TeSWeST" for short). He has undertaken to distribute the various aspects of texts over a battery of representational devices derived from formal logic. As the theory evolves, the number and complexity of its components steadily increases (see Petöfi 1980 for a current version). The trend is to integrate more and more factors relating to the users of texts rather than to the text as an isolated artifact. For example, the LEXICON, which originally contained little more than the vocabulary defined for the text at hand (see van Dijk, Ihwe, Petöfi & Rieser 1972), is made to incorporate steadily more "commonsense knowledge" about how the world at large is organized (cf. Petöfi 1978: 43). The logical status of text sense simply does not emerge unless we consider its interaction with the users' prior knowledge (see already Petöfi 1974).

34. In the 1980 version, components are offered for representing a text from nearly every perspective. To meet the demands of the logical basis, a "canonic" mode (a regularized,

idealized correlate) is set up alongside the "natural language" mode in which the text is in fact expressed. Rules and algorithms are provided for such operations as "formation", "composition", "construction", "description", "interpretation", and "translation".[15] The reference of the text to objects or situations in the world is handled by a "world-semantic" component; at least some correspondence is postulated between text-structure and world-structure.

35. Setting aside the technical details of Petöfi's evolving model, we can view it as illustrative of the issues which logic-based text theories will have to face. Either established logics are employed, so that much of the texts' nature is lost from view; or the logics are modified to capture texts more adequately (Petöfi 1978: 44f.). Petöfi foresees intricate mechanisms to mediate between real texts and logically adequate versions of texts. Whether this undertaking will succeed, and whether it will then clarify the interesting properties of texts, remains to be seen. Perhaps a less rigorous, formalized approach would do more justice to the approximative way humans use texts in everday communication.

36. Teun van Dijk's (1972*a*) monumental treatise, *Some Aspects of Text Grammars,* pursues a rather different range of considerations. Like Heidolph (1966) and Isenberg (1968, 1971), van Dijk marshalled the arguments for text grammars in terms of problems that sentence grammars could not treat satisfactorily. His main object of study was **literary** and **poetic** texts, which often do not conform to conventions of grammar and meaning and still belong indisputably to the set of texts of a language (cf. IX.9). He concluded that there must be "literary operations" applied to sound, syntax, and meaning in order to obtain such unconventional texts, e.g. *addition, deletion,* and *permutation* (i.e. inserting, leaving out, or changing the basic materials). Literary metaphors served as illustrations.

37. An important notion which sets van Dijk's work apart from studies of sentence sequences is that of MACRO-STRUCTURE:[16] a large-scale statement of the content of a text. Van Dijk reasoned that the generating of a text must begin with a main **idea** which gradually evolves into the detailed meanings that enter individual sentence-length stretches (cf. III.21). When a text is presented, there must be operations

which work in the other direction to extract the main idea back out again, such as *deletion* (direct removal of material), *generalization* (recasting material in a more general way), and *construction* (creating new material to subsume the presentation) (van Dijk 1977*a*).[17] Sentence grammars of course make no provision for any such operations concerning macro-structures, since the issue simply does not come up in the contemplation of isolated sentences. Accordingly, van Dijk turned to cognitive psychology for a *process-oriented* model of the text. In collaboration with Walter Kintsch, he investigated the operations people use to summarize texts of some length, notably stories (cf. Kintsch & van Dijk 1978; van Dijk & Kintsch 1978).[18] The typical summary for a text ought to be based on its macro-structure (see now van Dijk 1979*b*). However, research showed that the actual outcome involves both the macro-structure of the text and previously stored macro-structures based on knowledge of the organization of events and situations in the real world (cf. our discussion of "schemas" in IX.25–8).

38. A still different line has been adopted in the work of Igor Mel'čuk (cf. Mel'čuk 1974, 1976; Mel'čuk & Žolkovskij 1970). He argues that the transition between "meaning" (Russian "smysl") and text should be the central operation of a linguistic model, i.e. how meaning is expressed in or abstracted out of a text. "Meaning" is to be defined as "manifesting itself" in the "speaker's ability to express one and the same idea in a number of different ways and in the hearer's ability to identify a number of outwardly different synonymous utterances as having the same meaning" (Mel'čuk & Žolkovskij 1970: 11). As might be expected from this declaration, the mainstay of investigation is the construction of "paraphrasing systems" (on paraphrase, cf. IV.18–19).

39. Mel'čuk envisions a meaning representation with its own "syntax"; that is, with a connectivity not visible in the grammatical organization. He arrives at a network which is in some ways similar to those we shall discuss in Chapter V, though he subdivides concepts into simpler units upon occasion. The units are taken from a "deep lexicon", moved to the network, and then formatted with a "deep syntax" ("deep" in the sense of being composed of primitive, basic elements rather than words and phrases of the text itself).[19] To

create acceptable paraphrases, "weighted filters" are imposed on the selection of options.

40. The "text grammars" of Petöfi, van Dijk, and Mel'čuk are typical of recent attempts to redirect transformational generative grammar. Whereas the earlier research simply postulated the same kind of structures *among* sentences as those that had been established *within* sentences, allowing only small alterations (e.g. Heidolph 1966; Isenberg 1968, 1971; van Dijk, Ihwe, Petöfi & Rieser 1972), the recent trends reveal a search for a fundamentally different conception of grammar. Mel'čuk's model adapts the paraphrase potential built into the notion of "transformation" (see Ungeheuer 1969) to focus the direction of the language model toward "imitating human behaviour in a purely automatic manner" (Mel'čuk & Žolkovskij 1970: 10). For this task, he adopts a new kind of meaning representation to capture cognitive continuity (cf. V.2). Petöfi shifts the operation of transformation from its original domain on the syntactic level only and allows transformations *among different levels,* so that more elaborate correspondences throughout the language can be developed. Van Dijk expands transformations to describe cognitive processes that can render texts "literary" or produce summaries.

41. It is probably safe to conclude that virtually all models of texts and text grammars will make some use of the notion of "transformation", but probably not the same use made in Chomskyan grammar. Moreover, many assumptions found in the older grammar – such as the autonomy of syntax – are likely to be dropped as the demands of modelling human communication in real interaction become better defined. The trends indicated by the work of Petöfi, van Dijk, and Mel'čuk illustrate this kind of evolution in theory and method.

42. This chapter has not been intended as an exhaustive survey of research on texts. Instead, we have merely essayed to mention some representative work inside and outside linguistics. In particular, we intended to suggest the sort of approaches that arise when texts are investigated from various perspectives and for various motives. In most cases, the notion of "text" involved has been narrower than the one we are advocating ourselves (e.g.: unit bigger than the sentence; distribution of morphemes; sequence of well-formed sentences), but the scope is expanding steadily, as Petöfi and van

Dijk have demonstrated. Accordingly, we view our own approach as an outcome of continual evolution rather than a confrontation or even refutation of previous theories and methods.

Notes

1 We return to these matters in our sketch of text production (III.18–28).

2 The notion of a whole language having "style" seems out of place: how can the repertory itself be a selection? The selection involved here would be the characteristic means which one language offers among the totality that could be available to language in principle. The "comparative stylistics" of Vinay and Darbelnet (1958) (cf. X.23) is quite revealing.

3 On judging grammaticality or acceptability, cf. VI.21ff.

4 It will not help to view texts or discourses as super-long sentences (cf. Katz & Fodor 1963; II.28) or as sentence sequences joined with "punctuation morphemes" (periods) (cf. Ballmer 1975). Sentences are judged by their cohesion, whereas texts and discourses must possess all the standards of textuality enumerated in Chapter I.

5 Our own use of the term "discourse" is that explained here, and is more compatible with Sinclair and Coulthard's work than with that of Zellig Harris (1952), who also uses the term (cf. II.21–2). If, as we argue here, discourses inherit all the standards of textuality, we might want to make the discourse our central notion (see for example "discourse-world models" vs. "text-world models", IX.23). But we might incur some disadvantages for treating single texts occurring by themselves.

6 Later, the term "taxonomic linguistics" was applied to this approach by transformational grammarians, whose work was also the description of structures (a very special use of the notion of "generative") (cf. II.30). The most elaborate taxonomic work is that of Koch (1971), who devotes considerable attention to the implications of creating taxonomies.

7 We use the term "level" throughout to designate one of the systemic, simultaneously co-present aspects of a language or text, e.g. sound, syntax, meaning, planning, etc, and not a type of unit, e.g. morpheme, word, sentence, etc; the latter are better called **ranks.**

8 Like many early landmarks in text linguistics – Schmidt (1968), Koch (1971), Wienold (1971) – Harweg (1968) was a habilitation dissertation directed by Prof. Peter Hartmann at the University of Münster (West Germany). The publication dates are all substantially later than the actual work.

9 When citing from various sources, we try to use our own terminology rather than that of each individual researcher, provided there are discoverable correspondences, to save confusion and promote unity.

10 Most of these are found in the references in Dressler (1972*a*).

11 One example is "cataphora", in which the pro-form appears before any noun or noun phrase supplying its content (cf. IV.23–4).

12 The notion of "well-formedness" has rather indiscriminately been

expanded from grammar to domains where its application is rather doubtful. To prevent further confusion, we do not use the notion at all, assuming that all actually occurring texts are "well-formed" if intended and accepted as such; they may of course be inefficient, ineffective, or inappropriate (cf. I.23). We will have enough to do with these real samples and need not try to concoct deliberately "ill-formed" texts on our own.

13 Concerning the "lexicon", cf. II.33.

14 But this model only captures some activities of real production and reception of texts, dwelling with undue stress on linearization (cf. III.25f.).

15 Such elaborate machinery is probably required for any logic-based model of texts with as wide a scope as Petöfi's. Petöfi's basic representation is, surprisingly perhaps, still first-order predicate calculus. For a lengthy treatment, see Biasci & Fritsche (eds.) (1978).

16 In van Dijk (1972*a*), he used the term "deep structure" but dropped it later to save confusion with Chomskyan usage (cf. van Dijk 1979*b*). See note 19 to this chapter.

17 Van Dijk makes no attempt to bring these notions into contact with the similar work of David Ausubel or John Bransford. See also discussion in IX.28.

18 Concerning story understanding, see note 22 to Chapter IX.

19 In transformational grammars, "deep" entities are *primitive* ones not capable of further decomposition, e.g. the structures of axioms. In the procedural approach, "deep" entities are those removed from the surface presentation; "deeper" processing therefore entails less identification and more integration and organization than shallower processing (cf. III.9 and note 6 to Chapter III).

Chapter III

The procedural approach

1. For many years, syntax and semantics were studied with little regard for the ways people use grammar and meaning in communication. The use of language was relegated to the domain of PRAGMATICS and left largely unexplored. In a **procedural** approach, however, all the levels of language are to be described in terms of their utilization. Pragmatics is then the domain of PLANS and GOALS, and questions of use are freely treated in syntax and semantics as well. Our notions of "cohesion" and "coherence" can be helpful in studying a text only if they deal with how connections and relations are actually set up among communicative occurrences. The concerns of pragmatics are dealt with by exploring the attitudes of producers ("intentionality") and receivers ("acceptability"), and the communicative settings ("situationality").

2. Linguists of all persuasions seem to agree that a language should be viewed as a SYSTEM:[1] a set of elements each of which has a function of contributing to the workings of the whole. This definition is so general that its implications for language research can be highly diverse. For example, as noted in II.19, early study entailed extracting systems of minimal units for each aspect of a language; each unit had the function of being distinctive from all the others. However, no one would equate this kind of system with the operations of communicating: people are not combining distinctive units in any direct or obvious way. Indeed, empirical tests show that many abstract distinctions are not apperceptibly maintained in real speaking

and are recoverable only from context (cf. Pollack & Pickett 1964; Woods & Makhoul 1973; Walker (ed.) 1978).

3. One's outlook on an object of study depends upon the scientific tasks to be accomplished. The SYSTEMIZATION of the object (discovery or imposition of a system in some domain of study) – a notion advanced especially by Carl Hempel[2] – proceeds on the basic assumption that occurring manifestations are controlled by orderly principles rather than by randomness. The DESCRIPTION of an object requires that we identify those orderly principles to the extent that the classification of samples can be objectively and reliably performed. The EXPLANATION of the object, on the other hand, requires that we uncover the principles whereby the object assumed the characteristics it has and whereby the observable samples were created and used. A description of a language may be given quite independently of any stated or implied explanation. Indeed, descriptions can be simplified by deliberately excluding many considerations which an explanation would have to address.

4. A case in point is the opposition between MODULARITY, where the components of a model are viewed as independent of each other, and INTERACTION, where the components are seen to interlock and control each other (cf. Sussman 1973: 12f.; Winograd 1975: 192). Modular systems are far easier to design and keep track of, since additions or modifications affect only specific elements; in exchange, however, system operations are vastly cumbersome (cf. Levesque & Mylopoulos 1979: 94). Therefore, the largely modular models of language developed in both descriptive structural linguistics and transformational grammar would provide only very inefficient operating systems for the use of language in real time. Language users would appear to be floating in an endless sea of minute structures on different language levels; how syntax and grammar interact with meaning and purpose remains a mystery.

5. There can be no doubt that real communicative behaviour can be explained only if language is modelled as an interactive system (cf. Walker (ed.) 1978). The correlation between levels cannot be ignored or reserved for some after-the-fact phase of "interpretation". Tests show that a language model in which syntax is autonomous cannot function in real time because of

COMBINATORIAL EXPLOSION: an immense over-computation of alternative structures and readings that run into astronomically vast operation times.[3] The understanding of the road sign [1] ('slow children at play') – to take a very mild example – would demand too much processing if it had to be analyzed independently of the context where it occurs (cf. I.19). The production and reception of a text of greater length, if they had to be done without interaction of language levels and cognitive or situational factors, would seem to be little short of a miracle.

6. Considerations of this kind have led to the inception of a PROCEDURAL approach to the study of texts in communication. Here, the discovery of units and structural patterns, though still a central activity of investigation, is not a goal in itself. Instead, we are concerned with the operations which manipulate units and patterns during the utilization of language systems in application (cf. II.5). The TEXT figures as the actual outcome of these operations. Hence, a text cannot be explained as a configuration of morphemes or sentences (cf. Chapter II): we would rather say that morphemes and sentences function as operational units and patterns for signalling meanings and purposes during communication. The thoroughness with which text users actually organize and utilize morphemic and syntactic materials should be an issue for empirical research under realistic conditions, rather than an a priori assumption dictated by a particular theory.

7. As Manfred Bierwisch (1966: 130) notes, there is no definite constraint on the number of abstract grammars which could be set up for a language. It has been customary to argue in favour of one grammar over another on the basis of criteria such as simplicity, consistency, and generality. In the procedural approach, however, the decisive criteria must include operationality and human plausibility.[4] The intuitions of linguists can be no more than a heuristic, and do not constitute primary data (see discussion in Crystal 1971: 105ff.; Spencer 1973; Ringen 1975; Snow & Meijer 1977). The validity of theories and models must be demonstrated from natural human activities.

8. Research along these lines entails a shifting of priorities among the issues to be explored.[5] For example, the distinction between sentences and non-sentences is absolutely indis-

pensable for an abstract grammar, since it decides what the grammar should or should not allow. But if human language users are in fact demonstrably unable to make such a distinction consistently – as suggested by the research reviewed in VI.23ff. – grammaticality of sentences is only a DEFAULT in a theory of language as human activity, that is, something assumed in absence of contrary specification (cf. III.18). A presentation is likely to be rejected as a non-text only if the standards of textuality are so strongly defied (e.g. by total absence of discoverable cohesion, coherence, relevance to a situation, etc.) that communicative utilization is no longer feasible (cf. I.3). Such a borderline can depend on factors outside the text itself, e.g. tolerance and prior knowledge of the participants present, or type of text in use.

9. As the distinctions of sentence/non-sentence and text/non-text lose importance, the gradations of efficiency, effectiveness, and appropriateness gain (cf. I.23). Those factors control what people say at least as much as do the abstract rules of grammar and logic. Procedurally, **efficiency** contributes to *processing ease,* that is, the running of operations with a light load on resources of attention and access. **Effectiveness** elicits *processing depth,* that is, intense use of resources of attention and access on materials removed from the explicit surface representation.[6] **Appropriateness** is a factor determining the correlation between the current occasion and the standards of textuality such that reliable estimates can be made regarding ease or depth of participants' processing. Notice that efficiency and effectiveness tend to work against each other. Plain language and trite content are very easy to produce and receive, but cause boredom and leave little impression behind. In contrast, creative language and bizarre content can elicit a powerful effect, but may become unduly difficult to produce and receive. Hence, appropriateness must mediate between these opposed factors to indicate the proper balance between the conventional and the unconventional in each situation.

10. The quality of a text as efficient, effective, and appropriate would be sensitive to the extent of processing resources expended upon its production and reception (cf. III.28). In principle, there is no cut-off point where production is definitively accomplished, but at most a THRESHOLD OF TERMINATION where the producer finds the outcome satis-

factory for the intended purpose (cf. Flower & Hayes 1979: 17). Similarly, the receivers' judgement of text quality will affect the extent of resources they are disposed to expend on processing the presentation. There would be no absolute end to reception, but rather a threshold of termination where utilization appears satisfactory. In principle, someone else could come along and revise the text still further or analyze it yet more thoroughly.[7]

11. The considerations we have raised suggest how difficult it would be to limit the study of texts to the artifacts of speech or writing alone. Those artifacts are inherently incomplete when isolated from the processing operations performed upon them. If we view a text as a document of decision, selection, and combination, then many occurrences are significant by virtue of the other alternatives which might have occurred instead. Frequently, the basic organization of the language (e.g. its regularities of sound, grammar, vocabulary, etc.) provide no decisive guidelines about what should be chosen. We must constantly seek to discover and systemize the MOTIVATIONS and STRATEGIES according to which the creation and utilization of texts are kept in operation.

12. On the other hand, we must guard against allowing the text to vanish away behind mental processes. Recent debates over the role of the reader point up the dangers of assuming that text receivers can do whatever they like with a presentation.[8] If that notion were accurate, textual communication would be quite unreliable, perhaps even solipsistic. There must be definitive, though not absolute, controls on the variations among modes of utilizing a text by different receivers (cf. III.16). Beaugrande (1980*a*) proposes that the text itself be viewed as a system, being a set of elements functioning together.[9] Whereas a language is a VIRTUAL system of available options not yet in use, the text is an ACTUAL system in which options have been taken from their repertories and utilized in a particular STRUCTURE (relationship between or among elements). This utilization is carried out via procedures of ACTUALIZATION.[10]

13. Since descriptive structural linguistics and transformational grammar are both preoccupied with virtual systems, little research was expended on actualization procedures until recently. Even at this early stage of inquiry, it now seems clear

that actualization is organized in ways which are not directly applicable to virtual systems. For instance, there seems to be a very heavy interdependency of decisions and selections, both within one level and among different levels. This interdependency exerts powerful controls on possible variations in utilizing a single text. If one participant adopted an unconstrainedly idiosyncratic outlook on textual occurrences, communication would be seriously damaged.

14. From here, Beaugrande (1980*a*) concludes that a text constitutes a CYBERNETIC system which continually regulates the functions of its constituent occurrences. Whenever a textual occurrence falls outside the participants' systems of knowledge about language, content, and purpose, the STABILITY of the textual system is disturbed and must be restored by REGULATIVE INTEGRATION of that occurrence, e.g. via additions or modifications to one's store of knowledge. Text utilization is blocked only if regulative integration fails, e.g. if unresolvable discrepancies persist. Under normal conditions, participants uphold systemic stability in maintaining a CONTINUITY of cognitive experience by discovering the relations between each meaningful occurrence and its context.[11] Even where there are several possible relations that might be constructed, some are more satisfactory or probable than others and will therefore be given PREFERENCE.[12] To the extent that preference knowledge is shared by a communicative community (or indeed, serves to *identify* such a community), the processing outcome for a particular text will be quite similar among all members of the community. Any noticeably idiosyncratic outcome will elicit special regulation, so that in time, the language user becomes aware of community preferences.

15. The awareness of community preference knowledge is by no means a compulsion to conform to it. On the contrary, a text whose format and content were entirely in conformity with established knowledge would possess an extremely low degree of *informativity* in the sense of I.17f. (cf. also Chapter VII). Complete knownness – or, in cybernetic terms, **total stability** – is evidently uninteresting to the human cognitive disposition. Communication therefore acts as the *constant removal and restoration of stability through disturbing and restoring the continuity of occurrences*. Hence, the awareness of preference

knowledge cannot preclude creativity in textual communication; instead, it merely enables participants to find an orientation for creativity and to provide or recover its motivations within a given textual system.

16. The above line of argument suggests how a systems-theoretical approach would resolve the dilemma of admitting human processes as factors in the utilization or investigation of texts. The users of a system must be aware of the system's functional principles, or else utilization will be impaired or blocked. Certain classes of occurrences, e.g. ambiguities, contradictions, or discrepancies, which are likely to impede utilization or to render it hard to control, are therefore considered inopportune except for special effect (e.g. in jokes or paradoxes). The standards of textuality we set forth in this book are all *relational* in character, concerned with how occurrences are connected to others: via grammatical dependencies on the surface (cohesion); via conceptual dependencies in the textual world (coherence); via the attitudes of the participants toward the text (intentionality and acceptability); via the incorporation of the new and unexpected into the known and expected (informativity); via the setting (situationality); and via the mutual relevance of separate texts (intertextuality).

17. This emphasis upon relational continuity and connectivity allows us to study textuality and text processing in terms of formal PROBLEM-SOLVING in the sense of Newell and Simon (1972).[13] A PROBLEM is defined as a pair of states whose connecting pathway is subject to FAILURE (not being traversed) because it can't be found or identified. A SERIOUS PROBLEM would obtain if the chances of failure significantly outweigh those of success. The problem is said to be SOLVED when a pathway is found leading without interruption from the INITIAL STATE to the GOAL STATE. If a point is reached where the problem-solver cannot advance at all toward the goal, a BLOCK has occurred. Clearly, the crucial operation of problem solving is the SEARCH for connectivity between states. Three search types should be mentioned:[14]

(*a*) In DEPTH-FIRST SEARCH, the problem-solver tries to dash toward the goal along one continuous pathway, giving little heed to alternatives as long as progress moves forward. If a block is encountered, the problem-solver moves back only far enough to get moving again and then resumes its dash forward. Depth-first search is not very safe except when the pathway is obvious and uncontested.

(*b*) In BREADTH-FIRST SEARCH, the problem-solver looks ahead only up to a proximate sub-goal and weighs the various pathways to get there. The best path is attempted, and, if success ensues, the procedure is repeated with the next sub-goal, until the main goal is eventually attained. Breadth-first search is circumspect and safe, but may be inefficient and laborious if the pathway is obvious.

(*c*) In MEANS-END ANALYSIS, the problem-solver identifies the main differences between the initial state and the goal state, and tries to reduce them one by one. If the differences seem too great, an intermediate subgoal may be taken for comparison first. While depth-first and breadth-first search can be used in forward means-end analysis, efficiency can be increased by working both forward from the initial state and backward from the goal state as seems opportune. Indeed, any state along the way might be a useful CONTROL CENTRE to work out from in either direction.[15]

18. We can now sketch out a model of the production of texts, using the notions presented in this chapter so far (compare Beaugrande 1979*b*; Flower & Hayes 1979; Meyer 1979). The model foresees a loosely sequential set of PHASES OF PROCESSING DOMINANCE. We say "dominance" because it seems unlikely and unnecessary that the operations of one phase must shut down those of all the others; rather, there could be a *threshold* beyond which the **focus** of processing resources is directed to one phase of operations, while other operations are only reduced rather than suspended. The notion of "dominance" helps to resolve the opposition between modularity and interaction (III.4) by allowing the processor to distribute its activities in various proportions (see Winograd 1975). The interaction among levels (sound, syntax, meaning, etc.) is managed by a class of operations called MAPPING: the correlation of elements, structures, and relations of different types.[16] It is not yet decidable how much organizational activity must be done within a single level before mapping is carried out to other levels. There will often by ASYMMETRY (lack of one-to-one correspondence) between levels, but

DEFAULTS (assumptions made when no specifications are given) and PREFERENCES (dispositions toward one option over others) for mapping would help to reduce current processing load (cf. VII.12).

19. Under typical conditions, operations are probably not strongly tailored to the individual text materials. There ought to be powerful, general procedures capable of accepting and adapting to a substantial diversity of data and occasions (cf. X.5). Bobrow and Winograd's (1977) notion of PROCEDURAL ATTACHMENT (specification or modification of standard operations for current needs) seems to fit here. The procedures would be called by mechanisms of PATTERN-MATCHING that detect a reasonable fit between current and stored materials.[17] While the general procedures are running, specific details can be filled in where suitable.

20. The first phase of text production would usually be PLANNING (cf. Flower & Hayes 1979; Meyer 1979). The producer has the intention of pursuing some goal via the text, e.g. distributing knowledge or obtaining compliance with a plan (cf. I.13; VI.16ff.). In the most immediate sense, the production of the text is a sub-goal along the pathway to the main goal. Through **means-end analysis** (III.17(*c*)), the producer could try to calculate which of various possible texts would make the greatest contribution to reducing the differences between the current state and the goal state. If this question is hard to decide, one may try **breadth-first search** by offering several texts in succession and hoping that one of them will lead to success. The texts are integrated into the plan through PLAN ATTACHMENT (a subtype of procedural attachment as explained in III.19).

21. The setting of a goal and the choice of a text type will be closely followed by (or will overlap with) a phase of IDEATION. An IDEA would be an internally initiated (not environmentally forced) configuration of content providing CONTROL CENTRES for productive, meaningful behaviour, including text production. The mapping of a plan structure onto an idea (or vice-versa) is doubtless intricate, especially when it would not be expedient to talk about the plan too openly. For instance, the goal of persuading people may demand elaborate searching for ideas that would be appealing to the group's presumed view of the world, or that would change that view in a useful manner

(cf. VI.16; VIII.17ff.). One would hardly announce the plan itself (cf. VI.8; VIII.1)!

22. Following ideation, a phase of DEVELOPMENT can serve to expand, specify, elaborate, and interconnect the ideas obtained. Development can be envisioned as a searching of stored KNOWLEDGE SPACES, i.e. internally organized configurations of content in the mind. Development may vary between summoning forth more or less intact spaces and bringing together very unusual constellations. The problem-solving used to make content coherent by connecting it via relational pathways (demonstrated in Chapter V) would be correspondingly more intense in the latter case. Still, if the text is to be informative in the sense of Chapter VII, there would be at least some new configurations in its textual world.[18]

23. The results of ideation and development need not yet be committed to particular natural language expressions (cf. Flower & Hayes 1979: 24). They might, for instance, be composed of mental imagery[19] for scenes or event sequences. Hence, there must be a phase of EXPRESSION to which the content accruing so far is relayed. Search for expressions would be a special instance of problem-solving by constructing pathways from one level of organization to another. However, search would be supported if, as seems plausible, the activation of mental content naturally tends to spread out to the typical expressions stored for that content (cf. V.12). Already active expressions would then be taken as PREFERENCES in the sense of III.18.

24. A special kind of PROBLEM could arise here. Content such as mental imagery of a scene or of a sequence of gradual events might be CONTINUOUS, while the expressions are more or less DISCRETE elements – an important illustration of the **asymmetry** mentioned in III.18. The text producer must decide upon the boundaries that scene components or events should be assigned (cf. Halliday 1967–8; Miller & Johnson-Laird 1976; Talmy 1978). Different expressions will frequently suggest boundaries of greater or lesser extent and distinctness.

25. Since the presentation of texts is limited to the sequential media of sound or print, the final phase of production must be PARSING: putting the expressions relayed from the last phase into GRAMMATICAL DEPENDENCIES and arranging the latter in a LINEAR format for the SURFACE TEXT. The repertory of

grammatical dependencies in a language such as English is much smaller than the repertory of conceptual relations we would consider necessary (cf. IV.7ff. versus V.26), so that asymmetry enters once again. There would be less asymmetry in languages with many grammatical cases that signal conceptual relations (e.g. Finnish, Hungarian).[20]

26. The most prominent preference in **linearization** is that of *adjacency*, i.e. the elements in a grammatical dependency are arranged next to each other in the progressive series. **Active storage** (cf. IV.2; V.4) would be able to parse dependencies with maximum ease when the elements are kept in closely knit groups. However, many motivations readily override this preference. When a single element enters into several dependencies in a phrase or sentence, some of its dependent elements will have to be removed to some distance. In the opening of the 'rocket'-text from I.1, the sequence:

[4]*a* A great black and yellow V-2 rocket 46 feet long

contains one element 'rocket' entering into dependencies with a determiner ('a') and five modifiers ('great', 'black', 'yellow', 'V-2', 'long'). Since these dependent elements cannot all be adjacent, conventions are applied for the ordering of modifier types (cf. Vendler 1968; Martin 1969; Danks & Glucksberg 1971), e.g. size before colour. In another sequence from the same text:

[4]*b* With a great roar and burst of flame

knowledge of the world intervenes to indicate that 'great' modifies both 'roar' and 'burst' (the determiner 'a' not being repeated), but 'of flame' probably modifies only 'burst'. In contrast, the sequence of sample [6] running:

[6]*a* Great words or silences of love

would preferentially be construed as having 'great' and 'of love' depend on both 'words' and 'silences'. If the modifiers represented opposed concepts, however, for example:

[6]*b* Great words or silences of smallest size

we would link each modifier only with the element adjacent to it. We can see that adjacency is a useful but relatively weak preference in parsing.

27. We have briefly surveyed the phases that might plausibly

constitute text production: planning, ideation, development, expression, and parsing. As was cautioned in III.18, the phases should not be envisioned as running in a neat time sequence with clear-cut boundaries. It would be perfectly conceivable that all five phases could be interacting at once, with dominance shifting about rapidly. When difficult or unsatisfactory results emerge in one phase, dominance could shift back to a "deeper"[21] phase (i.e. one further removed from the surface text under production) for new modes of organization. Later decisions may reveal that previous ones were not advantageous; for instance, development and expression may call forth changes in planning and ideation.[22] Indeed, there may be some such principle as the "intention of the text" whereby the textual materials reveal organizational tendencies of their own during production and impose them upon the producer, provided operations are not terminated too soon (compare Iser (1980) on text intention in the reader's viewpoint). In III.10, we suggested that production is an inherently open-ended process whose termination is carried out when a threshold of satisfaction is attained. Perhaps that threshold could be evoked by the emergence of such material-specific tendencies as depicted here. Yet even then, there might be potential left for still more revising.

28. The continued practice of text production could lead to a telescoping of phases. A standard of text quality that once demanded much shifting among phases for revision might become attainable in a single straightforward run-through. Writers or speakers who are considered talented and important may not appear to expend extreme effort on production, but they may offset shorter duration with correspondingly greater intensity of processing. Even they presumably had to work through early stages where vast expenditures were conscious and manifest. The "intention of the text"–if there are grounds for such a notion–might become easier to discern through extended experience. That effect would explain why a practiced producer can improve upon other people's texts (not just on his or her own) without having actually participated in their mental processes.[22a]

29. The RECEIVING of texts could be modelled as a corresponding set of phases of processing dominance in the reverse direction.[23] The receiver would begin on the "surface"

with the presentation itself and work "downward" to the "deeper" phases.[24] The surface text would be PARSED from the linear string into grammatical dependencies (an operation we outline in IV.7ff.). The elements in those dependencies are the expressions which ACTIVATE concepts and relations in mental storage–a phase we could call CONCEPT RECOVERY (cf. V.4). As the conceptual configuration accrues and shows densities and dominances, the main IDEAS can be extracted in a phase of IDEA RECOVERY. The extraction of the PLANS which the text producer appears to be pursuing would be performed during PLAN RECOVERY. The receiver is now able to consider possible actions and reactions.

30. Since we explore the reception processes in detail in Chapters IV, V, and IX, we will not pursue them here at any length. We should however point out that the phases of reception, like those of production, need not be separated by rigid boundaries. There is more probably a shifting of dominance with extensive interaction and consultation among the phases, especially when the results in any phase are considered doubtful or disturbing. There would also be variation in the intensity and duration of the phases, depending on such factors as: (*a*) the receiver's judgement of the text's quality (cf. III.10); (*b*) the degree to which the text's content should be integrated into the receiver's store of prior knowledge (cf. Spiro 1977; Beaugrande 1980*c*); (*c*) the receiver's cognitive and emotional involvement in the communicative situation. For instance, the amount of **inferencing** done by the text receiver might vary considerably (cf. I.11; V.34).

31. Consequently, text reception would involve a THRESHOLD OF TERMINATION where the comprehension and integration of the text is deemed satisfactory (cf. III.10). If the text is important for the receiver, the threshold will be high. A professional literary critic, for example, would expend atypically great amounts of processing on specific literary samples, encompassing not only the most probable and easily recoverable aspects of format and content, but many more subtle subsidiary aspects as well. A still more extreme illustration would be the analysis performed by a professional linguist uncovering not only the actually intended structural organization, but many possible alternatives that normal text receivers would not be likely to notice.

32. In some respects, the reception of a text would not be a reversal of the procedures of production (cf. III.29). The receiver must try to anticipate the producer's activities in order to react rapidly and intelligently. Here, receiving has the same directionality as producing, i.e. the receiver is trying to emulate the production process,[25] thus making the recovery of main ideas and plans (III.29) more immediate. Without the continual creating and testing of **hypotheses** about what the producer is doing, the receiver could easily bog down in an undirected mass of alternatives and non-determinacies. There would be an EXPLOSION of structures and relations that processing could hardly handle in any realistic expanse of time.[26]

33. This very rough outline of production and reception will be filled in somewhat in later chapters. It is a difficult object of investigation because many operations are hard to observe and control in a reliable experimental setting. We must set up PROCEDURAL MODELS which reflect the operations that might be responsible for the means whereby texts are created and used. These models can be tested in two ways. First, their functioning can be *simulated* on computers, as is done in the field of research known as ARTIFICIAL INTELLIGENCE (cf. surveys in Minsky & Papert 1974; Goldstein & Papert 1977; Winston 1977; Winston & Brown (eds.) 1979; X.26ff.).[27] Terry Winograd (1972) demonstrated how a computer could be programmed to use a Halliday-style grammar to process English utterances about moving blocks on a table. Roger Schank's theory of "conceptual dependency" views language understanding as the application of knowledge about sequences of events and actions (cf. Schank et al. 1975; Schank & Abelson 1977). To the extent that they involve processing tasks, some issues of traditional text linguistics have been restated computationally, e.g. use of pronouns (cf. Grosz 1977; Webber 1978; Hobbs 1979). Although the human mind may not handle language processes in exactly the same way as the computers, these machines are indispensable for testing whether complex procedural models can operate (cf. X.27).

34. Another line of inquiry is developing in COGNITIVE PSYCHOLOGY, the branch of psychology concerned with acquisition, storage, and use of knowledge (survey in Kintsch 1977*a*).[28] Here, models are tested against the cognitive and linguistic behaviour of human subjects on such tasks as recog-

nizing and recalling what has been heard or read. Although most work was devoted to sentences (survey in Clark & Clark 1977), texts have become increasingly prominent objects of investigation. We shall review some trends in that domain in IX.24ff.

35. It would be wrong to imply that the production and reception of texts are well explored at this time. On the contrary, we are only gradually achieving a consensus about what the issues are. The true **complexity** of the operations involved doubtless exceeds by several orders of magnitude the most complex models developed so far (cf. X.28). For the present, we would like to imagine that complexity will still prove manageable (cf. X.29), due to principles like procedural attachment (III.19) and general problem-solving (III.17). Thus, although there would be a vast number of operations in text processing, there would be a reasonably small number of *operation types,* e.g. maintaining continuity and connectivity, testing hypotheses, matching patterns, computing probabilities, planning toward goals, solving problems, and so forth (cf. X.4f.). In the following discussion of the standards of textuality, we shall repeatedly return to these operation types as illustrated via naturally occurring texts of many kinds.

Notes

1 See for example Saussure (1916); Firth (1957); Hartmann (1963*a*, 1963*b*); Coseriu (1967); Halliday (1976); Berry (1977).

2 Cited in Stegmüller (1969: 205).

3 The importance of this factor emerged in early computer models of language processing, e.g. Petrick (1965); cf. Woods (1970).

4 cf. the notion of "procedural adequacy" in Schank & Wilensky (1977).

5 cf. O.6; X.6.

6 cf. Craik & Lockhart (1972); Mistler-Lachman (1974). We make no attempt to state just how many "depths" there are in all, but these seem fairly safe: (1) substance of sound/print; (2) linear surface presentation; (3) grammatical dependency structure; (4) conceptual-relational text-world; (5) main idea; (6) plan. These "depths" – moving from shallowest (1) to deepest (6) in the list – will (except for (1), cf. note 2 to Chapter I) be discussed later on in the chapter.

7 As Peter Hartmann (personal communication to RdB) observes, professional linguists have a disproportionately high threshold of processing and uncover far more structures than normal language users. Unfor-

tunately, the linguist's analysis has all too often been taken as a model of language comprehension, most drastically by transformationalists (cf. overview in Clark & Clark 1977).

8 See especially the papers in Warning (ed.) (1975).

9 cf. Hartmann (1963*a*: 85f.); Oomen (1969); Fowler (1977: 69).

10 Actualization was already treated by Coseriu (1955-6).

11 The vital importance of continuity has all too frequently been overlooked in linguists' preoccupation with analysis into units and constituents. All the standards of textuality are closely related to continuity (cf. for instance III.16; IV.1; V.2; VII.13; IX.29).

12 Our use of the term is rather broader than that of its originator, Yorick Wilks (see now Wilks 1979).

13 The "general problem-solver" was an early programme (Ernst & Newell 1969) in which powerful operations were decoupled from the specifics of tasks at hand. Our treatment is closer to that of Winston (1977) because of our network representations. See following note.

14 See Winston (1977: 90ff.; 130ff.).

15 The notion of "control centre" is crucial in understanding procedures of access (cf. for instance IV.7; V.24, 29f.; Beaugrande 1980*a*).

16 "Mapping" was originally a concept of formal logic, but it can also be operationalized (cf. Goldman, Balzer & Wile 1977).

17 On pattern-matching, cf. K.Colby & Parkinson (1974); Kuipers (1975); Pavlidis (1977); Rumelhart (1977*a*); Winston (1977).

18 To what degree a textual world (cf. I.6; V.2) ought to match or differ from prior stored knowledge, and how this matching is done, are among the most burning questions for a science of texts. See IX.31ff.

19 Mental imagery is an inordinately difficult issue (cf. Paivio 1971), but it can't be ignored (cf. VI.26; VII.10; IX.32).

20 Asymmetry would mean, in operational terms, problem-solving on interactive levels with units and paths of different size, range, and constitution. Still, the levels are mutually supportive at least some of the time (cf. V.30).

21 On this use of the notion "deeper", see note 6 to this chapter and note 19 to Chapter II.

22 The writer Peter von Tramin (personal communication to WD) maintains that, before he ever begins to write, he has already decided upon the content of the text, the course of events, the arrangement of the various segments, the assignment of materials to the foreground or the background, the use of retardation or expansion, the elements of dialogue, and the characters of the story line. Such an example is doubtless unusual: decisions like these would more often be made along the way during the writing. A more disturbing phenomenon is how *other* writers can weigh one's own decisions and suggest changes, even though they did not partake in the original planning at all (cf. III.28 and note 22a to this chapter).

22[a] Indeed, revision often seems *easier* for non-producers of the text because the producer already *knows* the intended ideas and fails to see cases of inefficient expression or downright error.

23 A reversible formalism which both parses the 'rocket'-text onto a net-

work and vice-versa is given in Simmons & Chester (1979); Beaugrande (1981*b*).

24 On "depth", see note 6 to this chapter.

25 A procedure called "analysis-by-synthesis" (cf. Neisser 1967).

26 On "explosion", cf. note 3 to this chapter.

27 "Intelligence" is taken to designate a human-like capacity to deal with a wide range of diverse tasks and input (as opposed to the computer-like slavish dependence on strict steps and rigid formats) (cf. Lenat 1977; Walker (ed.) 1978; Simon 1979). Compare X.5; X.26.

28 The co-operation of cognitive psychologists with computer scientists in artificial intelligence has fostered the discipline of "cognitive science" (cf. I.24; X.3).

Chapter IV

Cohesion

1. We suggested in III.14 that the STABILITY of the TEXT AS SYSTEM is upheld via a CONTINUITY OF OCCURRENCES. The notion of "continuity" as employed here is based on the supposition that the various occurrences in the text and its situation of utilization are related to each other, or in cognitive terms: each occurrence is instrumental in ACCESSING at least some other occurrences. The most obvious illustration is the language system of SYNTAX that imposes organizational patterns upon the SURFACE TEXT (the presented configuration of words). In using the term "cohesion" ("sticking together"), we wish to emphasize this function of syntax in communication.[1]

2. The human mind is rather limited in its capacity to store surface materials long enough to work on them (cf. Keele 1973; Loftus & Loftus 1976). Materials are placed in ACTIVE STORAGE, a "working memory" where processing resources are distributed among elements of a presentation according to their importance (cf. Eisenstadt & Kareev 1975: 338f.; III.26; V.4, 10). There appears to be a very short-lived imprint of visually or acoustically perceived materials upon which some provisional organization must be rapidly imposed (cf. Sperling 1960; Neisser 1967; Crowder & Morton 1969; Rumelhart 1970). These provisionally organized materials can then be retained for some longer periods of time, but still only within modest limits. It follows that text processing could not afford to run through the participants' vast stores of world

knowledge immediately; there must be some ancillary organizational system with far more limited options and patterns. In natural language texts, this system is that of syntax, whose classes and structures, though often more diversified than what is found in English, are still quite limited in number in comparison to the classes and structures for concepts and relations (cf. III.25ff.; V.30). This account is borne out by observations that surface structures are more predominantly maintained in a "short-term" storage, and conceptual content in a "long-term" storage (Wright 1968).

3. The functions of syntax reflect these cognitive factors. Since grammatical dependencies often obtain among elements not directly adjacent to each other (III.26), syntax must provide closely-knit patterns of various size and complexity into which current materials can be fit.[2] Hence, the major units of syntax are patterns of well-marked dependencies: the PHRASE (a head with at least one dependent element), the CLAUSE (a unit with at least one noun or noun-phrase and an agreeing verb or verb-phrase), and the SENTENCE (a bounded unit with at least one non-dependent clause).[3] These units can all be utilized in a short span of time and processing resources. For long-range stretches of text, there are devices for showing how already used structures and patterns can be re-used, modified, or compacted. These devices contribute to STABILITY (cf. III.14) and ECONOMY (cf. V.15) in respect to both materials and processing effort. RECURRENCE is the straightforward repetition of elements or patterns, while PARTIAL RECURRENCE is the shifting of already used elements to different classes (e.g. from noun to verb). Repeating a structure but filling it with new elements constitutes PARALLELISM. Repeating content but conveying it with different expressions constitutes PARAPHRASE. Replacing content-carrying elements with short placeholders of no independent content constitutes the use of PRO-FORMS. Repeating a structure and its content but omitting some of the surface expressions constitutes ELLIPSIS. One can also insert surface signals for the relationships among events or situations in a textual world, namely by using TENSE, ASPECT, and JUNCTION. The ordering of expressions to show the importance or newness of their content yields FUNCTIONAL SENTENCE PERSPECTIVE. In spoken texts, INTONATION can also signal importance or newness of content.

4. Cohesion *within* a phrase, clause, or sentence is more direct and obvious than cohesion *among* two or more such units. Even so, the issue of how these closely-knit units are built during the actual use of a text is worth our consideration. Procedurally, the basic phrases and clauses of English can be viewed as configurations of links between pairs of elements, many of them having further linkage (cf. Perlmutter & Postal 1978; Johnson & Postal 1980). The question is then: how and in what order are these links created?

5. Abstract grammars suggest various answers to the question, but in general, the real-time processes involved have not been prominent criteria for setting up such grammars. We would like to point out a different kind of syntax which has been demonstrated to perform the best in the simulation of language processing on computers: the AUGMENTED TRANSITION NETWORK (cf. Thorne, Bratley & Dewar 1968; D. Bobrow & Fraser 1969; Woods 1970; Christaller & Metzing (eds.) 1979). The network is a configuration of NODES, in this case, GRAMMAR STATES,[4] connected by LINKS, in this case, GRAMMATICAL DEPENDENCIES. To move from one node to another, the processor performs a TRANSITION across a link. This operation demands the identification of the link as one of a repertory of dependency types, e.g. "subject-to-verb" or "modifier-to-head". The transition can be AUGMENTED with any kind of search or access operation, such as specifying the exact category to which the upcoming node belongs (Winston 1977: 172). A special kind of augmenting could test what conceptual relation corresponds to the grammatical dependency being created (cf. V.30).

6. In a transition network, the structures of phrases and clauses are operationalized as means to build and test hypotheses about the types of elements to use or expect at any given time. Hence, these networks capture the grammatical STRATEGIES and EXPECTATIONS of language users; and they express the rules of grammar as PROCEDURES for *using* the rules (Rumelhart 1977*a*: 122). The phrase, clause, or sentence appears as an actually occurring grammatical MACRO-STATE in which elements are MICRO-STATES of the textual system.[5] The divergence between competence and performance is reconciled (vis-à-vis Chomsky 1965), because the rules are intended

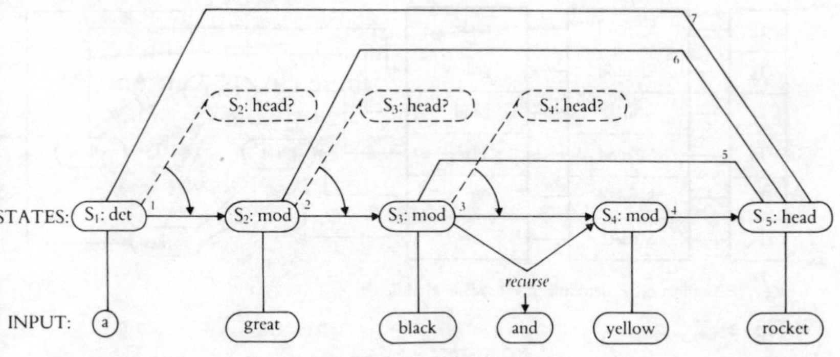

Fig. 1

to stipulate the ACTUAL rather than the VIRTUAL roles of grammatical dependencies (on actual/virtual, cf. III.12).[6]

7. We can provide here only a brief glimpse of the transition network in action (for more details, see Winston 1977; Rumelhart 1977*a*; Beaugrande 1980*a, b*). Let us model the processing of this simplified version of the opening of sample [4] in I.1:[7]

[4.1]*a* A great black and yellow rocket stood in a desert.

As we noted in III.26, the linear sequence is partly misleading, since the several modifiers are at unequal distances from their head 'rocket'. Therefore, one main operation will be to maintain the "modifier-to-head"[8] dependencies as direct links. As soon as the determiner 'a' is set up, the processor enters a NOUN-PHRASE NETWORK, i.e. a MACRO-STATE in which a head noun has at least one element depending on it. The processor sets up the goal of accessing the head; thereupon, the head will be used as a CONTROL CENTRE for the whole macro-state.[9]

8. Figure 1 shows the processor moving along through the noun-phrase network. It keeps predicting the head, but finding modifiers instead. Presumably, the hypothesis of head is given PREFERENCE, but the hypothesis of modifier is next in line to be tried (the order of preferences being of course subject to variation in different languages – we are only using English for our demonstration). We show this operation with a dotted-line link for the failed hypothesis, and a continuous link for the successful one. When the **junctive** 'and' occurs,[10] the processor can confidently predict that (*a*) another modifier is forthcoming, and (*b*) this will be the last modifier before the

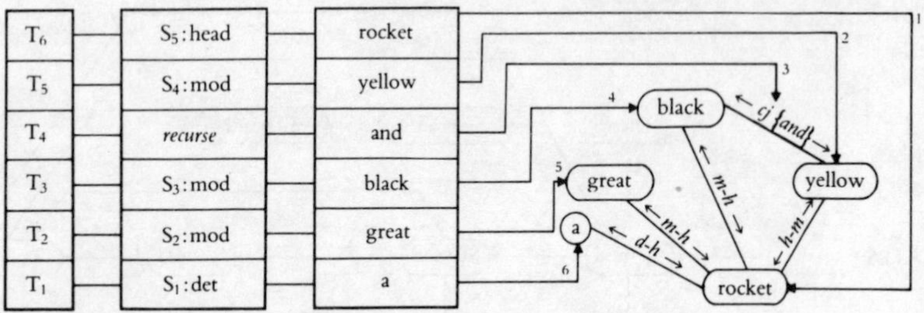

Key: *cj:* conjunction; *d:* determiner; *h:* head; *m:* modifier

Fig. 2

head. These predictions are confirmed, so that the head is attained and links between it and all its dependent elements can be filled in as shown in the upper part of Fig. 1. We can look at the operations in another perspective. The processor would place each occurrence of a single element on a HOLD STACK until the entire macro-state was constructed, and then would build a GRAMMATICAL DEPENDENCY NETWORK from the results. A "hold stack" can be used as a "pushdown" storage where elements are entered in a certain order and removed in the reverse order. Figure 2 illustrates the order for stacking our noun phrase: the times of entry are on the far left, the labels of states next to the times, and the states themselves in the middle. When the head is found, the processor creates the network structure to the right. Presumably, the elements would be taken off the stack in the reverse order from that of their entry. The small numbers along the lines are intended to indicate the order of the linkage according to that principle. However, the procedures actually used during communication may be more variable.[11]

9. The rest of our sample would be run as the construction of a VERB-PHRASE network. This macro-state is entered upon encountering the verb 'stood', which is already the head. The processor can safely anticipate a modifier, but it would be expedient to augment the search by shifting to a greater degree of detail and looking for subclasses of modifiers, e.g. adverb vs. prepositional phrase. If the adverb were the preference hypothesis, it would fail and yield to the prepositional phrase, the latter being a macro-state within the overall verb-phrase macro-state. The sub-goal is set up of finding the head of the phrase, which, in this sample, follows its determiner ('a')

Fig. 3

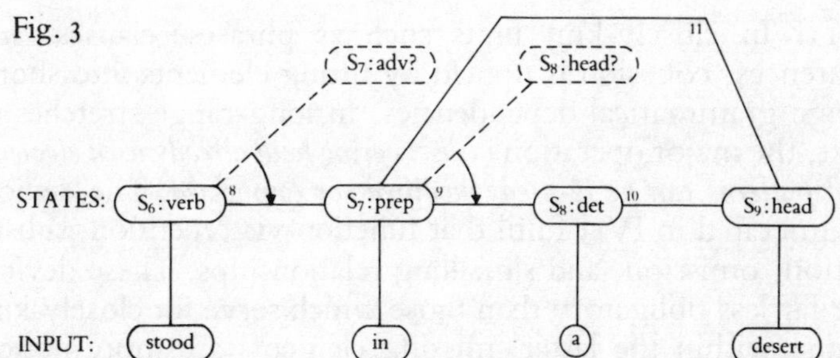

immediately ('desert'). Figure 3 shows the parsing out of the verb-phase in terms of a system of states, like Fig. 1.

10. We end up with the sentence shown not as a linear sequence, but as a labelled transition network. The nodes are the grammatical states and the links are the dependencies. Figure 4 illustrates the network in this fashion. The role of such a network would be to organize the surface structure according to the most direct access, so that the linear text could be read off it during production, or traced back to it during reception.[12] Although research on production is still very rare, there is some empirical evidence on reception that supports the model of the transition network. Stevens and Rumelhart (1975) found that people's syntactic predictions about how sentences would continue beyond a particular point agreed some 75 per cent of the time; and when readers altered a text while reading aloud,[13] their changes agreed 80 per cent of the time with their expectations established in the other tests. These proportions of agreement are strikingly high and would clearly be sufficient for workable processing. The application of expectations to the actual input would entail only minor specification and modification as foreseen by the notion of PROCEDURAL ATTACHMENT (cf. III.19). In terms of networks, the transitions could be augmented (cf. IV.9). The expected patterns would yield a reasonable match with current materials most of the time.

Fig. 4

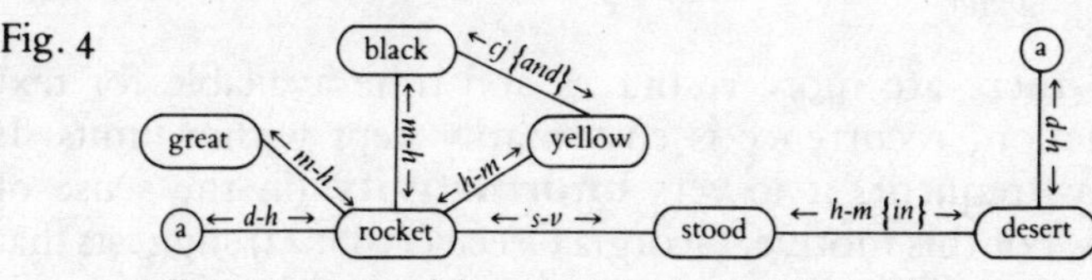

Key: *cj*: conjunction; *d*: determiner; *h*: head; *m*: modifier; *s*: subject; *v*: verb

11. In closely-knit units such as phrases, clauses, and sentences, cohesion is upheld by fitting elements into short-range grammatical dependencies. In long-range stretches of text, the major operation is *discovering how already used elements and patterns can be re-used, modified, or compacted.* The devices enumerated in IV.3 fulfil that function via repetition, substitution, omission, and signalling relationships. These devices are far less obligatory than those which serve for closely-knit units: within the latter, missing elements are more noticeable and disturbing in immediately active storage.[14] Failure to complete a clause or sentence would be more disorienting than failure to use recurrence, pro-forms, junctives, and so on. The long-range devices are thus contributors to **efficiency** rather than being grammatical obligations (Beaugrande 1980*a*): they render the utilization of the surface text stable and economic (IV.3).

12. The direct repetition of elements is called RECURRENCE, since the original occurrence merely happens again (cf. Plett 1975). Recurrence appears on various levels. Weinrich (1972) shows that grammatical categories tend to recur rather than shift – a finding obtained by Harris (1952) via a different approach (cf. II.21f.). Van Dijk (1969) suggests that components of concepts recur to support the coherence of texts. But we will glance here only at *lexical* recurrence, that is, repetition of the same words or expressions, as being the most noticeable sort.[15]

13. Recurrence is common in spontaneous speaking, where restatement results from short planning time and rapid loss of the surface text. Following a flash flood, a distraught county supervisor made this observation (reported in the *Gainesville Sun,* 20 Dec. 1978. We adopt the convention of placing demonstration elements in italics.):

[20] There's *water* through many homes – I would say almost all of them have *water* in them. It's just completely under *water*.

When there are more resources and time available for text production, recurrence is customarily kept within limits. If unduly frequent, it lowers **informativity** (in the sense of I.17f.). For this motive, Georgia Green (1968: 22) suggests that an utterance like:

[21] John ran home and John ran home.

would be unacceptable, since it is pointless to say exactly the same thing twice. However, recurrence is prominently used to assert and re-affirm one's viewpoint,[16] or to convey surprise at occurrences that seem to conflict with one's viewpoint. We have samples of both uses here:

[22] MARLOW: What, my good friend, if you gave us a glass of *punch* in the meantime? . . .
HARDCASTLE: *Punch*, sir! . . .
MARLOW: Yes, sir, *punch!* A glass of warm *punch*, after our journey, will be comfortable.
(Oliver Goldsmith *She Stoops to Conquer* 1773: 24)

Hardcastle is taken aback at being ordered around in his own house; he repeats the requested item as if he had not heard right, and Marlow repeats it twice to reassure him and to re-affirm the request. In a like manner, recurrence can be used in REPUDIATION as defined by Halliday and Hasan (1976): rejecting some material stated (or implied) in the previous discourse. The material is repeated to show exactly what is being rejected, e.g. (Deeping 1930: 729):

[23] "I think I told you that my name is Burnside."
"It might be *Smith*, sir, or *Jones*, or *Robinson*."
"It is neither *Smith*, nor *Jones*, nor *Robinson*."

In this dialogue, Mr Burnside is combating the other man's attempts to brush aside his identity with trivial, everyday names. Still another contextual factor eliciting recurrence is the need to overcome irrelevant interruptions and get on with a statement:

[24] HARDCASTLE: *He first summoned the garrison –*
MARLOW: Don't you think the ventre d'or waistcoat will do with the plain brown?
HARDCASTLE: *He first summoned the garrison, which might consist of about five thousand men –*
HASTINGS: I think not; brown and yellow mix but very poorly.
HARDCASTLE: I say, gentlemen, as I was telling you, *he summoned the garrison, which might consist of about five thousand men –*
(Goldsmith 1773: 23).

14. In poetic texts, the surface organization of the text is often motivated by special correspondences to the meaning and purpose of the whole communication.[17] In Tennyson's (1930: 237) well-known lines:

[25] Break, break, break
On thy cold grey stones, O Sea!

echoed in a later stanza with slight variation, the recurrences enact the motion of the waves being described. Frost (1969: 224) closes a poem with the lines:

[26] And miles to go before I sleep,
And miles to go before I sleep.

in order to evoke the even, continual motion of the speaker's journey in a sleigh through a snowy landscape at night. Uses like the above are instances of ICONICITY: an outward resemblance between surface expressions and their content.

15. In all of our illustrations [20 – 26], the recurring expression kept the same REFERENCE, that is, it continued to designate the same entity in the "world" of the text (or discourse).[18] Hence, stability was strongly upheld with obvious continuity (cf. III.14). If a recurrent expression has a quite different reference, the result can be disturbing, e.g. *(Wilton Times,* cited in Levin & Goldman 1978: 1):

[27] The bad news didn't surprise Miss Ankrom, who is *expecting* a baby. She said she had been half *expecting* it.

Here, the lexical recurrence is not correlated with conceptual recurrence, the element 'expect' being used in two different **senses** (cf. V.1f.).[19] The pronoun 'it' is non-determinate and might be carrying forward either 'news' or 'baby'. Although the latter alternative is bizarre, it forces itself on the receiver's attention because of the recurrence.

16. PARTIAL RECURRENCE entails using the same basic word-components but shifting them to a different word class (cf. the device of "polyptoton" in classical rhetoric). In this fashion, an already activated concept can be re-used while its expression is adapted to various settings. Here are examples from the American *Declaration of Independence:*

[28.1] . . . to assume among the powers of the earth the *separate* and equal station . . . the causes which impel them to the *separation.*

[28.2] *Governments* are instituted among Men, deriving their just powers from the consent of the *governed*.

[28.3] mankind are more disposed to *suffer*, while evils are *sufferable* . . . Such has been the patient *sufferance* of these Colonies

In his survey of partial recurrences like these, Dressler (1979*a*) notes that the presence of the one expression allows the other(s) to be rare or entirely novel. He cites the usage in Joachim Ringelnatz's story about 'The Whales and the Stranger':[20]

[29] The famous *skyscraper* made of toasted *banana* peels . . . south of the *banana-scraper*

The expression 'banana-scraper' would hardly be intelligible in the sense intended here without recourse to the co-referent expressions before it. Dressler also notes a story by Erich Fried (1975) where the title of *'Turtle-Turning'* and the expression *'turtle-turner'* are introduced without explanation until a later passage:

[30] Everywhere he finds a helpless *turtle* fallen on its back, he *turns* it over.

17. Recurrence has the disadvantage, noted in IV.13, of reducing informativity. Therefore, techniques are often used in which forms recur with somewhat different content, or content recurs with different forms. PARALLELISM entails re-using surface formats but filling them with different expressions.[21] In the *Declaration of Independence*, the British King is described as follows:

[31] He has plundered our seas, ravaged our coasts, burnt our towns.

Here, a series of similar, though not identical actions, are expressed in parallel clauses (verb – possessive pronoun – direct object) with a recurrent 'our' in the middle of each. In another passage of the same document, the king's various actions are all expressed via present participles preceded by 'for':

[32] For quartering large bodies of troops . . . For protecting them . . . For cutting off our trade . . . For imposing taxes . . . For depriving us . . . For transporting us . . . For abolishing the free System . . .

Once again, there is some relatedness among these actions (all abuses of power) which is emphasized by the parallelism of form. In addition, the repetition of formats evokes the repetition of the king's actions; indeed the expression 'repeated' is itself repeated shortly after:

[33] Our *repeated* Petitions have been answered only by *repeated* injury.

By the same token, a *reversal of form* can stress a *reversal of content,* as in the closing words of the cited passage:

[34] We must . . . hold them . . . *Enemies in War, in Peace Friends.*

18. PARAPHRASE is the recurrence of content with a change of expression,[22] as illustrated in this passage (Beerbohm 1958: 56ff.):

[35] I had never seen a *murderer* . . . the decent symbol which indemnifies the *taker of a life.*

While [35] shows the paraphrase of a single concept ('murderer'), [36] illustrates the paraphrasing of a more complex configuration (Govinda 1976: 206):

[36] When God became conscious of his omniscience, he suddenly felt terribly bored, because, *whatever happened, he knew the outcome. There was no more any surprise; there was nothing that was not known beforehand.*

It is not certain that the content of these italicized passages is the same. The question of paraphrase ultimately merges into the much debated question of SYNONYMY.[23] There seem to be only a few natural language expressions whose **virtual** meanings are identically the same. But there are many cases where contexts of occurrence determine the **actual** meanings (senses, cf. V.1) sufficiently that synonymy appears to be fulfilled, e.g. in [35] and [36].

19. **Situationality** can affect the outlook adopted on paraphrase and synonymy. Legal discourse, for instance, is intended to define certain kinds of behaviour beyond all doubt; accordingly, paraphrase is used richly in hopes of capturing every possible aspect of the intended content. The *Gainesville Telephone Directory* (1978–9: 16) quotes "Laws of Florida" which forbid using the telephone to make

[37] any comment, *request, suggestion,* or *proposal* which is *obscene, lewd, lascivious, filthy,* or *indecent.*

Under normal conditions, each series – 'request/suggestion/proposal', and 'obscene/lewd/lascivious/filthy/indecent' – would be taken as having elements meaning more or less the same (indeed, it might be hard to define one member of such a series without using other members in the definition). Still, the law is intended to cover all possible shadings and varieties of such behaviour, and thus prefers to be repetitious and pedantic if necessary. Shakespeare's Constable Dogberry provides an immortal parody of this legalistic tendency:

> [38] Marry, sir, *they have committed false report;* moreover, *they have spoken untruths;* secondarily, *they are slanderers;* sixth and lastly, *they have belied a lady;* thirdly, *they have verified unjust things;* and, to conclude, *they are lying knaves.*
>
> (*Much Ado about Nothing* V i 224–9)

The effect of this passage rests both on knowledge of the text type being spoofed (**intertextuality** supporting parody, cf. I.22) and on the failure of the Constable to maintain it (confusing the numbers, ending with a non-legal term 'lying knaves'). A textual discrepancy is matched with a discrepancy normally accepted in the "real world" (cf. IX.8; X.16).

20. Our examples should suggest the kinds of motivations that call for recurrence, partial recurrence, parallelism, and paraphrase. In general, these techniques are deployed in order to insist upon relationships among elements or configurations of content within the text, most often EQUIVALENCE (but opposition can be stressed also, cf. sample [34].[24] It follows that these techniques will be used above all in situations where stability and exactness of content can have important practical consequences, as in the application of legal texts to real life. Not surprisingly, text producers will strive to make texts fully determinate whenever a potential group of receivers is likely to contest detailed points. For instance, this passage is taken from a union contract:[25]

> [39] Except for discoveries or inventions made during the course of approved outside employment, a discovery or invention which is made in the field in which the investigator is employed by the university or by using university funds, facilities, materials, equipment, personnel, or proprietary technological information, is the property of the university, and the inventor shall share in the proceeds therefrom.

We see a veritable battery of the devices we have discussed above: recurrence ('discoveries/discovery', 'inventions/invention', 'made/made', 'university/university/university'), partial recurrence ('invention/inventor', 'employment/employed'), and paraphrase ('discovery/invention', 'investigator/inventor', 'facilities/materials/equipment'). Note that the text could have been clearer yet with parallelism:

[39]*a* a discovery or invention *which is made in the field* . . . or *which is made with the use* of . . .

21. Everyday communication does not demand this degree of certitude all the time. More often, cohesive devices are used which shorten and simplify the surface text, even though, along the way, there is a certain loss of determinacy (cf. IV.29; IV.37). One obvious device is the use of PRO-FORMS: economical, short words empty of their own particular content, which can stand in the surface text in place of more determinate, content-activating expressions (cf. Karttunen 1969; Padučeva 1970; Dressler 1972*a*: 27). These pro-forms allow text users to keep content current in active storage (cf. IV.2; V.4) without having to restate everything. The best-known pro-forms are the PRONOUNS which function in the place of the nouns or noun phrases with which they CO-REFER (i.e. share reference in the sense of IV.15).[26] In this well-known children's rhyme:

[40] There was an old woman who lived in a shoe.
She had so many children, *she* didn't know what to do.

the pronoun 'she' makes it unnecessary to keep saying 'the old woman who lived in a shoe', 'the old woman', or even 'the woman'.

22. Sample [40] illustrates ANAPHORA: using a pro-form *after* the co-referring expression (cf. Postal 1969; Bresnan 1971; Edmonson 1976; Hankamer & Sag 1976; Kaplan 1976; Bullwinkle 1977; Camarazza et al. 1977; Webber 1978). Anaphora is the most common directionality for co-reference, since the identity of the conceptual content being kept current is made plain in advance.[27] However, anaphora can still be troublesome if there is a lengthy stretch of text before the pro-form appears (cf. V.35ff.). By then, the original elements could have been displaced from active storage and other candidates may be mistakenly called.

23. The use of the pro-form *before* the co-referring expression is called CATAPHORA (cf. Halliday & Hasan 1976). Processing would require the creation of a temporarily empty slot – a position on a **hold stack,** perhaps, in the sense of IV.8 – until the required content is supplied. Such a mechanism would work best if the distance between the pro-form and the co-referring expression is kept within limits, e.g. inside the boundaries of a single sentence:

[41] I don't know if *he*'s serious, but my roommate wants to walk a tightrope over Niagara Falls.

Sample [41], taken from a student's essay, is not the only kind of cataphora. A pro-form may look ahead to an entire event rather than an individual object, as in Halliday and Hasan's (1976: 56) example:

[42] I would never have believed *it*. They've accepted the whole scheme.

Also, cataphora can be used to generate uncertainty and therefore to intensify receivers' interest (cf. VII.13). One story starts off like this:

[43] *He* was scarcely ten years old when *he* was first arrested as a vagabond.
He spoke thus to the judge: "I am called Jean François Leturc . . .
(François Coppée *The Substitute* (in Coppée 1891: 91))

A detailed self-description of the lad's life follows, removing all doubt about the identity carefully withheld in the opening sentence. Receivers will be stimulated to find out how a ten-year-old of whatever identity comes to be arrested – PROBLEMATIC knowledge because apparently not easy to connect (cf. III.17).[28] The cataphora raises a momentary problem in the surface text and helps to propel the readers into the story.

24. To test whether this interest effect can be empirically documented, an experiment with the 'rocket' text (to be depicted in more detail in IX.25ff.) entailed, among other things, showing a group of readers this rearrangement of the original [4] in I.1:

[4]*c* Empty, it weighed five tons. For fuel it carried eight tons of alcohol and liquid oxygen. There it stood in a New Mexico desert: a great black and yellow V-2 rocket 46 feet long. . . .

With the original opening sentence at the end of the paragraph, the pronoun 'it' in the new beginning is now cataphoric. The recall protocols did reveal a striking effect. Whereas only 30 per cent of the readers of the original recalled both fuels, 80 per cent did so after seeing the inversion. In exchange, 80 per cent reading the original recalled the colours, while only 30 per cent did so for the inversion. Apparently, the markedness of the inverted opening caused only a *redistribution* of the readers' **attention** rather than an absolute *increase*. This finding corresponds to the mechanism known as the "von Restorff effect" concerned with special markedness (cf. Wallace 1965). Still, the usefulness of cataphora for creating focus on some block of content – in this case, impelling readers to use content heavily in trying to figure out the co-referent for 'it' – does seem clear.[29]

25. Other elements besides nouns or noun phrases can be correlated with pro-forms. The verb 'do' is frequently employed as a PRO-VERB to keep current the content of a more determinate verb or verb phrase (cf. Karlsen 1959: 124ff.; Isačenko 1965: 172f.; Roggero 1968; Haskell 1973; Vater 1975: 37f.; Halliday & Hasan 1976: 125ff.). In this instance (Goldsmith 1773: 36):

[44] MISS HARDCASTLE: I understand you perfectly, sir.
MARLOW (aside): Egad! and that's more than I *do* myself.

the pro-verb 'do' stands for 'understanding Marlow perfectly'. The pro-verb can, as we see, co-refer with a considerable block of content. In this text:

[45] To this day I am ashamed that I did not spring up and pinion him, then and there. Had I possessed one ounce of physical courage, I should have *done so*. (Beerbohm 1958: 57)

the term PRO-MODIFIER might be used for 'so' in sample [45], or, more specifically, PRO-COMPLEMENT (cf. Steinitz 1968: 148ff.). The 'so' can stand for whatever modifiers were connected to the verb in the original verb phrase (cf. Bolinger 1970; Bouton 1970). In British English, 'so' is more often omitted in such usage than in American. In American, the Inspector's reply (Priestley 1950: 299):

[46] MRS BIRLING: I don't understand you, Inspector.
INSPECTOR: You mean you don't choose to *do*, Mrs Birling.

would more likely be:

[46]*a* INSPECTOR: You mean you don't choose to *do so,* Mrs Birling.

Another pro-form would be a pro-modifier like 'such' (cf. Hasan 1968: 78; Palek 1968: 61ff.; Figge 1971: 175), as in:

[47] Gerald Middleton was a man of mildly but persistently depressive temperament. *Such* men are not at their best at breakfast. (Wilson 1958: 3)

Here, 'such' co-refers with the entire depiction of the 'man'.

26. It would be wrong to imply that pro-forms must always co-refer with elements of the same type, e.g. pronouns with nouns, pro-verbs with verbs, pro-complements with complements, and pro-modifiers with modifiers. Such correspondences are at best PREFERENCES which have the advantage of making already parsed grammatical frameworks re-usable. The pro-forms must also fit into the grammatical settings where they are needed. Consider this well-known passage *(Julius Caesar* I ii 194–5):

[48] Yond Cassius has a lean and hungry look.
He thinks too much. *Such men* are dangerous.

The co-reference of 'Cassius/he' is entirely straightforward: noun followed by pronoun, both in the subject slot of their respective sentences. In contrast, the pro-modifier 'such' carries forward the content of 'has a lean and hungry look' plus 'thinks too much' – two verb phrases thus co-referring with a single pro-adjective. Some researchers (e.g. Lakoff 1968) would also classify 'men' as a pseudo-pronoun or quasi-pronoun on the grounds that it has only minimal content of little relevance, criteria that would include 'thing' as well as equivalents in other languages (German 'Ding', Italian and Spanish 'cosa', etc.) (cf. Green 1968: 25; Hasan 1968: 94f.; Dougherty 1969: 513f.).

27. In addition, the pro-forms often must be correlated with entire clauses ("clausal substitution" in Halliday & Hasan 1976: 130–141). The pro-form 'so' is especially versatile. In this stretch of text:

[49] "Are you to get in at all?" said the Footman. "That's the first question, you know."

It was no doubt; only Alice did not like to be told *so*.

(Carroll 1960: 81)

the 'so' carries forward the entire content of what the Footman said. In the following usage:

[50] "Of course you agree to have a battle?" Tweedledee said in a calmer tone.

"I suppose *so*," the other sulkily replied.

(Carroll 1960: 241)

'so' signals affirmation of the other person's utterance, and its converse would be 'not'.[30] The "substitution of clauses" is carried out by pro-forms which signal that the *content* of the clauses is to be kept active, not their *surface format*.

28. The settings of pro-forms also vary in regard to *specificity*. Lakoff (1968) suggests that the usual progression starts with the most specific and determinate content and moves toward the least. We might have a sequence of: (*a*) proper name, (*b*) specific description, (*c*) general class (pseudo-pronoun in the sense of IV.26), and (*d*) pro-form. An illustration might be:

[51] *Napoleon* arrived at the palace. The *conqueror of Austria* was in high spirits. I never saw such an elated *man*. *He* hardly ever stopped talking.

This progression is probable because the content should be most clearly specified at the first use before re-use later on. However, a reversal of the progression would be a striking means to reveal the identity of the referent bit by bit. That tactic is in fact used in a story by Nikolai Leskov (1961: 55):

[52] *Who* should walk in but a venerable old *man* in whom His Grace immediately recognized one of the *saints of the church*, no other than the *Right Reverend Sergius*.

Sample [52] shows how **effectiveness** can be increased by not following a convention set up for the sake of **efficiency** (cf. I.23; III.9).

29. The efficiency criterion is stressed in Beaugrande (1980*a*) as a prime motivation for pro-forms in general (cf. IV.11). At a certain point, however, a TRADE-OFF appears between compactness and clarity. Pro-forms save processing effort by being shorter than the expressions they replace, but if those expressions are hard to locate or determine, the savings are lost

again on search and matching operations. Various techniques can be applied in non-determinate cases. Chafe (1976: 47) suggests that a sample like:

[53] Ted saw Harry yesterday. *He* told *him* about the meeting

would be processed with a preference for keeping the subject status constant (Ted=he, Harry=him).[31] Another strategy would be to consult the organization of the situations, objects, or events in the textual world. When the *Declaration of Independence* says:

[54] He has constrained our fellow Citizens . . . to become executioners of *their* friends and Brethren, or to fall *themselves* by *their* Hands.

the pro-form 'their' is shifted in rapid succession from 'Citizens' to 'friends and Brethren'; any other reading would not fit the events. The same factor applies to the 'rocket' text that begins:

[4] A great black and yellow rocket stood in a New Mexico desert. Empty *it* weighed five tons.

From the standpoint of syntax alone, 'it' might co-refer with 'rocket', 'desert', or even 'New Mexico'. The **lexicon** would not help, since no reasonable definitions would stipulate what a rocket, a desert, or the state of New Mexico ought to weigh. The co-reference is simply resolved via the world-knowledge that the weight of a flying object such as a 'rocket' is **problematic**[32] (it may cause a flight to fail, cf. III.17) and hence likely to be mentioned; parts of the landscape are seldom moved, so that their weight would be irrelevant for normal tasks (and probably undiscoverable anyway).

30. The preference for problematic knowledge in textual discourse is a pervasive principle of organization because it determines what people consider **interesting** and hence worth talking about (cf. Schank 1977; Beaugrande 1980*a*). Consider this fragment of a conversation:

[55] "Next morning he gets up, has a fire lit, orders in three shillins' worth o' crumpets, toasts 'em all, eats 'em all, and blows his brains out."
"What did he *do that* for?" inquired Mr Pickwick abruptly
(Dickens 1947: 617)

The pro-forms 'do that' might refer to all of the mentioned actions in Sam's story ('gets up', 'has a fire lit', etc.), but there is little doubt that Mr. Pickwick's question is only directed to the last-mentioned one. 'Blowing one's brains out' is by far the most problematic, since no **reason** is apparent, whereas people 'get up', 'light fires', 'toast crumpets', etc., in the everyday course of life.

31. The same principle would apply to sorting out *homonyms* (words of the same outward format but differing in meaning or function), such as the pro-form 'one' and the numerical 'one'. The pro-form is often used for an unspecified member of a class, e.g. (Dickens 1948: 128):

[56] It's a very distressing case – very; I never knew *one* more so.

where 'one' designates any (unknown) 'case' meeting the description 'more distressing than the present case'. Similarly, 'one' can serve in place of an unspecified person, e.g. (Govinda 1976: 15):

[57] *One* should not form judgements on the ground of such perceptions, nor should *one* allow *one*'s thoughts to be determined and led by them.

Now consider this newspaper headline *(Gainesville Sun* 20 Dec. 1978):

[58] San Juan Gunfire Kills *One*

Text receivers will hardly construe 'one' as an unspecified person ('San Juan Gunfire Kills People'), since that would not be **informative:** it entails no problem because gunfire can be fatal in any city. Hence, 'one' will be preferentially taken as the numerical, being the number of entities affected by this particular shooting incident.

32. Another cohesive device contributing to compactness and efficiency is ELLIPSIS (cf. Karlsen 1959; Gunter 1963; Isačenko 1965; Crymes 1968; Dressler 1970; Halliday & Hasan 1976; Grosz 1977). An examination of the sources just cited will reveal considerable dispute over what constitutes ellipsis. The dispute is due to differences in the requirements of a grammar. If the criteria for well-formedness and logical stringency are very extensive, a great many real texts will appear elliptical.[33] In the procedural approach advocated here,

ellipsis is present only when text processing involves an *apperceptible discontinuity of the surface text*. The question of whether a given sample is truly elliptical must eventually be decided empirically (which surface structures do text users consider discontinuous?).

33. Usually, ellipsis functions via a sharing of structural components among clauses of the surface text. The typical case is *anaphoric,* i.e. the complete structure occurs before the elliptical one (cf. IV.22):

> [59] Mine be thy love, and thy love's use their treasure
> (Shakespeare *Sonnet XX*)

In [59], the verb 'be' from the first clause is needed to complete the second ('thy love's use *be* their treasure'). The complete structure should still be recoverable in such cases, so that the distance to the elliptical one must be kept within limits. Ellipsis does, however, often occur in a new utterance unit rather than in the same one:

> [60] The daughter is said to be well-bred and beautiful; the son an awkward booby, reared up and spoiled at his mother's apron strings. (Goldsmith 1773: 14)

A change of speaker may be involved:

> [61] BRUTUS: Let me tell you, Cassius, you yourself
> Are much condemned to have an itching palm;
> To sell and mart your offices for gold
> To undeservers.
> CASSIUS: I an itching palm?
> (*Julius Caesar* IV iii 9–12)

The recovery of the full forms ('the son is said to be an awkward booby', 'I am much condemned to have an itching palm?') is not difficult, even though, in [61], there is some distance between the complete stretch and the elliptical one.

34. Ellipsis is most noticeable when follow-up structures lack the verb – a relationship called *gapping* by Ross (1970) – because in English at any rate, the verb is the least dispensable element in a clause. The ellipsis of subjects in independent clauses is not uncommon:

> [62] He's always asleep. Goes on errands fast asleep . . . I'm proud of that boy – wouldn't part with him on any account.
> (Dickens 1947: 55)

The dispensability of subjects may be related to Chafe's observation about subject roles (cf. IV.29); the subject slot is the likely place to direct attention when completing elliptic structures like 'goes on errands' because this role is assumed to remain stable. All the same, Leech and Svartvik (1975: 168) note that ellipsis of subjects in dependent clauses is rare in English, e.g..

[63] He was so tired that went to sleep.[33a]

even though there would be no trouble supplying the subject.

35. The ellipsis of subjects or other dispensable elements illustrates the complexity of interaction between cognition and syntactic conventions. The identity of the missing subject is beyond all doubt in [63]; yet such a construction is seldom used. A **procedural approach** is concerned with discovering the conditions under which ellipsis becomes frequent. A **situation** such as sending a telegram will elicit heavily elliptic texts that are nonetheless comprehensible. The texts of Mr Alfred Jingle, though admittedly eccentric in their fragmented format, are not hard to follow:

[64] Fired a musket – fired with an idea – rushed into wine shop – wrote it down – back again – whiz, bang – another idea – wine shop again – pen and ink – back again – cut and slash – noble time, sir. (Dickens 1947: 11)

Yet if the function of syntax in communication is, as we argued in IV.2ff., to provide a surface organization that constrains hypotheses about the organization of underlying concepts and relations (a system with few options acting as a kind of "distant early warning" for a system with many more options), then partial use of syntax, as in [64], would constitute a substantial processing strain. The *problem-solving* that imposes cohesion and coherence on discourse (see Chapter III) would have to work unusually hard in all kinds of directions. Mr Jingle's utterances are easy enough to piece together when supplied in print, but they could be confusing if we heard them spoken.

36. Little research has been done on the processing of elliptical texts, because the well-formed sentence was usually taken as the obligatory unit for language experiments.[34] The dominant role of the sentence in linguistic theories engenders

the notion that "perhaps all utterances are derived from implicit complete sentences" (R. Brown 1973: 209). However, this notion is hardly convincing and certainly not empirically proven. The conversion of a text such as [64] to complete sentences would be useful, but not necessary for processing. Moreover, it would be difficult to agree upon any complete version. Quite possibly, processing might *bypass* some utilization of syntax whenever the expenditure of effort would outweigh the benefits; the processor would attempt to recover coherence more directly, doing only "fuzzy parsing" of the surface (cf. Burton 1976; VII.9). Exhaustive utilization of syntax, possibly done by augmenting the transitions of the grammar net (cf. IV.9), would be encouraged whenever other cues do not prove conclusive, e.g. in the presence of ambiguities.

37. Like the use of pro-forms, ellipsis illustrates the **trade-off** between compactness and clarity (cf. IV.29). Utilizing texts with no ellipsis consumes time and energy. At the other extreme, very heavy ellipsis cancels out any savings of time and energy by demanding intensive search and problem-solving. Text users must weigh the **appropriateness** of ellipsis to the setting to decide what extent will contribute to rather than damage **efficiency** (cf. III.9). This weighing operation is a typical difference between an abstract system of syntax and a procedural model of syntax in interaction with other factors of textuality.

38. Cohesion is further supported by TENSE and ASPECT (cf. Reichenbach 1947; Weinrich 1964; Wunderlich 1971; Dowty 1972).[35] These categories are organized very differently in various languages (cf. Dressler 1972*a*: 47ff.). Usually, there are means to distinguish: (*a*) past, present, and future times; (*b*) continuity vs. single points; (*c*) antecedent vs. subsequent; (*d*) finished vs. unfinished. Some of these distinctions arise mainly from the perspective of the text users at that moment (e.g. past, present, and future are relative to the situation), and others from the organization of text-world situations or events among themselves. When the verb systems do not make the distinctions explicit, modifiers or junctives must be used.

39. The strategies of text formation reflect some influences of the order in which tenses and aspects are used. In Hebrew, there is a sequence of tenses which must be used consecutively

(Harweg 1968: 284). In Bahinemo, a language of Papua New Guinea, the verb of a single dependent clause at the beginning sets the time for all events and situations mentioned in the paragraph (Longacre 1970). In Godie of the Ivory Coast, the time need be set only once for an entire text (Grimes 1975: 232). In Xavante of Brazil, two distinct aspect systems are used for events vs. non-events (Grimes 1975: 93). In Mumuye and Longuda of Nigeria, a progressive aspect is used for settings as opposed to the main sequence of events (Grimes 1975: 234).

40. Such striking variety points up the enormous complexity and subjectivity involved in the organization of **time** in a textual world (cf. Bruce 1972). The view that time is passing at a steady rate (a pre-Einsteinian, but commonly held view) is far less decisive than the interrelationships among situations and events that differ not only in duration, but also in structure and importance. As Talmy (1978: 21) points out, the same event can be expressed in different perspectives, e.g.:

[65]*a* The beacon flashed.

[65]*b* The beacon kept flashing.

[65]*c* The beacon flashed five times in a row.

In [65]*a*, the event is seen as a closed unit at a single point in time. In [65]*b*, the event is a multi-part unit extending over an unbounded expanse of time. In [65]*c*, the event is a multi-part unit with defined time boundaries. Fillmore (1977: 74) suggests that "any particular verb or other predicating word assumes, in each use, a given perspective" on a "scene". The need for envisioning "scenes" in order to process even syntactic surface formats (e.g. anaphora) has been eloquently illustrated by Dillon (1978: 70ff.).

41. Still, some consistent principles of time organization might be discoverable and relatable to systems of tense and aspect. If textuality rests on **continuity,** as claimed in III.14, text users would naturally see text-world events and situations as related (cf. I.11). Noticeable gaps could be filled by UPDATING, that is, making inferences (in the sense of I.11; cf. V.32-4) about how the text-world is evolving (cf. Sacerdoti 1977: 15; Winston 1977: 386). For instance, when the rocket 'rises' in sample [4], we update its location from 'desert' to 'sky', its fuel supply from 'eight tons' to less, etc., without

explicit statements. Some further principles of time organization have been proposed by Leonard Talmy (1978): (*a*) *plexity*, the capacity of having multiple parts; (*b*) *boundedness*, the capacity of having discernible limits; (*c*) *dividedness*, the lack of internal continuity; and (*d*) *distribution*, the pattern of actions/events in a time unit. Though considered by both Halliday and Talmy to be "grammatical" notions, they are clearly traceable back to human cognition about events and situations (cf. Miller & Johnson-Laird 1976). As in many other domains, the **cohesion** of the surface text rests on the presupposed **coherence** of the textual world (cf. Morgan 1978).

42. A clear device for signalling the relationships among events or situations is JUNCTION, the use of **junctive expressions** (in traditional grammars rather indiscriminately all called "conjunctions") (cf. Gleitman 1965; Dik 1968; Tai 1969; Harweg 1970; Dougherty 1970–1; R. Lakoff 1971; Halliday & Hasan 1976; Lang 1976; van Dijk 1977*b*). At least four major types should be discussed:

(*a*) CONJUNCTION links things which have the same status, e.g. both true in the textual world.
(*b*) DISJUNCTION links things which have alternative status, e.g. two things of which only one can be true in the textual world.
(*c*) CONTRAJUNCTION links things having the same status but appearing incongruous or incompatible in the textual world, e.g. a cause and an unanticipated effect.
(*d*) SUBORDINATION links things when the status of one depends on that of the other, e.g. things true under certain conditions or for certain motives (precondition/event, cause/effect, etc.).

43. These types are recognizable by the classes of **junctives** as **surface cues** for each. CONJUNCTION is most often signalled by 'and', and less often by 'moreover', 'also', 'in addition', 'besides', 'furthermore', etc. Conjunction is an *additive* relation, for instance, when connecting two interdependent events or situations mentioned within a sentence, e.g.:

[66] The great birds like to roost in trees in parks just outside the town, *and* since 1885 the local citizens have made the best of the situation. (*TIME* 26 March 1979)

Conjunction can carry across the boundaries of the sentence:

[67] Sadat called this a means of protecting the "human rights" of the Gaza Palestinians. *And* to ensure that Gaza attains autonomy, Sadat wanted a firm commitment. (*TIME* 26 March 1979)

Conjunction can link utterances not formatted as complete sentences at all, provided an additive or interdependent relationship obtains:

[68] After all I've done for law enforcement – *and* for them to treat me this way. (*TIME* 26 March 1979)

Conjunction is the **default** junction, since, unless specified otherwise, events and situations are combined additively in a textual world. There is no motive to place 'and', 'also', 'in addition', etc. between all clauses or sentences; in fact, such a practice renders the text dull except for occasional special effects (cf. the device of "polysyndeton" in classical rhetoric). The use of such junctives is more likely when interdependency is not obvious and should be stressed.

44. DISJUNCTION is nearly always signalled by 'or' (sometimes expanded to 'either/or', 'whether or not', etc.). It is most commonly employed within sentences:

[69] A man must not be too precipitate, *or* he runs over it [his hat]; he must not rush to the opposite extreme, *or* he loses it altogether. (Dickens 1948: 49f.)

Within a sentence, 'or' joins alternatives both of which are current in active storage, but only one of which obtains in the textual world. Between sentences, 'or' tends rather to announce an afterthought, an alternative not considered before:

[70] "Unless Mr Winkle feels aggrieved by the challenge; in which case, I submit, he has a right to satisfaction."
Mr Winkle, with great self-denial, expressed himself quite satisfied already.
"*Or* possibly," said the man, "the gentleman's second may feel himself affronted." (Dickens 1947: 31)

Disjunction is probably not easy to process, since text users would have to carry forward both alternatives in active storage until a resolution is found.

45. CONTRAJUNCTION is signalled most often by 'but' and less often by 'however', 'yet', 'nevertheless', etc. It is the function

of contrajunction to ease problematic transitions at points where seemingly improbable combinations of events or situations arise. In a sample like:

[71] Discouraged aides talked openly of the trip becoming a debacle. *But* at the last minute Carter achieved a victory of presidential diplomacy. (*TIME* 26 March 1979)

the text producer deploys 'but' to alert receivers that the expected 'debacle' became something totally different, a 'victory'. In this text:

[72] Carter was upset and angry. *But* Begin remained firm. (*TIME* 26 March 1979)

contrajunction signals that a natural response to the anger of a powerful personage, namely conciliation, was not the case.

46. SUBORDINATION is represented by a large repertory of junctive expressions: 'because', 'since', 'as', 'thus', 'while', 'therefore', etc. Subordinating junctives make common types of COHERENCE RELATIONS explicit, such as those outlined in I.6-11 (cf. also Chapter V). One type well represented by junctives is CAUSE (necessary conditions, cf. I.7):

[73] It would befoul Long Beach Harbour with oil spills and seriously worsen the local smog problem, *because* merely unloading the oil would release hydrocarbon fumes into the atmosphere. (*TIME* 26 March 1979)

REASON (rational human reaction, cf. I.8) is also frequent:

[74] The judge refused, *on the grounds that* he lacked authority.

47. The repertory of junctive expressions is large for the relation of TEMPORAL PROXIMITY (cf. I.10) as well: 'then', 'next', 'before', 'after', 'since', 'whenever', 'while', 'during', and so on. Proximity can be sequential if events or situations are ordered in respect to each other, e.g.:

[75] The President emotionally declared that he was "glad to be home". *Then* he told the gathering what it had come to hear. (*TIME* 26 March 1979)

Overlap can be indicated rather than sequentiality:

[76] The following day the Egyptian Cabinet also unanimously approved the final details of the agreement. *Meanwhile,* the Israeli and Egyptian Defense Ministers met in Washington. (*TIME* 26 March 1979)

Temporal proximity can involve a chaining where the termination of one event or situation coincides with the initiation of the next, possibly with causality implied as well.

[77] *When* Carter brought up Sadat's proposals, Begin said they were "completely unacceptable". (*TIME* 26 March 1979)

48. Still another use of subordination is to signal MODALITY, that is, the probability, possibility, or necessity (or the opposites of those) of events and situations (cf. Reichenbach 1976). The junctive 'if' marks a *condition* under which some event or situation would be true, e.g. in Mrs Thatcher's campaign remark (*Daily Telegraph* 26 April 1979):

[78] We can have German standards of living *if* we have German standards of work.

Modality is important for PROJECTED events and situations, those which might happen or might have happened in a textual world (cf. V.28). For past time, there is usually no longer any possibility for the projection to be true:

[79] *If* the principle tower of Rochester Castle *had* suddenly *walked* from its foundation, and stationed itself opposite the coffee-room window, Mr Winkle's surprise *would have been* nothing compared with the profound astonishment with which he heard this address. (Dickens 1947: 24)

The contrary-to-fact status of the walking tower and its results are, as we see, also signalled by marked verb tenses ('had walked', 'would have been').

49. The intricacies of junction are far greater than our sketch might imply. Except for disjunction, the use of junctives as explicit signals is rarely obligatory, because text users can recover relations such as additivity, incongruity, causality, etc. by applying world-knowledge. We could delete the junctives from samples [66], [67], [73], [76], and [77], adding punctuation occasionally, without rendering the texts doubtful. But by using junctives, text producers can exert control over how relations are recovered and set up by receivers. For instance, using 'then' in [75] makes it clear that the President's 'emotional declaration' was not (as might be assumed if 'then' were deleted) what 'the gathering had come to hear'; the producer can thus insert his or her own interpretation into the **monitoring** of the situation (cf. VIII.1).

50. In this perspective, junction demonstrates how com-

municative interaction, not just grammatically obligatory rules, decides what syntactic formats participants use. Junctives can be a simple token of courtesy to help make reception of a text efficient. They can assist the text producer as well during the organization and presentation of a textual world. They can, as we saw in IV.49, imply or impose a particular interpretation. Yet they are seldom to be found in every transition among events and situations of an entire textual world. Apparently, a certain degree of **informativity** is upheld by not using junctives incessantly. There are other surface categories which can fulfil the same functions, e.g. using causative verb forms (cf. Grimes (1964) for a comparison of Huichol and English) or inserting interjections (cf. Gülich 1970; Franck 1979).

51. A special aspect of interaction between syntax, informativity, and communicative settings has been stressed in FUNCTIONAL SENTENCE PERSPECTIVE mentioned in II.18. The mere placement of materials in the earlier or later stretches of clauses and sentences suggests the relative priorities and degrees of informativity of underlying content (for discussions and surveys, cf. Mathesius 1928; Firbas 1962, 1964, 1966, 1968, 1974, 1975; Halliday 1967-8; Beneš 1968; Chafe 1970, 1976; Sgall et al. 1973; Daneš (ed.) 1974; Dahl (ed.) 1974; Grossman, San & Vance (eds.) 1975; Grimes 1975; Firbas & Golková 1976; Li (ed.) 1976; Jones 1977). The extent to which this aspect controls syntax varies according to the number of other constraints that apply. In English, the lack of a differentiated morphemic system in many areas places heavy constraints on word-order patterns. In Czech, with its richer morphemic systems, word order can follow the functional perspective much more faithfully (Sgall et al. 1973).[36]

52. Since people tend to give a point of orientation before presenting new or surprising things, informativity tends to rise toward the end of a clause or sentence. Consider the opening of a story from the Tibetan biographies of the Eighty-Four Siddhas (Govinda 1976: 25).

[80.] There once was a hunter called Savari. [80.2] He was very proud of his strength and marksmanship. [80.3] The killing of animals was his sole occupation, [80.4] and this made his life one single sin. [80.5] One day, while he was out hunting, he saw a stranger.

The text begins with an empty expression 'there once was' that merely asserts the existence of the main character. The character's profession and name are saved until the end stretch, with the more specific name following the less specific profession [80.1]. The character now can appear as the subject of the next sentence, whose predicate offers more material about his traits. Of course, a hunter could be readily expected to possess 'strength' and 'marksmanship'; but in this story, the hunter will be defeated on precisely those two counts, such that the narrator is motivated to stress them here. A format such as:

[80.2]*a* His strength and marksmanship made him very proud.

would create less **focus** on the crucial elements. In [80.3], 'the killing of animals' makes a good beginning because it follows determinately from the already stated profession 'hunter'; the new material is that this activity is his 'sole occupation' (i.e. unredeemed by works of kindness), leading into [80.4]. An anaphoric 'this' (in [80.4]) keeps the content of the preceding sentence active so that a characterization ('a single sin') can be added. The opening of [80.5] presents Savari in his usual occupation; the sentence ends up with the expression of a new arrival ('stranger') on the scene.

53. We shall look into informativity in more detail in Chapter VII. We wanted to note here that, since cohesion rests on the assumption of underlying coherence (cf. IV.41), the sequencing of surface texts gives signals about the shared knowledge to be applied during a given stage of the communicative interaction. For example, due to the strategic usefulness of presenting known material first, the subjects of English sentences are often, though certainly not always, expressions (re)activating established or predictable content (cf. Firbas 1966*a*). The latter stretch of the predicate is, in turn, especially serviceable for creating **focus.**

54. A subsidiary cohesive system available only for spoken texts is INTONATION (cf. Halliday 1967; Crystal 1969; Lehiste 1970, 1975; Brazil 1975). In English, the usual pattern is a *rising* intonation toward the ends of clauses or sentences, notably reaching a peak on the last expression conveying substantive content. Although research was long centred on clauses and sentences, David Brazil (1975) has recently undertaken an

account of intonation in whole texts or in texts within discourses. He adopts Halliday's (1967) "tones" but re-names them to suggest the kinds of **discourse actions** (cf. VI.11) involved. INVOKING ("referring") is done when the speaker presents predominantly known or expected material, while INFORMING ("proclaiming") is done when the speaker presents predominantly new, unexpected, corrective, or contrastive material (cf. VIII.10). Hence, informing is more prone to elicit responses from other participants than is invoking. There is also a *neutral* option not deemed to qualify as either action.

55. The TONE is the rising or falling tendency of a TONE GROUP (a stretch of text uttered as a unit). The basic choice is between a *falling* tone and a *falling-rising* (falling, then rising) one (Tones 1 and 4 in Halliday's scheme). The falling tone is normally used for informing, and the falling-rising for invoking. If we use arrows pointing either down (fall) or down, then up (fall-rise), we could have four patterns for the same two-part utterance, as in Figure 5 (examples from Brazil 1975: 6) [81]*a* would be used if the hearer is assumed to know about the speaker's reading 'Middlemarch', but not about future plans. [81]*b* would be appropriate if the reading of 'Adam Bede' were already known, but not the intended occasion or time of the reading. The reversing of the clauses, intriguingly enough, does not alter this outlook: [81]*c* would work for [81]*a*, and [81]*d* for [81]*b*. Apparently, the contrasting intonation of the clauses makes the rising-falling one appear as background

Fig. 5

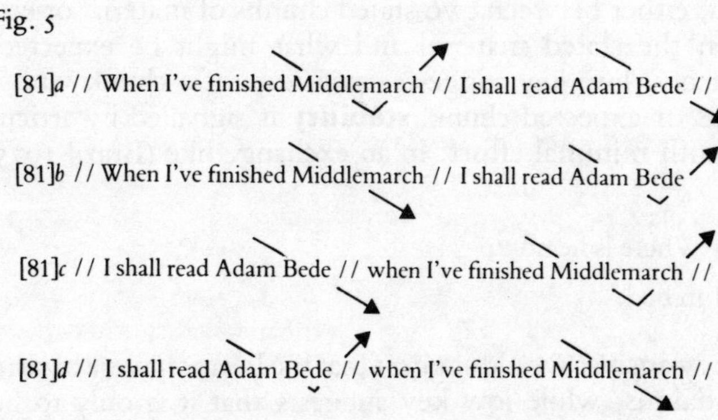

[81]*a* // When I've finished Middlemarch // I shall read Adam Bede //
[81]*b* // When I've finished Middlemarch // I shall read Adam Bede
[81]*c* // I shall read Adam Bede // when I've finished Middlemarch //
[81]*d* // I shall read Adam Bede // when I've finished Middlemarch //

Double bars mark boundaries of tone groups; arrows show tone movement.

material and the falling one as foreground, irrespective of their order of utterance.

56. In addition, Brazil (1975: 7f.) identifies two *marked* or *intensified* options indicating an extra measure of involvement on the part of the speaker. An intensified informing action would have a *rising, then falling* tone (Halliday's Tone 5). If placed on the opening clause of [81]*b*, rise-fall tone would stress the time of completing 'Middlemarch' (i.e. then and only then, then and not a moment sooner, etc.). Similarly, an intensified invoking action would have a simple *rising* tone (Halliday's Tone 2). If applied to the second clause of [81]*b*, the effect would be to turn the utterance into a question, or into a statement seeking support or confirmation in view of the speaker's own uncertainty. The rising tone is especially suited for an insistent question, or, in 'if'-clauses (cf. IV.48), an insistent condition. Finally, Brazil recognizes a *low rising* tone (i.e. rising only from low to mid key) (cf. IV.57) as a "neutral" option used to avoid committing oneself to one type of discourse action (Halliday's Tone 3).

57. This basic scheme is combined with a differentiation of KEYS going all the way back to Henry Sweet (1906). *Mid* key is the pitch considered normal for the circumstance, and *high* and *low* the pitches above and below the norm, respectively. Brazil argues that the usual discourse sequence is high-mid-low, because the high key suggests an intention to continue the current stretch of discourse, and the low key an intention to end. In particular, high key is prominently employed in *contrasts,* either between two stated chunks of material or else between the stated material and what might be expected. Conversely, low key suggests *equivalence* of a chunk with a previous or expected chunk; **stability** is signalled by articulation with minimal effort. In an exchange like (Brazil 1975: 28):

[82.1] Where is he now?
[82.2] In bed.

a high key answer would suggest that the location were bizarre or scandalous, while low key suggests that it is only to be expected. Hence, the high key would encourage further discussion, whereas the low key would indicate that no more need be said. The mid key is neutral and non-committal in this regard, and would therefore be used when one wishes to leave the option of continuing completely open.

58. Even our brief outline of Brazil's scheme should reveal its important implications for the study of texts as human activities. Intonation not only links together spoken surface texts; it also serves to *qualify* the linkage of concepts and relations both within the textual world and between the textual world and shared prior knowledge. Consider just the simple mechanisms of RECURRENCE and PARAPHRASE noted in IV.12–19 and IV.18–19, respectively. When one participant repeats or paraphrases a text just presented by another, the further development of the discourse depends crucially on intonation. A high-key recurrence or paraphrase elicits further explanation or justification, such as Hardcastle's exclamation 'Punch!' in sample [22]. A low-key recurrence or paraphrase would merely signal that the prior text has been heard and understood. A mid-key recurrence or paraphrase leaves it up to the producer of the prior text to decide whether anything more should be added. In this fashion, the choice of key is a gauge of **intentionality** and **acceptability** as speaker and hearer attitudes about **cohesion, coherence,** and **informativity.** As such, intonation contours have noteworthy influence upon **situationality** (what is going on in a particular communicative setting) and **intertextuality** (how to frame your text in regard to other people's texts in the same discourse). Moreover, any disregard for the demands of **efficiency, effectiveness,** and **appropriateness** can be immediately regulated; a high-key paraphrase would be used to respond to a severe disregard, while a low-key paraphrase would be used for a mild disregard.

59. This chapter has been devoted to the factors in text cohesion. We suggested that *short-range* stretches of surface structure are set up as closely-knit patterns of grammatical dependencies; *long-range* stretches, in contrast, could be handled by re-utilizing previous elements or patterns, economizing where possible. We progressed from cases where the surface occurrences simply happen again toward cases where greater compactness is attained. RECURRENCE entails the exact return of materials (IV.12–17). PARTIAL RECURRENCE involves different uses of the same basic language items

(word-stems) (IV.16). PARALLELISM is found when structures are re-used with different materials in them (IV.17). PARAPHRASE obtains via approximate conceptual equivalence among outwardly different materials (IV.18-19). We argued that these four devices are preferentially deployed when text producers wish to preclude uncertainty or contest. For everyday use, other devices serve to compact the surface text: PRO-FORMS are brief, empty elements that are employed to keep the content of fuller elements current and, where expedient, to re-use basic syntactic structures (or compacted versions of these) (IV.21-31); ELLIPSIS allows the omission of some structural components, provided that a complete version is recoverable (IV.32–7). Pro-forms and ellipsis evince a **trade-off** where compactness might become so extreme that no savings in effort are attained after all, because energy is drained away reconstructing things (IV.29ff.; IV.37).

60. We then progressed toward devices which overtly signal relations within or among events and situations of the textual world. TENSE and ASPECT can signal relative times, boundedness, unity, order, and modality of events and situations (cf. IV.38-41). JUNCTION offers explicit markers for relationships of additivity, alternativity, incompatibility, and subordination through causality, time, modality, and so on (IV.42-50). We concluded by reviewing the contributions of FUNCTIONAL SENTENCE PERSPECTIVE as a correlation between priorities of knowledge or informativity and the arrangement of words in clauses and sentences (IV.51-53); and of INTONATION as the imposition of characteristic audible contours of tone and key upon texts in discourse, providing major cues about expectations, attitudes, intentions, and reactions (IV.54-8).

61. Though by no means complete or exhaustive, our survey should make it clear why the notion of "text cohesion" is substantially broader than usual notions of "text syntax" or "text grammar." The broadening arises from two factors: the *operationalization* of syntactic or grammatical structures as configurations utilized in real time; and the *interaction* of syntax or grammar with other factors of textuality. Syntactic theories of the 1950s and 1960s were not intended to account for those two factors, so that we may be compelled to develop new theories rather than just "revising" or "extending" standard ones. We hope at least that we have raised some issues of the

kind that new theories of text cohesion ought to encompass; and that we have set forth motives for building such theories in the wider context of human interaction.

Notes

1 As pointed out by David Johnson (1977: 153), standard sentence grammars, centred around notions like "dominance" and "precedence", have made very little of relational linkage and dependency. "Relational grammar" (cf. Cole & Sadock (eds.) 1977) is intended to compensate for this neglect.

2 On pattern matching, see note 17 to Chaper III.

3 There are of course numerous other definitions of the sentence (survey in O'Connell 1977), many of them inconsistent and confused.

4 The "state" of a system is the point where operations are centred at a given moment. We can have "macro-states" or "micro-states" by adjusting our scope of operations toward larger or smaller. We can also have different types of states: grammar states in cohesion (cf. IV.6), knowledge states in coherence (V.31), plan states in intentionality (cf. VI.13f.), information states in informativity, states of objects and participants in situationality (see note 6 to Chapter VII), and so on. Like many theoretical notions, "state" also figures as an entity in textual worlds (cf. V.26(*a*)).

5 "Macro-states" could presumably join to yield a "macro-structure" in the sense of van Dijk (1979*b*); cf. II.37.

6 Note that the actual use may be different for the same element in different dependencies. For instance, 'in a desert' is a "modifier" of the "head" 'stood', but 'desert' is also a "head" for the "determiner" 'a' (see Fig. 4).

7 In principle, the transition network should be equally applicable to production and reception of texts, as has been logically and mathematically demonstrated by Simmons and Chester (1979). There would be some obvious distinctions in the type of **search**, since the producer is making the original decisions and the receiver only recovering them; but in both cases, linkages must be found and tested before use. We approach the matter here mostly from the standpoint of reception, since that is the use for which the formalism was designed in the first place (see references in IV.5).

8 It may be better to subdivide modifier types, e.g. "adjective", "adverb", and so on; this question will have to be resolved empirically: do language users always make those distinctions? And if they do, what about cases that normal speakers might find hard to decide, e.g. 'bright' in 'The moon shone bright'?

9 cf. note 15 to Chapter 3.

10 As noted in IV.43, conjunction with 'and' is essentially *additive:* it usually joins elements of the same type or status.

11 For example, there may be several transitions being tested and traversed in parallel.

12 See note 7 to this chapter.
13 These alterations are called MISCUES (cf. Goodman & Burke 1973).
14 We do not suppose that people would build transition networks for the grammatical dependencies of whole texts (they would rather build up conceptual-relational networks after each stretch of text was processed, cf. Chapter V). But they might well have traces left of a previously built network that would make re-use easier than building something new.
15 On recurrences of other kinds, see the demonstration in VII.29-42.
16 Of course, limited repertories of language systems, especially phonemes, make a certain amount of recurrence unavoidable (cf. Werth 1976; Beaugrande 1978*b*). Such recurrences would hardly be noticed. The use of recurrence for insistence is illustrated in VI.18; VIII.24, 26.
17 As noted in IX.9, poetic texts are definable according to their reorganization of mapping strategies onto the surface text. Receivers therefore focus more attention on recurrences of all kinds.
18 The discussions over reference among philosophers have been lengthy and seldom conclusive (survey in Lyons 1977: 174-229). The tendency is to try to explain all kinds of reference on the basis of the few marginal cases we can nail down, e.g. naming objects present. See V.40 for a different outlook, where reference is a property of textual worlds, not of words.
19 The "sense" is the actual knowledge conveyed by a text element within its continuity of coherence (cf. V.1f.). Doubtful reference of course follows from doubtful sense but not necessarily vice versa (see note 18 to this chapter).
20 Where it can be done without distorting the demonstration, we provide our own translations of non-English samples and citations. The *creative* use of partial recurrence is in conformity with the "general theory" of creativity outlined in Beaugrande (1979*c*).
21 For more illustrations, cf. VII.34.
22 For more illustrations, cf. VII.37, 41, and VIII.24.
23 See for instance Hirsch (1975). Some illustrations are noted in VII.37.
24 The notion of "equivalence" was central in descriptive linguistics (cf. II.21f.). In our usage, however, there is usually some degree of approximation; the important factor is the **stability** of an actual system when occurrences (or blocks of occurrences) belong to the same general type. Such is the case here.
25 From the *Agreement between the Board of Regents, State University System of Florida, and United Faculty of Florida, 1978-1981* (no date or place of publication), p. 22.
26 We use the term "co-refer" because it is well established, but we retain the reservations expressed in note 18. Perhaps "co-sense" would be more fitting than "co-reference" in some instances.
27 On different usage in Samoan, compare Chapin (1970).
28 The tendency to prefer problematic knowledge as discourse material is stressed again in IV.29f.; IX.14, 26.
29 There may also be effects of **primacy** (the first part of a presentation being favoured) at work (cf. Meyer 1977: 308f.). See IX.37.5 and note 23 to Chapter IX.

30 On the many uses of 'so', cf. Halliday & Hasan (1976: 140) and accompanying discussion.

31 Reichman (1978: 290) points out an interesting case where a proper name is used rather than a pro-form, even though no confusion would be possible, apparently because the person mentioned is outside the focus of attention; the person in focus is referred to via a pro-form.

32 See note 28 to this chapter.

33 The question is: "elliptical in comparison to what?" (Coseriu 1955–6). Alfred Whitehead was prone to condemning natural language because of its incompleteness.

33*a* This construction is in fact used in Spenser's *Faerie Queene* (I i 42): 'but he againe shooke him so hard, that forced him to speake'. Dillon (1978: 118) classes such usage as "ungrammatical".

34 The "cloze" procedure of omitting words periodically for test persons to supply is not really comparable to using ellipsis in spontaneous discourse.

35 In common usage, "tense" designates the inflection of verbs to show time relative to the act of discourse, while "aspect" subsumes the boundaries (beginning, completed) and duration of events as marked by verb inflections.

36 On many other languages, cf. Grimes (1975); Grossman, San & Vance (eds.) (1975); Li (ed.) (1976); Grimes (ed.) (1978).

Chapter V

Coherence

1. If MEANING is used to designate the *potential* of a language expression (or other sign) for representing and conveying knowledge (i.e., *virtual* meaning), then we can use SENSE to designate the knowledge that *actually* is conveyed by expressions occurring in a text. Many expressions have several virtual meanings, but under normal conditions, only one sense in a text. If the intended sense is not at once clear, NON-DETERMINACY is present. A lasting non-determinacy could be called AMBIGUITY if it is presumably not intended, or POLYVALENCE if the text producer did in fact intend to convey multiple senses at the same time. Though not yet well explained, the human ability to discover intended senses and preclude or resolve ambiguities is one of the most amazing and complex processes of communication (cf. for example Hayes 1977).

2. A text "makes sense" because there is a CONTINUITY OF SENSES among the knowledge activated by the expressions of the text (cf. Hörmann 1976). A "senseless" or "non-sensical" text is one in which text receivers can discover no such continuity, usually because there is a serious mismatch between the configuration of concepts and relations expressed and the receivers' prior knowledge of the world. We would define this continuity of senses as the foundation of COHERENCE, being the mutual access and relevance within a configuration of CONCEPTS and RELATIONS (cf. I.6). The configuration underlying a text is the TEXTUAL WORLD, which may or may not agree

with the established version of the "real world" (cf. VII.18.1), i.e. that version of the human situation considered valid by a society or social group. Note, however, that the textual world contains *more* than the sense of the expressions in the surface text: cognitive processes contribute a certain amount of COMMONSENSE knowledge derived from the participants' expectations and experience regarding the organization of events and situations. Hence, even though the senses of expressions are the most obvious and accessible contribution to the meaningfulness of texts, they cannot be the whole picture.

3. **Knowledge** is not identical with language expressions that represent or convey it, though confusion on this point is rife in linguistics and psychology.[1] This confusion arises from the enormous difficulty in envisioning and describing knowledge and meaning without constantly relying on language expressions. Many researchers agree that a language-independent representation would be highly desirable (cf. for example Schank, Goldman, Rieger & Riesbeck 1975). But so far, we cannot seem to agree on any representational mode already proposed. This stalemate is no mere accident: instead, it reflects the nature of the entities we are trying to **systemize** (in the sense of III.3).

4. As argued in I.6, a CONCEPT can be defined as a configuration of knowledge that can be recovered or activated with more or less consistency and unity. This definition is *operational,* based on the indisputable fact that language users, when employing or being confronted with a particular expression, tend to ACTIVATE roughly the same chunk of knowledge (i.e. place the chunk in ACTIVE STORAGE, cf. III.26; IV.2).[2] Variations among different language users do not seem to be substantial enough to occasion disturbances very often. It should follow from here that the meaning of a concept is the sum of its possible uses (cf. Schmidt 1968). Unfortunately, many concepts are so adaptable to differing environments that they remain quite FUZZY in regard to their components and boundaries.[3] Therefore, defining concepts involves working with comparative PROBABILITIES: weaker or stronger likelihood that the concept will subsume certain knowledge when actualized in a textual world, where each concept appears in one or more RELATIONS to others, e.g. "state of", "attribute

of", and so on (cf. V.26). These relations constitute the LINKAGE which delimits the use of each concept.

5. If concepts can indeed subsume different knowledge elements according to the conditions of activation, then concepts cannot be primitive, monolithic units. Instead, concepts must have their own components held together by a particular STRENGTH OF LINKAGE. Components essential to the very identity of the concept constitute DETERMINATE knowledge (e.g. all humans are mortal). Components true for most but not all instances of the concept constitute TYPICAL knowledge (e.g. humans usually live in communities). Components which happen to be true of random instances only constitute ACCIDENTAL knowledge (e.g. some humans happen to be blond).[4] As Loftus and Loftus (1976: 134) point out, this gradation is also fuzzy. Very few components, for example, turn out to be absolutely determinate: birds can be birds even if they can't fly or if their feathers are stripped off; tables might have all kinds of shapes and all numbers of legs; and so on. Labov (1973) tested the borderlines where people were willing to call a presented shape a 'cup' as opposed to other vessels ('jar', etc.), and found only partial agreement. Still, some gradation of strength of linkage is probably necessary if concepts are to be operational. The concept is, after all, designed to handle *normal* instances rather than bizarre counter-examples dreamed up in peculiar situations (e.g. philosophers' debates).

6. It is one thing to agree that concepts can be **decomposed** into more basic units; it is quite another to agree upon what those units might be (cf. le Ny 1979).[5] Even straightforward cases can become entangled in unresolvable debates. For example, it ought to be fully reasonable to view the concept 'kill' as composed of 'cause', 'become', 'not', and 'alive'; yet even here, controversy rages. And texts can be found where this simple analysis fails utterly:

[83] And though I kill him not, I am the cause
His death was so effected.

(*All's Well that Ends Well* III ii 118-9)

Evidently, the components of concepts are themselves not entirely stable, whether they be called "features", "markers", "primitives", "semes", "sememes", or whatever.[6]

7. Even if we could agree on the units which constitute concepts, we would not have shown that the decomposition of concepts is a routine activity of text processing. Evidence for such routines is at present slight (Kintsch 1974: 242; J. Anderson 1976: 74; Hayes-Roth & Hayes-Roth 1977). And the unsettled questions are alarming. How many units would be needed for all possible concepts? Would the same set of units work for concepts and expressions? Given that people communicate via expressions, how are units acquired? How can we define the units without having recourse to the same kinds of expressions or concepts that we are trying to decompose? Are there units which, in the worst case, are needed for only one concept or expression in the whole language?

8. Perhaps it would be more productive to try working in the other direction: rather than asking how expressions or concepts can be cut into the tiniest possible pieces, we might inquire how expressions are assigned conceptual **senses,** and how senses are put together into large configurations of a **textual world.** Certainly, the building of textual worlds is a documented routine activity in human communication. This reversal of outlook would shift attention away from questions which adjudication a priori cannot solve (such as those in V.7) toward questions which can be pursued empirically (e.g. via reading and recall of texts, cf. IX.24ff.). The fuzziness and instability of concepts and their possible components should become steadily less prominent when they appear in more and more determinate contexts of communication. In that perspective, the sense of an expression or the content of a concept are definable as *an ordered set of hypotheses about accessing and activating cognitive elements within a current pattern*. To describe such a sense or content, one would have to stand at that point in the configuration of concepts and relations and look out along all pathways (cf. Quillian 1966).

9. The study of language meaning via this approach is the concern of a recent trend known as PROCEDURAL SEMANTICS (cf. Miller & Johnson-Laird 1976; Winograd 1976; Johnson-Laird 1977; Levesque 1977; Schneider 1978; Levesque & Mylopoulos 1979). It is recognized that in addition to DECLARATIVE knowledge (statements of facts or beliefs about the organization of events and situations in the "real world"), communication requires PROCEDURAL knowledge (facts or beliefs stated in

formats intended for specific types of uses and operations) (cf. Winograd 1975; Winston 1977: 390ff.; Goldstein & Papert 1977; Bobrow & Winograd 1977). The meaningfulness of language in texts is just a special case of the acquisition, storage, and utilization of knowledge in all manner of human activities. Since language use is highly differentiated and reasonably well regulated by social agreement, the special case is perhaps the most promising approach to the general one (cf. X.7).

10. When expressions are used in communication, the corresponding concepts and relations are ACTIVATED in a mental workspace we can hence term ACTIVE STORAGE (cf. III.29; IV.2; V.4). George Armitage Miller (1956) reported that this workspace seems limited to only about seven items at a time. It follows, he observed, that efficiency would be promoted if the items were large, well-integrated CHUNKS of knowledge rather than single, unrelated elements. Consequently, the knowledge that underlies textual activities would normally figure as GLOBAL PATTERNS which are matched and specified to accommodate current output (in production) and input (in reception) (cf. V.16). The difficulty in processing non-expected or discrepant occurrences (cf. VII.13) presumably arises because they cannot be handled as parts of well-integrated stored patterns and must be held separately in active storage until they can be fitted in and accommodated.

11. These patterns of knowledge might well look different according to the demands of current processing tasks. Text receivers would use patterns for building and testing hypotheses about what the major TOPIC is (cf. V.23) and how the textual world is being organized. It follows that the topic pattern would be utilized more richly than subsidiary patterns of marginal usefulness for the text at hand (cf. V.16). Another scale of difference would be the importance and relevance of the text for the receiver's **situation:** as these factors rise, utilization of knowledge would become more detailed and thorough (cf. III.31).

12. When some item of knowledge is activated, it appears that other items closely associated with it in mental storage also become active (though perhaps not so active as the original item). This principle is often called SPREADING ACTIVATION (see Collins & Loftus 1975) and mediates between

the explicitly activated concepts or relations and the detailed richness which a textual world can assume. In production, spreading activation might work outward from concepts or relations toward natural language expressions that could be preferentially used (cf. III.23). In reception, spreading activation makes it possible to form elaborate associations, to create predictions and hypotheses, to deploy mental images, and so forth, far beyond what is actually made explicit in the surface text. DETERMINATE and TYPICAL knowledge should be especially prone to spreading activation (cf. V.5), though ACCIDENTAL knowledge might also be involved if imprinted forcefully enough in one's own experience.

13. There is some evidence of two different principles of storing and utilizing knowledge. Endel Tulving (1972) introduced the notions of EPISODIC MEMORY VS. SEMANTIC MEMORY to account for the distinction. Episodic memory contains the records of one's own experience ('what happened to me'), while semantic memory – at least in the most appealing sense of the term[7] – reflects the inherent patterns of the organization of knowledge, e.g. the structures of events and situations ('what is true about the world at large and how it all fits together'). Of course, one's experiences continually feed into one's general views about the world, while the latter impose organization upon experience. Still, episodic knowledge would be heavily tied to the original contexts of encounter and would thus manifest many accidental traits. Semantic knowledge, in contrast, would be more dominantly organized in terms of the characteristics which all or most individual instances have in common.

14. Since the times of Plato and Aristotle up through the Middle Ages even into the present, the comparative importance of experience vs. human reasoning powers in the acquisition of knowledge has been hotly debated. Whether concepts can exist independently of all particular instances of them (as Plato believed), or whether they must all be extracted from personal experience (as empiricists asserted), are questions which may be unresolvable in the framework of the usual discussions. Any view which denies either innate human reasoning powers or the effects of real experience would prove untenable if subjected to unbiased comprehensive investigations of human conduct – a recourse which generations of

philosophers hardly seem to have considered. The utilization of texts almost certainly involves steady interactions and compromises between the actual text materials being presented, and the participants' prior disposition, according to conditions which, though flexible and variable, are by no means unsystematic (cf. discussion in IX.37ff.).

15. In a procedural approach, arguments in favour of one model of knowledge over another should be couched in terms of tasks and operations. Consider for example the question of ECONOMY. On the one hand, each item of knowledge might be stored in a system only once, no matter how many configurations would contain the item. There would be either a very dense interlocking of configurations, or else a given configuration would have to be assembled every time need arose. This kind of system offers great economy of STORAGE, but heavy expenditure on SEARCH. On the other hand, items could be **redundantly** stored in each of the configurations which include them. This system would work very rapidly on search, but would be horrendously wasteful on storage. As Walter Kintsch (1977*a*: 290f.) notes, this **trade-off** between economy of storage and economy of search is probably resolved by compromise. Frequently used configurations would be stored as wholes, in spite of the redundancy involved; unusual, seldom required configurations would be assembled via searching out component items only when occasion arises.

16. Some types of **global** patterns would be stored as complete chunks because of their usefulness in many tasks. FRAMES are global patterns that contain commonsense knowledge about some central concept, e.g. 'piggy banks', 'birthday parties', etc. (cf. Charniak 1975*b*; Minsky 1975; Winograd 1975; Petöfi 1976; Scragg 1976; Metzing (ed.) 1979). Frames state what things belong together in principle, but not in what order things will be done or mentioned. SCHEMAS are global patterns of events and states in ordered sequences linked by time proximity and causality (cf. Bartlett 1932; Rumelhart 1975, 1977*b*; Kintsch 1977*b*; Mandler & Johnson 1977; Rumelhart & Ortony 1977; Spiro 1977; Thorndyke 1977; Kintsch & van Dijk 1978; Beaugrande & Colby 1979). Unlike frames, schemas are always arrayed in a progression, so that hypotheses can be set up about what will be done or mentioned next in a textual world. PLANS are global patterns of events and

states leading up to an intended GOAL (cf. Sussman 1973; Abelson 1975; Sacerdoti 1977; Schank & Abelson 1977; Cohen 1978; McCalla 1978; Wilensky 1978*a*; Allen 1979; Beaugrande 1979*a*, *b*). Plans differ from schemas in that a planner (e.g. a text producer) evaluates all elements in terms of how they advance toward the planner's goal. SCRIPTS are stabilized plans called up very frequently to specify the roles of participants and their expected actions (cf. Schank & Abelson 1977; Cullingford 1978; McCalla 1978). Scripts thus differ from plans by having a pre-established routine. The importance of these kinds of global patterns has become recognized in the **procedural attachment** of producing and receiving texts: how a topic might be developed (frames), how an event sequence will progress (schemas), how text users or characters in textual worlds will pursue their goals (plans), and how situations are set up so that certain texts can be presented at the opportune moment (scripts). Different pattern types might share the same basic knowledge in a variable perspective (e.g. a frame for 'structure of a house' versus a plan for 'building a house'). Using global patterns greatly reduces complexity over using local ones, and allows retaining much more material in active storage at one given time. We provide some demonstrations later on.[8]

17. A further issue in procedural models of knowledge is that of INHERITANCE: the transfer of knowledge among items of the same or similar types or sub-types (cf. Fahlman 1977; Hayes 1977; Brachman 1978; Levesque & Mylopoulos 1979). At least three kinds of inheritance should be noted. First, an INSTANCE inherits all the characteristics of its CLASS[9] unless expressly CANCELLED (Fahlman 1977). We assume that Napoleon had toes – to use a familiar example from Walter Kintsch (1974) – even though nobody (but Walter) has ever told us so, because Napoleon is an instance of the class 'human beings'. If he had had no toes, there would doubtless be some historical anecdote to cancel our assumption. Second, SUBCLASSES inherit from SUPERCLASSES only those characteristics that the narrower SPECIFICATION of the subclasses allows. For example, the subclass of 'ostriches' differs from the superclass of 'birds' in being unable to fly, but able to run extremely fast. Third, entities can inherit from those with which they stand in ANALOGY, i.e. they are of different classes but comparable in

some useful respects. For instance, researchers in cognitive science and artificial intelligence are making assumptions about the human mind by analogy to the computer (cf. X.26ff.). Without claiming that minds and computing machines are the same thing, we can still discover comparable characteristics that are helpful in building complex models of cognition.

18. Inheritance falls under the consideration of **economy** raised in V.15. If knowledge about classes/instances, subclasses/superclasses, or analogies were stored in a neat hierarchy, predictions should be possible about time needed to access certain facts. For example, [84]*a* should take longer to judge "true" or "false" than [84]*b* because the superclass 'animal' is higher up in the hierarchy than the subclass 'bird', and thus to connect them demands at least one more step:

[84]*a* A chicken is an animal.
[84]*b* A chicken is a bird.

However, testing failed to confirm such predictions (cf. Collins & Quillian 1972). For one thing, [84]*c* was regularly confirmed faster than [84]*b*, though 'chicken' and 'robin' should be on the same plane in the hierarchy:

[84]*c* A robin is a bird.

Smith, Shoben, and Rips (1974) explain this effect in terms of "features" as basic components of concepts like 'bird': the more determinate and typical features (cf. V.5) an instance or subclass has, the quicker it will be judged a member of a class or superclass. 'Robins', who fly and sing well, are thus easier to judge as 'birds' than are 'chickens', who do not. In a like fashion, people are more prone to misjudge [84]*d* as true than [84]*e*:

[84]*d* A bat is a bird.
[84]*e* A stone is a bird.

because of the shared feature 'can fly' which sets 'bats' and 'birds' into an analogy. Rosch and Mervis (1975) argue that "family resemblances" are responsible for such effects rather than defining features, because it is extremely difficult in many cases to decide what features every member of a class *must* have (cf. examples in V.5).

19. We can readily see that the procedural considerations we have outlined–activation (V.4, 10), strength of linkage (V.5),

decomposition (V.6-7), spreading activation (V.12), episodic vs. semantic memory (V.13), economy (V.15), global patterns (V.16), and inheritance (V.17–18)–all depend upon each other. They all must be treated in terms of whatever are taken as the basic units and operations upon knowledge. A very simple, limited model might accommodate the results of experiments on judging sentences like [84]*a* through [84]*e* and still tell us little about that larger question (Kintsch 1979*b*). Symptomatic of this disparity is the attempt to separate off a neatly organized "lexicon" or "dictionary" of words or concepts from the vast, messy maze of an "encyclopedia" of world knowledge (cf. Smith 1978). As Kintsch (1979*b*) points out, such a separation is a research fiction which hinders the development of really powerful, general models and breaks down eventually in view of a wider range of realistic data.

20. From here, some basic conclusions can be drawn. First of all, instead of trying to cut language off from everything else, we should strive to build models in which the use of language in real texts is explainable in terms comparable to the processes of apperception and cognition at large (cf. Minsky 1975; Miller & Johnson-Laird 1976; Kintsch 1977*a*; Rumelhart 1977*a*; Beaugrande 1980*a*). The restrictions upon research which reduce all issues to a matter of variations in time for performance on unrealistic tasks (including sentence judgements along the lines depicted in V.18) run counter to the main incentive for such an undertaking. We must work toward a diversity of experiment types among which the everyday utilization of texts plays a leading role.

21. A second conclusion is that efforts to encompass the study of texts and knowledge into the framework of logic since Aristotle may prove a mixed blessing. We should rather reverse our priorities by first building humanly plausible models and then inquiring after types of logic that can serve as formalisms (Petöfi 1978: 44f.). Humans are evidently capable of intricate reasoning processes that traditional logics simply cannot explain: jumping to conclusions, pursuing subjective analogies, and even reasoning in absence of knowledge (Collins 1978). For example, when confronted with a possible fact, people might say to themselves: "If this were true, I ought to know about it; since I don't know, it is probably false" – the *lack of knowledge inference* described by Collins.

The important standard here is not that such a procedure is logically unsound, but rather that the procedure works well enough in everyday affairs.

22. A third conclusion is that, as we have already stressed (V. 8), knowledge and meaning are extremely sensitive to the **contexts** where they are utilized. We would like to pursue some implications of that view for a candidate model of text coherence. Basically, the combination of concepts and relations activated by a text can be envisioned as PROBLEM-SOLVING in the sense of III.17. Given some fuzzy, unstable units of sense and content, text users must build up a configuration of pathways among them to create a TEXTUAL WORLD (V. 2). Only certain characteristics or "features" of the concepts involved are really necessary and relevant for these operations. Such procedures as decomposition, spreading activation, inferencing, and inheritance will be carried out in accordance with the current conditions of processing. The central question is how to classify and systemize those conditions (and not how to prove that all text users do the same things all the time). In this line of inquiry, we could ask: how do people extract and organize content from texts for use in storing and recalling? What factors of the interaction between the presented text and people's prior knowledge and disposition affect these activities? What regularities can be uncovered by varying factors such as the style of the surface text or the user groups to whom the text is presented? What is the role of expectations?

23. An initial step toward exploring these and similar questions is to find a basic representation for the coherence of texts. We shall suggest at least one possible means analogous to our proposals for a procedural model of syntax in IV.5-10. Coherence will be envisioned as the outcome of combining concepts and relations into a NETWORK composed of KNOWLEDGE SPACES centred around main TOPICS. Our demonstration text will be the 'rocket'-sample [4] from I.1, used already in our brief discussion of cohesion (IV.7ff., 24, 29) as well as in some earlier research.[10]

24. Before tackling the text itself, we should call to mind the requirements for representing the processing of texts. We focus now on reception rather than production, though, as we stressed in III.29, there are undoubtedly important similarities between the two activities. The imposition of coherence on

any stretch of text should be performed along the lines suggested in III.29ff. The surface text is PARSED onto a configuration of GRAMMATICAL DEPENDENCIES, as depicted in IV.5–10. The surface expressions are taken as cues to ACTIVATE concepts (V.4, 10). This phase cannot involve a straightforward lookup in a mental "dictionary" (cf. V.19). Instead, the concepts are treated as steps in the construction of a **continuity of sense** (V. 2), and the extent of processing expended will vary according to whatever is required and useful for that task. Attention would be directed particularly toward the discovery of CONTROL CENTRES, i.e. points from which accessing and processing can be strategically done.

25. The most likely candidates for control centres can be termed PRIMARY CONCEPTS:

(*a*) OBJECTS: conceptual entities with a stable identity and constitution;
(*b*) SITUATIONS: configurations of mutually present objects in their current states;
(*c*) EVENTS: occurrences which change a situation or a state within a situation;
(*d*) ACTIONS: events intentionally brought about by an agent.[11]

26. The other concepts would be assigned to a typology of SECONDARY CONCEPTS. The following set is taken from Beaugrande (1980*a*), where a more elaborate justification is offered:

(*a*) STATE: the temporary, rather than characteristic, condition of an entity;
(*b*) AGENT: the force-possessing entity that performs an action and thus changes a situation (cf. V.25*(d)*);
(*c*) AFFECTED ENTITY: the entity whose situation is changed by an event or action in which it figures as neither agent nor instrument;
(*d*) RELATION: a residual category for incidental, detailed relationships like 'father-child', 'boss-employee', etc.,
(*e*) ATTRIBUTE: the characteristic condition of an entity (cf. "state");
(*f*) LOCATION: spatial position of an entity;
(*g*) TIME: temporal position of a situation (state) or event (cf. I.10);
(*h*) MOTION: change of location;

(*i*) INSTRUMENT: a non-intentional object providing the means for an event;
(*j*) FORM: shape, contour, and the like;
(*k*) PART: a component or segment of an entity;
(*l*) SUBSTANCE: materials from which an entity is composed;
(*m*) CONTAINMENT: the location of one entity inside another but not as a part or substance;
(*n*) CAUSE: see I.7;
(*o*) ENABLEMENT: see I.7;
(*p*) REASON: see I.8;
(*q*) PURPOSE: see I.9;
(*r*) APPERCEPTION: operations of sensorially endowed entities during which knowledge is integrated via sensory organs;[12]
(*s*) COGNITION: storing, organizing, and using knowledge by sensorially endowed entity;
(*t*) EMOTION: an experientially or evaluatively non-neutral state of a sensorially endowed entity;
(*u*) VOLITION: activity of will or desire by a sensorially endowed entity;
(*v*) RECOGNITION: successful match between apperception and prior cognition;
(*w*) COMMUNICATION: activity of expressing and transmitting cognitions by a sensorially endowed entity;
(*x*) POSSESSION: relationship in which a sensorially endowed entity is believed (or believes itself) to own and control an entity;
(*y*) INSTANCE: a member of a class inheriting all non-cancelled traits of the class (cf. V.17);
(*z*) SPECIFICATION: relationship between a superclass and a subclass, with a statement of the narrower traits of the latter (cf. V.17);
(*aa*) QUANTITY: a concept of number, extent, scale, or measurement;[13]
(*bb*) MODALITY: concept of necessity, probability, possibility, permissibility, obligation, or of their opposites;
(*cc*) SIGNIFICANCE: a symbolic meaning assigned to an entity;
(*dd*) VALUE: assignment of the worth of an entity in terms of other entities;
(*ee*) EQUIVALENCE: equality, sameness, correspondence, and the like;

(*ff*) OPPOSITION: the converse of equivalence;
(*gg*) CO-REFERENCE: relationship where different expressions activate the same text-world entity (or configuration of entities) (cf. IV.21);
(*hh*) RECURRENCE: the relation where the same expression reactivates a concept, but not necessarily with the same reference to an entity, or with the same sense (cf. IV. 12–15).[14]

27. Most of these concept types are familiar from "case grammars"[15] that undertook to classify language relationships according to the organization of events and situations (cf. Fillmore 1968, 1977; Chafe 1970; Grimes 1975; Longacre 1976; Frederiksen 1977). At some point, these schemes tend to become a classification of knowledge and its organization, reflected in other domains besides language (cf. Kintsch 1974; Charniak 1975*a*; Schank et al. 1975; Woods 1975; Wilks 1977*b*). We incorporate some further concepts to encompass mental operations (apperception, cognition, emotion, volition, communication, possession), class inclusion (instance, specification), and notions inherent in systems of meaning per se (quantity, modality, significance, value, equivalence, opposition, co-reference, recurrence). We do not claim that this typology is exhaustive, or superior to others proposed before. It is merely useful for labeling the links among concepts, e.g. that one concept is the "state of" another, or the "agent of" another, etc.; and through various combinations, we can capture the notions of other typologies we have examined so far. One might easily work with typologies having greater or lesser detail than ours.[16]

28. In addition to a typology of concepts for labelling links, we might need a set of OPERATORS which further specify the status of linkage. For example, we could introduce operators for STRENGTH OF LINKAGE in the sense of V.5: (*a*) a DETERMINATENESS operator [δ] for components necessary to the identity of a concept; and (*b*) a TYPICALNESS operator [τ] for frequent, but not necessary components. These operators would apply to configurations of world knowledge, as shown in V.39. Furthermore, we could introduce operators for linkage which involves **boundaries:** (*a*) an INITIATION operator [ι] for an entity just being created or enacted; (*b*) a TERMINATION operator [†] for the converse; (*c*) an ENTRY

operator [ϵ] for an entity coming about on its own; and (*d*) a EXIT operator [χ] for the converse of entry. Finally, two operators are useful for dealing with approximative or contrary-to-fact linkage: (*a*) the PROXIMITY operator [π] for relationships with some distance or mediation (cf. temporal proximity in I.10, causal proximity in V.36, etc.); and (*b*) the PROJECTION operator [ρ] for relations which are possible or contingent, but not true in the textual world (cf. IV.48). To distinguish operators from the link labels formed out of the beginning letters of concept names (e.g. "ca" for cause, "ti" for time, etc.), operators are Greek letters from the first or second position of the respective words, joined to the other labels with the sign "÷".[17]

29. The motives and applications for our typologies presented above should become clearer through a demonstration. We start with the opening paragraph of our 'rocket' text:

> [4] [1.1] A great black and yellow V-2 rocket 46 feet long stood in a New Mexico desert. [1.2] Empty, it weighed five tons. [1.3] For fuel it carried eight tons of alcohol and liquid oxygen.

The CONTROL CENTRE for this passage is clearly the object concept 'rocket', to which are assigned attributes ('great', 'black', 'yellow', 'long'), a specification ('V-2'), and a state ('stood') with its locations ('New Mexico', 'desert'); the attribute 'long' has the quantities '46' and 'feet'. We could put all of these conceptual relations into a network such as that shown in Figure 6. Link labels announce the type of concept that is attained by traversing links in the directions shown by the arrows. The operations would be comparable to those depicted for the TRANSITION NETWORKS in IV.5–10. The processor works from a current state to a following state by trying to identify the type of the node to be attained. The strategies of PROBLEM-SOLVING (III.17) would apply, assisted by spreading activation (V.12), inferencing (cf. V.32ff.), and global patterns (V.16).

30. It is important to compare and contrast the conceptual network in Fig. 6 with the grammatical network in Fig. 4 in IV.10. Although we still use English words in the notation of Fig. 6, we are now representing *concepts* rather than *surface expressions*. It might be desirable to have some other repre-

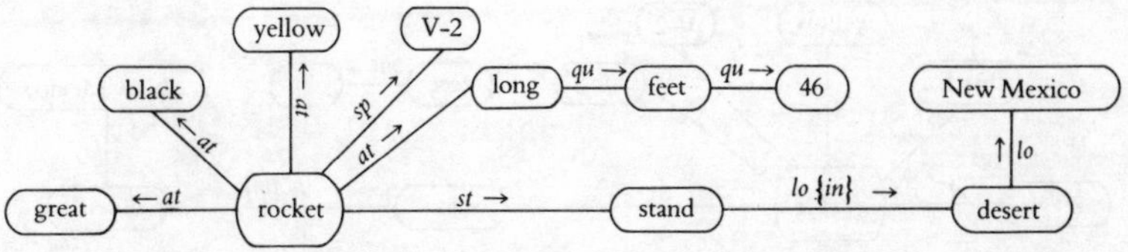

Key: *at:* attribute of; *lo:* location of; *qu:* quantity of; *sp:* specification of; *st:* state of; Fig. 6

sentation, but at present, researchers are manifestly unable to agree on any one. Notice that the general pattern of the two networks is similar: the **access** routes from node to node are much the same. Hence, it seems reasonable that text processing should make use of structural similarities on different levels as far as is expedient (cf. R. Bobrow 1978; Walker (ed.) 1978; Woods & Brachman 1978). For example, a hypothesis that *grammatical heads are usually primary concepts* would be confirmed often enough to merit its general application. Similarly, one could postulate that grammatical modifiers are attributes, states, locations, etc., in a certain preference order (on preferences, cf. III.18) as indicated by the nature of the primary concept at the control centre. Such hypotheses and preferences could serve to AUGMENT the transitions among nodes in the sense of IV.5. Where possible, the uncovering of grammatical and conceptual dependencies would interact heavily or even run in parallel rather than as two separate phases, though there would nearly always be some ASYMMETRY involved, since the grammatical repertory is smaller than the conceptual (cf. III.18, 25). In other terms: the problems on one level could be solved with the aid of more readily solvable or already solved pathways on another level.

31. Another distinction between the two network types just discussed is the *stretch of text* that they represent. It seems most unlikely that people would build grammatical networks for any whole texts other than very short ones.[18] The standard procedure would more probably be to build grammatical networks only for a convenient span of text retainable in active storage while the conceptual network is being constructed; hence, only the conceptual network would be assembled for the entire text. The whole paragraph of our 'rocket'-sample would be easy to assemble into a coherent KNOWLEDGE SPACE – a conceptual MACRO-STATE in which concepts are MICRO-STATES (cf. IV.6) – because the 'rocket' concept itself

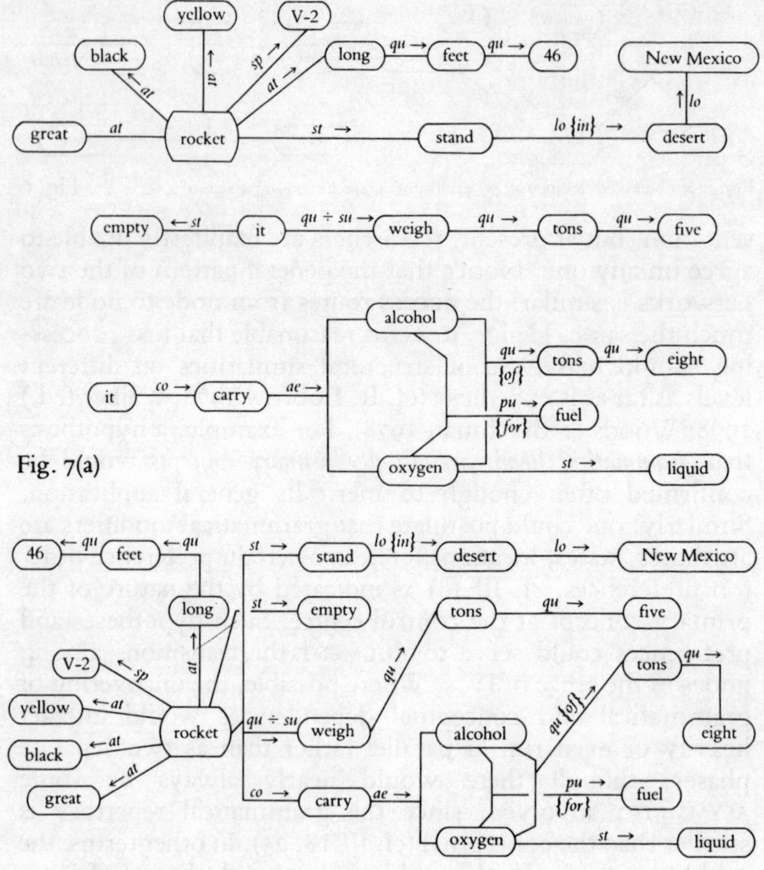

Fig. 7(a)

Fig. 7(b)

underlies something in each stretch of text. Thus, the addition of 'Empty, it weighed five tons' and 'For fuel, it carried eight tons of liquid oxygen' would merely involve attaching more content – viz. states, quantities, containment, substances, and so on – to the already created 'rocket' node. Figures 7a and 7b show the knowledge space first with separate configurations for sentence-length stretches, and then as an integrated unit. Of course, the pro-form 'it' is at once suppressed, since its content is derivative from the co-referent 'rocket'. Possibly, no such 'it' node is ever set up in such a straightforward case; the new material is immediately connected to the proper node of the co-referent.[19] In this manner, cohesion (e.g. pro-forms) supports coherence.

32. The integration of the underlying configuration of the next paragraph is more intricate:

> [4] [2.1] Everything was ready. [2.2] Scientists and generals withdrew to some distance and crouched behind earth mounds. [2.3] Two red flares rose as a signal to fire the rocket.

Here, there are no noticeable cohesive devices among the sentences. Nor is the underlying coherence at once obvious. A state of 'readiness' is mentioned, followed by two kinds of motion events ('withdraw/crouch', 'rise'). To bind things together, INFERENCING must be done (cf. I.11). This operation involves supplying reasonable concepts and relations to fill in a GAP OR DISCONTINUITY in a textual world. In contrast to SPREADING ACTIVATION (V.12), which ensues without specific demand, inferencing is always directed toward solving a problem in the sense of III.17: bridging a space where a pathway might fail to reach.[20] Reasonable inferences for our sample would be that the 'ready' state was the "reason" for the motions; that 'everything' subsumes whatever was needed to "enable" the 'take-off' of the 'rocket'; and that the 'scientists' and 'generals' were present in order to 'observe' the 'rocket'. If

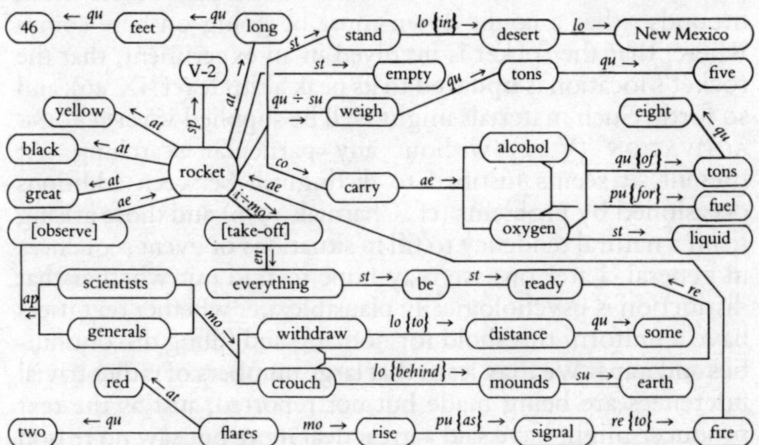

Key: *ae:* affected entity; *ap:* apperception of; *at:* attribute of; *co:* containment of; *en:* enablement of; *lo:* location of; *mo:* motion of; *pu:* purpose of; *qu:* quantity of; *re:* reason of; *sp:* specification of; *st:* state of; *su:* substance of; *ϵ:* entry; *ι:* initiation

Fig. 8

we now add this second model space to the first, with inference nodes placed in square brackets, we obtain the pattern given in Figure 8. Again, the links have labels explained in the key and marked with directional arrows.

33. Two possible objections should be noted here. First, it might be protested that the inferences we admitted are chosen arbitrarily. Yet, although intuition played some role in suggesting the inferences, they were heavily confirmed on empirical tests (discussed in IX.34), where readers reported them *as part of what they had read*. In one group of 72 readers, for instance, no less than 24 recalled the scientists 'observing' the rocket. Such a result suggests that the distinction between concepts directly activated by text expressions and concepts supplied for evident discontinuities may not be so clear-cut as we would like to think. Very few of the text-activated concepts fared as well in our tests as the inferred 'observe'. Perhaps it would be expedient to assign probability values to inference nodes and links, but, if so, this might well have to be done for the text-activated nodes and links also (cf. Beaugrande 1980*b*).

34. The second objection might be that the inferences we admit are rather too few than otherwise. Text users could make many more: that the 'fuel' will burn, so that 'scientists' and 'generals' must seek shelter behind non-flammable 'earth mounds'; that a count-down must be going on here somewhere; that the rocket is involved in an experiment; that the rocket's location is **updated** to its peak altitude (cf. IX.26); and so forth. Such materials might well be supplied via SPREADING ACTIVATION (V.12) without any particular searching. At present, it seems justified to distinguish between additions occasioned by problems (cf. Charniak 1976) and those arising from a natural tendency to fill in situations or event sequences in general. Later on, we may hope to find out whether that distinction is psychologically plausible, i.e. whether text users have a uniform threshold for noticing and filling discontinuities and gaps. We may learn that large numbers of rather trivial inferences are being made but not reported, just as the text producer might have said a great deal more but saw no reason to do so. The question would then be: how similar are the textual world of the producer and that of the typical receiver? Do they, for instance, agree on what is or not worth mention-

ing? Are there major differences in the richness of their mental representations for text-world situations and events? Just now, these questions are far from answered; but accumulating results with the 'rocket'-text indicate that the uniformity of different people's textual worlds is at best approximative though still reasonably reliable.

35. The third paragraph surpasses the first in its use of cohesive devices, here: **recurrence** ('flame', 'faster', 'yellow'), **paraphrase** ('rose . . . faster and faster'/'sped upward'), and **pro-forms** ('it'):

> [4] [3.1] With a great roar and burst of flame the giant rocket rose slowly at first and then faster and faster. [3.2] Behind it trailed sixty feet of yellow flame. [3.3] Soon the flame looked like a yellow star. [3.4] In a few seconds, it was too high to be seen, [3.5] but radar tracked it as it sped upward to 3,000 mph.

The placement of 'it' is not always very clear, for example in [3.4] and [3.5], where possible co-referents might be 'flame' or 'star'. Still, the tendency would be to attach doubtful pro-forms to the TOPIC node, which is of course 'rocket' (cf. V.38).

36. The model space for this paragraph might look something like Figure 9. The 'rising' motion of the 'rocket' is the

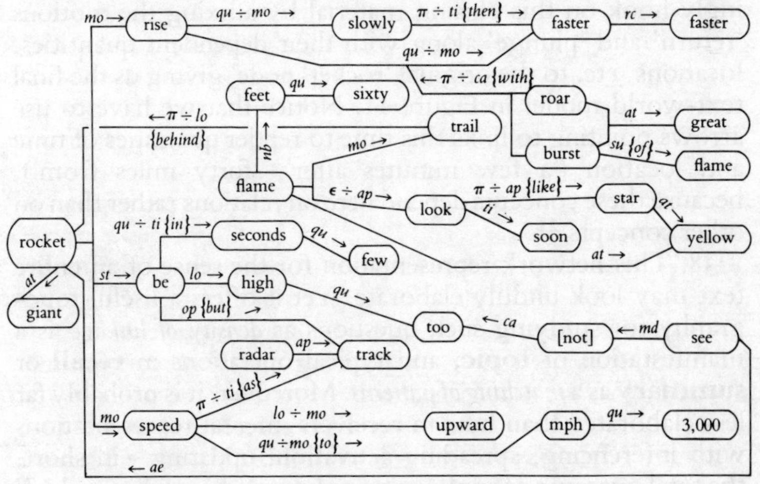

Key: *ae:* affected entity; *ap:* apperception of; *at:* attitude of; *ca:* cause of; *lo:* location of; *md:* modality of: *mo:* motion of; *op:* opposed to; *qu:* quantity of; *rc:* recurrence of; *su:* substance of; *ti:* time of; ε: entry; π: proximity

Fig. 9

proximate cause of the 'roar' and 'burst' and has as quantities of motion 'slowly' and 'faster and faster' (these quantities being temporally proximate to each other). In locational proximity to the 'rocket', the 'flame' with its attribute 'yellow' and quantities 'sixty feet' has the motion 'trail' and proximity of apperception ('look like') to a 'star'. The 'yellow' attribute is **inherited** via **analogy** from 'flame' to 'star' (cf. V.17). In the quantity of time 'few seconds', the 'rocket' is (state) at the location 'high' whose quantity 'too' is the cause that 'seeing' has the modality 'not' (inferred here). In opposition to that lack of apperception, the 'radar' still apperceives ('tracks') the 'rocket' in temporal proximity to the latter's 'speeding' with a location of motion 'upward' and quantities of motion '3,000 mph'. If we now connect this whole model space to the previous configuration, merging the 'rocket' nodes and assuming that the 'observers' were those that could 'not see' the rocket at great heights, we obtain Figure 10.

37. The single sentence of the final paragraph is cohesive with the preceding text via **recurrences** ('fired', 'speed', 'mph', 'saw') and the **pro-form** 'it' still co-referring with 'rocket'. This 'it' occurs at considerable distance from 'rocket' (after three intervening sentences), but is again likely to be connected to the topic node as before (V.35). We can accordingly hook on this closing material by affixing the motions 'return' and 'plunge' along with their dependent quantities, locations, etc. to the original 'rocket' node, giving us the final text-world model in Figure 11. Notice that we have to use arrows pointing to links this time to render quantities of time and location ('a few minutes after', 'forty miles from'), because these concepts depend here on relations rather than on other concepts.[21]

38. This network representation for the sense of an entire text may look unduly elaborate. Yet it offers a useful topography for studying such questions as *density of linkage* as a manifestation of **topic,** and typical operations in **recall** or **summary** as a *matching of patterns*. Moreover, it is probably far less elaborated than human receivers' mental representations with inferencing, spreading activation, updating – in short, the total outcome of applying prior knowledge of the world.[22] To be truly comprehensive, we might have to include time parameters for what is true at any moment (e.g. after 'rose',

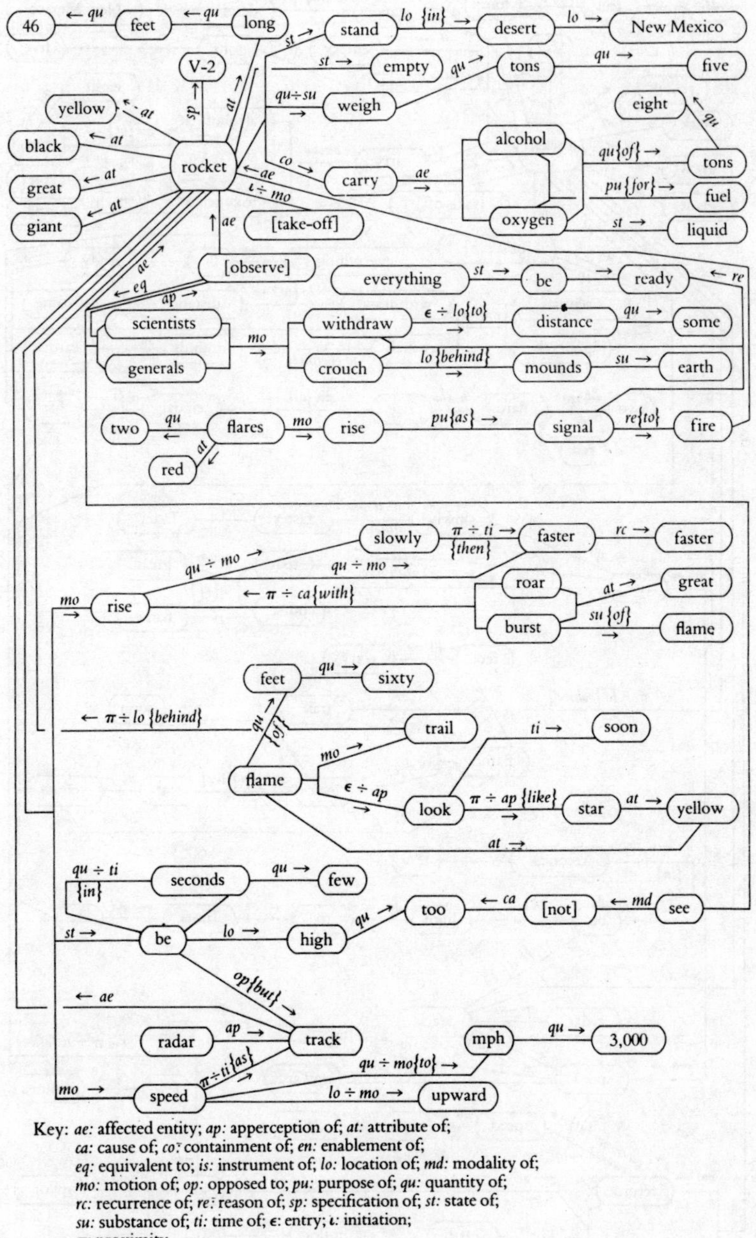

Key: *ae:* affected entity; *ap:* apperception of; *at:* attribute of;
ca: cause of; *co:* containment of; *en:* enablement of;
eq: equivalent to; *is:* instrument of; *lo:* location of; *md:* modality of;
mo: motion of; *op:* opposed to; *pu:* purpose of; *qu:* quantity of;
rc: recurrence of; *re:* reason of; *sp:* specification of; *st:* state of;
su: substance of; *ti:* time of; ϵ: entry; ι: initiation;
π: proximity

Fig. 10

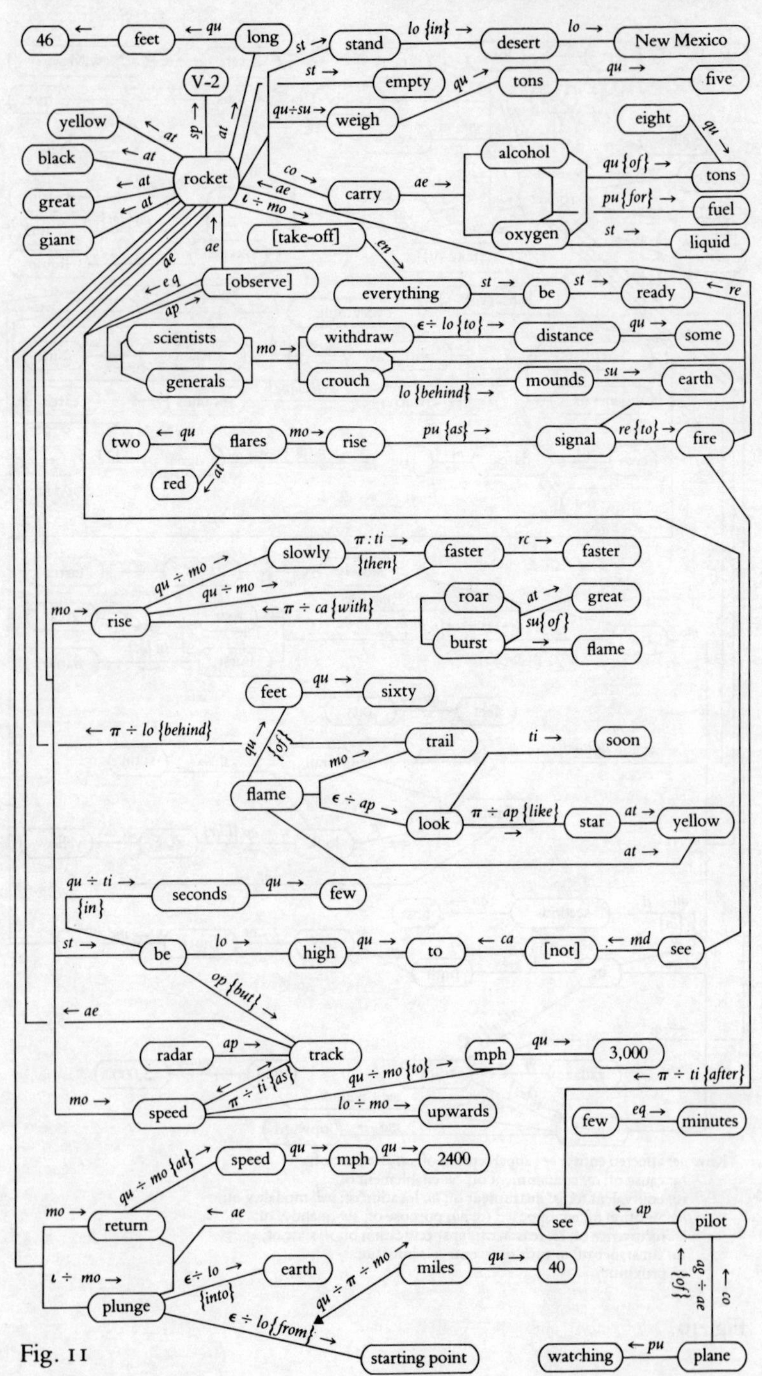

46
feet
qu
long
st
stand
lo {in}
desert
lo
New Mexico
V-2
st
empty
qu
tons
qu
five
yellow
at
sp
at
qu÷su
weigh
eight
qu
black
at
alcohol
rocket
co
qu {of}
tons
at
great
at
ae
carry
ae
pu {for}
fuel
ι ÷ mo
giant
ae
[take-off]
oxygen
st
liquid
ae
en
eq
[observe]
everything
st
be
st
ready
re
ap
scientists
withdraw
ϵ÷ lo {to}
distance
qu
some
mo
generals
crouch
mounds
su
earth
lo {behind}
two
qu
flares
mo
rise
pu {as}
signal
re {to}
fire
red
at
slowly
π : ti
faster
rc
faster
{then}
qu ÷ mo
qu ÷ mo
roar
at
great
mo
rise
π ÷ ca {with}
su{of}
burst
flame
feet
qu
sixty
π ÷ lo {behind}
trail
ti
soon
qu
{of}
mo
flame
ϵ ÷ ap
look
π ÷ ap {like}
star
at
yellow
at
qu ÷ ti
seconds
qu
few
{in}
st
be
lo
high
qu
to
ca
[not]
md
see
op {but}
ae
radar
ap
track
mph
qu
3,000
π ÷ ti {as}
qu ÷ mo {to}
π ÷ ti {after}
mo
speed
lo ÷ mo
upwards
few
eq
minutes
qu ÷ mo {at}
speed
qu
mph
qu
2400
mo
return
ae
see
ap
pilot
ι ÷ mo
ϵ÷ lo
earth
qu ÷ π ÷ mo
miles
qu
40
ag ÷ ae
{of}
co
plunge
{into}
ϵ ÷ lo{from}
starting point
watching
pu
plane

Fig. 11

the location 'in a New Mexico desert is no longer true until the 'plunge into earth') and probabilities for a wealth of incidental inferences (cf. V.34). Soon, the model would be in danger of exploding into unmanageable diffuseness and complexity. It would be better to limit the text-world model to only those concepts directly activated by text expressions and to only those inferences without which any portion of the model would not be connected to the rest at all. We shall propose to include world-knowledge being matched against the textual world in a pattern called the WORLD-KNOWLEDGE CORRELATE; and **global** knowledge in general patterns such as a schema about 'flight' that **attaches** text entries (cf. IX.25-8).

39. The world-knowledge correlate for our sample might look something like Figure 12, if we try to keep the same basic proportions for those elements also shown in Fig. 11. Other elements are in square brackets: this material would be supplied by spreading activation or, if discontinuities were apperceived, by inferencing. We undertake – as a suggestion at least – to distinguish DETERMINATE from TYPICAL linkage with the operators proposed in V.28.[23] For example, 'burning' must have 'fuel' and cause 'heat'. A 'signal' must be 'noticeable' if it is to be 'observed'. 'Seconds' are parts of 'minutes' by definition. In contrast, most links are merely typical: the 'isolated' 'site' for 'take-off' located in a 'desert' of 'New Mexico'; the 'explore' activities of 'scientists' and the 'attack' activities of 'generals' via the instrument 'rocket'; the locations, substances, and attributes of 'shelter' required for 'danger'; the purposes and attributes of 'flares' and 'signals'; and so forth, as shown in the diagram. Though **fuzzy** (V.5), the distinction between determinate and typical knowledge does appear useful. We also include recurrences in the sense of V.26(*hh*), rather than putting them in a separate graph. However, the global world-knowledge belonging to the notion of 'flight' as the overall framework for our text will be reserved for treatment under the notion of "schema" in IX.25-8.

40. We have presented our text-world model without clarifying the notion of REFERENCE, despite the prominence of

Key: ae: affected entity; *ag:* agent of; *ap:* apperception of; *at:* attribute of;
ca: cause of; *co:* containment of; *en:* enablement of; *eq:* equivalent to;
is: instrument of; *lo:* location of; modality of; *mo:* motion of;
op: opposed to; *pu:* purpose of; *qu:* quantity of; *rc:* recurrence of;
re: reason of; *sp:* specification of; *st;* state of; *su:* substance of;
ti: time of; ϵ: entry; ι: initiation; π: proximity

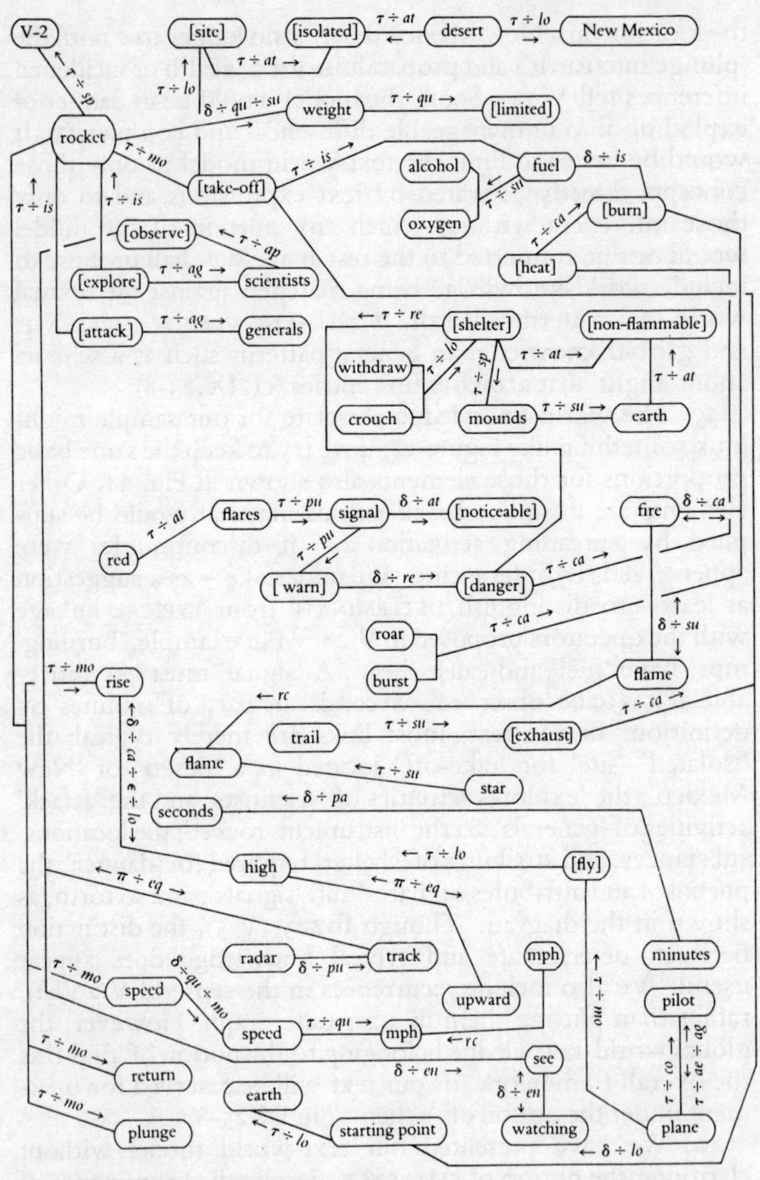

Key: *ae:* affected entity; *ag:* agent of; *ap:* apperception of;
at: attribute of; *ca:* cause of; *co:* containment of;
en: enablement of; *is:* instrument of; *lo:* location of;
mo: motion of; *pu:* purpose of; *qu:* quantity of;
rc: recurrence of; *re:* reason of; *sp:* specification of;
su: substance of; *ϵ:* entry; *π:* proximity
δ: determinate; *τ:* typical

Fig. 12

that notion in many philosophical theories of meaning.[24] In older semantics, it was hoped that meaning could be explained in terms of the "conditions" under which statements (misleadingly called "sentences") are "true". Thus, to know what something means is to know how to "verify" its "truth". This viewpoint, sometimes called "verificationism",[25] has unpleasant implications: for one thing, it is obviously wrong that people cannot understand a statement unless they can tell whether it is true; for another, people have no such immediate access to the "truth" as is being implied here. In the line of enquiry we are pursuing, however, the text-world is constructed from cognitive content ("knowledge")[26] collated against one's beliefs about the "real world" in a complex and often approximative manner. Hence, rather than saying that "words refer to objects" or the like, we prefer to say that "expressions activate knowledge". The act of referring is then an intricate process of **pattern-matching,** during which text users may decide that a text-world failing to match at a given threshold is FICTIONAL. There are numerous contingent factors that can influence this act of referring: type and purpose of text; importance of the text and its implications for one's situation; the believability of the text producer as encountered in past experience; and the topic materials in the textual world. Empirical research on these matters is still rare.

41. This chapter has been concerned with the means for exploring and representing coherence as the outcome of actualizing meanings in order to make "sense". To investigate human activities with texts, we should treat meaning and sense in terms of procedures for utilizing knowledge in a wide range of tasks. In that outlook, issues like these emerge: continuity (V.2), activation (V.4, 10), strength of linkage (V.5), spreading activation (V.12), episodic vs. semantic memory (V.13), economy (V.15), use of global patterns (V.16), inheritance (V.17f.), and compatibility between language in texts and apperception or cognition at large (V.20). Whereas the meanings of expressions or the content of concepts are highly disputable in isolation, their occurrence within a textual world where processing must be performed should be reasonably stabilizing and delimiting. We presented a mode for observing the construction of a text-world model for a sample, hoping to suggest and illustrate at least a few major

factors worth pursuing (V.23-40). We pointed out some cases where prior knowledge affects text processing in this manner (for more discussion, cf. IX.31ff.).

42. The study of coherence along such lines does not, of course, promise to be simple. But it is quite conceivable that the questions traditionally posed and disputed regarding meaning and sense are otherwise quite unanswerable. Certainly, dogmatic insistence upon extreme views, typical of so many discussions among philosophers and psychologists in the past, should yield to a flexible, realistic modelling of the diverse but systematic strategies people actually apply when using texts in everyday life.

Notes

1 We use the term "knowledge" throughout to designate cognitive content of all kinds, as opposed to "meaning" and "sense" of expressions (cf. discussion in V.1f.). Failure to make such a distinction leads to blurring the fact that knowledge must be selected and processed before it can be expressed and communicated.

2 The term "chunk" goes back to Miller (1956): a knowledge configuration processed as a unified block (cf. V.10). Bock (1979) points out that psycholinguistic theories have all too often made little use of memory research.

3 cf. Rosch (1973); Kintsch (1977*a*: 292ff.). One important use of "fuzzy set theory" has been the treatment of fuzzy concepts (cf. Zadeh 1972, 1975, 1979; Eikmeyer & Rieser 1979).

4 Smith, Shoben & Rips (1974) use the notions of "defining" and "characteristic features" similar to our notions here, though they insist that their model be based on set theory rather than on networks (see refutation in Hollan 1975). Rosch & Mervis (1975) argue instead in favour of "family resemblances", because "defining features" are often hard to discover (cf. V.18 and note 23 to this chapter).

5 The untenability of the initial proposals of Katz & Fodor (1963) has been repeatedly demonstrated (cf. Bolinger 1965; Hörmann 1976). We suspect that the whole undertaking of stipulating the *units themselves* may be misguided and hopeless; we can at best stipulate *unit types*, e.g. "attributes". See X.5 for some wider implications.

6 The terms "features" and "markers" were used by Katz & Fodor (1963); "primitives" by Wilks (1977*a*); "semes" in Greimas (1966); and "sememes" in Koch (1971). See the general survey in le Ny (1979).

7 Concerning some disadvantageous senses of the term, cf. Schank (1975); Kintsch (1979*b*). The term "conceptual memory" might be more useful (cf. Rieger 1975; Beaugrande 1980*a*).

8 cf. VI.11-20; VII.38; IX.25-8.

9 A "class" is a group of entities sharing some characteristic, whereas a "set" is simply defined by the members it has. Set theory has been proclaimed as a foundation for the study of meaning (e.g. by Smith et al. 1974), but perhaps it only passes over rather than settles the real question: what classificatory procedures are used to form sets in the first place?

10 cf. McCall & Crabbs (1961); Miller & Coleman (1967); Aquino (1969); Kintsch & Vipond (1979); Beaugrande (1979*f*, 1980*a*, *b*). For a new treatment in terms of computational logic, cf. Simmons & Chester (1979); Beaugrande (1981*b*).

11 It can easily be seen that "situations" subsume "objects", and "events" subsume "actions;" we therefore usually speak of "situations and events" as a cover-all designation of primary concepts and their organization.

12 Though "perception" is more usual in the literature, "apperception" stresses the common case of applying prior knowledge to what we experience.

13 It might well be expedient to subdivide this category into "numericals" and "measurements" in future research.

14 In most cases, there is no special need to draw in "co-reference" and "recurrence" in text-world models, since the nodes in question are usually merged anyway. But it may prove useful to mark these relations when exploring such factors as the effects of repetition and variation within surface texts upon processing and recall. See note 19 to this chapter.

15 The notion of "case" originated in languages (e.g. Latin) which mark the role of nouns in phrase structures via surface formatting. Often, there were no unified conceptual criteria for all the uses of a single grammatical case. Fillmore's early notion was that, in a language such as English, "cases" are "underlying" features of nouns in sentences. On Fillmore's new outlook, see Fillmore (1977).

16 In general, linguists' typologies have fewer categories than ours (e.g. Fillmore 1968; Chafe 1970; Longacre 1976), while those in artificial intelligence have more (e.g. Wilks 1977*a*).

17 We use the symbol "†" for "termination" to prevent confusion with "τ" for "typical".

18 See note 14 to Chapter IV.

19 We do not merge the two occurrences of 'tons', though it may turn out that we would be justified in doing so (compare note 14 to this chapter).

20 In terms of problem-solving procedures, spreading activation would be oriented more toward **breadth-first search** and inferencing more toward **means-end analysis** (cf. III.17).

21 We use two labels for the relation of 'pilot' to 'plane': the 'pilot' is in "containment of" the 'plane' and also the "agent" acting on the 'plane' as "affected entity". We could dodge the issue with a simple "relation-of" link called "pilot-of", but that doesn't really settle anything.

22 We review some material added by receivers in IX.31ff.

23 To see whether a recipient group could agree on this matter, Beaugrande conducted a test in which receivers of the 'rocket'-text were asked, six weeks after the original presentation, to select one of a set of choices in statements like: "Rockets must/should/don't need to burn fuel when

they fly"; "Rockets are always/often/seldom used to attack military targets". As was expected, agreement was consistent, but by no means unanimous. Only these two statements elicited unanimous agreement: "Without fuel, a rocket can't fly"; and "Launching sites usually are located on the earth". Many replies showed that the group (all university freshmen) are poorly informed about aviation and rocketry (e.g. thinking that 'alcohol' is a "worthless fuel"). Such results should render us mistrustful of studies in which receivers are all presumed to be as knowledgeable as a "lexicon".

24 cf. note 18 to Chapter IV.

25 For a discussion of this now discredited viewpoint, cf. Johnson-Laird (1978).

26 See note 1 to this chapter.

Chapter VI

Intentionality and acceptability

1. The **cohesion** of surface texts and the underlying **coherence** of textual worlds are the most obvious standards of textuality. They indicate how the component elements of the text fit together and make sense. However, they cannot provide absolute borderlines between texts and non-texts in real communication. People can and do use texts which, for various motives, do not seem fully cohesive and coherent. We should therefore include the *attitudes* of text users among the standards of textuality. A language configuration must be **intended** to be a text and **accepted** as such in order to be utilized in communicative interaction.[1] These attitudes involve some **tolerance** toward disturbances of cohesion or coherence, as long as the purposeful nature of the communication is upheld (cf. I.13f.). The production and reception of texts function as **discourse actions** relevant to some plan or goal (cf. VI.11).

2. In I.13, we introduced the notion of INTENTIONALITY to subsume the intentions of text producers. In the most immediate sense of the term, the producer INTENDS the language configuration under production to be a cohesive and coherent text. Some situations may place such limits on time and processing resources that this intention is not fully realized by the presentation. For example, cohesion is lacking on occasion in *conversation* (documented in Coulthard 1977: 53, 108, 89, 88–9):

[85] But that was – then you went to Fred's.

[86] Do you – what are you laughing at?
[87] You want to hear my – eh – my sister told me a story last night.
[88] When I say I want to be something, it's not just that I want to be this, it's just – I – I – I just – that's the only thing I tell people that I want to be an artist.

The inconsistent surface structures (whose use would be called "anacoluthon" in classical rhetoric) above signal the influence of such situational factors as the following. In [85], the speaker shifts the plan for the utterance in trying to reconstruct a still unclear event. In [86], the speaker abandons an utterance just begun and reacts to a disturbance from another participant. In [87], the speaker originally intends to offer 'my sister's story' and then decides that the 'story' should first be introduced as a recent and presumably newsworthy event. In [88], the text producer apparently feels some hesitation in expressing his true desires for a career. Such discontinuities and shifts are usually tolerated when they do not disturb communication, especially if their causes are readily apparent.

3. The same point can be made regarding reduced coherence. Text producers may become confused and inconsistent if the situation is in some way disorienting:

[89] "Well, sir," said the constable, "he's the man we were in search of, that's true; and yet he's not the man we were in search of. For the man we were in search of was not the man we wanted, sir, if you understand my everyday way." (Hardy 1977: 30)

This unlogical series of assertions arose from a case of mistaken identity. On occasion, a text producer may deliberately impair coherence for special effect. When Sherlock Holmes is pretending to be deliriously ill, his **plan** calls for deceiving Watson by appearing incoherent:

[90] "You will convey the very impression which is in your own mind – a dying man – a dying and delirious man. Indeed, I cannot think why the whole bed of the ocean is not one solid mass of oysters, so prolific the creatures seem. Ah, I am wandering!" (Conan Doyle 1967: 444)

Of course, Holmes is careful to maintain the intended topic in spite of the picturesque ramblings about 'oysters', so that the superior goal of his long-range plan is upheld. This kind of intentionality – attaining goals through deception – is not widely dealt with in philosophical discussions.

4. The interdependence of cohesion and coherence with intentionality can lead to complicated situations. For example, text producers may wish to conceal some knowledge and, along the way, they may betray themselves with disturbances of coherence:

[91] "I see that the big one was the deaf and dumb Spaniard . . . and the Spaniard swore he'd spoil her looks just as I told you and your two – "
"What? The deaf and dumb man said all that!"
Huck had made another terrible mistake!
(Twain 1922: 242f.)

This kind of situation should be distinguished from the kind where coherence is intended but not accepted, because the knowledge and roles of participants are too diverse. Mark Twain (1913: 45ff.) provides an extreme illustration where a miner-gambler is negotiating with a clergyman:[2]

[92] "Are you the duck that runs the gospel-mill next door?"
"Am I the – pardon me, I believe I do not understand?"
" . . . you are the head clerk of the doxology works next door."
"I am the shepherd in charge of the flock whose fold is next door."
"The which?"
"The spiritual advisor of the little company whose sanctuary adjoins these premises."
Scotty scratched his head, reflected a moment, and then said:
"You ruther hold over me, pard. I reckon I can't call that hand. Ante and pass the buck."
"How? I beg pardon. What did I understand you to say?"

Each uttered text is intended to be coherent by itself, but the *discourse* is non-communicative much of the time and neither participant can discover the coherence of the other's texts.

5. Twain's discourses here are of course extremes, and we must bear in mind that they form part of larger texts whose coherence is beyond dispute. Still, they illustrate typical **regulatory** actions that follow upon breaks in coherence as a continuity of sense (cf. III.14). In [91], the other participant uses a high-key **recurrence** combined with pro-forms to call attention to the disturbance (cf. IV.58). In [92], both partici-

pants signal lack of comprehension (the miner's signals being themselves obscurely expressed in gambling terminology), while the original question remains unanswered. In Chapter IX, we describe some types of SITUATION MONITORING where texts themselves are monitored for various motives (cf. IX.15ff.). In the wider perspective of INTERTEXTUALITY developed in that chapter, we would grant that cohesion and coherence of a single text may be derivative from that of another text in the same discourse. Hence, cases like [91] and [92] can be eventually resolved in the framework of the entire discourses in which they are located.

6. In a wider sense of the term, intentionality designates all the ways in which text producers utilize texts to pursue and fulfil their intentions. An extensive body of research has been devoted to intentions in various disciplines, e.g. sociology (cf. Heider 1958), psychology (cf. C. Schmidt 1976; Schlesinger 1977), philosophy (cf. Austin 1962; Searle 1969), and artificial intelligence (cf. Bruce 1975, 1977; Schank & Abelson 1977; Cohen 1978; McCalla 1978; Allen 1979). The function of texts is seen somewhat differently in these several fields. Sociologists would explore the use of texts in "speech exchange systems" where participants interact and allot speaking turns (Sacks, Schegloff & Jefferson 1974). Psychologists would emphasize the text producer's intention "to guide the consciousness of the hearer" (Jörg & Hormann 1978: 447; cf. Hörmann 1976). Philosophers have argued that a text producer who "means something" by a text "intends the utterance" of the text "to produce some effect in an audience by means of the recognition of this intention" (Grice 1971: 58). Artificial intelligence researchers are concerned with people's plans and goals in order "to better analyze the meanings of words whose subtlety lies in their intentions rather than in their physical manifestations" (Schank & Abelson 1977: 129).

7. Linguistics has been most profoundly affected by the philosophical approach, labouring over the question of how intentions are in fact correlated with the format and sense of utterances. Searle (1969: 43ff.) proposes that Grice's account of intention and meaning be amended[3] because it fails to respect the significant influence of *conventions* and *intended effects*. Searle builds upon Austin's (1962) work to develop the notion of "speech acts", i.e. actions which the utterance of a text inten-

tionally or conventionally performs. He distinguishes: (*a*) *utterance acts* as the simple uttering of words or sentences; (*b*) *propositional acts* as the use of content and reference; (*c*) *illocutionary acts* as conventional activities accomplished by discourse, e.g. promising, threatening, etc.; and (*d*) *perlocutionary acts* as the achieving of effects on text receivers, e.g. alarming or convincing them (Searle 1969: 23ff.). He undertakes to state the conventions which apply to the illocutionary acts. For example, *promising* entails stating your future action which the text receiver desires and which you would not do otherwise in the normal course of things; to be "sincere", you must really intend to do the action and to place yourself under the obligation to do it (Searle 1969: 57ff.).

8. Though speech-act theory has made impressive contributions to the study of PRAGMATICS in the sense of III.1, it has some inherent limitations. There is a vast difference between relatively well-defined acts such as "promising" or "threatening" and extremely diffuse acts such as "stating", "asserting", "describing", or "questioning"; yet all of these are grouped together as "illocutionary acts" (Searle 1969: 23). There is no obvious way to set down the conditions and intentions which must be given in order to "state" or "describe" according to criteria as exact as those provided for the action of "promising". If someone says:

[93] I promise.
[94] I apologize.

the action is transparent enough, because *the uttering is itself the action*. The verbs for such actions are often called PERFORMATIVES, and their use is common in legal and parliamentary transactions:

[95] I hereby adjourn the meeting.
[96] I now pronounce you man and wife.

Yet everyday communication is far more diversified and far less transparent. Many commonplace intentions are hardly ever made explicit. People are not likely to say things of this kind:

[97] I hereby try to get you to comply with my plan.
[98] I hereby try to persuade you to adopt the viewpoint most useful to me.

Yet these are some of the most frequent intentions of discourse participants. Speech act theory is therefore rather incomplete in its usual framework, and it fails to appreciate the interaction of conventions with current context (Cohen 1978: 26).

9. A more general approach has been worked out by Paul Grice (1975, 1978).[4] He offers a set of "maxims" that the producers of texts normally follow in conversation. The "maxims" are merely strategies and precepts, not "rules" as envisioned by Searle. We illustrate below the maxims as quoted from Grice (1975: 45ff.).

9.1 The principle of CO-OPERATION is stated as "make your conversational contribution such as is required, at the state at which it occurs, by the accepted purpose or direction of the talk exchange in which you are engaged". Co-operation would be clearly demanded in situations where someone is in need of advice or assistance. The following dialogue shows violations of the maxim (Carroll 1960: 80f.):

[99] "How am I to get in?" she repeated aloud.
"I shall sit here," the Footman remarked, "till to-morrow – or the next day, maybe."
"How am I to get in?" asked Alice again in a louder tone.
"*Are* you to get in at all?" said the Footman. "That's the first question, you know . . . I shall sit here," he said, "on and off, for days and days."
"But what am *I* to do?" said Alice.
"Anything you like," said the Footman, and began whistling.

Here, Alice's intentions are blocked by the Footman's refusal to accept her plan of 'getting in'; instead he muses over his own rather goalless plans.

9.2 The maxim of QUANTITY is given as "Make your contribution as informative as (but not more informative than) is required." Being "informative" would, we presume, involve giving someone new or unpredictable knowledge when occasion arises. In the following excerpt from a play (Shaffer 1976: 21f.), Alan refuses to be informative, first relying on silence and then singing a television commercial to Dysart, a psychiatrist:

[100] DYSART: So: did you have a good journey? I hope they gave you lunch at least. Not that there's much to choose between a British Rail meal and one here.
[ALAN stands staring at him.]

DYSART: Won't you sit down?
[Pause. He does not. Dysart consults his file.]
DYSART: Is this your full name? Alan Strang?
[Silence.]
DYSART: And you're seventeen. Is that right? Seventeen? . . . Well?
ALAN [singing low]: Double your pleasure, double your fun with Doublemint, Doublemint, Doublemint Gum.

Such discourse is naturally effective as a representation of communicating with a mentally disturbed participant.

9.3 The maxim of QUALITY is concerned with truthfulness: "Do not say what you believe to be false, or that for which you lack adequate evidence." This standard is more rigorously applied to scientific texts (cf. IX.10) than to conversation, but even in the latter, it is generally regarded as a social obligation. Disregard for truthfulness may be motivated by the intention of concealing one's own actions, as is often Tom Sawyer's situation:

[101] "What were you doing in there?"
"Nothing."
"Nothing! Look at your hands. And look at your mouth! What *is* that truck?"
"*I* don't know, aunt."
"Well, *I* know. It's jam – that's what it is. Forty times I've said if you didn't let that jam alone I'd skin you."
(Twain 1922: 2)

9.4 The maxim of RELATION is simply "be relevant". Relevance could have at least two aspects: (*a*) what kinds of knowledge are related to a given topic; or (*b*) what kinds of knowledge would be useful in attaining some goal. In Alice's dialogue with the Footman [99], both aspects are violated by the latter's utterances. In Holmes's speech to Watson [90], the remarks on 'oysters' are irrelevant to the topic about which Watson is being instructed, but highly relevant to Holmes's goal of appearing delirious. Still another case would be intentional irrelevance to divert a discourse in an unplanned direction, as in this exchange overheard on the University of Florida campus:

[102] BIBLE EVANGELIST: It's a fearful thing to meet with God the King!
STUDENT: Like when Godzilla meets King Kong?

The student seized upon surface similarities of unrelated expressions to steer the discourse toward an old movie recounting the battle of two imaginary but popular monsters.[5] The student perhaps considered the evangelist's remark, shouted in a park to nobody in particular, a violation of relevance in itself. Discourse participants do after all have a right to relevance, e.g. as an aid in reducing possible misunderstandings and non-determinacies. Tom Magner (personal communication to W.D.) adduces a passage from a letter received by the public health officials in Pittsburgh:

[103] I cannot collect my sick pay. I have six children. Can you tell me why?

The text producer is probably not asking for an explanation of why so many children are in the family, since that question would not be relevant for an inquiry to public health officials (though possibly worth asking in principle).

9.5 The maxim of MANNER includes several ways to arrange and deliver texts. "Be perspicuous" has been restated as "be such that the intentions you have for what you say are plainly served" (Grice, personal communication to RdB). This restatement looks back to Grice's original account of intentional meaning (cited in VI.6), adding a stipulation of clarity (cf. II.6). The same objections could be raised again, e.g. that intentions cannot override all convention; and it might be expedient to conceal them (cf. samples [90], [91], [97], [98], and [101] above, and [109] and [139] below).

9.6 The maxim of manner includes another injunction, namely to "avoid obscurity of expression". Here, the potential obstacle to communication lies in the phase of mapping already selected and organized content onto surface expression (cf. III.23), rather than in making the selection itself. We noted in example [92] that the intention to convey knowledge and attain a goal (finding a parson) was continually put out of effect by a mutual obscurity of expressions. However, a text producer might have motives for obscurity, such as the attempt to appear learned. Such is the striving of the schoolmaster Holofernes, who describes the speaking style of another person in that very style (*Love's Labour's Lost* V i 17f.):

[104] He draweth out the thread of his verbosity finer than the staple of his argument. I abhor such fanatical phantasims,

such insociable and point-devise companions; such rackers of orthography.

Another motivation would be the advantages which obscurity can create in preventing a distribution of knowledge. The obscurity of expression in tax laws is apparently a big money-saver for governments:

[105] According to Hubert Möckershoff, president of the Federal Tax Council, the approximately 90 laws and 100 regulations for taxes are often so complicated and incomprehensible that taxpayers certainly cannot recognize all the benefits for which they are eligible.

(*Neue Westfälische Zeitung* 8 May 1979)

9.7 A third part of the maxim of manner is "avoid ambiguity". Although many natural language expressions could have different senses under different conditions, ambiguity obtains only when it cannot be decided which sense is actually **intended** (V.1). If multiple senses are in fact intended, we would use the term "polyvalence" (V.1). While the processing of polyvalence is no doubt arduous, ambiguity has the additional annoyance of expending effort on materials neither intended nor useful. Consequently, participants hasten to eliminate ambiguity by regulative action, usually by paraphrasing the content into a non-ambiguous format. In this exchange between a railway official and a customer (Allen 1979: 3):

[106] CUSTOMER: When is the Windsor train?
OFFICIAL: To Windsor?
CUSTOMER: Yes.
OFFICIAL: 3:15.

the customer's opening question is unresolvably ambiguous, since in this situation, intentions to find out about trains either going to or coming from Windsor would be equally reasonable. The official at once reformulates the troublesome part of the question into a determinate format. Under normal conditions, participants would be motivated to remove occurring ambiguities as efficiently as possible. To insist on ambiguities would be to discourage communication.

9.8 The fourth part of the maxim of manner is "be brief". While the maxim of quantity concerns how much you say, brevity concerns how much you take to say it (Grice, personal communication to RdB). Constable Dogberry's speech quoted in IV.19 demonstrates the violation of brevity: five more restatements of the fact that the prisoners have 'committed false report'. Not surprisingly, communication breaks down over this violation:

[107] PEDRO: This learned constable is too cunning to be understood. (*Much Ado about Nothing* V i 234)

All the same, Dogberry was *intending* to be communicative; he was simply attempting to imitate legal language (cf. IV.19).

9.9 The final part of the maxim of manner is "be orderly", i.e. "present your materials in the order in which they are required" (Grice, personal communication to RdB). Obvious illustrations would be the NORMAL ORDERING STRATEGIES for mentioning events and situations, e.g. in the time sequence in which things happen (cf. VII.18.2). When test persons were given a passage running:

[108]*a* The rocket rose faster and faster after starting slowly.

40 per cent recalled the passage in the normal time sequence:

[108]*b* The rocket rose slowly and then faster and faster.

The favouring of normal ordering strategies seems to reflect the extent to which they make processing and storage easier: the mind does not have to strain itself by searching for an unconventional organizational mode.

9.10 Grice's concern regarding these maxims is particularly devoted to an account of CONVERSATIONAL IMPLICATURES, i.e. the knowledge conveyed when people "imply, suggest, mean, etc." something distinct from what they "say" (Grice 1975: 43). As long as participants are complying with the principle of co-operation and with the maxims of quantity, quality, relation, and manner, one can decide fairly easily what they intend to convey via a given contribution to conversation. When participants "unostentatiously violate" or "blatantly flout" a maxim, or simply "opt out of" it, conversational implicatures are likely to arise – especially in the case of "flouting" (Grice 1975: 49). In sample [99], the uncooperative Footman's contributions lead Alice to conclude that he is "perfectly idiotic" (Carroll 1960: 82). In [100], Alan conveys the implicature that he has no intention of giving any insights about himself, not even the most trivial. In [101],

Tom's utterances imply that he has in fact been doing something forbidden. In [102], the student is implying that the Evangelist is dealing with ideas as foolish and unsubstantial as sensationalist movie monsters. Grice (1975: 51ff.) provides a range of further examples, but the conclusion should be clear: conversational participants will infer unexpressed content rather than abandon their assumption that discourse is intended to be coherent, informative, relevant, and cooperative.

10. Grice's maxims undeniably cover a much wider range than the typologies of well-defined "speech acts" from Austin and Searle. By following the maxims, text producers are not committing themselves to performing special actions under conventionally established conditions; they are merely trying to communicate with a minimum of needless effort and disturbances. The application of the maxims would be a case of PROCEDURAL ATTACHMENT: the current materials of the discourse would be managed according to general procedures (cf. III.19). As we have seen, however, producers' intentions may lead them to violate the maxims when it seems expedient – a factor suggesting that the "sincerity" criteria of speech act theory are not a satisfactory account for discourse actions.

11. There is still an uncharted area between Grice's maxims and Searle's "speech acts". Grice suggested that people can pursue unexpressed goals via *conversational implicatures*, i.e. saying something which implies a belief or request. But this notion is still vague and fails to reflect the full importance of discourse goals. We could explore the correlation of actions with texts in a more direct and operational way. We could begin with von Wright's (1967) definition of an ACTION as an intentional act which changes a situation in a way that would not have happened otherwise (cf. V.25). The DISCOURSE ACTION would then be described in terms of the changes it effects upon the situation and the various states of participants: knowledge state, social state, emotional state, and so on. Among all the changes occurring through a single discourse, the focus of each participant would be on those states which are instrumental to his or her PLAN toward a GOAL. Thus, the states would be processed via PLAN ATTACHMENT (fitting actions into a planned sequence of states) (cf. III.20; VI.20).

12. In the outworn tradition of behaviourism (e.g. Watson

1930), the human organism figures as a mechanism continually "responding" to the "stimuli" of its environment. Theories of language (Skinner 1957) and meaning (Quine 1960) were set forth in these terms. One of the many human capacities ignored or even abrogated by this approach is PLANNING: the ability to envision alternative future states and to work toward a particular desired one.[6] Of course, human planners are not usually all-knowing or all-powerful, and hence one must also notice and react to environmental conditions. Yet even then, the "stimuli" being encountered are often understood in terms of their implications for one's plans.

13. The human mind is presumably endowed with what might be called a THRESHOLD OF PLAN ACTIVATION. This threshold would be the degree of awareness of possible future **states** that is required to start developing a plan. When a desired future state appears uncertain enough that its attainment might well fail, the planner has a PROBLEM in the sense of III.17. Hence, planning is an elaborated, comprehensive type of **problem-solving** applied to advancing the planner's own state toward a goal in an evolving situation. The plan might begin at the CURRENT STATE (the moment of making the plan) or at an INITIAL STATE where the plan will start running later on. As a DEFAULT, we could assume that the GOAL STATE should be DESIRABLE from the planner's standpoint (cf. Beaugrande 1979*a*, 1980*d*).

14. The amount and intensity of planning would vary according to several factors: (*a*) the probability or improbability of attaining the goal; (*b*) the presence or absence of stabilized social conventions for attaining the goal; (*c*) the possible interference of counter-planners (other agents whose goals conflict with one's own); and (*d*) the required range of planning, i.e. short-term vs. long-term (the number of steps needed to carry out the plan). Frequently occurring human problems, e.g. hunger, are handled via conventionalized plans where one needs merely to step into a ROLE (a framework of typical, expected actions and attributes) within a well-defined situation. Schank and Abelson (1977) employ the designation SCRIPT for these conventionalized plans (cf. V.16). Their famous "restaurant script" has roles for customer, waiter, cook, and cashier. Anyone able to pay can solve the hunger problem by stepping into the customer role, and no special

planning is needed henceforth, beyond such matters as selecting one dish from among alternatives (any meal would satisfy the main goal).

15. Robert Wilensky (1978*a*, *b*) points out that the majority of human situations are not well scripted. He suggests rather that people have flexible, powerful strategies for planning and for recovering other people's plans through their actions. Although Wilensky's work, like that of Schank and Abelson, is mostly concerned with the reception and processing of texts *about* actions (i.e. actions in textual worlds), we submit that it can be relevant also for the intentionality of text **production**. The DISCOURSE ACTION, which changes a situation (VI.11), would be plan-directed whenever the text producer is trying to steer the situation toward some goal. The term SITUATION MANAGEMENT can designate this activity, while the simple reaction to a situation by describing or narrating the available **evidence** would be SITUATION MONITORING (cf. VIII.1ff. for further discussion).

16. Since discourse is definable as a situation or event sequence in which various participants present texts as discourse actions, we can consider communication through discourse as an instance of INTERACTIVE PLANNING (cf. Bruce & Newman 1978). For example, your plan might require inducing **beliefs** in others such that they will be helpful in bringing about your goal. This plan would be problematic if those beliefs were contrary to available evidence, or not based on evidence at all. We shall look at such a case, namely where Rachael, a spinster aunt, is engaged in discourse with a gentleman she regards as a prospective lover or husband. Her problem is that he might be more drawn to her attractive young nieces if he considered the available evidence. Her solution to this problem is striking (Dickens 1947: 54f.):

[109] [1] "Do you think my nieces pretty?" whispered their affectionate aunt to Mr. Tupman.
[2] "I should, if their aunt wasn't here," replied the ready Pickwickian, with a passionate glance.
[3] "Oh, you naughty man – but really, if their complexions were a little *little* better, don't you think they would be nice-looking girls – by candle-light?"
[4] "Yes, I think they would," said Mr. Tupman, with an air of indifference.

[5] "Oh, you quiz – I know what you were going to say."

[6] "What?" inquired Mr. Tumpan, who had not precisely made up his mind to say anything at all.

[7] "You were going to say, that Isabel stoops – I know you were – you men are such observers. Well, so she does; it can't be denied; and certainly, if there is one thing more than another that makes a girl look ugly, it is stooping. I often tell her, that when she gets a little older, she'll be quite frightful. Well, you *are* a quiz!"

[8] Mr. Tupman had no objection to earning the reputation at so cheap a rate: so he looked very knowing, and smiled mysteriously.

[9] "What a sarcastic smile," said the admiring Rachael: "I declare I'm quite afraid of you."

[10] "Afraid of me!"

[11] "Oh, you can't disguise anything from me – I know what that smile means, very well."

[12] "What?" said Mr. Tupman, who had not the slightest notion himself.

[13] "You mean," said the amiable aunt, sinking her voice still lower – "You mean, that you don't think Isabella's stooping is as bad as Emily's boldness. Well, she *is* bold! You cannot think how wretched it makes me sometimes. I'm sure I cry about it for hours together – my dear brother is *so* good, and *so* unsuspicious, that he never sees it; if he did, I'm quite certain it would break his heart. I wish I could think it was only manner – I hope it may be – " (here the affectionate relative heaved a deep sigh, and shook her head despondingly.)

17. The first discourse action [109.1] is a simple ASK (cf. VIII.10): the aunt seems to be merely inquiring how Mr Tupman is MONITORING the situation. Her 'whispered' intonation, however, indicates that she is hoping for an answer that the nieces themselves would be dismayed to hear. Mr Tupman's reply [109.2] shows that he is in principle inclined to be co-operative and support her overall goal of amorous pursuit, but it is disquieting all the same as an admission that he is indeed comparing the nieces to the aunt. He even suggests that there is evidence for 'thinking' them 'pretty'. Alarmed, the aunt at once adduces a piece of disfavourable evidence: poor 'complexions' that, even if improved, would still be

'nice-looking' only under the attenuating illumination of 'candles' [109.3] Her criticism is disguised as a defence, as an attempt to minimize a defect rather than call attention to it – a case of *plan concealment*. Mr Tupman's response [109.4] is again only partially co-operative: he displays 'indifference' toward the nieces, but his answer is still an unrestricted 'yes'. Perhaps Mr Tupman feels committed to the objective evidence in a manner that might warm the otherwise dispassionate heart of a behaviourist.

18. In VIII.19 we suggest a strategy of discourse action bearing upon how situations are monitored. According to this strategy, if a monitoring is rejected or disapproved of, it should be replaced with a less MEDIATED version, i.e. a version based more directly on the available **evidence.** But in sample [109], we have just the reverse: Mr Tupman's reply [109.4] is *not mediated enough,* not sufficiently removed from the evidence to suit the aunt. She therefore implements a series of actions designed to replace his unmediated monitorings with versions mediated toward her plan. The first step is to simply reject [109.4] as not being 'what he was going to say'; at the same time, she offers a flattering monitoring of his apperceptive and cognitive abilities by calling him a 'quiz' [109.5]. In effect, she ascribes to him a planned discourse action which, as [109.6] makes plain, he had no set intention of performing. Since he therefore cannot co-operate to the desired extent, she is now free to supply her own material for the substituted discourse action in [109.7]. The steps in this miniature re-evaluation of evidence are instructive. She at first states the main idea that 'Isabel stoops', and immediately goes on to praise Mr Tupman's powers as an 'observer'. He must conclude that the proposition is in fact inescapable to anyone weighing the evidence; to reject it would be to deprecate his own perspicacity. The aunt's next two steps are both re-affirmations ('so she does', 'it can't be denied') just in case Mr Tupman has any inclination to disagree. A further step is to elevate this defect to the status of a major factor in 'making a girl look ugly'. The culmination is to stress that a 'frightful' state must ensue with the mere passage of time ('when she gets a little older' – 'little' to show that it will be soon); this tactic solves the problem that the girl is manifestly *not* 'frightful' at present. The finishing touch is to again flatter Mr Tupman's

perspicacity and thus to ensure co-operation: an instance of **recurrence** serving to re-assert a viewpoint (cf. IV.13).

19. As expected, Mr Tupman 'has no objection' to appearing more astute than he really is [109.8]; yet having nothing to add to the opinion ascribed to him, he can only assume a 'knowing' facial expression. The aunt is naturally led by the success of her first planning phase to run the same steps over again and discredit the second niece with the same tactics that worked so well before.[7] Again, she seizes upon a slight facial cue ('smile') to ascribe a plan-mediated monitoring to Mr Tupman [109.11, 13], though as before, he has no corresponding intentions [109.12]. This time, she dispenses with the flattery of his mental abilities, assuming no doubt that the earlier emphasis on that point will carry over. The step-by-step construction of the discourse action [109.13] is otherwise analogous to that of [109.7]. She begins with the idea of Emily's 'boldness', neatly tying it to the previous material by a disadvantageous comparison to 'stooping' (and incidentally, re-asserting the 'Isabel stoops' idea yet one more time). Again, she follows up with a re-affirmation ('she *is* bold'), pretending to agree with his view. To make this potentially harmless trait seem sufficiently grievous, she monitors her own response to it as well as the response which her 'brother' (Emily's father) would have if he only could 'see'. Her 'wretchedness' (leading to 'crying' for 'hours together') and his 'heartbreak' duly magnify the fault to such dimensions that only a 'good' and 'unsuspicious' person could possibly overlook it – that is,one unable to see the evil at work. Here, she equates any tendency to monitor the situation in any way but her own with simple blindness (not 'seeing') toward reality. She then resumes her apparent action of defending rather than defaming her niece by 'wishing' and 'hoping' that the fault is merely put on ('only manner') rather than deeply rooted. But her use of tenses ('could think', 'may be') carefully suggests that her 'hope' is contrary-to-fact (cf. IV.48). Her 'sighing' and 'head-shaking' are similarly intended to convey the realness of her reason for being 'despondent'. Notice that this closing touch simultaneously signals the aunt's own kindness and concern for others, so that she will not be suspected of the intention to defame.

20. The foregoing sample demonstrates how the aunt

MANAGES a situation while pretending only to MONITOR it (cf. VIII.1). The convincing nature of this fictional discourse is surely due to our ready ability to relate its component texts to plan steps via **plan attachment.** The presence of some disturbances in coherence, e.g. assigning to a smile a fully elaborated content that could not have been intended, and the aunt's clear violation of the maxim of QUALITY (cf. VI.9.3) do not render the discourse unacceptable, as long as such disturbances and violations are intentional actions toward a goal.

21. In I.15f., we introduced the notion of ACCEPTABILITY as the text receivers' attitude in communication. In the most immediate sense of the term, text receivers must ACCEPT a language configuration as a cohesive and coherent text capable of utilization. Like intentionality, acceptability includes a TOLERANCE range for such minor discontinuities or disturbances as illustrated in samples [85] through [90] (cf. VI.2ff.), provided that continuity can be restored by reasonable **problem-solving** (cf. III.14ff.). If we identify acceptability with the text receivers' "ability to extract operating instructions from the utterance" (Jörg & Hörmann 1978: 76), then it must be reasonably evident from the text and its situation of occurrence what those "instructions" are (cf. S. Schmidt 1971*b*, 1973; Weinrich 1976).

22. The importance of acceptability gradually emerged during research on how to verify a "grammar" as an account of all sentences allowed in a language (cf. II.27). Ostensibly, one should be able to present lists of sentences to *informants* (native speakers giving views on their language) to be judged either "grammatical" or "ungrammatical". The "grammar" must then be able to generate the former and exclude the latter. This requirement is vastly more ambitious than any in traditional school grammars, because it must expressly exclude vast numbers of sentences which nobody would "ever be in danger of forming" (Quirk & Svartvik 1966: 9f.).

23. Even in early investigations, uniform judgements about sentences were notoriously hard to obtain (cf. papers in Sebeok (ed.) 1960). More comprehensive and recent research has confirmed that difficulty beyond all dispute (cf. Heringer 1970; Ringen 1975; Greenbaum 1977; Mohan 1977; Snow & Meijer 1977). Lambek (1961: 167) sarcastically pointed out the disparity of attitudes: "At one extreme there are those who call

every utterance a sentence, that is, any string of words ever mouthed by poet or peasant. At the other extreme there are those who would declare cannibalism ungrammatical on the grounds that 'man' does not belong to the class of food-nouns." Lambek is addressing two opposed outlooks on language study: (*a*) the insistence on actually occurring grammatical data as all belonging to the language; and (*b*) the belief that a grammar can specify all possible relationships independently of actual occurrences. To mediate between these opposites, it has become customary to distinguish between **grammaticality** (what is stipulated by an abstract grammar) and **acceptability** (what is actually accepted in communication). So far, however, the correlation between these two notions is far from clear. We surmise that the crucial distinction is in fact between **virtual systems** and **actualization procedures** as explained in III.12. As noted already, actualization can apparently override the organization of virtual systems when appropriate motivation is present – a principle which sets language and communication apart from the objects of study in the natural sciences and mathematics (cf. 0.5).

24. It seems unlikely that theories of language can ignore the correlation between actual occurrences and theoretical models. We shall describe several means for bridging the gulf. One simple and frequent practice has been for linguists to invent and judge their own sentences, i.e. to become the informants themselves (cf. critique in Labov 1972: 199; Ringen 1975; J. Anderson 1976: 69; Schlesinger 1977: 210). Yet "it is dangerous", remarks Sidney Greenbaum (1977: 4), "for a linguist to depend on his own introspection as a means of obtaining data: lengthy exposure to a set of examples is likely to blur his judgements, and his reactions will inevitably be prejudiced by his general theoretical position and by the specific hypotheses that predict acceptability judgements". Spencer (1973) noticed that linguists often make different judgements of the same data than do non-linguists. Snow and Meijer (1977) suggest indeed that linguists can develop a special, exceptional ability not found in normal language users; their tests showed that linguists agreed with themselves and each other to a much larger degree, and were much more willing to mark sentences ungrammatical on the basis of

syntax alone. It has however been our experience that linguists also construct such elaborate examples and counter-examples that they may end up accepting sentences which everyday language users would find highly bizarre.[8]

25. A second means of correlating acceptability and grammaticality has been pursued especially by William Labov and his associates (see for instance Labov 1969, 1972). He argues that the divergencies of usage in various social groups can be accounted for by *variable* rules rather than strict, infallible ones. Depending upon social factors, text producers would be able to choose among alternative rules or sets of rules. Labov's approach would introduce diversity into a grammar without weakening the distinction between "grammatical" and "ungrammatical". Hence, it should still be possible for language users within a particular group to agree what sentences should or should not be allowed. This agreement is, as we have remarked (VI.23), precisely what is so hard to obtain.

26. A third means appears more promising than the first two, namely, to view the production and reception of texts (or sentences) as PROBABILISTIC operations. Grammar would be a set of "fuzzy" instructions in which well-formedness (conformity with the grammar) of sentences would be located somewhere on a graded scale (cf. Lakoff 1973; Mohan 1977). The really decisive consideration is the CONTEXT where sentences actually occur. Sentences are regularly judged "grammatical" by an informant when it is easy to imagine possible contexts for them (Bolinger 1968; McCawley 1976; Snow & Meijer 1977). In effect, "grammaticality" becomes a partial determiner of acceptability in interaction with other factors. For example, the order in which sentences are presented has been proven to affect people's judgements (Greenbaum 1973). Sentences are more readily accepted if their expressions elicit mental imagery, presumably because the images assist in devising contexts (cf. Levelt et al. 1977). In connected discourse, sentences can be influenced by the structures of neighbouring sentences (van Dijk 1977*c*); such is the case with ELLIPTICAL constructions like [60] and [61] in IV.33. Considerations of this kind suggest that the notion of acceptability in the narrow sense is really useful only for texts in situations, not for isolated sentences.

27. The correspondences between intentionality and acceptability are exceedingly intricate. Under stress or time pressure, people often produce utterances which they might feel disinclined to accept under normal circumstances; conversely, they accept utterances from other people which they would be most reluctant to produce (cf. van Dijk 1977*c*). It has been demonstrated that people may not be aware of their own speaking styles, or those of their social group, and be surprised to hear authentic recordings (Blom & Gumperz 1972: 430). Also, people often go back and "repair" their utterances when deemed unsatisfactory, even though their knowledge of the language has not changed at that moment (cf. Schegloff, Jefferson & Sacks 1977). And people may shift among **styles** of text production in order to project desired social **roles** in different settings, because of the social markedness of certain options (cf. Ervin-Tripp 1972; Fishman 1972; Tyler 1972). In view of all these considerations, the conclusion that language can scarcely be described or explained except in terms of texts in real settings again seems inescapable.

28. In a wider sense of the term, "acceptability" would subsume ACCEPTANCE as the active willingness to participate in a discourse and share a goal. Acceptance is thus an action in its own right (van Dijk 1977*c*), and entails entering into discourse interaction, with all attendant consequences. Refusing acceptance is conventionally accomplished by explicit signals, e.g.:

[110] I'm too busy for talking just now.
[111] I don't care to talk about it.

Otherwise, participation in discourse would, as a **default**, be assumed to imply acceptance.

29. The acceptance of other people's **goals** may arise from many diverse motivations (cf. Wilensky 1978*a*, *b*). We saw in sample [109] that Mr Tupman was willing to share the aunt's courtship goal, though he failed to support it as actively as she expected and desired. Successful communication clearly demands the ability to detect or infer other participants' goals on the basis of what they say (Allen 1979). By the same token, text producers must be able to anticipate the receivers' responses as supportive of or contrary to a plan, for example, by building an *internal model* of the receivers and their beliefs

and knowledge.[9] The following brief dialogue is imagined by Piglet as a means for freeing himself from an unpleasant situation: he believes himself caught in a trap built by a 'Heffalump' (a distortion of 'elephant'). Being a very small animal himself, he can only hope to outwit the large Heffalump by MONITORING the situation in the opposite way from the latter.[10] He hopes that the Heffalump will accept this reversal if delivered with sufficient self-confidence and offhandedness. In other words, he postulates an ideal and total attitude of acceptance on the Heffalump's part. Here is the dialogue as planned out by Piglet (Milne 1928: 44f.) (already cited as sample [5] in I.1):

[5] [1] HEFFALUMP *(gloatingly)*: Ho-ho!
[2] PIGLET *(carelessly)*: Tra-la-la, tra-la-la.
[3] HEFFALUMP *(surprised, and not quite so sure of himself)*: Ho-ho!
[4] PIGLET *(more carelessly still)*: Tiddle-um-tum, tiddle-um-tum.
[5] HEFFALUMP *(beginning to say 'Ho-ho' and turning it awkwardly into a cough)*: H'r'm! What's all this?
[6] PIGLET *(surprised)*: Hallo! This is a trap I've made, and I'm waiting for a Heffalump to fall into it.
[7] HEFFALUMP *(greatly disappointed)*: Oh! *(After a long silence)*: Are you sure?
[8] PIGLET: Yes.
[9] HEFFALUMP: Oh! (nervously): I – I thought it was a trap *I'd* made to catch Piglets.
[10] PIGLET *(surprised)*: Oh, no!
[11] HEFFALUMP: Oh! *(apologetically)*: I – must have got it wrong, then.
[12] PIGLET: I'm afraid so. *(politely)*: I'm sorry. *(He goes on humming.)*
[13] HEFFALUMP: Well – well – I – well. I suppose I'd better be getting back?
[14] PIGLET *(looking up carelessly)*: Must you? Well, if you see Christopher Robin anywhere, you might tell him I want him.
[15] HEFFALUMP *(eager to please)*: Certainly! Certainly! *(He hurries off.)*

30. The Heffalump's opening 'ho-ho!' [5.1] shows elation at attaining the goal of catching someone in his trap. Piglet is therefore motivated to avoid showing any indication of concern or fear which might confirm that monitoring. His humming

bits of songs [5.2, 4, 12] also suggests a carefree idleness that befits his own monitoring in [5.6]. The Heffalump duly begins to doubt his elation, and instead requests a monitoring from Piglet ('what's all this?') [5.5]. The latter is then privileged to deliver his own oddly mediated monitoring in [5.6]. Due to the strong acceptance attitude ascribed to him, the Heffalump does not protest, but merely asks if the new version is 'sure' [5.7] – the 'long silence' is presumably time spent adjusting his model of the situation. Upon confirmation [5.8], another 'oh' signals acquiescence, followed by a modest attempt to restore the original situation with a monitoring in [5.9]. The 'surprise' which greets this sally [5.10] underscores its improbability, just as the earlier 'surprise' [5.6] was to suggest that the Heffalump had no motive for being there at all. This finishing touch defeats the Heffalump's version altogether (the final 'oh!' marking this last step), leaving him to conclude that he 'must have got it wrong' [5.11]. Now Piglet can afford to be reserved – compare 'I'm afraid so' [5.12] to 'Yes' [5.8] and 'Oh, no!' [5.10] – and 'polite' to the downcast adversary [5.12]. Note that the insincerity of the apology renders it none the less relevant to Piglet's plan by suggesting his superior control over the situation (on sincerity, cf. VI.10). The Heffalump's speech hesitation, signalling his indecision about his role and situation model throughout [5.9, 11],[11] becomes extreme at this juncture [5.13], until he can think of nothing more but to withdraw from the interaction [5.13]. Still maintaining his 'carelessness', Piglet neatly elicits the Heffalump as a co-operative agent toward another, equally important goal: Christopher Robin's assistance is needed to get Piglet back out of the trap [5.14]. To make things perfect, the Heffalump evidently accepts this role as well and 'hurries off' to enact it [5.15].

31. The best-laid plans of Piglets go oft awry. When the time comes, the other participant does not provide the responses needed. In effect, Piglet has relied on running the situation like a SCRIPT; sudden replanning is hardly feasible. The other speaker (in reality, Christopher Robin, but Piglet can't see who it is) begins with 'Ho-ho!', but follows up Piglet's 'Tra-la-la' with another snatch from a song. The scripted plan is at once set off course:

[112] "He's said the wrong thing," thought Piglet anxiously, "he ought to have said 'Ho-ho!' again." (Milne 1928: 49)

Piglet's attempts to save the plan, e.g. by saying 'Ho-ho!' himself, fail to help, so that he is soon 'Completely Unsettled' and his texts lose some cohesion and a great deal of coherence:

[113] "This is a trap for Poohs, and I'm waiting to fall in it, ho-ho, what's all this, and then I say ho-ho again."
"What?" said Christopher Robin.
"A trap for ho-ho's," said Piglet huskily. "I've just made it, and I'm waiting for the ho-ho to come-come."
(Milne 1928: 49)

These jumbled texts arise from short-circuiting the components of the planned discourse across each other, so that bits of different texts appear together on the surface along with bits of the plan itself (e.g. 'then I say'). The notion 'trap for Poohs' stems from an earlier conversation in which Pooh had predicted the coming of the Heffalump. The interjection 'ho-ho' displaces 'Heffalump' apparently via a similarity of initial sound;[12] the doubling of syllables then spreads to 'come'.

32. This conversation, though somewhat fantastic, is a good illustration of how a discourse participant draws up a plan and predicts the contributions of others. If the others deny acceptance of the plan, thus violating the principle of **co-operation, textuality** can be impaired. It follows that an unwilling participant could block a discourse by refusing acceptance, e.g. by not recovering or upholding **coherence.** Here is an instructive sample in which Robert Benchley (1954: 106) prevents Mr Thwomly from recounting boring adventures abroad. Since the participants are in a moving railway carriage, Benchley cannot merely leave. His tactic is to fail to accept the main TOPIC concepts ('railway carriage', 'France', 'Frenchman'):

[114] [1] THWOMLY: We have been all summer in France, you know, and those French trains are all divided up into compartments. . . . On the way from Paris to Marseilles we had a funny experience. I was sitting next to a Frenchman who was getting off at Lyons . . . and he was dozing when we got in. So I –

[2] BENCHLEY: Did you get to France at all when you were away?

[3] THWOMLY: This was in *France* that I'm telling you about. On the way from Paris to Marseilles. We got into a railway carriage –

[4] BENCHLEY: The railway carriages there aren't like ours here, are they? I've seen pictures of them, and they seem to be more like compartments of some sort.
[5] THWOMLY *(a little discouraged)*: That was a French railway carriage I was just describing to you. I sat next to a man –
[6] BENCHLEY: A Frenchman?
[7] THWOMLY: Sure, a Frenchman. That's the *point*.
[8] BENCHLEY: Oh, I see.
[9] THWOMLY: Well, the Frenchman was asleep, and when we got in I stumbled over his feet. So he woke up and said something in French which I couldn't understand . . .
[10] BENCHLEY: You were across the border into France, then?
[11] THWOMLY *(giving the whole thing up as a bad job)*: And what did *you* do this summer? (Benchley 1954: 106)

33. In Chapter V, we used the notion of TOPIC to describe text-world concepts with the greatest density of linkage to other concepts (cf. V.38). Unless topic concepts are activated, the processing of the textual world is not feasible because there are no CONTROL CENTRES to show the main IDEAS. Thus, Mr Thwomly is blocked from recounting his dull 'experience' by the impression that his receiver audience has not grasped the concepts upon which he is trying to build. Benchley's questions would have been co-operative if they dealt with variable or unknown aspects of the textual world (cf. IX.14); but instead, they concern material which was plainly established just before. Thwomly has not violated the maxim of manner by being obscure or ambiguous (cf. VI.8ff.); yet the feedback seems to indicate that he has. He is forced to restate basic notions as if they were new [114.3, 5, 7], gradually becoming 'discouraged' at the slight chances of ever getting to the 'point' [114.7]. Just when he finally launches into the details of the trivial scene (trying to excuse oneself across a language barrier), he is thrown back to zero by a question about the most essential fact (location of the event sequence). Understandably, he 'gives the whole thing up' in the face of failing to make any headway [114.11]. In this fashion, Benchley has defeated the other participant's goal and attained his own (peace and quiet) via a lack of acceptance.

34. We can see from the examples in this chapter how great a role is played by the CONTEXT of communication with respect to intentionality and acceptability. Far more is involved than a

comparison of sentences with an all-purpose grammar. We must also consider factors like these: (*a*) how much knowledge is shared or conveyed among participants; (*b*) how the participants are trying to monitor or manage the situation; and (*c*) how the texts composing the discourse are related to each other. We shall devote the next three chapters to each of those factors in turn.

Notes

1 These standards apply in a special way to texts produced or received by computers. Here, the attitudes are located in the programmers rather than in the machine: the intending and accepting as activities are only simulated.

2 The clergyman has recently arrived from a 'theological seminary' in the East and is thus unused to the speech in the mining camp. The miner uses expressions from card games; 'you ruther hold over me, pard'='you are holding rather higher cards than I am, partner'; 'I can't call that hand'='I can't match your bet on your hand of cards'; 'ante and pass the buck'= 'put up some money and move on to another player'. The miner of course wants the clergyman to use easier vocabulary.

3 The Grice papers were produced much earlier than the dates we are citing. Grice (1971) was circulated as early as 1957; Grice (1975) was delivered as a lecture in 1967, but, according to Grice himself (personal communication to RdB) was composed several years before that.

4 See note 3 to this chapter. Our discussion incorporates some comments made by Grice himself to RdB at a colloquium in Bielefeld, June, 1979.

5 *King Kong vs. Godzilla* (1963).

6 A transition phase between the stimulus-response outlook and modern plan theory was brought about by the pivotal work of Miller, Galanter & Pribram (1960). Their model foresaw the organism "testing" the environment and "operating" on it until a goal was obtained.

7 If a plan works well and comes to be applied automatically, we can use the term SCRIPT (cf. V.16); such appears to be the case with Tom Sawyer's plan for bargaining other boys out of their possessions in return for the "privilege" of whitewashing (cf. VIII.27).

8 A notorious illustration is the "centre-embedded" sentence of the kind: 'The pen the author the editor liked used was new' (cf. Fodor & Garrett 1967). Since no reasonable person produces such sentences very often, it is hard to see why so much research has been lavished on how people process them.

9 cf. Goldman (1975: 346); Bernstein & Pike (1977: 3); Carbonell Jr. (1978); Cohen (1978: 16); McCalla (1978: 19); Rubin (1978*b*: 136); Allen (1979: 6).

10 Actually, the scene had been previously planned out by Pooh, so that Piglet's model is only borrowed. The monitorings here clearly qualify also as MANAGINGS of the situation (cf. VIII.1).

11 The loss of cohesion through indecision or surprise is not uncommon (cf. VI.2, 31).
12 The confusion of surface elements with similar or shared sounds is frequent in "miscues" (errors made by altering a text while reading it aloud, cf. note 13 to Chapter IV). Piglet's mistakes are rather unlikely from a linguistic standpoint, however.

Chapter VII

Informativity

1. As stated in I.17ff., we use the term INFORMATIVITY to designate the extent to which a presentation is new or unexpected for the receivers. Usually, the notion is applied to CONTENT; but occurrences in any language system might be informative. The emphasis on content arises from the dominant role of COHERENCE (as depicted in Chapter V) in textuality, while language systems like phonemes or syntax seem subsidiary or auxiliary and hence less often in the direct focus of ATTENTION. Here, "attention" would be defined as the expenditure of processing resources that restricts the potential for other tasks at the same time (Keele 1973). Hence, if attention is focused on the coherence of concepts and relations, other systems are not given prominence unless deliberately handled in noticeably non-expected ways. For example, some trends in twentieth-century poetry involve bizarre configurations of **sounds** that do not form known words, e.g. Ernst Jandl's:[1]

[115] la zeechn u bapp
iileo zunggi

Since coherence cannot be imposed, attention is free to dwell upon the sounds as such and set up unconfirmable hypotheses about possible senses. **Syntax** can also be focused by a markedly non-ordinary sequence such as God's command that His angels obey Christ in *Paradise Lost* (V 611-12):

[116] Him who disobeys, me disobeys.

In exchange, the content of [116] is quite straightforward (cf. VII.6).

2. Claude Shannon and Warren Weaver (1949) set forth an INFORMATION THEORY based primarily on the notion of STATISTICAL PROBABILITY. The greater the number of possible **alternatives** at a given point, the higher will be the information value when one of them is chosen. The most precise method for deciding what alternatives can appear is to look at all available sequences of the language and count up all occurrences of a pair of elements, say X followed by Y. If we then consider all occasions where X is followed by something else, we have the "transition probability" for X going to Y (i.e. the likelihood that the "state X" will pass over into the "state Y"). A sequence constituted according to these item-to-item transitions is called a MARKOV CHAIN.

3. It is fairly well agreed that this model of statistical probability is not applicable as such to natural language communication. It is out of the question to count up all the sequences of a language like English. Even if it were not, the occurrence of most elements depends on factors other than the occurrence of an element just before. We saw in IV.7ff., for example, that grammatical dependencies often extend over expressions not located next to each other. And the statistical approach ignores most aspects of the sense and purpose of texts in discourse.

4. Despite these reservations, realistic theories and models of texts in use can scarcely dispense with the notion of **probability** altogether. We have repeatedly appealed to such notions as "expectations", "hypotheses", "defaults", "preferences", and "predictions" as important controls upon what occurs in texts. For instance, the TRANSITION NETWORKS used to represent syntax in IV.5ff. and conceptual relations in V.29ff. work on the principle that certain linkages are more probable than others and hence worth trying out in a certain order. The use of PLANS in discourse similarly requires the planner to maintain a MODEL of current and future situations, and to design contingencies accordingly (cf. VIII.1).

5. The decisive step would be to replace the notion of *statistical* probability with that of *contextual* probability. The crucial consideration is then not how often things occur together in any absolute frequency, but rather what classes of occurrences are more or less likely under the influence of

systematic constellations of current factors. Quite possibly, a statistically rare configuration of surface expressions, underlying concepts, or plan steps, might be highly probable under appropriate conditions. At least, it seems safe to conclude that the contextual probabilities are different in strength for the different elements in the text (cf. Miller 1951; Shannon 1951; Sprung 1964). The question of how the various language systems interact to determine these probabilities is much less straightforward, and has not been well explored.

6. For one thing, the strength of probability might well be unequal in the several systems. A sequence might be composed of syntactically probable elements (hence, having low informativity in its cohesion) but conceptually improbable ones (hence, having high informativity in its coherence) (cf. Hess 1965). For instance, a sequence such as (*Macbeth* V v 22):

[117] All our yesterdays have lighted fools the way to dusty death

is conventional in cohesion, but quite unique in coherence, as contrasted with an ordinary statement in the same syntactic format:

[117]*a* All our western agencies have guided tours to dusty Death Valley.

In return, a sequence such as Milton's line already cited (VII.1):

[116] Him who disobeys, me disobeys.

is ordinary in its coherence, but non-ordinary in its cohesion, as opposed to an everyday rearrangement like this:

[116]*a* Whoever disobeys him is disobeying me.

Ordinariness supports easy processing, while non-ordinariness renders processing an interesting challenge.

7. It seems unlikely that extremely exact numerical values can or should be assigned to each occurrence on every level. More plausible would be the assumption of a *range of general probabilities,* that is, measurements of higher or lower on an approximate scale. For the time being at least, we might be content with a range of three ORDERS OF INFORMATIVITY, each sufficiently broad that human language users might be able to distinguish them during actual communication. If each occurrence is being selected from a **fuzzy** set of options, we

might divide the range into: (*a*) upper degree, (*b*) lower degree, and (*c*) apparently outside the set altogether.

8. The occurrence of an option in the upper range of probability, i.e, apperceptibly among the most likely candidates, would convey FIRST-ORDER informativity. An extreme illustration is the 'stop'-text found on a road sign: it is fully predictable in cohesion, coherence, and planning, the situation of occurrence is usually obvious, and the sign itself even has a unique shape and colour recognizable at considerable distance. Maximal predictability is motivated here in order to keep the motorists' attention free for current traffic conditions (cf. I.20).

9. First-order occurrences are rather TRIVIAL, that is, so well integrated into a system or setting that they receive very slight **attention** in the sense of VII.1. In English, the so-called FUNCTION WORDS (articles, prepositions, and conjunctions), all of which signal relations rather than content,[2] are usually so trivial that even frequent occurrences of them in a single text are hardly noticed. The slots where function words appear in a sequence are by and large well-defined. These considerations would have major implications for active processing. Function words are often pronounced so indistinctly that they would hardly be identifiable out of context (cf. Woods & Makhoul 1973). Clark and Clark (1977: 275) suggest that, during text production, function words are selected only after content-conveying words ("content words"). In text reception, people might skip over function words and piece content words together in a kind of "fuzzy parsing".[3] Text types requiring extreme economy, e.g. telegrams or road signs, often dispense with function words. It has been observed that aphasia (loss of language ability through brain disturbance) can lead its victims to omit function words in speaking (Goodglass & Blumstein 1973).

10. Content words, on the other hand, would generally be more informative. There is, for one thing, a much larger set to choose from than for function words (cf. the "statistical probability" cited in VII. 2). Content words activate more extensive and diverse cognitive materials (cf. V.8), and can elicit more pronounced emotions or mental images than can function words. However, a text producer might alter or reverse the normal roles of these two word types. For

example, the function words may be themselves ordinary, but still occur in very non-ordinary slots:

[118] wish by spirit and if by yes

(e. e. cummings 1972)

[119] long along the in and out of grey car

(Myra Cohn Livingston 1972)

The placement of such function words as 'if' in [118] and 'in' and 'out' in [119] creates a focus of attention in which special content can be assigned, e.g. 'if' as 'condition' and 'in' and 'out' as 'entry' and 'exit', respectively. It is no coincidence that we usually use content words to expound the role of function words in cases like these.

11. First-order informativity would always be present in any text, whether or not higher orders were attained. Any occurrence, no matter how trivial, represents the rejection of non-occurrence as an alternative. Moreover, every occurrence must have the property of being the same or different as the preceding occurrence in that same system (cf. Weinrich (1972) who shows that sameness of grammatical occurrences is more common than difference).[4] The simple oppositions of occurrence/non-occurrence and sameness/difference are in themselves quite trivial, though special focus may be created by breaking a repeated pattern. Many humans evidently subscribe to the so-called *gambler's fallacy* of expecting a series of the same occurrence to be broken fairly soon (cf. Kintsch 1977*a*: 91f.).

12. The standard procedures applied to first-order occurrences in communication would be DEFAULTS (operations or selections assumed to be stipulated in absence of contrary indicators) and PREFERENCES (operations or selections routinely favoured over competing alternatives) (cf. III.18). These procedures minimize processing load, so that attention is reserved for higher-order occurrences. When defaults or preferences are overridden, i.e. when occurrences are below the upper range of probability, we obtain SECOND-ORDER informativity. The presence of at least some second-order occurrences would be the normal standard for textual communication, since texts purely on the first order would be difficult to construct and extremely uninteresting. Upon occasion, first-order occurrences could be UPGRADED and

third-order ones DOWNGRADED to keep this medium order, as we shall see presently (cf. VII.13ff.).

13. Occurrences which at first appear to be *outside* the set of more or less probable options convey THIRD-ORDER informativity. These are comparatively infrequent occurrences which demand much attention and processing resources, but which are, in return, more INTERESTING.[5] DISCONTINUITIES, where material seems to be missing from a configuration, and DISCREPANCIES, where text-presented patterns don't match patterns of stored knowledge, would be the usual kinds of third-order occurrences. The text receiver must do a MOTIVATION SEARCH – a special case of **problem-solving** – to find out what these occurrences signify, why they were selected, and how they can be integrated back into the CONTINUITY that is the basis of communication (cf. III.14). In effect, a successful search will show that the occurrence in question was within the range of options after all, though accessible only via some mediation. Accordingly, the search has DOWNGRADED the third-order occurrence into the second order. Downgrading could have several DIRECTIONALITIES. If text receivers go back to find motivation in earlier occurrences, they are doing **backward** downgrading. If they wait to consider later occurrences, they are doing **forward** downgrading. If they move outside the current text or discourse, they are doing **outward** downgrading. The same distinction can be made for upgrading.

14. Such processing may well extend far beyond textual communication and apply to the human reaction to the world at large. As normal people, we would be astonished to receive a cheque in the mail for an enormous sum of money. We might think back if we had purchased a sweepstake ticket or the like (backward downgrading); we might wait to see if some notification will follow with an explanation (forward downgrading); or we might suppose that a mistake has happened with money intended for another person or purpose (outward downgrading). If none of these tactics downgrades the event, we will simply not be able to understand it. **Senselessness** (or **nonsense**) results from lack of continuity between an occurrence and the rest or our knowledge and experience, and is doubtless hard to tolerate (cf. V.2).

15. The degree to which a third-order occurrence is actually

disturbing would depend on the STRENGTH OF LINKAGE affected (cf. V.5). An occurrence that ran counter to DETERMINATE knowledge would be more disorienting than one that ran counter to TYPICAL; and a violation of typical knowledge would be more disturbing than that of ACCIDENTAL. In these well-known lines (Carroll 1960: 234):

[120] Their coats were brushed, their faces washed,
Their shoes were clean and neat –
And this was odd, because, you know,
They hadn't any feet.

the effect derives from the **determinate** knowledge that shoes must be worn on the feet. The presentation is motivated here by the intention to describe the young oysters in terms of human children on a holiday. If they had in fact been human children, their condition would not have been so 'odd', since the state of coats, faces, and shoes belonging to humans is purely **accidental** knowledge.

16. In I.18, we cited the following as a disturbing stretch of text:

[15] The sea is water

Apparently, determinate knowledge about the substance of the sea – it simply couldn't be the sea if not made of water – is being presented to no purpose. The text producer himself **upgrades** this **first-order** occurrence when he claims later on that the sea is 'actually' a 'solution of gases and salts' (cf. [15*a*] in I.18). The producer might have started out this way instead:

[15]*b* The sea is not water. It is actually a solution of gases and salts.

Then, the receiver is met right away with a **third-order** occurrence which can be easily integrated by **forward down-grading.** In both cases [15] and [15]*b*, the opening of the text creates an unstable INFORMATION STATE[6] which is presumably uncomfortable for the receiver. The regulative release from such a state is a prime illustration of how communication represents the continual removal and restoration of STABILITY (cf. III.15).

17. There must be a processing disposition which prevents text users from uncovering or accepting highly bizarre alterna-

tive readings of a single text. The example of Schank and Wilensky (1977: 141).

[121] Time flies like an arrow.

might be assigned various alternative readings beyond the obvious statement that time flies swiftly, e.g.: (*a*) someone is being ordered to measure the speed of flies in an arrow-like manner, or (*b*) a particular, oddly-named species of flies is fond of arrows. Yet either alternative would be of the third order, so that people would not be disposed to even consider them. At the other extreme of the informativity scale, a first-order reading of a line from a poem ('Richard Cory' by Edward Arlington Robinson (1914: 35)) is hardly likely to occur to receivers:

[122] And he was always human when he talked

Obviously, Mr Cory would belong determinately to the class of 'humans', and humans are the only ones likely to be 'talking' in this poem; informativity rises if Mr Cory is set so far apart from humans that his acting in a human manner is unexpected here. We argued on similar grounds in IV.31 that a first-order reading of the headline:

[58] San Juan Gunfire Kills One

wherein it is simply announced that gunfire is fatal in this particular town, will go unnoticed by the normal reader.

18. Contextual probability, even for this modest three-value scale, is a complex amalgam of factors. We might distinguish a progression of steadily more specialized HUMAN EXPECTATIONS applying in various degrees during communication (cf. Beaugrande 1978*b*):

18.1 The socially dominant model of the human situation and its environment constitutes what is commonly called the REAL WORLD. Propositions held to be **true** in that world (i.e. to match their organization with its own above a certain threshold) would be FACTS (cf. van Dijk 1978). The facts which a person or group consider to be generally applicable to some "real" or recoverable situation or event constitute their BELIEFS. The "real world" is accordingly the privileged source of beliefs underlying textual communication. Of course, we can produce and receive many texts which are not factual in this way;

but we still tend to use the "real" world as our point of orientation. Some "facts" are so firmly entrenched in our manner of thinking that they act as **defaults** for any textual world that might be presented: that causes have effects; that something cannot be both true and false, or existent and non-existent, at the same instant and under the same circumstances; that objects have identity, mass, and weight; and so forth. Should any such facts be violated in a textual world, there must be explicit, unmistakable signals. Even the less extreme case where shoes are worn without feet elicits Carroll's remark that 'this was odd' in sample [120]. The production and reception of a lengthy text in whose world cause and effect were suspended might prove not to be feasible, at least in English.

18.2 Humans seem to apply consistent strategies of apperceiving and arranging the real world, lest **complexity** become overwhelming. Humans do not experience the world as a bombardment of individual stimuli; they integrate their sensations into a MODEL of the world via a "highly skilled act of attention" (Miller & Johnson-Laird 1976: 29). Whatever knowledge is acquired is continually used as a bridge to annex further knowledge. We described in V.16, for instance, the use of GLOBAL PATTERNS such as FRAMES, SCHEMAS, PLANS, and SCRIPTS for matching, integrating, and controlling large amounts of current materials.[7] In addition, there is some evidence of NORMAL ORDERING STRATEGIES for apperceiving and talking about the world (real or imaginary). If asked to MONITOR a visual **scene** (cf. VIII.1), people tended to move from the top downward (DeSoto, London & Handel 1965; Clark & Chase 1974). In describing their own apartments, people mentally walked through them, mentioning each room in the order it would have been seen or entered; they placed major rooms more often in expressions filling the subject slot of sentences, whereas minor rooms were more often expressed in predicates (Linde & Labov 1975). Mobile objects tended to be mentioned via grammatical subjects more often than stationary ones in the same scene (Osgood 1971). Focus of attention on the agent as opposed to the affected entity of events has been found to correlate with preferences for active v. passive sentence formats (Olson & Filby 1972). Event sequences are normally recounted in the same temporal order in which they happened (Labov & Waletzky 1967; Clark & Clark 1968). All these tendencies are only PREFERENCES (cf. VII.12), however, and can be modified in appropriate contexts, expecially if signals to that effect accompany the presentation.[8]

18.3 The second source of expectations is the organization of the LANGUAGE to be used in a text. In a language such as English, many conventions for combining forms are ARBITRARY; that is, the organization of events and situations is not reflected directly in the organization of language (but cf. VII.18.2). Arbitrary conventions impel speakers to consider certain sound clusters unpronounceable because their language lacks them. Speakers of English, for example, would not try to pronounce clusters like 'Ltd', 'bbl', 'FBI', or 'lb' as written, but would at once recognize them as abbreviations of longer forms with more convenient sound patterns. On the same principle, the radically disordered sequences used by grammarians to stress the importance of syntax, e.g. Dresher and Hornstein's (1976: 365):

[123] Tall man the hit small round ball a.

would scarcely occur or be accepted outside linguistic debates. If such odd configurations of sound or syntax were presented, they would figure as non-downgradable third-order occurrences for most receivers. If sound and syntax are used only for their FUNCTIONS in organizing content (cf. VII.9),[9] then a denial of their organization seems pointless unless some new function is discoverable (cf. samples [118] and [119] in VII.10).

18.4 A third source of expectations arises from the techniques for arranging sequences according to the informativity of elements or groups of elements. In Chapter IV, we glanced at FUNCTIONAL SENTENCE PERSPECTIVE (IV.51-3) and INTONATION (IV.54-8) as means for signalling what is considered new, important, or unexpected within clauses or tone groups. We noted, for instance, that highly informative elements tend to appear toward the end of a clause and to receive a high key. In contrast, elements of low informativity tend to appear toward the beginning of clauses and receive a low key; or to be compacted via PRO-FORMS (IV.21-31) or omitted via ELLIPSIS (IV.32-7). These techniques provide for a balance between two opposing tendencies: maintaining a clear point of orientation, and keeping informativity reasonably high (cf. III.15).

18.5 It might be concluded that the first source of expectations about the "real world" and its "facts" would be independent of language altogether, whereas the second source (formal conventions) and the third (informativity signalling) would vary from one language to another. This issue is, however, in great dispute. The diversity of formal conventions among languages is uncontested; but there is little agreement about whether this diversity also compels the users of language to organize the world in different ways, as claimed by Whorf (1956). Similarly, if meaning of expressions and sense of texts are heavily tied to acquisition and use of knowledge, then they must be subject to the influence of cultural and social factors – a notion explored in "ethnographic semantics" (cf. Colby 1966). Therefore, there is doubtless substantial interaction among the three sources of expectations outlined above, but each source exerts distinctive effects corresponding to its particular organizational principles. On occasion, it might be possible to isolate the sources via specially constructed examples, although humans normally have no motivation to do so.

18.6 The fourth source of expectations is TEXT TYPE. As will be argued later on (IX.1ff.), text types are global frameworks controlling the range of options likely to be utilized. Such rare patterns of sound or syntax as noted in [115] and [116] (VII.1) are acceptable in **poetic** texts, where conventions of expression are characteristically modified and downgrading is frequently performed (cf. IX.9). In the sub-type "nonsense poem",[10] the presence of 'clean and neat' shoes without feet [120] is also tolerable. It would be quite disturbing if a science report were constructed along these lines:

[120]*a* This treatise examines the data gathered at the Scripts Institute of Oceanographic Research on cleanliness of shoes among footless mollusks of the genus *Ostreidae*.

The type **scientific text** (cf. IX.10) resists the suspension of basic "facts" in the organization of the world, e.g. things (like 'feet') being both absent and present (cf. VII.18.1). Hence, a sample like [120]*a* could not be utilized in scientific discourse.

18.7 The fifth and final source of expectations is the

IMMEDIATE CONTEXT where the text occurs and is utilized (cf. Dressler 1978). If, as we claim, ACTUALIZATION can override the conventional organization of VIRTUAL SYSTEMS,[11] this source might modify the expectations drawn from the other four sources. The notion of STYLE has been employed to reflect the assumption that a single text or set of texts manifests characteristic tendencies of selection (cf. II.7). Accordingly, receivers can expect some sorts of occurrences to be more dominant and frequent than others. **Literary** and **poetic** texts (cf. IX. 8f.) will draw special focus toward their styles, so that producers must expend considerable care and attention upon selection procedures. However, informativity can be increased on occasion by breaking out of one's own established style (Riffaterre 1959, 1960). If this tactic is pursued intensely and often, receivers may become so disoriented that they are unable to utilize a text (e.g. James Joyce's novel *Ulysses* is difficult for many readers): there are no stable patterns to form a background into which non-expected occurrences could be integrated via downgrading.

19. Although our scheme of expectations is not elaborate, it should already reveal why the notion of "statistical probability" sketched in VII.2 is a highly impoverished account of informativity. The correlation between information value and any absolute frequency of the occurrence is certainly not straightforward. The actual effects of an occurrence in its context can always be upgraded or downgraded via appropriately planned settings. Hence, frequency is useful, especially if computed for a very large set of texts, but neither sufficient nor reliable.

20. The appeal of frequency counts was doubtless due to their conciseness and simplicity. The discovery of text users' expectations, on the other hand, is a messy and intricate task (cf. IX.24ff.). Only on certain occasions do people actually declare what they are expecting. It follows that we shall have to work largely in the other direction. After identifying language techniques which serve to indicate expectations, we can proceed to trace out the latter from textual evidence. A fairly obvious illustration is the use of NEGATION, which typically is found only when there exists some motive to believe something is otherwise true (cf. Wason 1965; Osgood 1971; Givón 1978). We need merely locate and analyze

negations to see what kinds of content are being presupposed (cf. VII.38). Other signals include the cohesive devices enumerated in VII.18.4.

21. We demonstrate this approach with sample [3] from I.1, a brief excerpt from *TIME* (22 Jan. 1979):

> [3] [1] Twenty-year-old Willie B. is a diehard TV addict. [2] He hates news and talk shows, but he loves football and gets so excited over food commercials that he sometimes charges at the set, waving a fist. [3] Says a friend: [4] "He's like a little child."
>
> [5] Willie B. is a 450-lb gorilla at the Atlanta Zoo. [6] In December a Tennessee TV dealer heard about Willie B.'s lonely life as the zoo's only gorilla and gave him a TV set.

We shall undertake to sort out the flow of expectations according to what we can extract from the text itself.

22. One important factor is DEFINITENESS:[12] the status of text-world entities which are identifiable, accessible, and recoverable. This status is conventionally marked in English texts by the "definite" article, while the "indefinite" article is reserved for entities just being activated. The distinction is in fact vastly more intricate than this. Some entities are deemed definite because everyone knows about them, e.g. 'the sun' and 'the moon'. Some entities can be indefinite because they are unspecified members of a class, even if they are well-known or recently mentioned. In our sample above, 'the Atlanta Zoo' [5] is well-known and unique, and 'the zoo' [6] is an already mentioned entity – both are thus definite. INDEFINITENESS is usually assigned to entities upon their first mention: 'addict' [1], 'fist' [2], 'friend' [3], 'child' [4], 'gorilla' [5], and 'dealer' [6]. However, there are other explanations here besides first mention. Notice that 'child' and 'gorilla' are new designations for the already mentioned 'Willie B.'. On the other hand, 'a TV set' is indefinite in [6] despite previous mention of 'the [definite!] set' in [2].

23. These uses suggest that definiteness and indefiniteness might be more adequately treated in terms of PROCEDURAL ACCESS. If an entity is in active storage as explained in IV.2, then **determinate** and **typical** knowledge about the entity is easy to access; or it even may be already accessed by SPREADING ACTIVATION (cf. V.12). Thus, the mentioned 'TV addict' [1] can be expected to have a 'set', yielding the definiteness in [2].

In contrast, 'a fist' and 'a friend' are **accidental** members of **classes.** Now, Willie might be expected to have fists and friends; but by singling out one member of a class, the text producer is adding an "instance-of" link (V.26(*y*)) to "part-of" ('fist') (V.26(*k*)) or "relation-of" ('friend') (V.26(*d*)) links; and definiteness seems reluctant to spread more than one link.[13] 'A child' [4] is both first mention and an accidental instance. 'A gorilla' is first mention, but not an accidental member, since there is only one unique gorilla at the Zoo; hence, we could in fact have 'the gorilla', but not 'the fist', 'the friend', or 'the child'. 'A TV set' [6] is indefinite only if we consider this stretch of text beginning 'In December' a new departure, as it would be if it formed the opening sentence; we could equally well look back to Willie's description in the first paragraph and have 'the TV set' here at the end. Perhaps the indefinite usage arises from the perspective of the real sequence of events (cf. VII.18.2), since the 'giving' came before the 'charging' and thus at a time when the 'set' was not yet definite.

24. In addition to definiteness, the *sequencing* of sentences and clauses can be consulted (cf. IV.51ff.). The opening sentence [1] has of course no previous material to build on. The placement of 'Willie B.' in subject position signals that he will be the TOPIC character (cf. the 'rocket' topic appearing as the subject of the opening sentence in sample [4] of I.1). And this entity actually does serve in the subject slot of five more clauses: three in [2] and one each in [4] and [5]. The new or not yet established materials about Willie fill the predicates of all six clauses. These materials are organized among themselves with the aid of JUNCTIVES (cf. IV.42ff.): the 'but' smoothes the transition between the opposites of 'hates' and 'loves' (**contra-junction**, cf. IV.45), and 'so . . . that' signals a causal relation between 'excited' and 'charges' (**subordination**, cf. IV.46).

25. The coherence of the text is supported by the use of some expected material within two individual paragraphs, so that production and reception would be supported in part at least by spreading activation. A 'diehard TV addict' [1] is expected to have detailed likes and dislikes and to get very 'excited' over certain kinds of programs [2]. The extreme behaviour over 'food commercials' [2] is more easily compatible with a 'little child' [4] than with a 'twenty-year-old' [1]. Once Willie B. is

revealed as a 'gorilla' in [5], we expect to hear how the 'TV set' made it to the zoo [6]. 'December' is a likely time for Christmas gifts, particularly ones that promote business for a 'dealer'. And a 'lonely life' is expected for the 'only' one of a group [6].

26. Against this background of well-organized cohesion and coherence, the text producer is able to present a substantial surprise: that Willie B. is not the human being suggested throughout the entire first paragraph. 'Willie B.' is itself one such suggestive signal, since animals are less likely than humans to have last names, at least in America. The terms 'addict', 'talk', 'fist', 'friend', and 'child' all indicate human status with greater or lesser subtlety. The explicit comparison of Willie to 'a little child' is an outstandingly skilful touch for the text producer's intention. The distinctions of Willie's tastes in programs [2] lead us to suppose that he can understand their content; and for 'talk shows', he would of course have to understand language. Any signals that would betray the status of 'gorilla' are studiously avoided, e.g. 'paw' for 'fist', or 'frequent zoo visitor' for 'friend', though the reference to objects in the world would be the same.[14] The age of 'twenty years', quite substantial for a gorilla, is perfectly reasonable for humans.

27. The second paragraph then hits us with a series of expressions whose content demolishes the belief nurtured so far: '450 lb gorilla at the Atlanta Zoo' [5]. The immediate effect is an occurrence with **third-order informativity**, followed up by **backward downgrading** (cf. VII.13): the receiver can regress and find that the preceding material deals with only **typical**, not **determinate** knowledge about humans–though atypical for gorillas. **Forward downgrading** is also provided for via the material expressed in the final sentence [6]. The atypical situation and actions of the gorilla are revealed as caused and enabled by a human agent. These downgradings thus prevent the text from being really disturbing.

28. The use which this text producer has made of receivers' expectations markedly increases the INTERESTINGNESS of the text (cf. VII.13). The second paragraph might easily have been placed before the first one, but the EFFECTIVENESS of the text would have been much lower (cf. I.23). Such tactics are doubtless common in journalistic text production, where interest

must be upheld even when the events and situations to be depicted are not in themselves momentous. In addition, this particular text producer has a special motivation for the tactic. The situation in this textual world reflects people's belief that animal loneliness can be cured with the same technology as human loneliness. Parallel to that view, the striking imagery of a gorilla 'addicted' to television even to the point of 'charging at the set' during short, insignificant messages ('food commercials') projects back on the bizarre, childish conduct of many human TV watchers. By forcing us to confuse the gorilla with a human, the text producer validates his own analogy and suggests that the human TV watchers are acting below the standards of human intelligence and abilities, i.e. like animals who can hardly understand what is going on. And by forcing us to recover and build up that message from subtle cues, the text producer renders the argument especially persuasive (cf. I.16; VII.42; VIII.20).

29. As remarked at the outset, the everyday usage of "informativity" applies mostly to content (VII.1). We will now consider a text where the notion is useful for several language systems in concerted interaction. Our sample is the sonnet quoted as [6] in I.1 (Jennings 1967: 55) (cf. discussions in Beaugrande 1978b; Quirk 1978):

[6] GHOSTS

[1] Those houses haunt in which we leave
[2] Something undone. It is not those
[3] Great words or silences of love

[4] That spread their echoes through a place
[5] And fill the locked-up unbreathed gloom.
[6] Ghosts do not haunt with any face

[7] That we have known; they only come
[8] With arrogance to thrust at us
[9] Our own omissions in a room.

[10] The words we would not speak they use,
[11] The deeds we dared not act they flaunt,
[12] Our nervous silences they bruise;

[13] It is our helplessness they choose
[14] And our refusals that they haunt.

30. The format of the text on the page at once activates

expectations about **text type** (cf. VII.18.6). A **poetic** text is one in which, for special motives, the selection and mapping of language options is typically modified as compared with the conventional organization of language overall (cf. IX.9). An arrangement of fourteen lines of comparable length and rhythm suggests the sub-type "sonnet"; already, some expectations about the sub-type are to be violated. Instead of usual divisions such as eight lines (often two four-line stanzas) followed by six (often two three-line stanzas) – the so-called "Italian" or "Petrarchian" sonnet – or twelve lines (usually three four-line stanzas) followed by a couplet of two lines – the so-called "Shakespearean" sonnet – we have an odd-numbered division of nine lines (three three-line stanzas) followed by five (three-line stanza followed by two lines that do not form a rhyming couplet). The rhyme pattern is also hard to reconcile with the sonnet format: a "terza rima" scheme in which each new rhyme appears locked between two lines with the preceding rhyme. However, with the series of aba–bcb– cdc–ded–de, even this scheme is oddly imbalanced by a rhyme with four appearances, two of them in adjacent lines ('us/use/bruise/choose'). The rhymes themselves are only approximate in the first part of the text: 'leave/love', 'gloom/come', 'us/use' (the last being a rhyme more for the eye than the ear). A receiver would set up expectations that approximate rhymes are going to be the standard in the whole text; yet in the last five lines, there is a shift to full, regular rhymes. The line in which the lack of full rhyme becomes evident (line 3) contains the word 'silences'; the line initiating a pair with full rhymes (line 4) contains the word 'echoes'. Another oddity is that the title may be itself intended to rhyme with the second line, being closer to it than line 4 '(ghosts/ those' vs. 'those/place').

31. The progression of rhymes reveals a trend we can observe on other language levels as well: irregularity and unevenness in the first part (usually lines 1–9) yielding to regularity and expectedness in the last part (usually lines 10–14). For example, the full rhymes of the final five lines are reinforced by grammatical equivalence: all rhyme words are verbs with the same subject 'they' having identical reference to 'ghosts'. The closing word 'haunt' fulfils expectations on multiple levels: (*a*) it is in the closest possible association with

the poem's TOPIC of 'ghosts'; (*b*) it is a predictable verb for the subject 'they', i.e. the 'ghosts'; and (*c*) it is one of a small number of available rhymes for 'flaunt' in line 11. Yet the element is conceptually non-expected in its setting, since 'haunt refusals' is a far less probable combination than the 'haunt houses' at the poem's outset. As we shall claim later on (VII.41f.), the correspondences of expectation flow on different levels is apparently a result of the text producer's well-designed PLAN. The initial rejection of strict poetic conventions in the early stretch of the text is supportive of a refusal to adopt a conventional outlook.

32. The grammar/syntax[15] of the text is subtly organized. The object of the opening sentence would at first seem to be 'those houses', the element directly preceding the verb 'haunt'; on closer inspection, the subject is in the poem's title, and 'those houses' is the direct object displaced from its conventional slot after the verb. This displacement matches the fact that these are not the 'houses' that 'ghosts' would be expected to 'haunt' (cf. VII.38). (On the level of sound, 'something' breaks the rhythm pattern in line 2 and also designates an unexpected kind of action, i.e. 'undone'.)

33. The "cleft construction" is so called because it "cleaves" what could otherwise be a single sentence into two clauses, each with its own subject and verb (cf. Jespersen 1961: 147f.: Quirk et al. 1972: 951). The first clause usually opens with the conceptually empty expression 'it is' so that a focused element can have the rest of the predicate slot where high-informational items are expected to appear (cf. IV.52). The material connected to the focused element can then be added on in a relative clause introduced by 'who', 'which', 'that', or the like. In the sequence of the poem's second sentence ('it is not those great words . . . ', lines 2–5), attention is heightened in order to stress that (*a*) the 'great words and silences of love', a common topic for sonnets, will not be the topic this time; and (*b*) the events which ghosts are conventionally thought to re-enact (cf. VII.38) will not be considered here.

34. The first nine lines have a largely irregular formatting, so that syntactic constructions fail to coincide with line boundaries. The opening sentence apparently encompasses the title (cf. VII.32) and fills out one and a half lines. A similar transition from one major clause to the next in the middle of

the line is found in the third stanza too. Even closely-knit grammatical dependencies overrun line ends: verb-to-direct object in 1–2, determiner-to-head in 2–3, and head (verb)-to-modifier in 7–8. In contrast, the last five lines show heavy agreement between syntactic units and line organization. Each major clause in the fourth stanza fills exactly one line, with lines 10 and 11 being entirely PARALLEL (cf. IV.17). All five lines contain in their first stretch the direct object of the verbs placed at line end, while the next-to-last word is always the subject 'they'. Hence, the non-conventional, improbable English sentence order "direct object-subject-verb" becomes expected and probable – an illustration of statistical probabilities being overturned by context (cf. VII.5). Each occurrence of these parallel structures steadily downgrades their informativity.

35. The two groups of agents are expressed chiefly through **pro-forms**: 'we' versus 'they'. Whenever one of those groups is parsed onto the subject of a verb, the other one is brought into grammatical dependency with the verb's direct object: (*a*) *'ghosts'* haunt the 'houses' 'in which *we* leave something undone'; (*b*) *they* do so with no 'face' that *'we* have known'; (*c*) *'they'* thrust 'at *us'* *'our'* 'omissions'; (*d*) *'they'* use the 'words *we* would not speak'; (*e*) *'they'* flaunt the 'deeds *we* dared not act'; (*f*) *'they'* bruise *'our'* 'silences'; (*g*) *'they'* choose *'our'* helplessness'; and (*h*) *'they'* haunt *'our* refusals'. As indicated a moment ago (VII.34), the last five lines manifest a peak of regularity by making these dependencies parallel. The effect is to evoke on the grammatical level the correspondence between 'our' own 'deeds' and the ghosts' re-enactment.

36. The pattern formed by number of words per line also shifts between the early and later sections of the text. The first three stanzas have the word counts of 7–6–6, 7–6–7, and 7–6–6, yielding an even balance (first and third stanzas the same, middle stanza internally balanced). These lines contain mostly one-syllable words, with the multi-syllable ones distributed unevenly. In contrast, the last section opens with two lines of exclusively one-syllable words (10-11) that add up to the high word count of 8. There follows a line with the markedly low count of 5, and the final lines both have 6. The pattern of word-counts is thus another means of setting the first stretch of text off from the conclusion.

37. The selection of lexical expressions for the surface text was also carefully planned. RECURRENCE (cf. IV.12) is used, evoking the ghostly re-enactments: 'ghosts', 'haunt', 'those', 'words', 'silences', 'not', 'we', 'they', 'our'. The first occurrence of 'words' and 'silences' (line 3) is soon followed by 'echoes' (line 4); later on, the 'words' (line 10) and 'silences' (line 12) are of a very different kind, mocking perhaps those from the domain of 'love'. The recurrence of 'ghosts' and 'haunt' adds still more emphasis to the imitative nature of those activities. Besides recurrence, there is some degree of PARAPHRASE and SYNONYMITY (cf. IV.18; VII.41) among 'undone', 'omissions', 'helplessness', and 'refusals'. And the arrangement of thematic materials has its own patterning of alternation between the predominantly audible – 'words', 'silences', and 'echoes' in lines 3–4, and 'words', 'speak', 'silences', and 'refusals' in lines 10, 12, and 14–and the predominantly visual – 'face', 'arrogance', 'thrust', in lines 6–9, 'deeds', 'act', 'flaunt' in line 10, and 'helplessness' in line 13. Not surprisingly, this alternation becomes swift and regular in the last five lines: 10-audible, 11-visual, 12-audible, 13-visual, and 14-audible.

38. The various levels we have looked at so far (sound, syntax/grammar, lexical expression, and their correlations) are eminently supportive of the flow of expectations in the actual content and argument of the text. The title announces 'ghosts' as the TOPIC, activating the global knowledge configuration we have called a FRAME (cf. V.16). A reasonable 'ghost'-frame might contain common beliefs such as: (*a*) that ghosts haunt houses where something dreadful has been done; (*b*) that ghosts bear the faces of people involved in the dreadful events; and (*c*) that ghosts re-enact the events. These beliefs are of course not stated here, but the NEGATION of them in lines 1–7 shows that one would otherwise be inclined to hold such beliefs (cf. VII.20). The text contains four occurrences of 'not' (lines 2, 6, 10, and 11), a limiting 'only', and a series of expressions whose definition includes some kind of negation or absence: 'undone' (line 2), 'silences' (lines 3 and 12) 'unbreathed' (line 5), 'omissions' (line 9), 'helplessness' (line 13), and 'refusals' (line 14).

39. Since these denials of common beliefs come unexpectedly, a MOTIVATION SEARCH is required to DOWNGRADE

them (cf. VII.13). Receivers cannot, in most societies, verify beliefs about 'ghosts' via recourse to the "real world" as defined in VII.18.1; the motivation for the text's assertions cannot be "factual" and so must be discovered in terms of the text-world itself. This task can be done only if the identity of both the 'ghosts' and the group designated 'we', 'us', 'our' is established. The latter group can be defined in this context as 'those of us who have left something undone'. The 'ghosts' can be defined as entities which re-enact the omitted events.

40. A **discrepancy** arises here (cf. VII.13): how can something be re-enacted or even known about if it was never done in the first place? The only records of such events would be kept in the minds of those who intended or wanted to act but failed. If follows that the ghosts' activities can only be in those same minds. Accordingly, the poem's argument might be downgraded into something like:

[124] People who fail to act at the proper moment will keep on re-enacting those occasions in their minds.

This version would be attained by the sequence of processing steps we have outlined: (*a*) the title and some related expressions activate the 'ghost'-frame; (*b*) some basic beliefs in that frame are negated; (*c*) a discrepancy is noticed regarding the omitted events; (*d*) motivation search is instituted to downgrade the discrepancies in (*b*) and (*c*); (*e*) the identities of 'ghosts' and 'we' are reconstructed from the available material; (*f*) both the events and the ghosts are identified as located in the minds of the people who fail to act. This process entails **outward** downgrading (cf. VII.13) rather than the **backward** and **forward** downgrading noted for the 'gorilla' text in VII.27.[16]

41. The ARGUMENT proceeds as follows. The first lines declare the kinds of houses that ghosts haunt (1–2). Other possible occasions for haunting are denied (lines 2–7), and the opening declaration then returns in a PARAPHRASE (lines 7–9). The last five lines are used to develop and re-affirm what has already been stated. The 'words' and 'silences' depicted here supplant those rejected (lines 2–5). The 'deeds we dared not act' (line 11) look back to 'something undone' (line 2). The 'helplessness' (line 13) and 'refusals' (line 14) are predictable reasons for the various 'omissions'. The motivation of the

elaborate expectation patterning on the levels of sound, syntax/grammar, and expression now becomes obvious. In the opening stretch of text (lines 1–9), the receiver must be motivated to resolve discrepancies; accordingly, the planned irregularities and shifts prevent a relaxation of **attention** and **processing depth.** In the concluding stretch (lines 10–14), the receiver is to accept the argument as now established; hence, the various levels become regular, and expectations of all sorts are confirmed. What might otherwise appear a discrepant and debatable viewpoint attains a subtle but forceful inevitability, culminating with the fulfilment of multi-level expectations upon the final word 'haunt' (VII.31).

42. In VII.28, we suggested that careful use of expectation flow can be supportive of a text producer's intention. In the 'gorilla'-text, something seemingly human proved to be non-human. In the 'ghosts'-text, the reverse happens when non-human 'ghosts' prove to be human thoughts. In both texts, discrepancies are employed to force a recognition of ANALOGIES (cf. V.17), such that insights are provided into the human situation. The 'gorilla'-text is a **factual** news report, and thus committed to the organization of the "real world" (VII.18.1). The 'ghost'-text belongs to the **literary** type and is thus free to present a fundamentally different, alternative world (cf. IX.8). By monitoring an undesirable human situation via a frame of beliefs about unreal beings, the producer signals that the situation has no real justification. People could spare themselves mental re-enactment and regret by acting despite hesitation and overcoming 'nervous silences' and 'helplessness'. Notice that here again the text receivers are being persuaded by the line of argument that they have supplied and reconstructed themselves (cf. VII.28; VIII.20).

43. We hope that our discussion of informativity in this chapter has at least raised some worthwhile issues in the study of texts. We have argued that informativity, being the extent to which presented materials are new or unexpected, exerts important controls on the selection and arrangement of options in texts. The usual standard of informativity is a medium degree we called "second-order"; occurrences of the first order can be upgraded, and those of the third order downgraded. We suggested that text producers can create a planned flow of expectations in order to uphold interest and

fulfil an intention, and we undertook to illustrate the claim with two very different texts. We conclude that the controls exerted by informativity must be a vastly important factor in limiting and motivating the use of particular options in all sorts of contexts.

Notes

1 Cited in Karl Riha, "'Schntzgrmm.' Zu Ernst Jandl." *Replik* 3/4 1970, 54–6.

2 The so-called "function words" derive their name from the dominance of their contribution to the organization of actual systems over their contribution of stable content. This notion of "function" is the basic one in systems theory.

3 cf. IV.36. In effect, people would be inferring functions on the basis of preferential configurations of sense, rather than following the function cues in the surface text. The "content words" can thus contribute more to the functional organization of a text than the old dichotomy of "content words" versus "functions words" would seem to suggest.

4 The tendencies uncovered by Weinrich may be due to the tendencies of texual systems and subsystems to remain STABLE (cf. III.14f.).

5 Interest is not decided solely by improbability: we must also consider factors such as the inherent potential for strong impact on human sensory apperception, i.e. SALIENCE (cf. VIII.3); and the importance of an occurrence for the apperceiver's personal goals (cf. VI.12; le Ny & Denhière 1980).

6 The "information state" is only one of several important states in which a communicative participant may enter (cf. note 4 to Chapter IV). Beaugrande (1979*a, b*) suggests that humans decide their actions in order to attain or maintain *desirable* states along various dimensions. The desire for interestingness constantly conflicts with the desire for knownness.

7 Cf. VI.11-16; VII.38; IX.25-8.

8 For example, one can narrate events out of their original order in time if cues of tense, junctives, or time modifiers are employed (cf. IV.38ff.).

9 See note 2 to this chapter.

10 On "nonsense", cf. V.2; VII.14. It follows from our definition there that "non-sense" is a matter of receivers' expectations and prior knowledge, and it may well vary from one individual or group to another.

11 See the examples in VI.2f.; VII.1.

12 We do not treat definiteness in any detail in this book, since it falls between informativity and cohesion (selection of articles). See Beaugrande (1980*a*) for a more extensive discussion.

13 See again Beaugrande (1980*a*: 137–44) for details.

14 Considerations like this – why people are motivated to use different expressions in referring acts – should have been more prominently raised in the long dispute over 'Morning Star/Evening Star' since Frege (1892) (cf. Carnap 1947: 119; Quine 1953: 21; Linsky 1971: 83ff.). The issue

cannot be settled in terms of the names and existence of objects themselves.

15 We occasionally use the term "grammar/syntax" because the distinction between the two notions has been reduced in generative linguistics and fades still more in a linguistics of texts. In semiotics, syntax subsumes grammar entirely.

16 Here also, text-world discrepancies are intended to point up discrepancies in the "real world" (cf. IV.19; IX.8; X.16).

Chapter VIII

Situationality

1. The term SITUATIONALITY is a general designation for the factors which render a text relevant to a current or recoverable situation of occurrence (cf. I.19f.). Very rarely are the effects of a situational setting exerted without MEDIATION: the extent to which one feeds one's own beliefs and goals into one's MODEL of the current communicative situation (cf. IX.1). The accessible EVIDENCE in the situation is fed into the model along with our prior knowledge and expectations about how the "real world" is organized (cf. VII.18.1). If the dominant function of a text is to provide a reasonably unmediated account of the situation model, SITUATION MONITORING is being performed. If the dominant function is to guide the situation in a manner favourable to the text producer's goals, SITUATION MANAGEMENT is being carried out. The borderline between monitoring and managing is extremely fuzzy and can vary according to the views of the individual participants. Indeed, people seem to prefer disguising their managings as monitorings, creating the impression that things are going the desired way in the normal course of events. For instance, the spinster aunt managed the situation with her suitor in sample [109] (VI.16) by pretending to only monitor the situation of her nieces. In sample [5] (VI.29), Piglet managed a difficult situation by compelling the other participant to accept a certain kind of monitoring. If it had become apparent in either case that these monitorings were in reality highly mediated and contrary to available evidence, the plans of the monitoring

participants would have failed. Despite such cases of plan concealment (cf. VI.17), the distinction between monitoring and managing, if viewed in terms of DOMINANCES, is a useful one.[1]

2. One obvious variety of monitoring would be "simply describing" in the sense of Osgood's (1971) well-known experiments where people were asked to describe objects and events presented before them.[2] Even here, the texts are more than mere "responses" to the "stimuli" of the scene. For one thing, people have established beliefs about what is worth NOTICING, i.e. expending processing resources on registering and identifying something present. The ways in which noticed material is expressed in texts is often influenced by NORMAL ORDERING STRATEGIES like those cited in VII.18.2. Erving Goffman (1974) suggests that situations are sorted into various "tracks" of objects or events worth "attending" or "disattending". For instance, some gestures of a speaker are deemed significant, e.g. pointing to objects or indicating directions, while others are not, e.g. scratching oneself. However, normal ordering strategies and conventions for distributing attention could be overridden by some highly IMPROBABLE (and hence informative) object or event.

3. One very basic kind of improbability would be a disproportion in FREQUENCY, as stressed by the statistical approach to information theory (cf. VII.2). If a person present does something much more often than normal, monitoring is likely to follow:

> [125] "Damn that boy," said the old gentleman, "he's gone to sleep again."
> "Very extraordinary boy, that," said Mr. Pickwick, "does he always sleep in this way?"
> "Sleep!" said the old gentleman, "he's always asleep. Goes on errands fast asleep, and snores as he waits at table."
> "How very odd!" said Mr. Pickwick.
> "Ah! odd indeed," returned the old gentleman.
>
> (Dickens 1947: 55)

The monitoring may be accompanied by some attempt to account for the unusual frequency of events or objects and hence to **downgrade** it:

> [126] "Look here, sir; here's a oyster stall to every half-dozen houses. The street's lined with 'em. Blessed if I don't

think that when a man's very poor, he rushes out of his lodgings, and eats oysters in regular desperation."
(Dickens 1947: 301f.)

Monitoring can also serve to point out some lack of **continuity** to be downgraded, e.g. when people's actions seem to have no **reason:**

[127] The twelve jurors were all writing very busily on slates. "What are they doing?" Alice whispered to the Gryphon. "They can't have anything to put down yet, before the trial's begun."
"They're putting down their names," the Gryphon whispered in reply, "for fear they should forget them before the end of the trial."
"Stupid things!" Alice began in a loud indignant voice.
(Carroll 1960: 144f.)

The Gryphon downgrades the seemingly unmotivated action and elicits another monitoring. Alice's exclamation "Stupid things!" is typical of how SALIENT objects and events are likely to be monitored (i.e. those which represent striking extremes on some scale).[3] Salience may be subsequently downgraded into a predictable standard:

[128] "What curious attitudes he goes into!" (For the Messenger kept skipping up and down, and wriggling like an eel. . . .
"Not at all," said the King. "He's an Anglo-Saxon Messenger – and those are Anglo-Saxon attitudes."
(Carroll 1960: 279)

Fillmore (1977) suggests that salience affects surface formatting. Salient objects are readily assigned to the subject or direct object slots of English sentences to bring them into a prominent perspective.[3a]

4. Situation monitoring as observed in our samples is akin to PROBLEM-SOLVING as treated in III.17. The text producer notices some non-expected object or event and makes it the TOPIC of the text. There are two normal outcomes. Either the matter is left as observed – as 'odd' in [125] or 'stupid' in [127] – or a means is found to downgrade it such that it does not appear to be a violation of expectations after all – the outcome in [126] and [128] ([127] remaining in dispute). On the face of it, only the latter outcome would seem to actually solve the problem by integrating the occurrence. But by simply commenting on non-expected occurrences, the par-

ticipants re-affirm their own standards and seek similar affirmation from the others. Hence, expectations are validated at the very moment when they seem to have failed in a confrontation with an actual situation. Such a process belongs to the means for NEGOTIATING the socially accepted model of reality and its norms (cf. VII.18.1). Situation monitoring is thus extremely likely whenever different participants have opposed notions about what is going on:

[129] 1st SERVANT: Will't please your lordship drink a cup of sack?
2nd SERVANT: Will't please your honour taste of these conserves?
3rd SERVANT: What raiment will your honour wear to-day?
SLY: I am Christophero Sly; call not me 'honour' nor 'lordship.' I ne'er drank sack in my life; and if you give me any conserves, give me conserves of beef. Ne'er ask me what raiment I'll wear; for I have no more doublets than backs, no more stockings than legs, nor no more shoes than feet . . .
LORD: Heaven cease this idle humour in your honour!
O that a mighty man of such descent,
Of such possessions and so high esteem,
Should be infused with so foul a spirit!
SLY: What, would you make me mad?
(*The Taming of the Shrew* Induction [sic] ii 2-17)

Until some agreement is reached, even very basic human goals – in [129], the provision of drink, food, and clothing – may be suspended while the participants keep asserting their own outlooks. Notice the tendency to consider people 'mad' who arrive at a divergent view on the "real" situation – another mechanism for defending society's expectations.

5. Departures from the evidence of the situation are, however, allowed for certain text types, notably **dramatic** texts. As a subclass of **literary** texts, dramatic texts have the prerogative of presenting alternative organizations for objects and events (cf. IX.8); due to their mode of live presentation, they draw the receivers into a situation whose monitoring often requires extremely high mediation (in the sense of VIII.1). Dramatic texts usually provide an "exposition" early on to specify the kind and extent of mediation needed. The most famous example might be Shakespeare's *Prologue* to *King Henry the Fifth* (lines 19-31):

[130] Suppose within the girdle of these walls
Are now confin'd two mighty monarchies,
Whose high upreared and abutting fronts
The perilous narrow ocean parts asunder.
Piece out our imperfections with your thoughts:
Into a thousand parts divide one man,
And make imaginary puissance.
Think, when we talk of horses, that you see them
Printing their proud hoofs i' th' receiving earth;
For 'tis your thoughts that now must deck our kings,
Carry them here and there, jumping o'er times,
Turning th' accomplishment of many years
Into an hour-glass.

Although dramatic texts are a special sub-type, they nonetheless provide illuminating demonstrations of how situational evidence can be negotiated by participants in social interaction (cf. Goffman 1974).

6. Situation monitoring can be simplified by the use of PRO-FORMS rather than conceptual names for objects or events present. Halliday and Hasan (1976) suggest the term EXOPHORA for this usage (in analogy to "anaphora" and "cataphora", cf. IV.22ff.). Exophora is not strictly co-reference (IV.21), since there is no other expression in the text besides the pro-form; one could argue that there is some corresponding expression held in active storage without being uttered, but this argument is certainly contestable.

7. The first and second person pronouns are by nature exophoric, singling out the text producer and receiver(s) and sometimes signalling their social relationship:

[131] 2nd CITIZEN: Nay, *I* beseech *you*, sir, be not out with *me*; yet, if *you* be out, *I* can mend *you*.
MARULLUS: What mean'st *thou* by that? Mend *me, thou* saucy fellow! (*Julius Caesar* I i 16–19)

The workman must say 'you' to the government official, who responds with 'thou' to show social dominance (cf. Brown & Gilman 1960). Exophora can designate other participants besides producer and receiver, for instance, via third-person pronouns or DEICTICS ("pointing words") like 'this' and 'that':

[132] CASSIUS: *This* is Trebonius.
BRUTUS: He is welcome hither.
CASSIUS: *This,* Decius Brutus.

BRUTUS: He is welcome too.
CASSIUS: *This*, Casca; *this*, Cinna; and *this* Metellus Cimber.
BRUTUS: They all are welcome. (*Julius Caesar* II i 94–7)

In [132], Cassius first identifies men wearing masks and hence not recognizable from outward evidence. Once identity is clarified, Brutus can use the simple anaphoric pro-forms 'he' and 'they'; the reverse order, with pro-form *before* deictic, would be extremely bizarre. Deictics are useful for pointing to an entire situation or set of events:

[133] HARDCASTLE: *This* may be modern modesty, but I never saw anything look so much like old-fashioned impudence. (Goldsmith 1773: 29)

Mr Hardcastle is designating all of the actions of his guests since the time of their arrival.

8. We proposed in VIII.1 the term SITUATION MANAGEMENT for the use of texts in discourse to steer the situation toward the participants' goals. We noted that the border between monitoring and management is fuzzy and can best be described in terms of **dominances.** Monitoring, we suggested, is typically done when the situation fails to match expectations, so that the text producer's goal is predominantly to resolve discrepancies and discontinuities or at least to reaffirm one's expectations (VIII.4). In management, there are superordinate goals of the kind we saw in the conversation between the spinster aunt and Mr Tupman (cf. VI.16ff.). For example, goals provide heavy mediation when totally disparate monitorings are made of the same situation or event, in this case a primary election in Florida (*Gainesville Sun* 15 Oct. 1979):

[134] Kennedy supporters term the Florida showing "one of the greatest political upsets of the century".

[135] "They put in the best they had and we put in the best we had and we beat them and beat them bad", offered Jody Powell [Carter supporter].

Obviously, both sides could not be right, and their goals are so unmistakable that management clearly dominates monitoring. Notice the heavy RECURRENCE in Powell's statement, intended to reinforce his version (cf. IV.13). A still more decisive example was provided by armed men confronting the drivers of a money convoy with (*Gainesville Sun* 20 Dec. 1978):

[136] This is a holdup. We're not kidding.

They are describing the situation solely in terms of their 'steal money' plan, hoping that firearms would override everyone else's version of the situation.[4]

9. Such samples lead us to conclude that situation management can be profitably explored in terms of PLAN theory (cf. VI.11ff.). The stabilized plans often called SCRIPTS are developed only for situations whose management is routinely demanded in a given society (VI.14f.). In other situations, participants must adapt to a range of variable factors and protect their goals as best they can. They can scan texts from other participants to recognize the latter's goals (cf. Allen 1979). Or they can simply postulate DEFAULT goals by assuming that most people will have the same **desires** as they do themselves.[5] If resources are too limited for fulfilling every participant's goals, CONFLICT can be expected to result (cf. Wilensky 1978*a*).[6] As is evident in the statements from the supporters of Kennedy [134] and Carter [135], conflicting goals lead to conflicts in how the same event or situation is monitored.

10. Since many goals are not obtainable through the actions of one agent, situation management must entail GOAL NEGOTIATION: methods of obtaining the compliance and co-operation of others. Schank and Abelson (1977) discuss a set of "planboxes"[7] containing plans frequently used in goal negotiation. You might simply ASK other people to do things or to give you something. You might INVOKE some theme (where "invoking" is a discourse action of mentioning what is already known, as opposed to "informing" something new (cf. IV.54); and a "theme" is a topic recurring in various parts of a discourse), e.g. long-standing friendship or special fondness for an item you want. You might INFORM the people of a REASON (I.8) why they should be co-operative (or, if the reason is already known, you INVOKE it). You could BARGAIN to do them a FAVOUR in return, or you could BARGAIN to give them some OBJECT they would desire. If all these **discourse actions** (VI.11) FAIL, you could THREATEN people, OVERPOWER them, or STEAL what you want. When a planner moves down

this list toward steadily more extreme actions, we can use the term PLANBOX ESCALATION.[8] Such escalation could occur within a single planbox as well. You could make your ASK, INVOKE THEME, or INFORM REASON more detailed. You could raise a BARGAIN by offering bigger FAVOURS or more valuable OBJECTS. You could THREATEN steadily more violent actions, or intensify OVERPOWER with more destructive weapons.

11. Like many other procedures,[9] planbox escalation entails a **trade-off.** The planner must find a balance between EFFICIENCY (ease, minimum effort) and EFFECTIVENESS (maximum success chances) that will be APPROPRIATE to the situation and to the participants' roles (cf. I.23). Asking, invoking, and informing are easy and demand no expenditure except of the *processing* resources needed to produce the text. Bargaining commits you to an expenditure of *material* resources, but it provides a greater incentive in many cases (it might, however, offend close friends by suggesting that they won't help out without reward). Threatening, overpowering, and stealing commit you to an expenditure of *physical* resources, but they suppress further negotiation; their real disadvantage is that they render the goal *unstable* (cf. Wilensky 1978*a*: 253), because people will often try to avenge themselves or recover their property. Many societies have institutional measures for discouraging the extreme planboxes of overpowering and stealing. Threatening is easier to carry out and conceal, but also highly problematic (cf. Apeltauer 1977). Once compliance has been refused, the threatener has little to gain by carrying out the threat, and the goal will usually remain as far away as ever. If threatened people don't believe in your ability to carry out the threat, it matters little whether you can or not – your goal will not be reached.

12. Planbox escalation is therefore a normal response to continued failure, but must be kept within limits. Wilensky (1978*a*: 28) proposes to model the computer understanding of stories upon knowledge about escalation, e.g.:

[137] John wanted Bill's bicycle. He walked over to Bill and asked him if he would give it to him. Bill refused. Then John told Bill he would give him five dollars for it, but Bill would not agree. John told Bill he would break his arm if he didn't let him have it. Bill let John have the bicycle.

Bill's continued blocking of John's 'have-bicycle'-goal leads to a steady escalation from ASK to BARGAIN OBJECT to THREATEN. Notice that our knowledge of plans and goals enables us to sort out the vague **pro-forms** ('*he* would give *him*'; '*he* would break *his* arm if *he*'). John's goal is at length attained, but Bill will hardly be disposed toward co-operation in the future, and he may attempt to get his bicycle back. In [138], Tom Sawyer ASKs for another boy's name and, upon refusal, immediately escalates to THREATEN:

[138] "What's your name?"
"Tisn't any of your business, maybe."
"Well I allow I'll *make* it my business."
"Well why don't you?"
"If you say much, I will."
"Much – much – *much*. There now."
"Oh, you think you're mighty smart, *don't* you? I could lick you with one hand tied behind me, if I wanted to."
"Well why don't you *do* it? You *say* you can do it.".

(Twain 1922: 7f.)

Predictably enough, the encounter ends with a fist-fight (a recourse to OVERPOWER). Although Tom finally does 'lick' the other boy, the name is never revealed. INVOKING a spirit of courtesy and comradeship, or BARGAINING a favour might have worked better.

13. We shall now essay to describe situation management in terms of planned negotiation and escalation. By analyzing a goal-directed conversation, we shall undertake to extract some plausible strategies of situation management. We make no claim that these strategies would work in all cases or would cover all conceivable discourse actions. The implementation of any one strategy might be performed with a range of possible texts or even of non-verbal actions. The fitting of strategies to the actual situation would be an instance of PROCEDURAL ATTACHMENT as defined in III.19.

14. Our demonstration text is the celebrated occasion in *The Adventures of Tom Sawyer* (Twain 1922: 16ff.) where Tom has been ordered to whitewash a fence on Saturday, the very time he longs to be engaged in leisure activities. He is not an industrious boy to begin with, and will have to endure the additional torment of other boys passing down the street near the fence on their way to sports. We listen in at the point where

Tom has begun whitewashing, and a neighbour lad (Ben) happens to come along:[10]

[139] [1] Ben stared a moment, and said:
[2] "Hi-*yi*! You're up a stump, ain't you?"
[3] No answer. [4] Tom surveyed his last touch with the eye of an artist, then he gave his brush another gentle sweep and surveyed the result, as before. [5] Ben ranged up alongside of him. [6] Tom's mouth watered for [Ben's] apple, [7] but he stuck to his work.
[8] Ben said:
[9] "Hello, old chap, [10] you got to work, hey?"
[11] Tom wheeled suddenly and said:
[12] "Why, it's you, Ben! I warn't noticing."
[13] "Say – *I'm* going in a-swimming, *I* am. [14] Don't you wish you could? [15] But of course you'd druther *work* – wouldn't you? 'Course you would!"
[16] Tom contemplated the boy a bit, and said:
[17] "What do you call work?"
[18] "Why, ain't *that* work?"
[19] Tom resumed his whitewashing, [20] and answered carelessly:
[21] "Well, maybe it is, and maybe it ain't. [22] All I know is, [23] it suits Tom Sawyer."
[24] "Oh come now, you don't mean to let on that you *like* it?"
[25] The brush continued to move.
[26] "Like it? [27] Well, I don't see why I oughtn't to like it. [28] Does a boy get a chance to whitewash a fence every day?"
[29] That put things in a new light. [30] Ben stopped nibbling his apple.
[31] Tom swept his brush daintily back and forth – stepped back to note the effect – added a touch here and there – criticized the effect again – [32] Ben watching every move and getting more and more interested, more and more absorbed. [33] Presently he said:
[34] "Say, Tom, let *me* whitewash a little."
[35] Tom considered, [36] was about to consent; [37] but he altered his mind:
[38] "No – no – I reckon it would hardly do, Ben. [39] You see, Aunt Polly's awful particular about this fence – right here on the street, you know – but if it was the

back fence I wouldn't mind and *she* wouldn't. [40] Yes, she's awful particular about this fence; [41] it's got to be done very careful; [42] I reckon there ain't one boy in a thousand, maybe two thousand, that can do it the way it's got to be done."

[43] "No – is that so? [44] Oh come, now, – [45] lemme just try. [46] Only just a little – [47] I'd let *you*, if it was me, Tom."

[48] "Ben, I'd like to, honest injun; [49] but Aunt Polly – [50] well, Jim wanted to do it, but she wouldn't let him; [51] Sid wanted to do it, but she wouldn't let Sid. [52] Now don't you see how I'm fixed? [53] If you was to tackle this fence and anything was to happen to it – "

[54] "Oh shucks, I'll be just as careful. [55] Now lemme try. [56] Say – I'll give you the core of my apple."

[57] "Well, here – [58] "No, Ben, now don't. [59] I'm afeard – "

[60] "I'll give you *all* of it!"

[61] Tom gave up the brush with reluctance in his face, but alacrity in his heart.

15. This situation is decisively more elaborate than the samples we have explored so far. In contrast to the conversation between Mr Tupman and the aunt (in VI.16ff.), the participants in this scene are not previously disposed to co-operate. To obtain his own goal of relaxing rather than working, Tom must manage the situation such that Ben will set up an artificially induced goal of being allowed to whitewash. Whereas Mr Tupman was expected only to accept beliefs, Ben will have to expend substantial physical resources that he would not normally exert of his own free will. The negotiation must be correspondingly intricate and well-planned.

16. The first step to open an interactive situation is that the participants NOTICE each other in the sense of VIII.2. Ben 'stares' at Tom 'a moment' [139.1] before the conversation begins. The initial text [139.2] illustrates a common strategy:

Strategy 1: *Use a situation monitoring to begin a discourse.*

One very common example is to open with a remark about the weather. Such a remark is low in informativity, since most people can see for themselves what the weather is like, but at least conflicting opinions aren't likely (cf. VIII.4). A weather monitoring can be UPGRADED by assuming that a more informative occurrence will ensue, as shown here (Wilde 1956: 14):

[140] JACK: Charming day it has been, Miss Fairfax.
GWENDOLYN: Pray don't talk to me about the weather, Mr. Worthing. Whenever people talk to me about the weather, I always feel certain that they mean something else. And that makes me so nervous.
JACK: I do mean something else.

And [140] is in fact followed up by nothing less than a marriage proposal.

17. Ben's opening monitor-text is highly MEDIATED by his own outlook on work (cf. VIII.1), as compared with something like:

[139.2]*a* "Hi! You got to whitewash that fence, don't you?"

Mediated monitorings are **problematic** when receivers do not share the outlook of the text producer (cf. VI.18). The receivers then have several options:

Strategy 2: *If someone else's monitoring does not match your own outlook, do not accept it. You may: (a) reject it outright; (b) question it; (c) ignore it; or (d) replace it with your own monitoring.*

The selection of one of the options (*a*) through (*d*) would depend in part on the **social dominance** among participants and the rate of **escalation** that your plan calls for. A highly dominant participant not worrying about possible escalation would be prone to use outright rejection (*a*):

[141] "Being so many different sizes in a day is very confusing."
"It isn't," said the Caterpillar. (Carroll 1960: 68)

The number of situations where outright rejection is advisable is not large. Utterances of rejection are most common in closely-knit social groups where participants are not likely to take serious offence, e.g.:

[142] Nonsense!
[143] You're way off!
[144] Are you out of your mind?

In other kinds of groups, more indirect negotiation is usually done with the questioning option (*b*), e.g.:

[145] Are you sure?
[146] What makes you think so?
[147] Couldn't we see that another way?

18. Since Tom's goal requires Ben's willing co-operation, he can't fit the rejection option (*a*) of Strategy 2 into his plan. Instead, he selects the other three: questioning the monitoring [139.17], ignoring it [139.3], and eventually replacing it [139.26–8]. The "ignoring" option is particularly suitable for the opening phase of a conversation, since one can always claim not to have noticed the other participants, and can thus escape seeming rude. Tom's 'no answer' [139.3] is accordingly a realization of Strategy 2(*c*). This option also fits with a THEME he will INVOKE many times later on: that whitewashing is a skilled and difficult activity. He pretends to be so engrossed [139.4] that his **attention** is not free for conversation (cf. VII.1). This state is intended to **upgrade** the activity from a tedious, everyday one into a valuable rare one.[11] A general strategy for deciding when to perform upgrading could be:

Strategy 3: *To encourage planbox escalation, upgrade the object or event that you are being asked to give or perform.*

This strategy is prominent and successful in our sample, at least.

19. Ben realizes that his monitoring is not being acknowledged. He 'ranges up alongside of' Tom [139.5] to make **noticing** more probable. What is in fact noticed is his apple, causing Tom to set up a SUBGOAL 'have apple' [139.6] (this subgoal will be watching for an opportunity to assert itself in the course of the interaction). Ben applies another strategy:

Strategy 4: *If your monitoring is not accepted, replace it with a less mediated version.*

This strategy is based on the assumption that participants are more likely to agree when a text follows the available **evidence** more closely. Ben repeats his greeting [139.9] in case he hasn't been noticed, and then replaces his monitoring [139.2] with a less mediated version [139.10]. Tom is now willing to notice Ben [139.11], but not to accept the less mediated monitoring – he wants a version mediated toward his own plan. He pursues his **upgrading theme** by claiming that he 'warn't noticing', presumably being too enthralled by his whitewashing [139.12].

20. Now that the conversation has gotten under way, Ben monitors his own situation and plans [139.13]. His next remark [139.14] illustrates this strategy (cf. VIII.9).

Strategy 5: *Project your own desires and goals onto other participants except where there is evidence to the contrary.*

Feeling secure of his opinion, Ben ironically assigns to Tom an outlook deemed highly improbable [139.15]; he answers his own question ('wouldn't you? 'Course you would!') to reinforce its absurdity. At this point, Tom shifts to the "questioning" option (*b*) of Strategy 2 [139.17], and applies it in combination with another strategy:

Strategy 6: *When the monitorings of participants fail to match, negotiate the sense of the topic concepts involved.*

In this case, the **topic** concept to be negotiated is 'work' as a proposed description of Tom's current activity [139.18]. Tom cannot reject this concept outright (Strategy 2(*a*)), since he would sacrifice his believability. He therefore leaves the question of applying the concept entirely open by attaching 'maybe' to a statement of each possibility [139.21]. A strategy for this tactic might be:

Strategy 7: *If your own plan-directed monitoring would be disbelieved, don't advance it, but don't commit yourself to its opposite either.*

The monitoring cannot be contradicted as long as it has not been asserted. Apparently, text receivers are more easily persuaded by content which they have to infer or supply themselves (cf. I.16; VII.28, 42). Tom has already 'resumed his whitewashing' [139.19] as if he couldn't bear to be deprived of it for a moment. He limits himself to asserting that the activity 'suits' him, which is all he needs to 'know' [139.2–3]. His use of his own full name rather than the pro-form 'me' might suggest that whitewashing is flattering to his social role at large.

21. It is now Ben's turn to apply the "questioning" option (*b*) of Strategy 2, since the notion that Tom 'likes' the job [139.24] is incompatible with Strategy 5 as well as with common knowledge about Tom's disposition. Tom's response [139.26–7] follows a modified version of Strategy 7:

Strategy 8: *If your monitoring might be disbelieved, don't advance it directly, but ask others for reasons why it would not be plausible.*

Tom thus proclaims himself unable to find a reason why he 'oughtn't to like it' [139.27]. He goes on to upgrade the task as being available only on rare occasions [139.28]. His choice of expressions supports the upgrading by suggesting that the task is a 'chance' for enjoyment rather than a chore.

22. As we can see, Tom's monitorings, in contrast to Ben's, have all been dominated by **managing** (cf. VIII.1). He has succeeded in 'putting' the situation 'in a new light' [139.29] while seeming to do nothing more than monitor available evidence. The outcome is a CONCORD of goals (Wilensky 1978*a*), in which both participants want Ben to be doing the whitewashing. Ben already focuses his **attention** so heavily on Tom's motions [139.31–2] that the apple-eating is forgotten [139.30] (cf. definition of "attention" in VII.1.). Tom's intricate motions [139.31] are intended to invoke once more the upgrading theme (VIII.18) by imitating an 'artist' [139.4].

23. Ben first advances his newly-created goal with an ASK [139.34]. At this point, Tom could hand the brush over, and his own main goal would be attained. But he would destroy his subgoal 'have apple', set up early in the scene (cf. VIII.19), if he accepted Ben's ASK.[11a] He therefore follows Strategy 3 in order to encourage escalation. A specific strategy in this case would be:

Strategy 9: *If you desire objects or favours from people, reject their* ASK*s,* INVOKE THEME*s, and* INFORM REASON*s until planbox escalation reaches* BARGAIN*s.*

This strategy must be applied carefully to prevent two undesirable outcomes: (*a*) the people may abandon their goals at once; or (*b*) escalation may shoot past the BARGAIN stage into the violent extremes. In sample [137], Bill clung to his bicycle so long that he nearly got hurt and lost it anyway, whereas he might have at least obtained a bargain value of five dollars. In sample [138], the ASK was rejected so emphatically that escalation immediately moved to THREATEN. You must be able to judge other people's patience and the extent to which they are willing to pursue their goals. A corresponding strategy might be:

Strategy 10: *Prevent goal abandonment or extreme escalation by showing indecision in your refusals.*[12]

Tom signals his indecision both by gestures or facial expressions [139.35, 36, 61] and by utterances [139.38–9, 48, 52–3, 57–9].

24. To motivate his initial rejection of Ben's ASK, Tom INVOKES THEMES and INFORMS REASONS. His first REASON is Aunt Polly's strong concern for a conspicuous fence along the street in front of her house [139.39]. This tactic, which will be used again (cf. VIII.26), seems to represent a strategy like this:

Strategy 11: *To upgrade your contribution and steer escalation toward a good* BARGAIN, INFORM *or* INVOKE *outlooks of people who are absent and can't contradict you, so that you will not seem unreasonable or greedy.*[13]

Aunt Polly's purported outlook supports the now familiar THEME about the skill and artistry required to whitewash a fence (VIII.18). For added effect, Tom follows up with a RECURRENCE [139.40] (cf. IV.12ff.) and then a PARAPHRASE [139.41] (cf. IV.18f.) of his previously presented material. His culmination is comparing himself ('one boy') to 'a thousand' or even 'two thousand' less competent boys [139.42]. These numerical proportions suggest the dimensions which an adequate bargain ought to meet.

25. If a claim such as [139.42] had been made earlier in the conversation, it would doubtless have been energetically rejected by Ben. But thanks to extensive development of the upgrading theme, Ben shows only momentary scepticism [139.43-4] and then returns to his ASK with a partial limitation ('only just a little') [139.45-6]. A corresponding strategy could be:

Strategy 12: *To encourage co-operation, downgrade the expenditure of time and resources that others must make to further your goal.*

In [137], John might have persuaded Bill to relinquish the bicycle for a few minutes rather than permanently.

26. Ben's next discourse action [139.47] might be both INVOKE THEME (that Ben and Tom are old friends) and INFORM REASON (that Tom should be as generous as other people would be in the same circumstances). Tom follows suit by assuming the role of a helper anxious to remove obstacles to

Ben's goal. Though disposed to help out, Tom reverts to his upgrading theme, this time comparing himself to two known persons ('Jim', 'Sid') rather than to 'thousands' of unknown ones – a further realization of Strategy 11 (cf. VIII.24). Again, RECURRENCE is deployed as reinforcement, with the experience of 'Jim' and 'Sid' expressed in almost identical terms [139.50–1]. Ben is led to suppose that whitewashing would therefore elevate him also over Jim and Sid. From here, Tom moves yet once again to his upgrading theme by indicating that something bad would 'happen' if a less talented boy were to 'tackle this fence' [139.53].

27. Of course, all of Tom's discourse actions are designed to goad Ben into a BARGAIN OBJECT with the apple. Ben remains obtuse for a minute, renewing his ASK with a promise to 'be just as careful' as Tom [139.54–5]. Finally, it occurs to him to offer a BARGAIN [139.56], though the apple core is understandably not Tom's goal. Accordingly, Tom falls back on Strategy 10 and manifests his indecision by first assenting [139.57] and then refusing [139.58]. As he begins anew on his outworn upgrading theme [139.59], Ben interrupts (no doubt sick of hearing about it) with an escalated bargain object for the whole apple [139.60]. Having obtained both his major goal and his subgoal, Tom at last agrees, not forgetting to signal reluctance with a facial expression [139.61] and thus to uphold his theme to the very end; perhaps too much rejoicing on Tom's part would have alerted Ben even now to the extent of manipulation being perpetrated. Impressed by the success of his plan, Tom stabilizes it into a SCRIPT and practises it on all the boys passing by, so that, 'if he hadn't run out of whitewash, he would have bankrupted every boy in the village' (Twain 1922: 18).

28. This chapter has been devoted to describing some significant ways in which texts are correlated with discourse actions and applied to a situation. The correlations involved are far from simple reflections of the apperceivable evidence in the situation alone. Instead, the content of texts is usually removed via MEDIATION from the evidence according to the producer's outlook, beliefs, plans, and goals. Whether a text is acceptable may depend not on the "correctness" of its "reference" to the "real world," but rather on its *believability* and *relevance* to the *participants' outlook* regarding the *situation*.

We have argued that discourse actions can be viewed as realizations of general strategies for monitoring and managing all sorts of situations in which people communicate and interact.

Notes

1 The notions of "monitoring" and "managing" as used here are common in automatic data processing, but not well developed in linguistics so far.

2 To be precise, Osgood's experiments entailed both "describing" and "narrating" (in the senses set forth in IX.6), because both situations and event sequences were involved.

3 On salience, cf. Kintsch (1977*a*: 397ff.). See also note 5 to Chapter VII.

3[a] This approach finally allows a satisfactory explanation of the much-discussed sentence pairs like 'I smeared the wall with mud' versus 'I smeared mud on the wall': the element in the direct object slot is given more prominence than that in the prepositional phrase. Hence, one assumes that the first sentence of the pair implies the entire wall was smeared (cf. Fillmore 1977: 79).

4 On the use of firearms in re-defining situations, cf. Goffman (1974: 447).

5 On desirability, cf. VI.13; note 6 to Chapter VII.

6 Wilensky distinguishes between cases where one agent has conflicting goals ("goal conflict") and cases where goals of two or more agents work against each other ("goal competition"). The latter type of case is computationally more interesting and hence is used more often in **stories** (cf. Beaugrande & Colby 1979). We see both types in sample [139] below.

7 Schank & Abelson (1977: 90) define "planboxes" as a "key action that will accomplish the goals", plus three kinds of "preconditions": "controllable", "uncontrollable", and "mediating". They would view "escalation" as a means for creating "mediating" preconditions (see note 8 to this chapter).

8 Schank & Abelson (1977: 90) speak of "invoking some other planbox farther up the scale of potential benefit or potential danger" in order to create some "mediating precondition" for a goal, e.g. "willingness".

9 cf. IV.29, 37; V.15.

10 The numberings in this sample mostly follow the borderlines of actions and discourse actions rather than single sentences, as far as we could determine. Sentence boundaries can be used as boundaries of discourse actions, but there is no obligation to do so. There are a number of dialect forms: 'warn't' [12] = 'wasn't'; 'a-swimming' [13] = 'swimming'; 'druther' [15] = 'would rather'; 'lemme' [45] = 'let me'; 'honest injun' [48] = 'honest as an Indian' (an avowal of one's truthfulness); 'afeard' [59] = 'afraid'.

11 Notice that Tom never actually describes his action in such terms – the closest he comes is in [139.28]. In VIII.20, we suggest a strategic rationale for Tom's actions (what isn't asserted can't be contradicted).

11[a] This is a case of "goal conflict" in the sense of Wilensky (1978*a*); see note 6 to this chapter.

12 As recently witnessed by one of the authors (RdB), sellers are prone to intersperse into their negotiations utterances like: 'I don't believe I really want to sell it, sir.' The utterances are not of course intended to be taken seriously, but only to drive up the price of the sale. However, in this case the prospective buyer did take them seriously and abandoned the negotiation altogether.

13 This manoeuvre is used in a memorable scene in Molière's play *The Miser (L'Avare)* Act II Scene i.

Chapter IX

Intertextuality

1. We introduced the term INTERTEXTUALITY in I.21f. to subsume the ways in which the production and reception of a given text depends upon the participants' knowledge of other texts. This knowledge can be applied by a process describable in terms of MEDIATION (the extent to which one feeds one's current beliefs and goals into the model of the communicative situation, cf. VIII.1): the greater the expanse of time and of processing activities between the use of the current text and the use of previously encountered texts, the greater the mediation. Extensive mediation is illustrated by the development and use of TEXT TYPES, being classes of texts expected to have certain traits for certain purposes. Mediation is much smaller when people quote from or refer to specific well-known texts, e.g. famous speeches or works of literature. Mediation is extremely slight in activities such as replying, refuting, reporting, summarizing, or evaluating other texts, as we find them especially in CONVERSATION.

2. The question of TEXT TYPES offers a severe challenge to LINGUISTIC TYPOLOGY, i.e. systemization and classification of language samples. In older linguistics, typologies were set up for the sounds and forms of a language (cf. II.19). More recently, linguistics has been preoccupied with typologies of sentences.[1] Another approach is the construction of cross-cultural typologies for languages of similar construction (cf. Romportl et al. 1977). All of these typologies are devoted to VIRTUAL SYSTEMS, being the abstract potential of languages; a

text typology must deal with ACTUAL SYSTEMS in which selections and decisions have already been made (cf. III.12). The major difficulty in this new domain is that *many actualized instances do not manifest complete or exact characteristics of an ideal type*. The demands or expectations associated with a text type can be modified or even overridden by the requirements of the context of occurrence (cf. VII.18.7). In a larger perspective, of course, discrepancies between ideal language types and actual occurrences are always immanent. The issues in phonetics, for instance, are not yet resolved by constructing a typology of phonemes. And individual languages have their own versions of the types they share (cf. Skalička 1977).

3. In 1972, a colloquium on text types was held at the University of Bielefeld, Germany (proceedings in Gülich & Raible (eds.) 1972). Attempts to apply or convert traditional linguistic methods failed to meet the special needs of a typology of texts. We might count the proportions of nouns, verbs, etc. or measure the length and complexity of sentences (cf. Mistrík 1973; Grosse 1976) without really defining the type – we need to know how and why these traits evolve. Statistical linguistic analysis of this kind ignores the functions of texts in communication and the pursuit of human goals. Presumably, those factors must be correlated with the linguistic proportions (Schmidt 1978: 55).

4. Siegfried J. Schmidt (1978: 55) envisions "two basic possibilities" for the study of text types. One can either start out with the traditionally defined types as observable objects and try to reconstruct them via a consistent text theory; or one can begin with a text theory which sets up theoretical types to be compared with empirical samples. For a science of texts as human activities, it seems impossible to dispense with the traditional text types that people actually use as heuristics in the procedures of production and reception. If our typology turns out to be fuzzy and diffuse, it is only reflecting the state of affairs in real communication.

5. A typology of texts must be correlated with typologies of discourse actions and situations. Unless the **appropriateness** of a text type to its setting of occurrence is judged (cf. I.23), participants cannot even determine the means and extent of upholding the criteria of textuality. For example, the demands for cohesion and coherence are less strict in conversation (cf.

VI.2ff.), while they are elaborately upheld in scientific texts (cf. Huddleston 1971). In poetic texts, cohesion can be sporadically reorganized along non-conventional principles (cf. IX.9). If these various types were presented in inappropriate settings, communication would be disturbed or damaged.

6. Some traditionally established text types could be defined along FUNCTIONAL lines, i.e. according to the contributions of texts to human interaction.[2] We would at least be able to identify some DOMINANCES, though without obtaining a strict categorization for every conceivable example. DESCRIPTIVE texts would be those utilized to enrich knowledge spaces whose **control centres** are **objects** or **situations.** Often, there will be a frequency of conceptual relations for **attributes, states, instances,** and **specifications.** The surface text should reflect a corresponding density of **modifiers.** The most commonly applied global pattern would be the **frame** (cf. V.16; VII.38). NARRATIVE texts, in contrast, would be those utilized to arrange **actions** and **events** in a particular sequential order. There will be a frequency of conceptual relations for **cause, reason, purpose, enablement,** and **time proximity** (cf. Labov & Waletzky 1967; Beaugrande & Colby 1979; Stein & Glenn 1979). The surface text should reflect a corresponding density of **subordinations.** The most commonly applied global knowledge pattern would be the **schema** (cf. V.16; IX.25ff.).[3] ARGUMENTATIVE texts are those utilized to promote the acceptance or evaluation of certain **beliefs** or **ideas** as true vs. false, or positive vs. negative. Conceptual relations such as **reason, significance, volition, value,** and **opposition** should be frequent. The surface texts will often show cohesive devices for emphasis and insistence, e.g. recurrence, parallelism, and paraphrase, as we saw in the *Declaration of Independence* (IV.16f.). The most commonly applied global knowledge pattern will be the **plan** for inducing belief (cf. V.16; VI.11–16; VII.18.1).[4]

7. The foregoing proposals deal with typical traits and uses of text types and can at most provide a general heuristic. In many texts, we would find a mixture of the descriptive, narrative, and argumentative functions. For example, the *Declaration of Independence* contains descriptions of the situation of the American colonies, and brief narrations of British actions; yet

the DOMINANT function is undeniably argumentative, i.e. to induce the belief that America was justified in 'dissolving' its 'political bands'. The text producers openly declare their 'decent respect to the opinions of mankind' and the 'rectitude' of their 'intentions'. In another category, the automobile repair manual *How to Keep your Volkswagen Alive* (Muir 1969), though it contains more narration and argumentation than most such manuals, is still predominantly intended to describe the construction and maintenance of the Volkswagen. The assignment of a text to a type clearly depends on the FUNCTION of the text in communication, not merely on the surface format.

8. LITERARY texts also contain various constellations of description, narration, and argumentation. We therefore need some other distinguishing criteria. The most comprehensive definition of "literary text" might be: a text whose world stands in a principled *alternativity* relationship to the accepted version of the "real world" (cf. VII.18.1).[5] This alternativity is intended to motivate insights into the organization of the "real world" not as something objectively given, but as something evolving from social cognition, interaction, and negotiation. Often, literary text-worlds contain discrepancies which sharpen our awareness of discrepancies in the socially accepted model of the "real world" (cf. IV.19; VII.40; X.16). Even literary trends such as realism, naturalism, and documentary art – where care is expended to make the text-world match the "real world" – are motivated by this intention to elicit insights; the text world is still not "real", but at most *exemplary* for an alternative outlook on "reality". Only to the extent that this intention dominates the intention to report "facts" (cf. IX.10) is the text considered literary.

9. POETIC texts would then be that subclass of literary texts in which alternativity is expanded to re-organize the strategies for mapping plans and content onto the surface text. The cohesion of a poetic text is upheld partly in opposition to the cohesion of other text types and partly in accordance with type-specific conventions (cf. VII.30ff.). In Chapter VII, we undertook to show how the flow of expectations being fulfilled or disappointed is controlled by the detailed organization of the surface text. The poetic function is therefore intended to motivate insights into the organization of expression as in-

teractive and negotiable. Not surprisingly, many literary texts not presented as poems avail themselves of the poetic function to underscore the interactive, negotiable nature of discourse about the "real world" (IX.8).

10. Literary and poetic texts could be seen in opposition to text types intended to increase and distribute knowledge about the currently accepted "real world". SCIENTIFIC texts serve this purpose in their attempt to explore, extend, or clarify society's knowledge store of a special domain of "facts" (in the sense of VII.18.1) by presenting and examining evidence drawn from observation or documentation. DIDACTIC texts do not reach beyond society's current knowledge store, but only serve to distribute established knowledge to a non-specialized or learning audience of text receivers. This intention requires the presentation of more abundant and explicit background knowledge than is customary in scientific texts.

11. Even this modest beginning for a typology of texts is far from straightforward. The sets of texts and their characteristics remain **fuzzy.** Constellations of functions in varying degrees of dominance can be highly intricate. A single text can even be shifted to another type via a special means of presentation. For instance, it has become fashionable to "find" poems by publishing non-poems in a literary setting (e.g. Porter 1972); the text receivers' processing reaction should be quite unlike that in the original setting. Like so many other issues, the question of text types goes beyond conventional linguistic methods (IX.3) and merges with the larger conditions of utilizing texts in human interaction. A "text type" is a set of heuristics for producing, predicting, and processing textual occurrences, and hence acts as a prominent determiner of efficiency, effectiveness, and appropriateness (in the sense of I.23). But the type can hardly provide absolute borderlines between its members and non-members, any more than the notion of "text" can do (cf. III.8). The conditions of communicating are simply too diverse to allow such a rigorous categorization.

12. A second issue in intertextuality is TEXT ALLUSION: the ways people use or refer to well-known texts (IX.1). In principle a text producer can draw upon *any* available prior text; but in practice, *well-known* texts are more suitable as being more readily accessible to the receiver audience. The expanse of actual time between the production of the original

text and that of the follow-up text may vary enormously. In 1600,[6] Christopher Marlowe wrote the plea of a 'passionate shepherd to his love', beginning:

[148] Come live with me and be my love,
And we will all the pleasures prove
That valleys, groves, hills, and fields,
Woods, or steepy mountain yields.

The shepherd goes on to offer the lady a fanciful catalogue of flowers and rustic apparel. That same year, Sir Walter Ralegh penned 'the nymph's reply to the shepherd':

[149] If all the world and love were young,
And truth in every shepherd's tongue,
These pretty pleasures might me move
To live with thee and be thy love.

and remarking that the shepherd's offerings would soon 'fade', 'break', 'wither', and be 'forgotten'. Ralegh's reply preserves the surface format (rhyme scheme, rhythm, number of stanzas) and many expressions of Marlowe's original. Obviously, the utilization of the follow-up text demands detailed knowledge of the original and of the conventions that brought forth the latter. In 1612, John Donne borrowed Marlowe's general scheme for an elaborate, fanciful proposal of an improbable fisherman, beginning:

[150] Come live with me and be my love,
And we will all the pleasures prove,
Of golden sands and crystal brooks:
With silken lines, and silver hooks.

The fisherman suggests that by undressing and bathing in the river, the young lady will attract 'each fish, which every channel hath' and hence make it possible to dispense with fishing tackle. Although the mediation is greater between Marlowe's text and Donne's than between Marlowe's and Ralegh's, the reliance upon the original is still unmistakable. If Donne's first two lines had not been a near quote of Marlowe's, however, that reliance would be less crucial. Much later, in 1935, Cecil Day Lewis wrote an ironic new version in which the speaker is an unskilled labourer, beginning:

[151] Come, live with me and be my love,
And we will all the pleasures prove

Of peace and plenty, bed and board,
That chance employment may afford.

I'll handle dainties on the docks
And thou shalt read of summer frocks:
At evening by the sour canals
We'll hope to hear some madrigals.

The force of this text is its opposition to the very principles and conventions underlying Marlowe's original: the view that the lives of shepherds or other working classes are spent in ornate dalliance and merriment, with nature as a purveyor of luxurious toys and trinkets. In [151], the lady can only 'read' about the summer clothes promised so opulently by Marlowe's shepherd; and the hope of hearing 'madrigals' (an archaic song form) on contemporary 'canals' is absolutely unfounded — compare Marlowe's idyllic scene

[152] By shallow rivers to whose falls
Melodious birds sing madrigals.

Cecil Day Lewis's poem is far more devastating than Ralegh's rebuttal or Donne's sarcasm, because it attacks that whole alternativity relationship upon which the literary status of Marlowe's text was based; Ralegh and Donne had mocked the shepherd's proposals, not Marlowe's mode of selecting and communicating about a topic. In cases like this, the alternativity of a literary or poetic text is reinforced by opposition to previous conventions for that text type. Notice that in the sample just cited, it is the conventional organization of the "real world" of 1935 – economic slump – that asserts itself over the literary and poetic alternative of past tradition.[7]

13. Intertextuality prevails with the least mediation in CONVERSATION. We explored some ways in which the organization of conversation arises from **intentionality** (VI.16ff.) and **situationality** (VIII.13ff.). Neither of these factors can offer a full account, however; a text must be relevant to other texts in the same discourse and not just to participants' intentions and to the situational setting. **Topics** must be selected, developed, and shifted. Texts may be used to **monitor** other texts or the roles and beliefs implied by those texts (cf. Posner 1972, 1980). Monitoring is particularly likely if a text appears to violate conventions such as the conversational "maxims" cited in VI.9ff.

14. A TOPIC of conversation emerges from the density of concepts and relations within the worlds of constituent texts. Therefore, a single text might have only potential topics pending further development (Schank 1977: 424). To decide what is worth saying about any topic, participants presumably consider the **informativity** of potential contributions. The most suitable aspects of a topic to be developed are those involving PROBLEMS and VARIABLES, i.e. things not yet established because they are subject to difficulties or changes.[8] In the form of a Gricean "maxim" we would have: *Pursue those aspects of the presented topic which you consider problematic or variable*. We can illustrate some applications of this maxim to "small talk", where a participant merely reacts to an event or situation already expressed as a topic (cf. Schank 1977). One often asks a follow-up question whose connection to the previous text-world is a relation among concepts of the kind we presented in V.26. The following exchanges from contemporary dramas[9] show the following up of the concept type given in square brackets:

[153] SAMMY: When's he coming to see his chair?
DAVE: Who, Selby? [agent-of]

[154] PHOEBE: They want us to go out there, and for Archie to manage the hotel in Ottowa . . .
JEAN: When did they write this to you? [time-of]

[155] MARTIN: . . . "She entered heaven the moment she died." So I asked him, "How do you know that?" [cognition-of]

[156] JIMMY: Going out?
ALISON: That's right.
JIMMY: On a Sunday evening in this town? Where on earth are you going? [location-of]

[157] HELENA: She's going to church.
JIMMY: You're doing what? Have you gone out of your mind or something? [reason-of]

Variables are requested in [153] and [154]: the reference of a pro-form is variable in cohesion (cf. IV.29) and must be made recoverable if no longer available in active storage; and time is variable in coherence because few events and situations occur at fixed moments. Problems are aired in [155], [156], and [157]. People can hardly be expected to know about arrivals in heaven [155]. In a small town on a Sunday evening, it is hard to imagine a place anyone could go [156]. A declared atheist can of course not recover a reason why his own brainwashed wife would go to church [157]. Thus, in each case, a problematic aspect of a topic – 'going to heaven', 'going out on Sunday evening', and 'going to church'–is seized upon as the material for a follow-up question.

15. Texts often give rise to problems inherent more in the presentation than in the content of the textual world. If participants appear to be violating social conventions or conversational principles, or if their intentions and beliefs seem discrepant or unmotivated – either case brings **problems** – another participant may resort to **monitoring. Managing** is involved also when the monitoring participant hopes to correct the situation and restore conformity (cf. VIII.1). We shall illustrate, again with samples from modern plays,[10] some typical cases of this sort.

16. Text presentation is monitored if **social conventions** are being disregarded:

[158] GUS: One bottle of milk! Half a pint! Express Dairy!
BEN: You shouldn't shout like that.
GUS: Why not?
BEN: It isn't done.

Monitoring is also done if a participant seems to be focusing inadequate **attention** on the presentation:

[159] CATHERINE: During vacation, I do think Leonora ought to take a look at reality. Are you listening, Charlie?
CHARLIE: Yes, Catherine.
CATHERINE: What was I saying?
CHARLIE: Leonora ought to take a look at reality.

In [159], the inattentive participant is obliged to provide a **recurrence** of the other's text to prove attention. Monitoring will also occur if the **motivation** for a presentation seems unwarranted in the situation:[11]

[160] HANS: I'm losing a son; mark: a son.
LUCAS: How can you say that?
HANS: How can I say it? I do say it, that's how.

This monitoring elicits the evasive tactic of treating 'saying' as the topic rather than 'losing a son'. And finally, monitoring can be addressed to the **style** of the presentation rather than to the content:[12]

[161] FAY: I have had nothing but heartache ever since. I am sorry for my dreadful crime.
TRUSCOTT: Very good. Your style is simple and direct. It's a theme which less skilfully handled could've given offence.

17. The **state** of a participant may become the object of monitoring, based on the evidence of his or her texts:[13]

[162] DAPHNE: Get out of my life, Charlie . . .
LEONORA: Daphne, I know you're in difficulties, but I think you're most unpleasant.

A participant's state may be monitored as inadequate for the discourse:

[163] ESTHER: So where's the ideals gone all of a sudden?
CISSIE: Esther, you're a stall-owner, you don't understand these things.

Monitoring may include comments on conditions that favour or impede the participants' communicative abilities:

[164] HANS: You don't know what you're talking about. You've not had enough wine, that's your trouble . . .
MARTIN: You're drinking too much wine –

18. The participants' **intentions** may be monitored if a contributed text seems to serve no plan or goal:

[165] HAL: If, as you claim, your wife is a woman, you certainly need a larger income.
TRUSCOTT: Where is this Jesuitical twittering leading us?
HAL: I'm about to suggest bribery.

If the apparent intention is to be misleading, monitoring can serve to point out a refusal to be misled:

[166] STAUPITZ: It serves very nicely as protection for you.
MARTIN: What protection?
STAUPITZ: You know perfectly well what I mean, Brother Martin, so don't pretend to be innocent.

A participant may be intentionally **ambiguous** and thus elicit monitorings from others:

[167] PAULINE: Pamela's a bit special too, isn't she?
EDITH: How do you mean?
PAULINE: Well, she's not a raving beauty exactly but she's not ugly but you don't know what to *do* with her.

In [167], Pauline's original text is deliberately vague about the topic 'Pamela', partly because there is a real difficulty of classifying her along the scale 'beautiful-ugly'. Monitoring can be used also to aver or disclaim intentions underlying one's own previous texts:

[168] CATHERINE: You said that Leonora was putting on an act.
CHARLIE: I didn't mean it.
CATHERINE: It's a strange admission for a prospective professor of economics to say that he said what he didn't mean.
CHARLIE: I was not on the lecture platform. One is entitled to say what one doesn't mean in one's own home.

19. The **beliefs** and **prior knowledge** of participants can be monitored if a presented text presupposes as fact something still in dispute:

[169] MARTIN: Father, why do you hate me being here?
HANS: Eh? What do you mean? I don't hate you being here.

One may explicitly denounce some belief as false:

[170] FAY: I'm innocent till I'm proved guilty. This is a free country. The law is impartial.
TRUSCOTT: Who's been filling your head with that rubbish?

One may refuse a request for confirming someone else's beliefs on the grounds that they conflict with one's own:

[171] MCLEAVY: Is the world mad? Tell me it's not.
TRUSCOTT: I'm not paid to quarrel with accepted facts.

Notice the typical tendency to equate one's own beliefs with "facts" about the "real world" in [171] (cf. VII.18.1). However, one can also refute attributed beliefs without actually committing oneself to "facts" (cf. VIII.21):

[172] SARAH: What do they want to hold two meetings for?
HARRY: Well, why shouldn't they hold two meetings?
SARAH: What, *you* think they should hold two meetings?
HARRY: It's not what I think.

One's own avowed lack of belief can be attributed to the inherent non-believability of events or situations:

[173] MCLEAVY: Is it likely they'd fit eyes to a sewing machine? Does that convince you?

TRUSCOTT: Nothing ever convinces me. I choose the least unlikely explanation and file it in our records.

Similarly, one can point out unbelievability as grounds for not accepting other people's texts as appropriate contributions to the discourse:

[174] MCLEAVY: How does the water board go about making an arrest?

TRUSCOTT: You must have realized by now, sir, that I am not from the water board?

20. These excerpts of dialogue illustrate how textuality is upheld in discourse despite problems and disturbances. The content of texts seems not to match the roles, intentions, and beliefs attributed to the participants. Conversational principles such as Grice's "maxims" may be violated. For example, the maxim of QUALITY (VI.9.3) is endangered if a participant's text implies unfounded beliefs, as in [169], [170], [171], and [174]. The maxim of RELATION (VI.9.4) is threatened by a seemingly pointless contribution, as in [165]. The maxim of MANNER (VI.9.5ff.) must be reasserted to regulate ambiguity, as in [167]. And the various concerns of politeness [158], [162], attention [159], participant state [163], [164], and evasion of a topic [166] or of one's responsibilities [168], would presumably all affect the principle of CO-OPERATION (VI.9.1).

21. In VIII.4, we noted some similarities between **situation monitoring** and **problem-solving:** by making some non-expected object or event a text topic, a participant may integrate it into the usual shared version of the "real world" or at least defend that version against an apparent refutation. This principle might apply equally to the aspects of monitoring discussed here in IX.16-20: the function of monitoring the roles, intentions, and beliefs implied by texts is again to negotiate the basic conditions of communicating and to integrate potential deviations or obstacles. In **situation** monitoring, the non-expected occurrences arise in the external setting of the discourse. In **intertextual** monitoring, on the other hand, those occurrences are part of the discourse actions in progress. A text receiver can call the producer to account and request to know the MOTIVATION behind the non-expected occurrence at hand; hence, producer and receiver can interact in solving the problem (cf. VII.13 on "motivation search").

Many such problems arise simply because discourse participants can serve their goals better by departing from the conventions of conversation, e.g. from the Gricean "maxims": they might want to attribute unfounded beliefs to others, or to evade their own responsibilities, and so on. Other problems arise because standards for belief and behaviour need to be negotiated from time to time anyway.

22. Rachael Reichman (1978) argues that the **coherence** of conversation is not necessarily obvious on the basis of concepts shared among its component texts. She proposes to distinguish between general "issues of concern" (i.e. typical human activities and viewpoints) and the specific events and situations that participants have encountered and want to talk about. Her samples demonstrate transitions between the general and the specific as typical "context space relationships". An ILLUSTRATIVE relation obtains if a general issue is followed by some specific example from the participants' own experience; if a discussion of a specific event or situation is followed by citing a general issue that appears to be at stake, we have a GENERALIZATION relation. There are combinations where an event or a situation illustrates several issues at once – a SUBISSUE relation; or a single issue is illustrated by several events and situations – a JOINING relation. Reichman's relations further illuminate the interaction between participants' current concerns and topics or the "facts" which are held to be true in the "real world" at large (in the sense of VII.18.1).

23. In view of these considerations, the notion of "text-world model" advanced in Chapter V might well be expanded to that of a DISCOURSE-WORLD MODEL (cf. "discourse model" in Bullwinkle 1977; Reichman 1978; Rubin 1978*b*; Webber 1978). This entity would be the integrated configuration of concepts and relations underlying all the texts in a discourse. However, allowances would have to be made for possible disagreements among the discourse-world models of different participants. The monitoring of situations and texts demonstrated in VIII.14ff. and IX.16ff. would help to minimize conflicts among these models, notably by addressing assumptions and standards not mentioned explicitly in the text.

24. It can be rightly objected that people's implicit knowledge is inordinately difficult to observe and study. In most of our examples, such knowledge only emerged when it

led to some disturbance or discrepancy; there is obviously a vast amount that goes unnoticed even though it is indispensable for making sense. We opine, however, that properly designed experiments can bring a substantial amount of implicit commonsense knowledge to light. For instance, if people are required to listen to or read a text and then to recall the content, there will be a systematic pattern of additions, omissions, and changes manifested in their reports. The making of reports and summaries of texts one has read represents another important domain of intertextuality and can accordingly serve to conclude our discussion here.

25. The 'rocket'-text already treated in Chapter V was used in a series of tests with diverse groups of receivers.[14] The text runs like this:

[4] [1.1] A great black and yellow V-2 rocket 46 feet long stood in a New Mexico desert. [1.2] Empty it weighed five tons. [1.3] For fuel it carried eight tons of alcohol and liquid oxygen.

[2.1] Everything was ready. [2.2] Scientists and generals withdrew to some distance and crouched behind earth mounds. [2.3] Two red flares rose as a signal to fire the rocket.

[3.1] With a great roar and burst of flame the giant rocket rose slowly and then faster and faster. [3.2] Behind it trailed sixty feet of yellow flame. [3.3] Soon the flame looked like a yellow star. [3.4] In a few seconds, it was too high to be seen, [3.5] but radar tracked it as it sped upward to 3,000 mph.

[4.1] A few minutes after it was fired, [4.2] the pilot of a watching plane saw it return at a speed of 2,400 mph and plunge into earth forty miles from the starting point.

Our test subjects often began their reports with statements such as: 'This was the story of a rocket's flight.' Accordingly, the reception process would have been guided by attachment to a SCHEMA for flight (cf. V.16).[15] The schema would contain an ordered progression of the EVENTS and STATES that constitute 'flight'. The events would include at least: 'take-off', 'ascent', 'reaching a peak', 'descent', and 'landing'; each motion event brings the rocket into a new state of location. Figure 13 shows the 'flight'-schema as a network graph with the components just named. However, as our sample [4] shows, the events need not all be made explicit (in the sense of I.6).

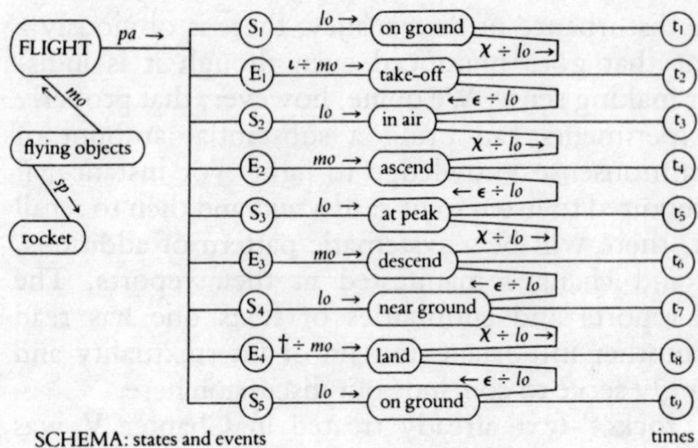

Fig. 13

The 'take-off' and 'ascend' events are both included under 'rise' in [4.3.1], and the 'reaching a peak' can only be **inferred** to have happened in the time between 'sped upward' [4.3.5] and 'return' [4.4.2]. Nonetheless, the schema can be shown to act as an "advance organizer" for the text material (cf. Ausubel 1960). Its application would be another instance of the PROCEDURAL ATTACHMENT proposed in III.19 as a powerful mechanism for fitting general strategies to current tasks. Figure 14 offers a graphic illustration of how the nodes from the text-world model (cf. Fig. 11) would be attached to those of the schema (Fig. 13).

26. The effects of the schema were unmistakably documented in our test protocols. The original text opens with a simple description of the scene, in which no events are narrated (cf. IX.6 on description vs. narration). Our test persons recalled the opening already in terms of the 'take-off' event that their schema foresaw for the 'rocket'. They seldom reported the rocket merely 'standing' there [4.1.1]; they more often had it 'on a launch pad', 'waiting for blastoff'. Many persons began right away with: 'A rocket fired up into the air'; 'It was a missile that fired'; 'In a New Mexico desert, a rocket was launched'. Evidently, material not deemed essential to the schema was often not noticed or not considered worth mentioning. Moreover, the original 'rise' concept [4.3.1] was usually replaced by 'take-off' under a variety of expressions ('take off', 'lift off', 'shoot off', 'launch', etc.) all conveying

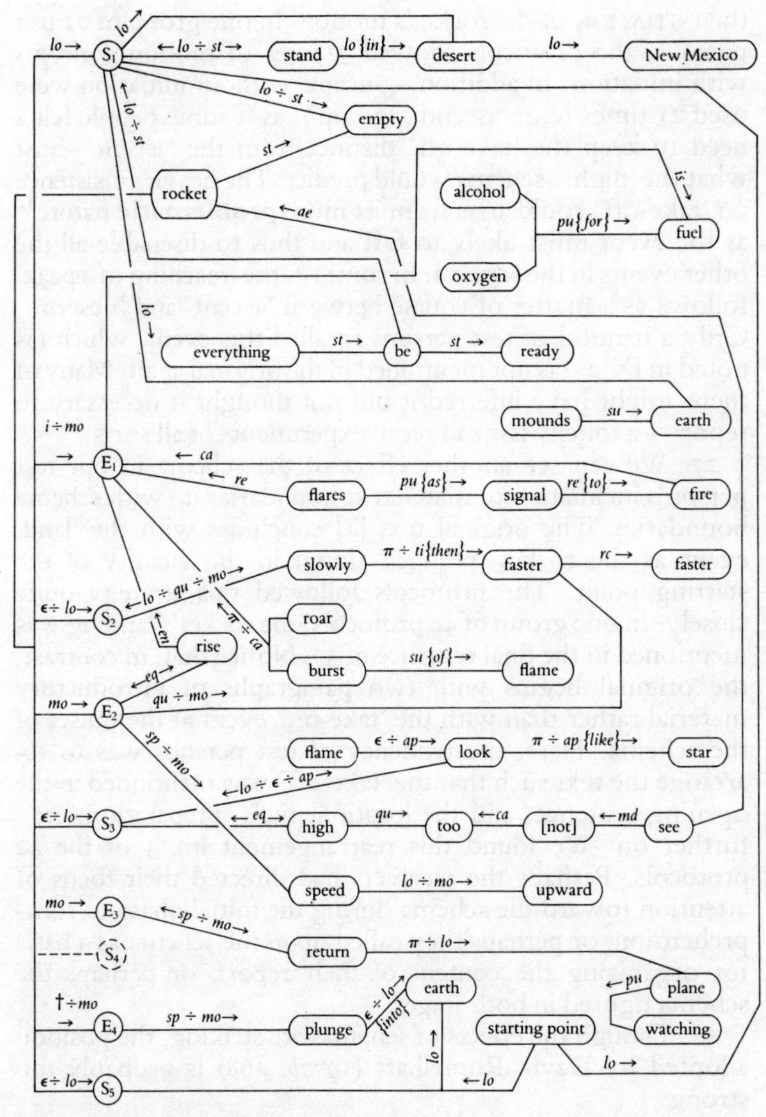

Key: S_1: on the ground; E_1: take off; S_2: in the air; E_2: ascend;
S_3: at peak; E_3: descend; S_4: near the ground; E_4: land;
S_5: on the ground; *ae:* affected entity; *ap:* apperception of;
ca: cause of; *en:* enablement of; *eq:* equivalent to;
is: instrument of; *lo:* location of; *md:* modality of;
mo: motion of; *pu:* purpose of: *qu:* quantity of;
rc: recurrence of; *re:* reason of; *sp:* specification of;
st: state of; *su:* substance of; *ti:* time of; ϵ: entry;
ι: initiation; π: proximity; †: termination

Fig. 14

the INITIATION of the rocket's motion. In one group of 72 test persons, the protocols showed 71 uses of motion concepts with initiation. In addition, concepts without initiation were used 21 times (e.g. 'ascend', 'go up'), as if some people felt a need to keep the 'take-off' distinct from the 'ascent' – just what the 'flight'-schema would predict. The heavier insistence on 'take-off' could arise from its more **problematic** nature[16] as the event most likely to **fail** and thus to disenable all the other events in the schema. In contrast, the 'reaching of a peak' follows as a matter of course between 'ascent' and 'descent'. Only a handful of test persons recalled this event, which (as noted in IX.25) is not mentioned in the original at all. Many of them might have inferred it but not thought it necessary to report – a touchy issue in recall experiments of all sorts.[17]

27. We can see another effect of the schema in our test person's inclination to match text boundaries up with schema boundaries. The original text [4] concludes with the 'land' event as the rocket 'plunges' down in the vicinity of the starting point. The protocols followed this strategy quite closely. In one group of 42 protocols, the rocket's landing was mentioned in the final sentence of 37. Notice that, in contrast, the original begins with two paragraphs of introductory material rather than with the 'take-off' event at the outset of the schema. Here, the tendency of test persons was to rearrange the text such that the 'take-off' was mentioned in the opening sentence, and the location, fuels, preparation, etc., further on. We found this rearrangement in 13 of the 42 protocols. Perhaps the receivers had directed their focus of attention toward the schema during the initial phase of comprehension; or perhaps they called upon the schema as a basis for organizing the content of their report; or perhaps the schema figured in both stages.

28. Though the effects of schemas are striking, the position adopted by David Rumelhart (1977*b*: 268) is probably too strong:

> "The process of comprehension is taken to be identical to the process of selecting and verifying conceptual schemata to account for the situation or text to be understood."

More probably, the selecting and verifying of schemas *contributes* to comprehension without being *identical* to it. There is a steady compromise between text-presented knowledge and the stored organizational knowledge patterns and cognitive disposition of the understander. Royer (1977) proposes to distinguish among three theoretical outlooks on remembering materials such as the content of texts. TRACE ABSTRACTION entails storing away traces of the original presentation as a sensory experience; recalling requires reviving traces (cf. Gomulicki 1956). Presumably, the understander decides along the way what sort of traces are worth attending to and disregards others (cf. Neisser 1967) – otherwise, storage would be chaotic and cluttered. CONSTRUCTION allows for the use of one's current knowledge patterns for organizing traces (cf. Bransford, Barclay & Franks 1972); construction theory could thus explain how different readers would recall their own versions of content, whereas trace abstraction theory could explain only omissions or errors. RECONSTRUCTION entails using one's stored schemas (or frames, plans, etc.) in their current state to reconstruct some presentation encountered in the past; the actual traces would no longer have any separate identity (cf. Spiro 1977). Rumelhart's view seems to project reconstruction theory into the very act of understanding the content being presented. He should then predict that conflicts between a schema and a presentation – for example, the inexact match of the 'rocket'-text to the 'flight'-schema (cf. IX.25ff.) – should always be resolved in favour of the schema; and that schema-related materials should always be recalled better than others. Our own results suggest that such trends are far less pronounced and certainly not infallible. There is evidently a gradation in which trace abstraction, construction, and reconstruction all participate to some extent. Traces such as the exact colours and speeds of the rocket could not be stored in anyone's schema, yet they were frequently abstracted, stored, and recalled. Construction was plainly at work when people noticed and remembered the 'desert' location, but added 'sunshine' and 'sand' on their own. Hence, reconstruction cannot be a full account unless we agree to consider *any* stored or recoverable pattern a "schema" (a trend unfortunately noticeable in some recent discussions) and thus render the term pointless.

29. In III.14, we suggested that a text might be regarded as a CYBERNETIC SYSTEM in which processing is devoted to a maintenance of CONTINUITY. Our criteria of textuality are thus

basically all centred around relation and access among elements within a level or on different levels. In this, perspective, the major priority in understanding and recalling text content would be keeping whatever is being noticed, stored, and recovered, in a continuous pattern. Whenever the actual traces of the presentation seem discontinuous, the understander draws freely on prior knowledge (including schemas and frames). Under normal conditions, a text receiver has no clear motivation to create a complete or exact trace of content from a particular text, nor to keep such a trace separated from other knowledge (cf. I.11; V.12, 34ff.). The motivation is rather to uphold a continuity of sense (V.2).

30. It follows from these considerations that one can design experiments to obtain support for any of the three theories we outlined in IX.28. Trace abstraction can be proven with closely-knit texts whose content matches typical world knowledge quite well. At the other extreme, a bizarre story such as Bartlett's (1932) 'War of the Ghosts' will demonstrate the importance of reconstruction (as Bartlett in fact did conclude). Still, the average standard will be a compromise between these extremes, such as was evinced by our 'rocket'-sample – its content is largely, but by no means entirely, conventional.

31. The processes of INFERENCING and SPREADING ACTIVATION have been studied as mechanisms which expand, update, develop, or complement the content expressed in a text. (cf. I.11; V.12, 34ff.). Inferencing is deployed for specific discontinuities and problems, while spreading activation results simply from making one point active inside a stored knowledge pattern. We can see these processes at work in the 'rocket' protocols. The additions seem to access links to the same concept types we outlined in V.26 for representing knowledge in textual worlds. The type of linkage followed most heavily evidently corresponds to the topic material and the frames or schemas that apply. Since a 'flight'-schema involves frequent changes of **location,** that concept should – and did – appear frequently in additions or alterations.

32. Location would also be enriched and developed by MENTAL IMAGERY (cf. Paivio 1971).[18] Following along a narrative of events or a description of situations can be accom-

panied by envisioning SCENES (cf. Fillmore 1975, 1977).[19] The 'desert' of our sample was recalled as *'sandy plains'*, sometimes *'far out'* in *'isolation'*, and sometimes *'outside a city'*.[20] The rocket was sent off *'under a bright sun'* from a *'launching pad'*. The 'mounds' were remembered as *'mountains'*, requiring further changes in order to keep things coherent: 'a rocket is *in front of a mountain in Arizona'*; or 'a rocket is *in front of a mountain where the people that control it are'*. The 'flight'-schema was doubtless consulted when a test person wrote: 'the rocket blasted *off, up,* and *away from the launch pad . . . at its peak* it reversed and plummeted downward *on its journey back to earth'*.

33. **Time** was also employed to link events together in a continuous pattern: the 'scientists crouched behind mounds *as* the rocket was launched'; *'When* the time came for the rocket to be launched, two red flares were sent up'; *'While* it was ascending, radar tracked the rocket'; there was 'a plane flying *at the same time* the rocket was'. In return, the time expressions of the original ('soon', 'in a few seconds', and 'a few minutes after') were seldom recalled or used. People apparently create their own time relations as needed for organizing a sequence of events in a textual world.

34. As remarked in V.33, **apperception** inferences were often made to the effect that 'scientists' and (less often) 'generals' were 'observing' or 'watching' the rocket. Other apperception links were also added with striking insistence: 'they *watched* the take-off and *paid attention to* the flames until they could not be *seen* any more and then they *looked* into a radar *detector* to find the distance of the rocket'; 'we can *see it by satellite,* but it speeds up and we *lose track of* it'. The early part of the flight was told from the ground perspective, whereas the 'pilot' of the observation plane was the point of orientation for the ending. Many protocols claimed that the pilot *'reported'* what he had seen (**communication** concept-linkage).

35. There was a variety of other concept types involved in such modifications. **Cause** was followed up to conclude that the rocket 'crashed' or 'exploded' upon landing; one person surmised: 'Going approximately 2,400 mph, *it must have made quite a recess in the earth's crust'*. **Purpose** was frequently assigned to the 'flight' as an *'experiment'* or a *'test'* of a *'new'* kind of rocket. **Agency** was attributed to the 'scientists' who were asserted to have set off the flares or even fired the rocket

themselves. The rocket's 'trail' was given **substances:** 'bright yellow *smoke*', or '*exhaust*'.

36. The additions and changes we have surveyed all rest upon commonsense knowledge about the organization of situations and events. The question that now seems crucial is: are there systematic strategies which control the interaction of text-presented knowledge and commonsense knowledge, so that predictions could be made and tested for the outcome of recalling a particular presentation? On the one hand, there certainly must be some systematic tendencies, or else communication would be totally unreliable from one text receiver to the next. On the other hand, there may be sufficient variations and gradations among different strategies and different personal expectations and knowledge stores that predictions could never surpass a rough degree of approximation. For instance, we might say that for the 'rocket' text, the inference that the 'scientists' were 'observing' the rocket would be *reported* by about 33 per cent of the test persons (the proportions generally obtained so far with over 300 persons); but we would not yet know how many actually *made* the inference without reporting it, nor whether proportions might rise or sink if any one of numerous factors were altered.[21] For the time being, we will have to rate *qualitative* predictions over *quantitative* ones.

37. In the last part of this chapter, we shall suggest what appear to be systematic tendencies in the interaction of stored world-knowledge and text-presented knowledge, based on the results of various tests so far.

37.1 *Text-presented knowledge is privileged in understanding and recall if it matches patterns of stored knowledge.* Since most rockets are powered by combustion, the recall of 'flame' by 48 out of 72 test persons, one of the highest frequencies we obtained for any concept, is not surprising. The prominent mention of 'desert' in 36 protocols is reasonable, since testing grounds should be, and usually have been, far from population centres or valuable farmland. The use of 'radar', recalled by 26 test receivers, is well-known in all kinds of aviation.

37.2 *Text-presented knowledge is privileged if it is attachable to the main entries of an applied global pattern, such as a frame, schema, plan, or script.* This tendency is a specialized corollary of the preceding one, but it claims priority for global patterns over local ones; the global patterns would make a more pervasive and constraining contribution to the understanding processes than would the local. We reviewed the effects of the 'flight'-schema upon the receivers of the 'rocket'-text in IX.26f. There is a very substantial body of research unequivocally documenting the usefulness of schemas in understanding STORIES, where a small number of common patterns underlie an enormous variety of actual texts.[22]

37.3 *Text-presented knowledge is altered to produce a better match with patterns of stored knowledge*. The 'rocket'-sample hardly seems to contain disturbing incongruities. But the 'earth mounds' [4.2.2] were noticeably treated as incongruous, perhaps because 'earth' suggests dark soil not found in a desert. These 'mounds' were recalled as *'sand hills', 'sand dunes', 'rocks', 'rock formations'*, and *'mountains'* – all common in deserts. Persons who recalled *'barriers'* or even *'concrete bunkers'* must have been focussing on the purpose of the 'mounds' to protect the personnel. Another discrepancy in the original sample was the claim that the rocket's trail 'looked like a yellow star' [4.3.3]. Test persons recalled the flame instead as a *'glow'*, a *'blur'*, or a *'dot'*; to get in the rocket's motion, others had a 'star *rising in the sky'*, or a *'shooting* star'. A striking alteration was performed by someone who must have encountered 'V-2' rockets in reports of World War II: he said that 'the paragraph was about the launching of a *captured German* V-2 rocket'.

37.4 *Distinct elements of text-presented knowledge become conflated or confused with each other if they are closely associated in stored knowledge*. The most widespread instance of this tendency was the conflation and confusion of the 'red flares' used as a 'signal' with the 'yellow flame' emitted by the rocket, e.g.: 'the rocket went off in a burst of *flares*'; 'when the rocket was launched, *it looked like a red flare*'; 'it sped upward to great heights, leaving a spectacular trail of yellow *and red* flames'. This conflating may have been assisted by surface similarities. The words 'flare' and 'flame' look and sound almost alike, and both are said to 'rise' in the original [4.2.3] vs. [4.3.1].

37.5 *Text-presented knowledge decays and becomes unrecoverable if it is designated accidental or variable in world knowledge*. This tendency was unmistakably prominent in the treatment our test persons accorded the various **quantities.** Their rockets weighed between 5 and 50,000 tons, and telescoped between

26 and 1,000 feet in length. Speeds wavered between 300 feet per minute (a measly 3.13 mph) and 300,000 miles per hour. The distance between launching and landing ranged from 60 feet to 164 miles. Speeds were converted to altitudes, and weights to numbers of gallons. Some people artfully dodged the whole issue by recalling '*lots of* fuel', 'a *certain* speed', or '*very* fast'. One person even remembered a quantity with nothing to measure: 'there was something about 2,400'. The rocket's colours fared little better, though their prominent placement at the beginning of the text may have supported their retention over many other details – an effect known as PRIMACY in learning experiments.[23] No one would be likely to know in advance that a V-2 rocket ought to be 'black' and 'yellow'. In one group, half of the test persons recovered no colours. A fourth recovered the correct ones, and the other fourth roamed across the colour spectrum, citing *'red', 'green', 'white', 'blue',* and *'silver'.* Only 'silver' is an inherently probable colour for a metal rocket.

37.6 *Additions, modifications, and changes performed via spreading activation or inferencing become indistinguishable from text-presented knowledge.* If, as was claimed in IX.29, text receivers normally have no motivation to preserve a separate trace for a single text or text-world, then people should eventually be unable to tell what they heard or read apart from their own contributions. The passage of time seems to intensify this tendency. When we had test persons wait just five minutes before making protocols, the additions and alterations were more pronounced than in a control group that started right after presentation. Harry Kay (1955) found that people would stick to their own versions even when given an opportunity to study the original again; the longer the intervening time, the more his people would cling to their versions rather than try to improve accuracy. The elapse of time seems to strengthen the *confidence* people place in their alterations.[24]

38. These six tendencies have been found for receiver groups of different ages. A set of tests was also run with native German speakers recalling a German translation.[25] The same results were obtained, e.g. the inference that 'scientists' were 'observing', or the insertion of 'take-off' as an initial schema event, so that the data cannot be specific to the English language. Of course, the German groups would have somewhat dif-

ferent background knowledge. Unlike the Americans, they seldom conflated 'New Mexico' with 'Arizona' or 'Nevada' (as predicted by IX.35.4), but they changed the 'earth mounds' to 'sand hills' just as often; they were no doubt better acquainted with the notion of 'desert' than with the geography of the southwestern United States. Their knowledge of chemistry was better than that of the Americans, who listed 'nitrogen' (a non-flammable substance) as a fuel; the 'liquid hydrogen' given by mistake in the German translation was either recalled exactly or corrected to 'liquid oxygen'.[26] The Germans tended to remember the presence of 'generals' at the launching far more often than the Americans (who concentrated on the 'scientists'), perhaps because of clearer memories of warfare rocketry. Still, the tendencies themselves were comparable for both nationalities, despite variations in commonsense knowledge stores.

39. The six processing tendencies would not, as far as we can judge, be able to make exact predictions for a specific case and receiver. In fact, they could easily interact in complex and unforeseen ways. For example, a given pattern of text-presented knowledge might match a pattern in stored knowledge so well that the privileged status of the good match (IX.37.1) could be offset by utter effacement of a few non-matching (IX.37.3) or variable (IX.37.5) elements; the overall result might be no more accurate recall than a modest match would elicit. Or, a particular person's experience might lead to a wholly unpredictable treatment of text-world elements, e.g. when the American reader remembered a 'captured German' rocket.

40. Furthermore, the fact that a recall protocol is a text in its own right has important implications (cf. Kintsch & van Dijk 1978: 374). A certain degree of variation between the original text and a given protocol can arise simply because the test person is striving to uphold TEXTUALITY at the moment of making the report. The current demands of **cohesion** and **coherence** will call for additions, changes, and omissions of material. In real-life settings, **situationality** will be influential according to the circumstances under which people must recall things. There may even be a trend toward upholding **informativity** by embellishing or exaggerating the content over that of the original; certainly some such process appears to operate in the "tall tales" narrated in rural areas.[27]

41. Such considerations indicate that intertextuality should not be disregarded as a factor in any experimental or empirical research on texts or on the transmission of knowledge via texts. Communication serves a myriad of purposes under all sorts of conditions, but with surprisingly economic means and surprisingly few disturbances and misunderstandings. At one extreme, we must not try to define the function of language elements for all conceivable contexts; at the other extreme, we must not conclude that every context is so unique that no systematic regularities can be distilled. The central task for a science of texts is rather to find the regularities according to which conventional functions are either re-affirmed or adapted in actual usage. The whole notion of **textuality** may depend upon exploring the influence of **intertextuality** as a procedural control upon communicative activities at large.

Notes

1 In addition to the sentence typologies of transformational grammar, sentence typologies have been offered by Admoni and Brinkmann, among others (cf. survey in Helbig 1974).
2 The notion of "function" here is again based on that in systems theory: the contribution of an element to the workings of the entire system (in this case, the system of communication). See note 2 to Chapter VII.
3 Freedle & Hale (1979) found that narrative schemas can be acquired and transferred to the processing of descriptive ("expository") texts.
4 A major question we have pointed out on occasion (cf. I.16; VII.28, 42; VIII.20) is the extent to which text receivers are persuaded by content they have to supply themselves – an important factor in argumentative texts. Yet as we suggested in Chapter VII, all texts should be studied in consideration of what they do not say, but might be expected to say.
5 Literary texts are often called *fiction* to signal their non-agreement with the "real world". But there are fictional texts which are not literary, e.g. simple lies; fictionality is not a sufficient condition for literariness. The sufficient condition is the intentional awareness of organizational principles that evolves from the various degrees of non-agreement between the text-world and the "real world" (cf. Iser 1975; Ihwe 1976).
6 The dates used here are those given in *The Norton Introduction to Literature* ed. J. Paul Hunter (New York: Norton, 1973) pp. 78ff. The dates are those of the first publication, which, according to the editor, do not "differ substantially" from the dates of actual writing (p. xliii).
7 Here again, a text-world discrepancy deliberately points up a discrepancy in the real world (cf. IV.19; IX.8; X.16).

8 On preferences for problematic knowledge, cf. IV.23, 29; IX.26. On the treatment of variables in recall, cf. IX.37.5.
9 The sources of these excerpts are as follows: [153] from Wesker (1964: 189); [154] from Osborne (1961*b*: 67); [155] from Osborne (1961*a*: 58); and [156] and [157] from Osborne (1960: 51).
10 The sources of these excerpts are as follows: [158] from Pinter (1960: 108); [159] from Spark (1963: 1); [160] from Osborne (1961*a*: 15); [161] from Orton (1967: 67]; [162] from Spark (1963: 100); [163] from Wesker (1964: 200); [164] from Osborne (1961*a*: 39); [165] from Orton (1967: 82); [166] from Osborne (1961*a*: 53); [167] from Osborne (1968: 16); [168] from Spark (1963: 76); [169] from Osborne (1961*a*: 38); [170] from Orton (1967: 66); [171] from Orton (1967: 70); [172] from Wesker (1964: 17); [173] from Orton (1967: 72); and [174] from Orton (1967: 62).
11 We noted the function of **motivation search** in VII.13; here, a participant is delegating the search task back to the producer of the problematic text (cf. IX.21).
12 If style is, as we asserted (cf. I.7), the outcome of selection and decision processes, then it could well be treated as **problematic** and **variable** and hence as a suitable topic of discourse (cf. IX.14).
13 On the states of participants, cf. note 6 to Chapter VII.
14 On earlier work about this text, cf. note 10 to Chapter V. Thanks are due to all those who participated in running these experiments: Manfred Buge, Roger Drury, Richard Hersh, Walter Kintsch, Genevieve Miller, and Althea Turner; and to the students who acted as test subjects at the Universities of Colorado and Florida, and at the Gymnasium am Wall (Verden an der Aller, West Germany).
15 The text is essentially **narrative** and thus predominantly, though not exclusively, guided by a schema (cf. IX.6).
16 See note 8 to this chapter.
17 The event would be recoverable via **updating** (cf. V.34).
18 A new test for the effects of mental imagery is now being designed by Robert de Beaugrande and Zofia Solczak-Roberts at the University of Florida. The presentation of the 'rocket'-text is accompanied by pictures whose effects on recall are often striking.
19 Fillmore's use of the term "scenes" is much broader: "any coherent segment of human beliefs, actions, experiences, or imaginings" (Fillmore, 1975: 143) (cf. IV.40). We prefer the narrow sense: coherent images of situations.
20 We italicize the items changed or added by our test subjects.
21 The passage 'too high to be seen' may have been influential here. But how can we *test* inferences without *eliciting* them by our questions?
22 cf. Rumelhart (1975, 1977*b*); Bower (1976); Anderson (1977); Kintsch (1977*b*); Mandler & Johnson (1977); Meyer (1977); Rumelhart & Ortony (1977); Thorndyke (1977); Kintsch & van Dijk (1978); Mandler (1978); Stein & Nezworski (1978); Adams & Collins (1979); Beaugrande & Colby (1979); Freedle & Hale (1979); Stein & Glenn (1979); Beaugrande & Miller (1980); Thorndyke & Yekovich (1980). Compare V.16.
23 The evidence for primacy effects on recalling texts is still inconclusive (Meyer 1977: 308ff.) (but cf. IV.24). Conversely, *recency* effects would

appear if the final passage of a text were favoured in recall; here again, definite proof is lacking (Meyer 1977: 309).

24 Bransford and Franks (1971) found that receivers were most confident about those altered versions which made explicit the greatest number of implied associations.

25 Thanks are due to Manfred Buge, of the Gymnasium am Wall (Verden an der Aller), for running these tests; and to Dany Paul for the translation.

26 One subject even commented that the presented text was in error, and pointed out that the V-2 required oxygen rather than hydrogen.

27 The tendency to depict preternaturally large or small objects in literary texts has been discussed in Weinrich (1966). Our own test readers quite often made the rocket much larger and faster in their reports (cf. IX.37.5). When one group was later assigned to write *their own* stories about a 'rocket', there were far greater exaggerations, e.g. flying from the earth to Mars in six hours.

Chapter X

Research and schooling

1. In the past, linguistic theories and models were often constructed according to purely internal considerations of describing language structures. Whether these theories and models would be useful to other disciplines concerned with language, and whether they would contribute to methodologies for improving language-based skills among society at large, were issues of small concern. A linguistics of TEXTS, on the other hand, as a sector of an integrated science of texts, places heavy emphasis on addressing these issues. After all, text linguistics needs the co-operation of adjacent disciplines in order to come to terms with its most essential objects of inquiry. And if the strategies and procedures which operate during the production and reception of texts are indeed controlled by standards of efficiency, effectiveness, and appropriateness (I.23), then a linguistics of texts should have considerable potential for contributing to language training (cf. Kohonen & Enkvist (eds.) 1978). We shall attempt to outline in this chapter some ways in which the approach presented so far might be useful in interdisciplinary *research* and language-related *schooling*.

2. The full extent of the implications that could be explored might well demand a separate book. We will only pass in review over a few concerns of those domains in which texts are either an object of inquiry or a means of management: COGNITIVE SCIENCE, SOCIOLOGY, ANTHROPOLOGY, CONSULTING PSYCHOLOGY, READING, WRITING, LITERARY STUDIES, TRANSLATION STUDIES, CONTRASTIVE LINGUISTICS, FOREIGN-LANGUAGE

TEACHING, SEMIOTICS, and COMPUTER SCIENCE.

3. COGNITIVE SCIENCE is a comparatively new field integrating the concerns of cognitive psychology (cf. III.34) and computer science (cf. X.26ff.) (see I.24; Bobrow & Collins (eds.) 1975; Collins 1977*b*). Texts are only one of the centres of interest in this field. Important progress has also been attained in the study of the organization of world knowledge in human memory and access; and of the procedural utilization of meaning (cf. Chapter V). We cannot yet observe the mechanisms of learning, knowing, and recalling meaningful material within the mind itself. But we can safely assume that the observable activities of textual communication must be in part determined by the organization of memory and the nature of meaningful behaviour.[1]

4. Plainly, textual communication is a crucial domain for building theories of cognition at large. Texts are essential for *reporting mental events* as far as the latter are accessible to conscious awareness. Textual communication is *the most elaborately and subtly differentiated system of human symbolic behaviour:* it allows people to maintain and agree upon distinctions that are unmanageably fuzzy or disputable in other modes of behaviour. Quite possibly, textual communication entails *all the major skills for rational human behaviour in general:* (*a*) PROBLEM-SOLVING capacities; (*b*) PLANNING capacities; (*c*) capacities for GENERATING, TESTING, and REVISING HYPOTHESES; (*d*) capacities for PATTERN-MATCHING; (*e*) PROCESSING EASE for expected or probable occurrences; (*f*) PROCESSING DEPTH for non-expected or improbable occurrences; (*g*) capacities for REDUCING COMPLEXITY to meet PROCESSING LIMITATIONS; (*h*) capacities for selective FOCUS OF ATTENTION; (*i*) capacities for maintaining CONTINUITY of experience; and (*j*) capacities for projecting or inferring these various dispositions and activities among the other participants in interaction.[2]

5. INTELLIGENCE arises, we believe, not merely from rapid, accurate storage and recovery of specific knowledge – an unfortunate misconception in both psychology and education – but rather from the *ability to apply or adapt a small set of powerful skills and procedures to any particular task at hand* (Beaugrande 1980*a*; Papert 1980). It is the capacity to work with high POWER (in the sense of Minsky & Papert 1974: 59) by recognizing and performing any given task as *an instantiation of a general opera-*

tion type, such as those enumerated in X.4. The decision and selection processes demanded in textual communication must function at this deep a level, so that content can be conveyed and situations can be managed without relying on predetermined texts. People can recall the purpose of a discourse after forgetting the surface texts used (Schweller, Brewer & Dahl 1976). On the level of conscious attention, syntax, meaning, information, and planning are processed in terms of *high-power typologies of occurrences and relationships,* not in terms of particular words and structures (cf. III.14, 17, 35; IV.3; V.25ff.; VII.7ff.; VIII.10ff.; etc.). Research on textual communication may well lead to processing models with powerful implications for the development of intelligence at large.

6. To meet these changing priorities, a new perspective may evolve upon issues treated in traditional linguistics (cf. 0.6). The isolation of "distinctive features", practised extensively in descriptive linguistics (cf. II.19), may be redirected toward those features which are *actually consulted* during language operations. The structural analysis of potentially ambiguous sentences, a frequent exercise in transformational grammar, may be re-oriented toward human processing strategies that *preclude* or *resolve* ambiguities in actual usage.[3] The notion of "presuppositions" as prior knowledge entailed by a single sentence, a topic of numerous discussions among philosophers (cf. Petöfi & Franck (eds.) 1974), might be superseded by the development of a general theory of how *world-knowledge* is utilized in communication. The logicians' preoccupation with the "existence" of individual objects and the "truth conditions" for sentences could be supplanted by the investigation of the *cognitive thresholds* at which humans are disposed to *recognize* objects and *believe* statements (cf. V.40). Perhaps the issues which have resisted conclusive treatment from *speculative* or *formalistic* standpoints may become decidable from an *empirical* one.

7. If, as we suggested in X.4, textual communication entails all major skills found in rational human behaviour at large, the usefulness of a science of texts should be extremely wide and versatile. Many disciplines besides linguistics deal with aspects of problem-solving, planning, hypothesis-testing, and attention. Moreover, texts are the most widespread *vehicle* of scientific exploration and discussion. The status of theories

and models in most sciences is no better than the status of the accepted mode of discourse.[4] The scientists themselves cannot belong to a scientific community until they have acquired its conventions of discourse and argumentation. Instruction, description, explanation, examination, interviews, questionnaires, research reports – all these commonplace uses of texts are as indispensible to science as the most elaborate technological instruments.

8. In many disciplines, texts themselves are among the objects of inquiry. SOCIOLOGISTS are concerned with notions like *"symbolic interaction"* as expounded by George Henry Mead, and *"strategic interaction"* as expounded by Erving Goffman.[5] Language skills figure prominently in the sociology of *schooling,* and the study of *social class differences.*[6] ANTHROPOLOGISTS investigate *folktales, rituals, litigation,* and other cultural institutions centred around the use of certain text types.[7] PSYCHIATRISTS and CONSULTING PSYCHOLOGISTS depend upon *therapeutic* discourse for the discovery and treatment of mental illness.[8]

9. The study of READING has advanced considerably in recent years. A science of texts should be able to assist in defining READABILITY as the extent to which a presentation is suitable for reception among given groups. Early probes relied heavily on surface aspects, such as length and frequency of words and complexity of sentences (cf. surveys in Klare 1963; Groeben 1978). Such simple methods were straightforward in their application, but rather inconclusive as accurate measurements. As Rothkopf (1976: 108) remarks, "the lexical characteristic chiefly tapped is familiarity. Vividness and concreteness are neglected. Exposition and organization are disregarded completely. Content factors are ignored." In effect, the early measures took no account of **textuality** beyond some obvious factors in **cohesion.**

10. To appreciate coherence, readability measures would have to consider how text-presented knowledge interacts with world-knowledge (cf. IX.37ff.). For example, readability has been shown to suffer if material needed to match elements of a STORY SCHEMA is removed (Thorndyke 1977); schemas are evidently used even by very young children.[9] The hierarchical organization of material according to its importance and generality affects readability also (Meyer 1975, 1977): passages

rated by judges as the most important were shown to be the best remembered by various groups of readers.

11. On the other hand, readability cannot be optimized simply by striving for the best possible match between text-presented knowledge and prior world knowledge. The resulting text would possess radically low **informativity** and hence be devoid of **interest.** This flaw pervades much of the reading materials now used in education. Readers will gladly expend additional effort upon a text if the unexpected occurrences lead to rewarding insights. We discussed in VII.21ff. how the 'gorilla'-text was constructed according to that principle. Readability must therefore *not* be defined as the expenditure of the least effort (despite Hirsch 1977), but rather as *the appropriate proportion between required effort and resulting insights.*[10]

12. The situation is similar in the research on and the teaching of WRITING. Older methods dwelt heavily on surface mechanics, such as punctuation, subject-verb agreement, or disordered syntax. Often, the suppressing of errors in surface mechanics was equated with writing well. Later, scholars (e.g. Christensen 1967) began to study the formal arrangement of extended discourse, and found various typical patterns. But "the reasons for the effectiveness of different patterns, the ways in which their parts interact, the most useful techniques of deciding upon particular sequences of steps in composing . . . have been dealt with slightly, hesitantly, or not at all" (Larson 1976: 71). A **procedural** investigation of the **decision-making processes** would be helpful in offsetting this deficit.[11] The ways that a writer can build and use a reasonable model of the intended reader audience should also be presented and explored. Unlike spoken language, writing cannot rely on immediate feedback and must therefore be far more closely planned and critically evaluated (cf. Rubin 1978*a*). The subsidiary factors of voice quality, intonation, facial expressions, and gestures must be compensated with purely textual means of creating focus and interest.

13. LITERARY STUDIES have been applying linguistic methods of inquiry for many years (see II.11). The methods corresponded to the contemporary trends in linguistics proper. The description of structures was carried out in early studies such as those of the "Russian Formalists" (e.g. Eichenbaum, Jakobson, Jakubinskij, Propp, Šklovskij, Tomasevškij,

Tynjanov, Vinogradov), and the "Prague Structuralists" (e.g. Havránek, Mathesius, Mukařovský, Trnka).[12] Description focused on the elements and configurations which set literary or poetic language apart from everyday language and thus remove it from "automatic" processing. This "de-automatization" (Mukařovský 1964) could be achieved both via "deviations" such as rare neologisms or displaced syntax, and via the imposition of detailed "equivalences" which everyday language would not manifest.[13] In either case, the structures involved were described from an essentially static viewpoint.

14. During the ascendancy of transformational grammar, proposals were advanced for a "generative poetics": a special grammar designed to "generate" literary structures via modified rules.[14] However, it gradually became evident that no such grammar could be set up for any large set of texts. The diversity of literature and poetry would lead to an explosion of special rules, some of which, in the worst case, would be required for one single instance. The rules would also generate many undesirable structures not found in any samples. Indeed, the explosion of the grammar would eventually allow the generating of every conceivable structure, so that nothing would have been explained at all.[15]

15. Neither the descriptive nor the transformational approach made any concerted attempt to deal with the alternativity of textual worlds which we consider a distinctive trait of literature and poetry (cf. IX.8f.). Consequently, the epistemological and social functions of literary discourse were neglected or treated only marginally. The poetic text was thought to revolve around itself, drawing all of the receivers attention to the formatting of the message and hence freeing them from any practical consequences of communicative interaction.

16. Deviations for their own sake or for the sake of tinkering with language would hardly suffice to account for the prestigious status of literary and poetic texts within the overall context of social discourse. The history of literature shows that the value assigned to a literary text over the years is not a direct outcome of its degree of deviation; otherwise, we should all rate Gertrude Stein over Ernest Hemingway. Evaluation rather reflects the enriching nature of the insights provided in **downgrading** unexpected occurrences by finding their communicative motivations (cf. VII.13ff.) and

upgrading expected occurrences by noting their special significance. Discrepancies and discontinuities in literary texts are most **effective** if they are matched to discrepancies and discontinuities in the socially established model of the "real world" (cf. IV.19; VII.40; IX.8). For example, the enduring appeal of Lewis Carroll's *Alice* books arises from the entertaining way in which the nonsensical occurrences in the text-world point up the arbitrary, often foolish conventions of Victorian society and its treatment of children.

17. Experimental classes conducted by R. de Beaugrande at the University of Florida have demonstrated that this outlook is quite useful in teaching literature to a wide audience of non-specialized receivers. Students rapidly become skilled at discovering the motivations for all sorts of non-ordinary occurrences in poetry. These motivations may not have been present in the conscious control of the text producer. Often, we have no reliable access to the text producer's real intentions other than through the evidence of the text itself. Indeed, the best of intentions would not be relevant if the text could not be utilized by its contemporaries without detailed personal knowledge from other sources.[16] There does seem to be a correlation between common intuitive value judgements, literary texts, and the interestingness of motivations and insights uncovered in the fashion described above.

18. This approach admittedly exceeds the traditional scope of linguistics. Literary studies could profit greatly from a general, interdisciplinary science of texts. Siegfried J. Schmidt (1979, 1981) has provided a theoretical framework for literary studies in the broader context of social action and interaction. The investigation of literary texts would be expanded to the investigation of the *use* of literary texts (cf. Wienold 1972): literary criticism would become an object of inquiry as well as a means. Even when critics cannot agree on the motivation for certain occurrences in a given text, critical reactions still document the presence and interestingness of the occurrences themselves.[17] Criticism is basically an activity of DOWNGRADING (finding motivations that integrate improbable occurrences) and UPGRADING (finding more specialized motivations for everyday occurrences): the more rewarding the text, the more numerous and fulfilling will be the spread of upgradings and downgradings. In Shakespeare's texts, for instance, there are

striking, many-sided motivations for the selection and arrangement of language options.[18] One critic's downgradings would not be "correct" or "incorrect", but rather more or less *probable, convincing,* and *enriching.*

19. A science of texts can also contribute to TRANSLATION STUDIES.[19] Translating entails above all **actualization** of language, and the traditional linguistic preoccupation with virtual, self-contained systems impeded the development of translation theory.[20] This point became dramatically clear when virtual systems were used as the sole basis for machine translation: a computer working only with a grammar and lexicon (both virtual systems) was found unable to operate reliably, because it could not evaluate **context.** A computer equipped with prior knowledge of the world fares much better, being able to decide what concepts and relations will be **preferentially** combined in text-worlds.[21] A preference model for *all* language operations would work better still, e.g. with preferences for mapping text-worlds onto the surface texts; for realizing intentions and plans via discourse actions; for relating texts to situations of occurrence; and so on. The high costs of programming all these preferences into a computer would be offset in the long run by more intelligent, satisfactory translating.

20. Human translating has been the object of a longstanding controversy over "literal" versus "free" approaches. This discussion reflects the inaccurate views that there can be an equivalence of language elements independently of their setting of occurrence; and that such equivalence is somehow relevant to actual usage. The "literal" translator decomposes the text into single elements (or small groups of elements) and replaces each with a corresponding element (or group) in the goal language. The "free" translator judges the function of the whole text in discourse and searches for elements that could fulfil that function in a goal-language situation. The success or failure of either approach is uncertain: an unduly "literal" translation may be awkward or even unintelligible, while an unduly "free" one may cause the original text to disintegrate and disappear altogether.

21. The equivalence of a translation with its original can only be an equivalence in the *experience of the participants.*[22] The major source of non-equivalence arises when the translator

incorporates his or her own experience into the text itself, leaving the receivers with little to do. To counteract this tendency, translators must strive to convey the same kind of experience with the same kind of language material, and to expand, reduce, or modify textual components only as far as necessary to minimize a divergence of experience. Whether or not the elements in the goal language text occupy the same positions in their **virtual** systems as do the elements of the original text in theirs, is a secondary matter, often leading to irresolvable and unnecessary conflicts.

22. LITERARY translating illustrates these considerations quite forcefully. As we have suggested before, literary and poetic texts make use of alternative organizations of the world or of discourse about the world in order to elicit special processing activities from the receivers.[23] If a literary or poetic translator interferes with those organizations, equivalence of experience is rendered impossible. All too often, translators will incorporate into the text their own processing activities: solving the problems, reducing polyvalence, explaining away any discrepancies or discontinuities, and so forth. Soon, the receivers of the translation find their mental tasks pre-empted. Translators must instead analyze both the text and the range of plausible receiver reactions, in order to preserve as much of that range as possible. This task would obviously be assisted by a science of texts in which language elements and structures are viewed in terms of processes and operations.

23. CONTRASTIVE LINGUISTICS, concerned with the differences between languages,[24] should be expanded to a confrontation of textual strategies. The contrasting of virtual systems alone – carried to extremes by John Catford (1964), for instance – fails to show how different languages can be used for the same or similar purposes in human interaction. Indeed, as Georges Mounin (1963) points out, a preoccupation with the divergencies among virtual systems, especially grammar/syntax and lexicon, would lead one to suppose that translating should be impossible in both theory and practice. The "comparative stylistics" developed by Vinay and Darbelnet (1958), on the other hand, illustrates correspondences and divergencies among cultural patterns of actual usage. Although their criteria are often impressionistic, Vinay and Darbelnet capture some important regularities that could

be empirically elaborated by psychological and sociological research.

24. FOREIGN-LANGUAGE TEACHING is at present in a precarious condition. All too often, the failure of most learners to acquire the new language adequately is accepted as the normal state of affairs. A radically behaviouristic approach – known as the "audio-lingual" or "direct" method – in which language use is considered a simplistic stimulus-response mechanism has survived in America despite the downfall of behaviouristic learning theories in psychology proper (cf. VI.12) – and despite the discrediting of this approach in Great Britain and Europe, where communication-oriented language methods are preferred (cf. Wienold 1973; Wilkins 1976). Apparently, the ability to communicate in a language is equated with the ability to form grammatical paradigms and syntactic patterns with the help of unsystematically compiled vocabulary lists. The learners are given no thorough exposure to the actualization strategies without which these virtual systems of grammar/syntax and lexicon are of little practical value: how to relate texts to situations or to plans and goals. Learners are forced to act as if grammatical perfection were the highest priority for saying anything (such is at least the usual standard for evaluation and testing),[24a] so that they easily become tongue-tied and helpless. A science of texts could help to set new priorities and to select those rules, procedures, and domains which are sufficient for textual communication on a limited scale (cf. Wikberg 1978).

25. The emerging super-discipline of SEMIOTICS, the study of signs, still lacks a general, unified theory. There is a great diversity among types of signs: written words, graphic images, musical notes, paintings, hand signals, and so forth. The unity of signs (and thus of semiotics) lies in the *systemic* nature of their *occurrence* in the context of human activities. In the broadest sense, any meaningful sign configuration is a text, and must possess textuality. Each individual sign occurs in an actual system that regulates and determines its function and sense. A science of linguistic texts might well be expanded and generalized to deal with semiotic texts of all sorts. Films, art works, billboards, concerts, political rallies, games – all these events (and many more) are composed of cohesive and coherent elements with relevance to the participants' attitudes

and goals within the situation. Presumably, it is a basic precondition of acquiring, storing, and using signs that they must contribute to the textuality of their respective settings of occurrence.

26. COMPUTER SCIENCE is currently in a state of rapid evolution. Terry Winograd (1979) discusses the rising demand for "higher-level" programming concerned not with detailed numerical operations, but with "manipulating complex systems and components". As long as computers can only carry out well-defined sequences of steps on precisely preformatted data, programmers will have to keep modifying or replacing expensive software capable of only a few specific tasks. An INTELLIGENT computer would be programmed to manage a wide range of tasks without severe restrictions upon the formatting of data (cf. Lenat 1977; Walker (ed.) 1978; Simon 1979; see discussion in X.5). For example, computers should be able to operate from an "informal" description of a task domain (Goldman, Balzer & Wile 1977). This kind of program will require "world views" (Winograd 1979: 395), i.e. knowledge of how real-world events and situations are organized, in order to *understand* its tasks and act without incessant inspection and guidance.

27. Research toward the development of such "intelligent" computer systems has important implications for a science of texts. We have already availed ourselves in this volume of many notions and proposals for "artificial intelligence" in computers.[25] These contributions are intended to improve the interactions of humans with machines, particularly where the abilities of the two groups complement each other. Computers offer rapid computation and expensive storage, while humans have vast storage and rather slow computational abilities (Loftus & Loftus 1976: 128). Computers can recall any desired amount of material without loss or error over long periods of time, while most humans cannot. Humans can recognize subtle analogies and correlations which still evade the computer (Collins & Quillian 1972). Whereas no absolute improvements of human memory capacity and computational speed are yet in sight, computer abilities have been enormously expanded in the past ten years. Humans apparently cannot become more machine-like, but machines can become more human.

28. On the other hand, artificial intelligence can also be construed as a source of models for human processes. In the new field of cognitive science (cf. X.3ff.), theories about the mental activities of humans are frequently tested by building computer models. Researchers agree that presently operating models are simpler than their corresponding human processes by several degrees of magnitude (cf. III.35), but those models already have attained a complexity far beyond the scope of traditional theories in linguistics and psychology. Only the computer allows us to test immediately whether a mathematical or procedural theory of cognition or communication actually operates in real time; we can and must specify exact details that may remain hidden in human experiments. In short, computers can lead us from *understanding data* toward the broader domain of *understanding understanding*.[26]

29. On this optimistic note, we must conclude our survey of text linguistics. We hope to have outlined the basic issues in a useful and not unduly technical manner. Although those issues are far from resolved, researchers are gradually acquiring important insights into the nature of the questions worth investigating. The nature of texts as objects of inquiry clearly calls for a re-evaluation of traditional linguistic methodology. By defining texts as actual communicative occurrences, we are obliged to consider all the factors of control and processing in realistic settings. Perhaps this expansion of our domain will not heighten the complexity of research and application as much as one might suppose. The fact that humans can and do communicate successfully in a staggering range of settings indicates that there must be a limited set of powerful, regular strategies at work, some of which we suggested in X.4. In its attempts to isolate single systems (phonology, morphology, syntax, etc.) and to keep language distinct from everything else, linguistic research may have remained on a superficial plane that *increased* complexity of study rather than reducing it. On a more powerful plane, a simpler and more unified account of human language may yet be forthcoming.

Notes

1 Bock (1979) suggests that some parallels may exist between text processing and the language tasks assigned in traditional psychological experiments, e.g. the learning of word-lists. A study by Mary Kircher (cited in Meyer 1977: 308), however, reports the contrary.

2 We appeal to these notions repeatedly in the present volume; see the Index of Terms for listings of the passages involved. See Beaugrande (1980*a*) for further details.

3 Peter Hartman (personal communication to RdB) observes that linguistic analysis tends naturally to proliferate ambiguities that play no role in real communication; cf. note 7 to Chapter III.

4 Groeben (1978) argues that linguistic and psychological tests can be deployed to improve didactic texts for scientific instruction.

5 cf. Blumer (ed.) (1969); Goffman (1974).

6 cf. Gumperz & Hymes (eds.) (1972); Cicourel et al. (1974).

7 cf. Frake (1972); Colby (1973*a*, *b*); Salmond (1974); Leodolter (1975); Wodak (1980).

8 cf. Dressler & Stark (1976); Engel (1977); Labov & Fanshel (1977); Wodak-Leodolter (1979).

9 cf. Kintsch (1977*b*). In a comparative study with fourth-graders and tenth-graders, Beaugrande & Miller (1980) found that the different stores of prior knowledge caused consistent variations in the interaction of a schema with prior cognitive dispositions. On schemas, cf. V.16; note 22 to Chapter IX. On modelling reading, cf. Beaugrande (1981*a*).

10 In more general terms: humans enjoy solving difficult **problems** if there are correspondingly intense rewards. On the preference for problematic knowledge in texts, see note 8 to Chapter IX.

11 cf. II.4; III.20–8; IV.20; VI.10–20; VIII.13–27. A similarly conceived model has been proposed by Flower & Hayes (1979) (cf. also Bruce, Collins, Rubin & Gentner 1978).

12 Some papers of the Russian Formalists are surveyed in Erlich (1955); Matejka & Pomorska (eds.) (1971); Hansen-Löve (1978); some from the Prague Structuralists are in Garvin (ed.) (1964).

13 On deviation, cf. Mukařovsky (1964); Levin (1963, 1965). On equivalence, cf. Levin (1962); Jakobson & Jones (1970); on some problems inherent in these and related approaches, cf. Werth (1976); Beaugrande (1978*b*, *d*, 1979*c*).

14 The major force in this movement was the work of Teun van Dijk (1972*a*, *b*); but some earlier short works (e.g. Bierwisch 1965*b*; Žolkovskij & Ščeglov 1967; Hendricks 1969; Thorne 1969; Levý 1971) were also influential.

15 There would also be **combinatorial explosion** if any text producer attempted to apply such a grammar (cf. III.5, 32).

16 The hopes of explaining literature away by analyzing the personal biographies of authors is a special case of **downgrading,** namely: assigning the motivations for special views of the world or of language about the world to external experiences (cf. X.18). But the causality of these experiences is at best doubtful, and not necessarily relevant in any case.

17 See discussion in Riffaterre (1959: 162).
18 cf. Jakobson & Jones (1970); Beaugrande (1979*c*).
19 cf. Dressler (1970, 1972*b*, 1974*b*); Beaugrande (1978*a*, 1980*e*).
20 This problem was already clear in the critique from Mounin (1963); cf. X.23.
21 This approach has been advocated especially in the work of Yorick Wilks (1972, 1979); the translation component of the Yale group (cf. Goldman 1975; Schank & Abelson 1977; Cullingford 1978) works on comparable principles in its application of knowledge about events and actions to the understanding process.
22 Beaugrande (1978*a*) undertakes to consider some implications of this thesis for literary translating in terms of research on reader phonomenology, e.g. the preservation of polyvalence. A treatment in terms of network coherence can be found in Beaugrande (1980*e*).
23 cf. VII.29-42; IX.8-9; X.13-18.
24 cf. Nickel (ed.) (1971, 1972). At present, contrastive linguistics is in a state of some confusion after the downfall of transformational grammar as the accepted "paradigm". Contrasts can only be made in terms of some linguistic theory or model (cf. Coseriu 1972).
24[a] Ulijn (1980) found that syntactic problems were in fact not as important barriers to comprehension as were semantic, at least in reading a second language.
25 The notions of "access", "control centre", "default", "frame", "goal", "hold stack", "management", "monitoring", "network", "operator", "problem-solving", "search", and "space", for example, are all borrowed from computer science in general and artificial intelligence in particular.
26 The shift away from "facts" toward the procedures for acquiring or demonstrating facts has finally begun in the sciences at large (cf. Stegmüller 1969, 1976; Kuhn 1970; Lakatos 1976; Spinner 1977; Feyerabend 1978). This trend, so long overdue, has proven enormously productive in opening the foundations of sciences to critical discussion at a time when a point of diminishing returns has become noticeable in many fields. For an application to linguistic theory, see Finke (1979); Beaugrande (1981*b*). On a more detailed plane, the same trend is emerging in education (cf. Collins, Warnock, Aiello & Miller 1975; Collins 1977*a*; Brown, Collins & Harris 1978; Papert 1980).

Table of Abbreviations for references

AI: Laboratory or program for artificial intelligence
AI: Artificial Intelligence
AJCLing: American Journal of Computational Linguistics
BBN: Bolt, Beranek & Newman Inc., 50 Moulton St, Cambridge, Massachusetts, 02138
BritJPsy: British Journal of Psychology
BrnStud: Brno Studies in English
CACM: Communications of the Association for Computing Machinery
CanJPsy: Canadian Journal of Psychology
CCC: College Composition and Communication
CLS: Proceedings from the Regional Meeting of the Chicago Linguistic Society
CogPsy: Cognitive Psychology
CogSci: Cognitive Science
CS: Department of computer science(s)
CS-TR: Department of computer science(s) technical report
DisPro: Discourse Processes
FoundLang: Foundations of Language
IJCAI: Proceedings of the International Joint Conference on Artificial Intelligence
IntJAL: International Journal of American Linguistics
IRAL: International Review of Applied Linguistics
ISCS: Institute for Semantic and Cognitive Studies, Castagnola, Switzerland (now at the University of Geneva, Geneva, Switzerland)
JApPsy: Journal of Applied Psychology
JEdPsy: Journal of Educational Psychology
JExPsy: Journal of Experimental Psychology

JGenPsy: Journal of General Psychology
JLing: Journal of Linguistics
JMathPsy: Journal of Mathematical Psychology
JPersSocPsy: Journal of Personality and Social Psychology
JPrag: Journal of Pragmatics
JTWC: Journal of Technical Writing and Communication
JVLVB: Journal of Verbal Learning and Verbal Behaviour
LangSty: Language and Style
LingBer: Linguistische Berichte
LingInq: Linguistic Inquiry
MechTrans: Mechanical Translation
MemCog: Memory and Cognition
PerPsyp: Perception and Psychophysics
PICL: Proceedings of the International Congress of Linguists
PsynSci: Psychonomic Science
PsyR: Psychological Review
PTL: Journal of Descriptive Poetics and Theory of Literature
QJExPsy: Quarterly Journal of Experimental Psychology
RRQ: Reading Research Quarterly
SborPra: Sborník Pracť Filozofické Fakulty Brněnské Univerzity: Řada Jazykovědena
SRI: Stanford Research Institute, 333 Ravenswood Ave, Menlo Park, California, 94025
TINLAP-2: *Theoretical Issues in Natural Language Processing – 2* New York: Association for Computing Machinery, P.O. Box 12105 Church Street Station, New York, NY 10249
TR: Technical report
TraLing: Travaux Linguistiques de Prague

References

For the convenience of readers in different disciplines, we give the first names of scholars, both here and in the Index of Names. All abbreviations are explained on pp. 223–4.

ABELSON, ROBERT (1975). 'Concepts for representing mundane reality in plans'. In Bobrow & Collins (eds.), 273–309

ADAMS, MARILYN & COLLINS, ALLAN (1979). 'A schema-theoretic view of reading'. In Freedle (ed.), 1–22

ALLEN, JAMES (1979). *A Plan-based Approach to Speech Act Recognition*. Toronto: University of Toronto CS-TR 131/79

ANDERSON, JOHN (1976). *Language, Memory, and Thought*. Hillsdale, N.J.: Erlbaum

ANDERSON, RICHARD (1977). 'The notion of schemata and the educational enterprise'. In Anderson, Spiro & Montague (eds.) 415–31

ANDERSON, RICHARD, SPIRO, RAND & MONTAGUE, WILLIAM (eds.) (1977) *Schooling and the Acquisition of Knowledge*. Hillsdale, N.J.: Erlbaum

APELTAUER, ERNST (1977). 'Drohen'. In Sprengel, Konrad, et al. (eds.) *Semantik und Pragmatik*. Tübingen: Niemeyer, 187–98

AQUINO, MILAGROS (1969). 'The validity of the Miller-Coleman readability scale'. *RRQ*, 4, 342–57

AUSTIN, JOHN (1962). *How to Do Things with Words*. London: Oxford

AUSUBEL, DAVID (1960). 'The use of advance organizers in the learning and retention of meaningful verbal material'. *JEdPsy*, 51, 267–72

BALLMER, THOMAS (1975). *Sprachrekonstruktionssysteme*. Kronberg: Scriptor

BARTLETT, FREDERICK (1932). *Remembering*. Cambridge, England: Cambridge

BAUMAN, RICHARD & SCHERZER, JOEL (eds.) (1974). *Explorations in the Ethnography of Speaking*. London: Cambridge

BEAUGRANDE, ROBERT DE (1981*a*). 'Design criteria for process models of reading'. *RRQ*, 16

BEAUGRANDE, ROBERT DE (1981*b*). 'Linguistic theory and meta-theory for a science of texts'. *Text*, 1

BEAUGRANDE, ROBERT DE (1980*a*). *Text, Discourse, and Process*. Norwood, N.J.: Ablex; London: Longman

BEAUGRANDE, ROBERT DE (1980*b*). 'Modelling cognitive processes in research on texts.' For *DisPro*

BEAUGRANDE, ROBERT DE (1980*c*). 'The status of texts in reading research'. In Tierney, Robert, Anders, Patricia & Mitchell, Judy (eds.), *Understanding a Reader's Understanding*. In press

BEAUGRANDE, ROBERT DE (1980*d*). 'The pragmatics of discourse planning'. *JPrag*, 4, 15–42

BEAUGRANDE, ROBERT DE (1980*e*). 'Towards a semiotics of literary translating'. In Wilss, Wolfram (ed.), *Semiotik und Übersetzen*. Tübingen: Narr, 23–42

BEAUGRANDE, ROBERT DE (1979*a*). 'Text and sentence in discourse planning'. In Petöfi (ed.), 467–94

BEAUGRANDE, ROBERT DE (1979*b*). 'Theoretical foundations for the automatic production and processing of technical reports.' *JTWC*, 9,239–68

BEAUGRANDE, ROBERT DE (1979*c*). 'Toward a general theory of creativity'. *Poetics*, 8, 269–306

BEAUGRANDE, ROBERT DE (1979*d*). 'A rhetorical theory of audience response'. In Brown, Robert & Steinmann, Martin (eds.), 9–20

BEAUGRANDE, ROBERT DE (1979*e*). 'Psychology and composition'. *CCC*, 30, 50–57

BEAUGRANDE, ROBERT DE (1978*a*). *Factors in a Theory of Poetic Translating*. Assen: van Gorcum

BEAUGRANDE, ROBERT DE (1978*b*). 'Information, expectation, and processing'. *Poetics*, 7, 3–44

BEAUGRANDE, ROBERT DE (1978*c*). 'Linguistic theory and composition'. *CCC*, 29, 134–40

BEAUGRANDE, ROBERT DE (1978*d*). 'Semantic evaluation of grammar in poetry'. *PTL*, 3, 315–25

BEAUGRANDE, ROBERT DE (ed.) (1980). *European Approaches to the Study of Text and Discourse*. *Discourse Processes*, 4, vol. I (special issue)

BEAUGRANDE, ROBERT DE & COLBY, BENJAMIN (1979). 'Narrative models of action and interaction'. *CogSci*, 3, 46–66

BEAUGRANDE, ROBERT DE & MILLER, GENEVIEVE (1980). 'Processing models for children's story comprehension'. *Poetics,* 9, 181–201

BEERBOHM, MAX (1958). *Selected Essays.* London: Heinemann

BELLERT, IRENE (1970). 'On a condition of the coherence of texts'. *Semiotica,* 2, 335–63

BENCHLEY, ROBERT (1954). *The Benchley Roundup.* New York: Harper and Row

BENEŠ, EDUARD (1968). 'On two aspects of functional sentence perspective'. *TraLing,* 3, 267–74

BERNSTEIN, JARED & PIKE, KENNETH (1977). 'The emic structure of individuals in relation to dialogue'. In van Dijk & Petöfi (eds.), 1–10

BERRY, MARGARET (1977). *Introduction to Systemic Linguistics.* London: Batsford

BIASCI, CLAUDIA & FRITSCHE, JOHANNES (eds.) (1978). *Texttheorie–Textrepräsentation: Theoretische Grundlagen der kanonischen sinnsemantischen Repräsentation von Texten.* Hamburg: Buske

BIERWISCH, MANFRED (1966). 'Strukturalismus: Geschichte, Probleme, Methoden'. *Kursbuch,* 5, 77–152. Also in Ihwe (ed.) (1971), 19–90

BIERWISCH, MANFRED (1965*a*). 'Rezension zu Z.S. Harris, "Discourse Analysis"'. *Linguistics,* 13, 61–73

BIERWISCH, MANFRED (1965*b*). 'Poetik und Linguistik'. In Kreuzer, Helmut & Gunzenhäuser, Rul (eds.), *Mathematik und Dichtung.* Munich: Nymphenburger, 46–66

BLOM, JAN-PETTER & GUMPERZ, JOHN (1972). 'Social meaning in linguistic structures: code switching in Norway'. In Gumperz & Hymes (eds.), 407–34

BLOOMFIELD, LEONARD (1933). *Language.* New York: Holt

BLUMER, HERBERT (ed.) (1969). *Symbolic Interactionism.* Englewood Cliffs, N.J.: Prentice-Hall

BOBROW, DANIEL & COLLINS, ALLAN (eds.) (1975). *Representation and Understanding: Studies in Cognitive Science.* New York: Academic

BOBROW, DANIEL & FRASER, BRUCE (1969). 'An augmented state transition network analysis procedure'. *First IJCAI,* 557

BOBROW, DANIEL & WINOGRAD, TERRY (1977). 'An overview of KRL: A knowledge representation language'. *CogSci,* 1, 3–46

BOBROW, ROBERT (1978). 'The RUS System'. In Webber, Bonnie & Bobrow, Robert, *Research in Natural Language Understanding.* Cambridge: BBN TR 3878

BOCK, WOLFGANG (1979). *Wort-, Satz-, Textverarbeitung.* Stuttgart: Kohlhammer

BOLINGER, DWIGHT (1970).'The meaning of "do so"'. *LingInq,* 1, 140–44

BOLINGER, DWIGHT (1968). 'Judgements of grammaticality'. *Lingua,* 21, 34–40

BOLINGER, DWIGHT (1965). 'The atomization of meaning'. *Language,* 41, 555–73

BOUTON, LAWRENCE (1970). 'Do so: do+adverb'. In Sadock, Jerrold & Vanek, Anthony (eds.), *Studies Presented to R.B. Lees.* Edmonton, Alberta: Linguistic Research Institute, 17–38

BOWER, GORDON (1976). 'Experiments on story understanding and recall'. *QJExPsy,* 28, 511–34

BRACHMAN, RONALD (1978). *A Structural Paradigm for Representing Knowledge.* Cambridge: BBN TR 3605

BRANSFORD, JOHN, BARCLAY, RICHARD & FRANKS, JEFFREY (1972). 'Sentence memory: A constructive versus interpretative approach'. *CogPsy,* 3, 193–209

BRANSFORD, JOHN, & FRANKS, JEFFREY (1971). 'Abstraction of linguistic ideas'. *CogPsy,* 2, 331–50

BRAZIL, DAVID (1975). *Discourse Intonation.* Birmingham: English Langage Research (Discourse Analysis Monographs, 1)

BREMOND, CLAUDE (1964). 'Le message narratif'. *Communications,* 4, 4–32

BRESNAN, JOAN (1971). 'A note on the notion "identity of sense anaphora"'. *LingInq,* 2, 589–97

BROWN, JOHN SEELY, COLLINS, ALLAN & HARRIS, GREGORY (1978). 'Artificial intelligence and learning strategies'. In O'Neill, Harry (ed.), *Learning Strategies.* New York: Academic, 107–39

BROWN, ROBERT & STEINMANN, MARTIN (eds.) (1979). *Rhetoric 1978: An Interdisciplinary Conference.* Minneapolis: University of Minnesota Center for Advanced Studies in Language, Style, and Literary Theory

BROWN, ROGER (1973). *A First Language: The Early Stages.* Cambridge: Harvard

BROWN, ROGER & GILMAN, ALBERT (1960). 'The pronouns of power and solidarity'. In Sebeok (ed.), 253–76

BRUCE, BERTRAM (1977). *Plans and Social Actions.* Cambridge: BBN TR 3550

BRUCE, BERTRAM (1975). *Belief Systems and Language Understanding.* Cambridge: BBN TR 2973

BRUCE, BERTRAM (1972). 'A model for temporal references and its application in a question answering program.' *AI,* 3, 1–25

BRUCE, BERTRAM, COLLINS, ALLAN, RUBIN, ANDEE & GENTNER, DEDRE (1978). *A Cognitive Science Approach to Writing.* Cambridge: BBN TR 3816

BRUCE, BERTRAM & NEWMAN, DENIS (1978). 'Interacting plans'. *CogSci,* 195–234

BULLWINKLE, CANDACE (1977). 'Levels of complexity in discourse for anaphora disambiguation and speech act interpretation'. *Fifth IJCAI*, 43–9

BURTON, RICHARD (1976). *Semantic Grammar: An Engineering Technique for Constructing Natural Language Understanding Systems* Cambridge: BBN TR 3453

CAMARAZZA, ALFONSO, GROBER, ELLEN, CATHERINE & YATES, JACK (1977). 'Comprehension of anaphoric pronouns'. *JVLVB*, 16, 601–9

CARBONELL, JAIME JR. (1978). 'Intentionality and human conversations'. *TINLAP-2*, 141–8

CARNAP, RUDOLF (1947). *Meaning and Necessity*. Chicago: University of Chicago Press

CARROLL, LEWIS (1960). *The Annotated Alice: Alice's Adventures in Wonderland and Through the Looking-Glass*. New York: Potter

CATFORD, JOHN (1964). *A Linguistic Theory of Translation*. London: Oxford

CHAFE, WALLACE (1976). 'Givenness, contrastiveness, definiteness, subjects, topics, and point of view'. In Li (ed.), 27–55

CHAFE, WALLACE (1970). *Meaning and the Structure of Language*. Chicago: University of Chicago Press

CHANSLOR, J.W. (1969). 'Treasure from the Sea'. In *Science and the Sea*. Washington, D.C.: U.S. Naval Oceanographic Office, 9–16

CHAPIN, PAUL (1970). 'Samoan pronominalization'. *Language*, 46, 366–78

CHARNIAK, EUGENE (1976). 'Inference and knowledge'. In Charniak & Wilks (eds), 1–21 and 129–54

CHARNIAK, EUGENE (1975*a*). *A Brief on Case*. Castagnola: ISCS

CHARNIAK, EUGENE (1975*b*). *Organization and Inference in a Frame-Like System of Common-Sense Knowledge*. Catagnola: ISCS

CHARNIAK, EUGENE & WILKS, YORICK (eds.) (1976). *Computational Semantics: An Introduction to Artificial Intelligence and Natural Language Communication*. Amsterdam: North Holland

CHATMAN, SEYMOUR & LEVIN, SAMUEL (eds.) (1967). *Essays on the Language of Literature*. Boston: Houghton Mifflin

CHOMSKY, NOAM (1965). *Aspects of the Theory of Syntax*. Cambridge: MIT Press

CHRISTALLER, THOMAS & METZING, DIETER (eds.) (1979). *Augmented Transition Network Grammatiken*. Berlin: Einhorn

CHRISTENSEN, FRANCIS (1967). *Notes toward a New Rhetoric*. New York: Harper & Row

CICOUREL, AARON, JENNINGS, KENNETH, JENNINGS, SYBILLYN, LEITER, KENNETH, MACKAY, ROBERT, MEHAN, HUGH & ROTH, DAVID (1974). *Language Use and School Performance*. New York: Academic

CLARK, HERBERT & CHASE, WILLIAM (1974). 'Perceptual coding strategies in the formation and verification of descriptions'. *MemCog,* 2, 101–111

CLARK, HERBERT & CLARK, EVE (1977). *Language and Psychology*. New York: Harcourt, Brace, and Jovanovich

CLARK, HERBERT & CLARK, EVE (1968). 'Semantic distinctions among memory for complex sentences'. *QJExPsy,* 20, 129–38

COHEN, PHILIP (1978). *On Knowing What to Say: Planning Speech Acts.* Toronto: University of Toronto CS-TR 118

COLBY, BENJAMIN (1973*b*). 'Analytical procedures in eidochronic study'. *Journal of American Folklore,* 86, 14–24

COLBY, BENJAMIN (1973*a*). 'A partial grammar of Eskimo folktales.' *American Anthropologist,* 75, 645–62

COLBY, BENJAMIN (1966). 'Ethnographic semantics'. *Current Anthropology,* 7, 3–32

COLBY, KENNETH & PARKINSON, RICHARD (1974). 'Pattern-matching rules for the recognition of natural language dialogue expressions'. *AJCLing,* 1, 1–70

COLE, PETER (ed.) (1978). *Syntax and Semantics IX: Pragmatics*. New York: Academic

COLE, PETER & MORGAN, JERRY (eds.) (1975). *Syntax and Semantics III: Speech Acts*. New York: Academic

COLE, PETER & SADOCK, JERROLD (eds.) (1977). *Syntax and Semantics VIII: Grammatical Relations*. New York: Academic

COLLINS, ALLAN (1978). 'Fragments of a theory of human plausible reasoning'. *TINLAP*-2, 194–201

COLLINS, ALLAN (1977*a*). 'Processes in acquiring knowledge'. In Anderson, Spiro & Montague (eds), 339–63

COLLINS, ALLAN (1977*b*). 'Why cognitive science.' *CogSci,* 1, 1–2

COLLINS, ALLAN & LOFTUS, ELIZABETH (1975). 'A spreading-activation theory of semantic processing'. *PsyR,* 82, 407–428

COLLINS, ALLAN & QUILLIAN, ROSS (1972). 'How to make a language user'. In Tulving & Donaldson (eds.), 309–351

COLLINS, ALLAN, WARNOCK, ELEANOR, AIELLO, NELLEKE & MILLER, MARK (1975). 'Reasoning from incomplete knowledge'. In Bobrow & Collins (eds.), 383–415

CONAN DOYLE, ARTHUR (1967). *The Annotated Sherlock Holmes*. New York: Potter

COPPEE, FRANÇOIS (1891). *Ten Tales.* Freeport, N.Y.: Books for Libraries

CORBETT, EDWARD (1971). *Classical Rhetoric for the Modern Student.* New York: Oxford

COSERIU, EUGENIO (1972). Über Leistung und Grenzen der kontrastiven Grammatik'. In Nickel (ed.), 39–58

COSERIU, EUGENIO (1967). *Theoría del Lenguaje y Lingüística General*. Madrid: Gredos

COSERIU, EUGENIO (1955–6). 'Determinación y entorno'. *Romanistisches. Jahrbuch*, 7, 29-54. Also in Coseriu (1967), 282-323

COULTHARD, MALCOLM (1977). *An Introduction to Discourse Analysis*. London: Longman

CRAIK, FERGUS & LOCKHART, RICHARD (1972). 'A framework for memory research'. *JVLVB*, 11, 671–84

CROWDER, ROBERT & MORTON, JOHN (1969). 'Precategorical acoustic storage'. *PerPsyp*, 5, 365–73

CRYMES, RUTH (1968). *Some Systems of Substitution Relations in Modern English*. The Hague: Mouton

CRYSTAL, DAVID (1971). *Linguistics*. Harmondsworth: Penguin

CRYSTAL, DAVID (1969). *Prosodic Systems and Intonation in English*. Cambridge, England: Cambridge UP

CULLINGFORD, RICHARD (1978). *Script Application: Computer Understanding of Newspaper Stories*. New Haven: Yale CS-TR 116

CUMMINGS, EDWARD ESTLIN (1972). 'Anyone lived in a pretty how town'. In *Complete Poems*. New York: Harcourt, Brace, and Jovanovich, 515

DAHL, ÖSTEN (ed.) (1974). *Topic and Comment, Contextual Boundness, and Focus*. Hamburg: Buske

DANEŠ, FRANTIŠEK (ed.) (1974). *Papers on Functional Sentence Perspective*. Prague: Academia

DANEŠ, FRANTIŠEK & VIEHWEGER, DIETER (eds.) (1976). *Probleme der Textgrammatik*. Berlin: Akademie der Wissenschaften

DANKS, JOSEPH & GLUCKSBERG, SAM (1971). 'Psychological scaling of adjective orders'. *JVLVB*, 10, 63–7

DASCAL, MARCELO & MARGALIT, AVISHAI (1974). 'Text grammars: A critical view'. In Projektgruppe Textlinguistik Konstanz (eds), *Probleme und Perspektiven der neueren textgrammatischen Forschung I*. Hamburg: Buske, 81–120

DEEPING, WARWICK (1930). *The Short Stories of Warwick Deeping*. London: Cassell

DESOTO, CLINTON, LONDON, MARVIN & HANDEL, STEPHEN (1965). 'Social reasoning and spatial paralogic'. *JPersSocPsy*, 2, 513–21

DICKENS, CHARLES (1947). *The Posthumous Papers of the Pickwick Club*. London: Oxford

DIJK, TEUN VAN (1979*a*). *The Structures and Functions of Discourse*. Lectures at the University of Puerto Rico, Rio Piedras

DIJK, TEUN VAN (1979*b*). *Macro-structures*. Hillsdale, N.J.: Erlbaum

DIJK, TEUN VAN (1978). *Facts: The Organization of Propositions in Discourse Comprehension*. Amsterdam: University of Amsterdam Institute for General Literary Studies

DIJK, TEUN VAN (1977*a*). *Text and Context*. London: Longman

DIJK, TEUN VAN (1977*b*). 'Connectives in text grammar'. In van Dijk & Petöfi (eds.), 11–63

DIJK, TEUN VAN (1977*c*). 'Acceptability in context'. In Greenbaum (ed.), 39–61

DIJK, TEUN VAN (1972*a*). *Some Aspects of Text Grammars*. The Hague: Mouton

DIJK, TEUN VAN (1972*b*). 'On the foundations of poetics: Methodological prolegomena to a generative grammar of literary texts'. *Poetics*, 1, 89–123

DIJK, TEUN VAN (1969). 'Sémantique structurale et analyse thématique'. *Lingua*, 23, 28–53

DIJK, TEUN VAN, IHWE, JENS, PETÖFI, JÁNOS & RIESER, HANNES (1972). *Zur Bestimmung narrativer Strukturen auf der Grundlage von Textgrammatiken*. Hamburg: Buske

DIJK, TEUN VAN & PETÖFI, JANOS (eds.) (1977). *Grammars and Descriptions*. Berlin: de Gruyter

DIJK, TEUN VAN & KINTSCH, WALTER (1978). 'Cognitive psychology and discourse: Recalling and summarizing stories'. In Dressler (ed.), 61–80

DIK, SIMON (1968). *Coordination*. Amsterdam: North Holland

DILLON, GEORGE (1978). *Language Processing and the Reading of Literature*. Bloomington: Indiana UP

DITTMAR, NORBERT (1976). *A Critical Survey of Sociolinguistics*. New York: St. Martin's

DOLEŽEL, LUBOMIR & BAILEY, RICHARD (eds.) (1969). *Statistics and Style*. New York: American Elsevier

DOUGHERTY, RAY (1970-1). 'A grammar of coordinate conjoined structures'. *Language*, 46, 850–98; and 47, 298–339

DOUGHERTY, RAY (1969). 'An interpretive theory of pronominal reference'. *FoundLang*, 5, 488–519

DOWTY, DAVID (1972). *Studies in the Logic of Verb Aspect and Time Reference in English*. Austin: University of Texas

DRESHER, ELAN & HORNSTEIN, NORBERT (1976). 'On some supposed contributions of artificial intelligence to the scientific study of language'. *Cognition*, 4, 321–98

DRESSLER, WOLFGANG (1979*a*). 'Zum Verhältnis von Wortbildung und Texlinguistik'. In Petöfi (ed.)

DRESSLER, WOLFGANG (1979*b*). *Naturalness as a Principle in Genetic and Typological Linguistics*. Vienna: University of Vienna Institute for Language Studies

DRESSLER, WOLFGANG (1978). 'Aspekte der Textlinguistik'. In *Germanistik II*. Vienna: Österreichischer Bundesverlag, 23–37

DRESSLER, WOLFGANG (1977). 'Elements of a polycentristic theory of word formation'. *Wiener linguistische Gazette*, 15, 13–32

DRESSLER, WOLFGANG (1974*a*). 'Funktionelle Satzperspektive und Texttheorie'. In Danes (ed.), 87–105

DRESSLER, WOLFGANG (1974*b*). 'Der Beitrag der Textlinguistik zur Ubersetzungstheorie'. In Völker Kapp (ed.), *Übersetzer und Dolmetscher*. Heidelberg: Quelle and Meyer, 61–71

DRESSLER, WOLFGANG (1972*a*). *Einführung in die Textlinguistik*. Tübingen: Niemeyer

DRESSLER, WOLFGANG (1972*b*). 'Textgrammatische Invarianz in Übersetzungen?' In Gülich & Raible (eds.), 98–106

DRESSLER, WOLFGANG (1970). 'Textsyntax und Übersetzung'. In Hartmann, Peter & Vernay, Henri (eds.), *Sprachwissenschaft und Ubersetzen*. Munich: Hueber, 64–71

DRESSLER, WOLFGANG (ed.) (1978). *Current Trends in Text Linguistics*. Berlin: de Gruyter

DRESSLER, WOLFGANG & SCHMIDT, SIEGFRIED (eds) (1973). *Textlinguistik: Kommentierte Bibliographie*. Munich: Fink

DRESSLER, WOLFGANG & STARK, JACQUELINE (1976). 'Störungen der Textkompetenz bei Aphasie'. In Meid, Wolfgang & Heller, Karin (eds.), *Textlinguistik und Semantik*. Innsbruck: Institut für Sprachwissenschaft, 265–68

DUNDES, ALAN (1962). 'From etic to emic units in the structural study of folktales'. *Journal of American Folklore*, 75, 95–105

EDMONSON, JERRY (1976). 'Semantics, games, and anaphoric chains'. In Bartsch, Renate et al. (eds.). *Amsterdam Papers on Formal Grammars*. Amsterdam: University of Amsterdam

EIKMEYER, HANS-JÜRGEN & RIESER, HANNES (1979). *Vagheitstheorie*. Bielefeld: University of Bielefeld Faculty of Linguistics

EISENSTADT, MARC & KAREEV, YAAKOV (1975). 'Aspects of human problem solving: The use of internal representations'. In Norman, Donald et al., *Explorations in Cognition*. San Francisco: Freeman, 308–346

ENGEL, DOROTHEA (1977). *Textexperimente mit Aphatikern*. Tübingen: Narr

ENKVIST, NILS-ERIK (1973). *Linguistic Stylistics*. The Hague: Mouton

ERLICH, VICTOR (1955). *Russian Formalism*. The Hague: Mouton

ERNST, GEORGE & NEWELL, ALLAN (1969). *GPS: A Case Study in Problem Solving*. New York: Academic

ERVIN-TRIPP, SUSAN (1972). 'On sociolinguistic rules: Alternation and co-occurrence'. In Gumperz & Hymes (eds), 213–50

FAHLMAN, SCOTT (1979). *NETL: A System for Representing and Using Real-World Knowledge*. Cambridge: MIT Press

FAHLMAN, SCOTT (1977). *A System for Representing and Using Real-World Knowledge*. Cambridge: MIT AI Laboratory TR 450 (now Falhman 1979)

FEYERABEND, PAUL (1978). *Der wissenschaftstheoretische Realismus und die Autorität der Wissenschaften*. Brunswick: Vieweg

FIGGE, UDO (1971). 'Syntagmatik, Distribution, und Text'. In Stempel (ed.), 159–74

FILLMORE, CHARLES (1977). 'The case for case reopened.' In Cole & Sadock (eds.), 59–81

FILLMORE, CHARLES (1975). 'An alternative to checklist theories of meaning'. In *Proceedings of the First Annual Meeting of the Berkeley Linguistic Society*. Berkeley: University of California Institute of Human Learning, 123–31

FILLMORE, CHARLES (1968). 'The case for case'. In Bach, Emmon & Harms, Robert (eds.), *Universals in Linguistic Theory*. New York: Holt, Rinehart, and Winston, 1–88

FINDLER, NICHOLAS (ed.) (1979). *Associative Networks: Representation and Use of Knowledge in Computers*. New York: Academic

FINKE, PETER (1979). *Grundlagen einer linguistischen Theorie: Empirie und Begründung in der Sprachwissenschaft*. Brunswick: Vieweg

FIRBAS, JAN (1975). 'On the thematic and the non-thematic section of the sentence'. In Ringbom, Håkon, et al. (eds.) *Style and Text: Studies Presented to Nils-Erik Enkvist*. Stockholm: Skriptor, 317–34

FIRBAS, JAN (1974). 'Some aspects of the Czechoslovak approach to problems of functional sentence perspective'. In Danes (ed.), 11–37

FIRBAS, JAN (1968). 'On the prosodic features of the modern English finite verb as means of functional sentence perspective'. *BrnStud*, 7, 11–47

FIRBAS, JAN (1966). 'On defining the theme in functional sentence analysis'. *TraLing*, 2, 267–80

FIRBAS, JAN (1964). 'Non-thematic subjects in contemporary English'. *TraLing*, 1, 239–56

FIRBAS, JAN (1962). 'Notes on the function of the sentence in the act of communication'. *SborPra*, 9, 133–47

FIRBAS, JAN & GOLKOVÁ, EVA (1976). *An Analytical Bibliography of Czechoslovak Studies in Functional Sentence Perspective*. Brno: Purkyna University Faculty of Philosophy

FIRTH, JOHN (1957). 'A synopsis of linguistic theory'. In *Studies in Linguistic Analysis*. Oxford: Blackwell, 1–32

FISHMAN, JOSHUA (1972). 'Domains and the relationship between micro- and macrosociolinguistics'. In Gumperz & Hymes (eds.), 435–53

FLOWER, LINDA & HAYES, JOHN RICHARD (1979). *A Process Model of Composition*. Pittsburgh: Carnegie-Mellon University Document Design Project TR 1

FODOR, JERRY & GARRETT, MERRILL (1967). 'Some syntactic determinants of sentential complexity'. *PerPsyp*, 2, 289–96

FOWLER, ROGER (1977). 'Cohesive, progressive, and localizing aspects of text structure'. In van Dijk & Petöfi (eds.), 64–84

FRAKE, CHARLES (1972). 'Struck by speech: The Yakan concept of litigation'. In Gumperz & Hymes (eds.), 106–29

FRANCK, DOROTHEA (1979). *Grammatik und Konversation: Stilistische Pragmatik des Dialogs und die Bedeutung deutscher Modalpartikeln*. Amsterdam: University of Amsterdam Faculty of Letters

FREDERIKSEN, CARL (1977). 'Semantic processing unit in understanding text'. In Freedle (ed.), 57–88

FREEDLE, ROY (ed.) (1979). *New Directions in Discourse Processing*. Norwood, N.J.: Ablex

FREEDLE, ROY (ed.) (1977). *Discourse Production and Comprehension*. Norwood, N.J.: Ablex

FREEDLE, ROY & HALE, GORDON (1979). 'Acquisition of new comprehension schemata for expository prose by transfer of a narrative schema'. In Freedle (ed.), 121–35

FREGE, GOTTLOB (1892). 'Über Sinn und Bedeutung'. *Zeitschrift für Philosophie und philosophische Kritik*, 100, 25–50

FRIED, ERICH (1975). *Fast alles Mögliche*. Berlin: Wagenbach

FRIES, UDO (1975). *Studien zur Textlinguistik: Frage- und Antwortsätze*. Vienna: Braumüller

FRIES, UDO (1972). 'Textlinguistik'. *Linguistik und Didaktik*, 7, 219–34

FROST, ROBERT (1969). *Poetry of Robert Frost*. New York: Holt, Rinehart, and Winston

GARVIN, PAUL (ed.) (1964). *A Prague School Reader on Aesthetics, Literary Structure, and Style*. Washington, D.C.: Georgetown UP

GINDIN, SERGEI (1978). 'Contributions to text linguistics in the Soviet Union'. In Dressler (ed.), 261–74

GIVÓN, TALMY (1978). 'Negation in language: Pragmatics, function, ontology'. In Cole (ed.), 69–112

GLEITMAN, LILA (1965). 'Coordinating conjunctions in English'. *Language*, 41, 260–93

GLINZ, HANS (1973). *Textanalyse und Verstehenstheorie*. Wiesbaden: Athenaion

GOFFMAN, ERVING (1974). *Frame Analysis*. New York: Harper and Row

GOLDMAN, NEIL (1975). 'Conceptual generation'. In Schank et al., 289–371

GOLDMAN, NEIL, BALZER, ROBERT & WILE, DAVID (1977). *The Inference of Domain Structure from Informal Process Descriptions*. Marina del Rey: University of Southern California Information Sciences Institute TR 77–64

GOLDSMITH, OLIVER (1773). *She Stoops to Conquer*. London: Newberry

GOLDSTEIN, IRA & PAPERT, SEYMOUR (1977). 'Artificial intelligence, language, and the study of knowledge'. *CogSci*, 1, 84–123

GOMULICKI, BRONISLAW (1956). 'Recall as an abstractive process'. *Acta Psychologica*, 12, 77–94

GOODGLASS, HAROLD & BLUMSTEIN SHEILA (1973). *Psycholinguistics and Aphasia*. Baltimore: John Hopkins UP

GOODMAN, KENNETH & BURKE, CAROLYNE (1973). *Theoretically Based Studies of Patterns of Miscues in Oral Reading Performance*. Washington, D.C.: Department of Health, Education, and Welfare

GOVINDA LAMA ANAGARIKA (1976). *Creative Meditation and Multi-Dimensional Consciousness*. Wheaton, Ill.: Theosophical Publishing

GREEN, GEORGIA (1968). 'On "too" and "either" and not just "too" and "either" either'. *Fourth CLS*, 22–39

GREENBAUM, SIDNEY (1977). 'Introduction'. In Greenbaum (ed.), 1–11

GREENBAUM, SIDNEY (1973). 'Informant elicitation of data on syntactic variation'. *Lingua*, 31, 201–12

GREENBAUM, SIDNEY (ed.) (1977). *Acceptability in Language*. The Hague: Mouton

GREIMAS, ALGIRDAS (1967). 'La structure des actants du récit: Essai d'approche générative'. *Word*, 23, 221–38

GREIMAS, ALGIRDAS (1966). *Sémantique structurale: Recherches de méthode*. Paris: Larousse

GRICE, PAUL (1978). 'Further notes on logic and conversation'. In Cole (ed.), 113–27

GRICE, PAUL (1975). 'Logic and conversation'. In Cole & Morgan (eds.), 41–58

GRICE, PAUL (1971). 'Meaning'. In Steinberg & Jakobovits (eds.), 53–9

GRIMES, JOSEPH (1975). *The Thread of Discourse*. The Hague: Mouton

GRIMES, JOSEPH (1964). *Huichol Syntax*. The Hague: Mouton

GRIMES, JOSEPH (ed.) (1978). *Papers on Discourse*. Dallas: Summer Institute of Linguistics

GROEBEN, NORBERT (1978). *Die Verständlichkeit von Unterrichtstexten*. Münster: Aschendorff

GROSSE, ERNST-ULRICH (1978). 'French Structuralist views on narrative grammar'. In Dressler (ed.), 155–73

GROSSE, ERNST-ULRICH (1976). *Texttypen: Linguistik nichtliterarischer Kommunikation*. Freiburg: University of Freiburg dissertation

GROSSMAN, ROBIN, SAN, JAMES & VANCE, TIMOTHY (eds.) (1975). *Papers of the Parasession on Functionalism*. Chicago: Chicago Linguistic Society

GROSZ, BARBARA (1977). *The Representation and Use of Focus in Dialogue Understanding*. Menlo Park: SRI AI-TR 151

GÜLICH, ELISABETH (1970). *Makrosyntax der Gliederungssignale im gesprochenen Französisch*. Munich: Fink

GÜLICH, ELISABETH & RAIBLE, WOLFGANG (1977). *Linguistische Textmodelle*. Munich: Fink

GÜLICH, ELISABETH & RAIBLE, WOLFGANG (eds.) (1972). *Textsorten*. Frankfurt: Athenäum

GUMPERZ, JOHN & HYMES, DELL (eds.) (1972). *Directions in Sociolinguistics: The Ethnography of Communication*. New York: Holt, Rinehart, and Winston

GUNTER, RICHARD (1963). 'Elliptical sentences in American English'. *Lingua*, 12, 137–50

HALLIDAY, MICHAEL (1976). *System and Function in Language*. London: Oxford

HALLIDAY, MICHAEL (1967-8). 'Notes on transitivity and theme in English'. *Journal of Linguistics*, 3, 37–81; 3, 199–244; and 4, 179–215

HALLIDAY, MICHAEL (1967). *Intonation and Grammar in British English*. The Hague: Mouton

HALLIDAY, MICHAEL (1964). 'The linguistic study of literary texts'. In Lunt (ed.), 302–307

HALLIDAY, MICHAEL & HASAN, RUQAIYA (1976). *Cohesion in English*. London: Longman

HANKAMER, JORGE & SAG, IVAN (1976). 'Deep and surface anaphora'. *LingInq*, 7, 391–428

HANSEN-LOVE, AAGE (1978). *Der russische Formalismus: Rekonstruktion seiner Entwicklung aus dem Prinzip der Verfremdung*. Vienna: Österreichische Akademie der Wissenschaften

HARDY, THOMAS (1977). *Wessex Tales and a Group of Noble Dames*. London: Macmillan

HARRIS, ZELLIG (1963). *Discourse Analysis Reprints*. The Hague: Mouton

HARRIS, ZELLIG (1952). 'Discourse analysis'. *Language*, 28, 1–30 and 474–94

HARTMANN, PETER (1979). 'Text und Satz'. In Petöfi (ed.)

HARTMANN, PETER (1975). 'Textlinguistische Tendenzen in der Sprachwissenschaft'. *Folio Linguistica*, 8, 1–49

HARTMANN, PETER (1970). *Aufgaben und Perspektiven der Linguistik*. Konstanz: University of Konstanz Press

HARTMANN, PETER (1963*a*). *Theorie der Grammatik*. The Hague: Mouton

HARTMANN, PETER (1963*b*). *Theorie der Sprachwissenschaft*. Assen: van Gorcum

HARWEG, ROLAND (1978). 'Substitutional text linguistics'. In Dressler (ed.), 247–60

HARWEG, ROLAND (1974). 'Textlinguistik'. In Koch, Walter (ed.), *Perspektiven der Linguistik II*. Stuttgart: Kroner, 88–116

HARWEG, ROLAND (1970). 'Phrasale "und"-Koordination in der generativen Grammatik'. *Zeitschrift für Phonetik*, 23, 192–214

HARWEG, ROLAND (1968). *Pronomina und Textkonstitution*. Munich: Fink

HASAN, RUQAIYA (1968). *Grammatical Cohesion in Spoken and Written English*. London: Longman

HASKELL, JOCELYN (1973). 'In search of the German pro-verb'. *Language Sciences*, 25, 41–5

HAYES, PHILIP (1977). *Some Association-Based Techniques for Lexical Disambiguation by Machine*. Rochester: University of Rochester CS-TR 25

HAYES-ROTH, BARBARA & HAYES-ROTH, FREDERICK (1977). 'The prominence of lexical information in memory representations of meaning'. *JVLVB*, 16, 119–36

HEGER, KLAUS (1976). *Monem, Wort, Satz, und Text*. Tübingen: Niemeyer

HEIDER, FRITZ (1958). *The Psychology of Interpersonal Relations*. New York: Wiley

HEIDOLPH, KARL-ERICH (1966). 'Kontextbeziehungen zwischen Sätzen in einer generativen Grammatik'. *Kybernetika*, 2, 274–81

HELBIG, GERHARD (1974). *Geschichte der neueren Sprachwissenschaft*. Hamburg; Rowohlt

HENDRICKS, WILLIAM (1969). 'Three models for the description of poetry'. *JLing*, 5, 1–22

HERINGER, JAMES (1970). 'Research on quantifier-negative idiolects'. *Sixth CLS*, 287–96

HESS, HELGA (1965). 'Zur Psychologie des Gedächntnisses IV: Determination und Behalten sinnvollen sprachlichen Materials bei Berücksichtigung von gestörtem Kontext'. *Zeitschrift für Psychologie*, 80, 152–70

HIRSCH, ERIC DONALD (1977). *The Philosophy of Composition*. Chicago: University of Chicago Press

HIRSCH, ERIC DONALD (1975). 'Stylistics and synonymy'. *Critical Inquiry*, 1, 559–79

HOBBS, JERRY (1979). 'Coherence and co-reference'. *CogSci*, 3, 67–90

HOBBS, JERRY (1976). *A Computational Approach to Discourse Analysis*. New York: City University of New York CS-TR 76–2

HOLLAN, JAMES (1975). 'Features and semantic memory: Set-theoretical or network model?' *PsyR*, 82, 154–5

HÖRMANN, HANS (1976). *Meinen und Verstehen*. Frankfurt: Suhrkamp

HUDDLESTON, RODNEY (1971). *The Sentence in Written English: A*

Syntactic Study Based on an Analysis of Scientific Texts. London: Cambridge UP

IHWE, JENS (1976). 'The philosophy of literary criticism reconsidered: On the "logic" of interpretation'. *Poetics*, 5/4, 339–72

IHWE, JENS (1972). *Linguistik in der Literaturwissenschaft*. Munich: Bayerischer Schulbuchverlag

IHWE, JENS (ed.) (1971). *Literaturwissenschaft und Linguistik: Ergebnisse und Perspektiven*. Frankfurt: Athenäum

IHWE, JENS & RIESER, HANNES (1972). 'Versuch einer Exploration des "Versuchs einer Exploration der neuentdeckten Formelwälder von der Insel Mainau" von Werner Kummer'. *LingBer*, 18, 56–8

ISAČENKO, ALEXANDER (1965). 'Kontextbedingte Ellipse und Pronominalisierung im Deutschen'. In *Beiträge zur Sprachwissenschaft, Volkskunde, und Literaturforschung*. Berlin: Akademie, 163–73

ISENBERG, HORST (1971). 'Uberlegungen zur Texttheorie'. In Ihwe (ed.), 150–73

ISENBERG, HORST (1968). 'Motivierungen zur "Texttheorie"'. *Replik*, 2, 13–17

ISER, WOLFGANG (1980). 'Texts and Readers'. In Beaugrande (ed.), 327–43

ISER, WOLFGANG (1975). 'Die Wirklichkeit der Fiktion'. In Warning (ed.), 277–324

JAKOBSON, ROMAN & JONES, LAWRENCE (1970). *Shakespeare's Verbal Art in "Th'Expence of Spirit"*. The Hague: Mouton

JELITTE, HERBERT (1976). *Sowjetrussische Textlinguistik*. Bern: Lang

JELITTE, HERBERT (1973-4). 'Kommentierte Bibliographie zur Sowjetrussischen Textlinguistik'. *LingBer*, 28, 83–100; and 29, 74–92

JENNINGS, ELIZABETH (1967). *Collected Poems 1967*. London: Macmillan

JESPERSĖN, OTTO (1961). *A Modern English Grammar on Historical Principles*. London: Allen and Unwin

JOHNSON, DAVID (1977). 'On relational constraints on grammar'. In Cole & Sadock (eds), 151–78

JOHNSON, DAVID & POSTAL, PAUL (1980). *Arc-Pair Grammar*. Princeton: Princeton UP

JOHNSON-LAIRD, PHILIP (1978). 'What's wrong with Grandma's guide to procedural semantics: A reply to Jerry Fodor'. *Cognition*, 6, 249–61

JOHNSON-LAIRD, PHILIP (1977). 'Procedural semantics'. *Cognition*, 5, 189–214

JONES, LINDA (1977). *Theme in English Expository Discourse*. Lake Bluff, Ill.: Jupiter

JÖRG, SABINE & HÖRMANN, HANS (1978). 'The influence of general and specific verbal labels on the recognition of labelled and unlabelled parts of pictures'. *JVLVB*, 17, 455–54

KALLMEYER, WERNER, KLEIN, WOLFGANG, MEYER-HERRMANN, REINHARD, NETZER, KLAUS & SIEBERT, HANS-JÜRGEN (1974). *Lektürekolleg zur Textlinguistik*. Frankfurt: Athenäum-Fischer

KAPLAN, JEFFREY (1976). 'The variability of phrasal anaphoric islands'. *Twelfth CLS*, 337–50

KARLSEN, ROLF (1959). *Studies in the Connection of Clauses in Current English: Zero, Ellipsis, and Explicit Form*. Bergen: Eides Boktrykkeri

KARTTUNEN, LAURI (1969). 'Pronouns and variables'. *Fifth CLS*, 108–116

KARTTUNEN, LAURI (1968). *What Makes Noun Phrases Definite?* Santa Monica: Rand Corporation TR P-3871

KATZ, JERROLD & FODOR, JERRY (1963). 'The structure of semantic theory'. *Language*, 39, 170–210

KAY, HARRY (1955). 'Learning and retaining verbal material'. *BritJPsy*, 46, 81–100

KEELE, STEVEN (1973). *Attention and Human Performance*. Pacific Palisades: Goodyear

KINTSCH, WALTER (1979*a*). 'Learning from text, levels of comprehension, or: Why anyone would read a story anyway'. *Poetics*, 9, 87–98

KINTSCH, WALTER (1979*b*). 'Semantic memory: A tutorial'. In Nickerson, Raymond (ed.), *Attention and Performance VIII*. Hillsdale, N.J.: Erlbaum

KINTSCH, WALTER (1977*a*). *Memory and Cognition*. New York: Wiley

KINTSCH, WALTER (1977*b*). 'On comprehending stories'. In Just, Marcel & Carpenter, Patricia (eds), *Cognitive Processes in Comprehension*. Hillsdale, N.J.: Erlbaum, 33–62

KINTSCH, WALTER (1974). *The Representation of Meaning in Memory*. Hillsdale, N.J.: Erlbaum

KINTSCH, WALTER & DIJK, TEUN VAN (1978). 'Toward a model of text comprehension and production'. *PsyR*, 85, 363–94

KINTSCH, WALTER, MANDEL, THEODORE & KOZMINSKY, ELY (1977). 'Summarizing scrambled stories'. *MemCog*, 5, 547–52

KINTSCH, WALTER & VIPOND, DOUGLAS (1979). 'Reading comprehension and readability in educational practice'. In Nilsson, Lars-Gören (ed.), *Memory: Process and Problems*. Hillsdale, N.J.: Erlbaum, 329–65

KLARE, GEORGE (1963). *The Measurement of Readability*. Ames: Iowa State University

KLOEPFER, ROLF (1975). *Poetik und Linguistik*. Munich: Fink

KOCH, WALTER (1978). 'Poetizität zwischen Metaphysik und Metasprache'. *Poetica*, 10, 285–341

KOCH, WALTER (1973). *Das Textem*. Hildesheim: Olms

KOCH, WALTER (1971). *Taxologie des Englischen*. Munich: Fink

KOCH, WALTER (ed.) (1972). *Strukturelle Textanalyse.* Hildesheim: Olms

KOHONEN, VILJO & ENKVIST, NILS-ERIK (eds.) (1978). *Text Linguistics, Cognitive Learning, and Language Teaching.* Åbo, Finnland: Åbo Akademi

KRISTEVA, JULIA (1968). 'Problèmes de la structuration du texte'. *Linguistique et Littérature,* 12, 55–64

KUHN, THOMAS (1970). *The Structure of Scientific Revolutions.* Chicago: University of Chicago

KUIPERS, BENJAMIN (1975). 'A frame for frames: Representing knowledge for retrieval'. In Bobrow & Collins (eds.), 151–84

KUMMER, WERNER (1975). *Grundlagen der Texttheorie.* Hamburg: Rowohlt

KUMMER, WERNER (1972*a*). 'Versuch einer Exploration der neuentdeckten Formelwälder von der Insel Mainau'. *LingBer,* 18, 53–5

KUMMER, WERNER (1972*b*). 'Zum "Versuch einer Exploration des 'Versuchs einer Exploration der neuentdeckten formelwälder von der Insel Mainau' von W. Kummer"'. *LingBer,* 19, 78–9

KUNO, SUSUMU (1978). 'Generative discourse analysis in America'. In Dressler (ed.), 275–94

LABERGE, DAVID & SAMUELS, JAY (eds.) (1977). *Basic Processes in Reading: Perception and Comprehension.* Hillsdale, N.J.: Erlbaum

LABOV, WILLIAM (1973). 'The boundaries of words and their meanings'. In Bailey, Charles & Shuy, Roger (eds.), *New Ways of Analyzing Variation in English.* Washington, D.C.: Georgetown UP, 340–73

LABOV, WILLIAM (1972). *Sociolinguistic Patterns.* Philadelphia: University of Pennsylvania Press

LABOV, WILLIAM (1969). 'Contraction, deletion, and inherent variability of the English copula'. *Language,* 45, 715–62

LABOV, WILLIAM & FANSHEL, DAVID (1977). *Therapeutic Discourse.* New York: Academic

LABOV, WILLIAM & WALETZKY, JOSHUA (1967). 'Narrative analysis: Oral versions of personal experience'. In Helm, June (ed.), *Essays on the Verbal and Visual Arts.* Seattle: University of Washington Press, 12–44

LAKATOS, IMRE (1976). *Proofs and Refutations.* London: Cambridge UP

LAKOFF, GEORGE (1973). 'Fuzzy grammar and the performance/competence terminology game'. *Ninth CLS,* 271–91

LAKOFF, GEORGE (1971). 'On generative semantics'. In Steinberg & Jakobovits (eds.), 232–96

LAKOFF, GEORGE (1968). *Pronouns and Reference.* Bloomington: Indiana University Linguistics Club

LAKOFF, ROBIN (1971). 'If's, and's, and but's about conjunction'. In Fillmore, Charles & Langendoen, Terence (eds.), *Studies in*

Linguistic Semantics. New York: Holt, Rinehart & Winston, 114–49

LAMBEK, JOACHIM (1961). 'On the calculus of syntactic types'. In *Procedings of Symposia in Applied Mathematics*, 12, 25–42

LANG, EWALD (1976). *Semantik der koordinativen Verknüpfung*. Berlin: Akademie der Wissenschaften

LARSON, RICHARD (1976). 'Structure and form in non-fiction prose'. In Tate (ed.), 47–71

LEECH, GEOFFREY & SVARTVIK, JAN (1975). *A Communicative Grammar of English*. London: Longman

LEHISTE, ILSE (1975). 'The phonetic structure of the paragraph'. In Cohen, Antonie & Nooteboom, Sibout (eds.). *Structure and Process in Speech Perception*. Berlin: Springer, 195–203

LEHISTE, ILSE (1970). *Suprasegmentals*. Cambridge: MIT Press

LENAT, DOUGLAS (1977). 'The ubiquity of discovery'. *Fifth IJCAI*, 1093–1105

LEODOLTER, RUTH (1975). *Das Sprachverhalten von Angeklagten vor Gericht*. Kronberg: Scriptor

LESKOV, NIKOLAI (1961). *Selected Tales*. New York: Noonday

LEVELT, WILLEM, ET AL. (1977). 'Grammaticality, paraphrase, and imagery'. In Greenbaum (ed.), 1977, 87–102

LEVESQUE, HECTOR (1977). *A Procedural Approach to Semantic Networks*. Toronto: University of Toronto CS-TR 105

LEVESQUE, HECTOR & MYLOPOULOS, JOHN (1979). 'A procedural semantics for semantic networks'. In Findler (ed.), 93–120

LEVIN, JAMES & GOLDMAN, NEIL (1977). *Process Models of Reference in Context*. Marina del Rey: University of Southern California Information Sciences Institute AI-TR 78–72

LEVIN, SAMUEL (1965). 'Internal and external deviation in poetry'. *Word*, 21, 225–37

LEVIN, SAMUEL (1963). 'Deviation – statistical and determinate – in poetic language'. *Lingua*, 21, 276–90

LEVIN, SAMUEL (1962). *Linguistic Structures in Poetry*. The Hague: Mouton

LEVÝ, JIŘI (1971). 'Generative Poetik'. In Ihwe (ed.), 924–37

LÉVI-STRAUSS, CLAUDE (1960). 'La structure et la forme'. *Cahiers de l'Institut de Science Économique Appliquée*, 99, 3–36

LI, CHARLES (ed.) (1976). *Subject and Topic*. New York: Academic

LINDE, CHARLOTTE & LABOV, WILLIAM (1975). 'Spatial networks as a site for the study of language and thought'. *Language*, 51, 924–39

LINSKY, LEONARD (1971). 'Reference and referents'. In Steinberg & Jakobovits (eds.), 76–85

LIVINGSTON, MYRA COHN (1972). 'Driving'. In *The Malibu and Other Poems*. New York: Atheneum

LOFTUS, GEOFFREY & LOFTUS, ELIZABETH (1976). *Human Memory: The Processing of Information*. Hillsdale, N.J.: Erlbaum

LONGACRE, ROBERT (1976). *An Anatomy of Speech Notions*. Lisse: de Ridder

LONGACRE, ROBERT (1970). *Discourse, Paragraph, and Sentence Structure*. Santa Ana: Summer Institute of Linguistics

LONGACRE, ROBERT (1964). *Grammar Discovery Procedures*. The Hague: Mouton

LUNT, HORACE (ed.) (1964). *Proceedings of the Ninth International Congress of Linguists*. The Hague: Mouton

LYONS, JOHN (1977). *Semantics*. London: Cambridge

MALINOWSKI, BRONISLAW(1923). 'The problem of meaning in primitive languages'. In Ogden, Charles & Richards, Ivor, *The Meaning of Meaning*. London: Oxford, 296–336

MANDLER, JEAN (1978). 'A code in the node: The use of story schema in retrieval'. *DisPro*, 1, 14–35

MANDLER, JEAN & JOHNSON, NANCY (1977). 'Remembrance of things parsed: Story structure and recall'. *CogPsy*, 9, 111–51

MARTIN, JUDITH (1969). 'Semantic determinants of preferred adjective order'. *JVLVB*, 8, 697–704

MATEJKA, LADISLAV & POMORSKA, KRYSTYNA (eds.) (1971). *Readings in Russian Poetics: Formalist and Structuralist Views*. Cambridge: MIT Press

MATHESIUS, VILÉM (1928). 'On linguistic characterology with illustrations from modern English'. In *Actes du Ier Congrés International des Linguistes*, 56–63

MCCALL, WILLIAM & CRABBS, LELAH (1961). *Standard Test Lessons in Readability*. New York: Columbia University Bureau of Publications

MCCALLA, GORDON (1978). *An Approach to the Organization of Knowledge for the Modelling of Conversation*. Vancouver: University of British Columbia CT-TR 78–4

MCCAWLEY, JAMES (1976). 'Some ideas not to live by'. *Die neueren Sprachen*, 75, 151–65

MEL'ČUK, IGOR (1976). 'Ein linguistisches Modell des Typs "Smysl-Text".' In Gierke, Wolfgang & Jachnow, Helmut (eds.), *Theoretische Linguistik in Osteuropa*. Tübingen: Niemeyer, 49–67

MEL'ČUK, IGOR (1974). *Opyt Teorii Lingvističeskix Modelej "Smysl—Tekst": Semantika, Sintaksis*. Moskau: Nauka

MEL'ČUK, IGOR & ŽOLKOVSKIJ, ALEXANDER (1970). 'Towards a functioning meaning-text model of language'. *Linguistics*, 57, 10–47

METZING, DIETER (ed.) (1979). *Frame Conceptions and Text Understanding*. Berlin: de Gruyter

MEYER, BONNIE (1979). *Research on Prose Comprehension: Applications for Composition Teachers*. Tempe: Arizona State University

Department of Educational Psychology Prose Learning Series TR 2

MEYER, BONNIE (1977). 'What is remembered from prose: A function of passage structure'. In Freedle (ed.), 307–336

MEYER, BONNIE (1975). *The Organization of Prose and its Effects on Memory*. Amsterdam: North Holland

MILLER, GEORGE (1956). 'The magical number seven, plus or minus two'. *PsyR,* 63, 81–97

MILLER, GEORGE (1951). *Language and Communication*. New York: McGraw-Hill

MILLER, GEORGE, GALANTER, EUGENE & PRIBRAM, KARL (1960). *Plans and the Structure of Behavior*. New York: Holt, Rinehart, and Winston

MILLER, GEORGE & JOHNSON-LAIRD, PHILIP (1976). *Language and Perception*. Cambridge: Harvard UP

MILLER, GERALD & COLEMAN, EDMUND (1979). 'A set of 36 prose passages calibrated for complexity'. *JVLVB,* 6, 851–4

MILNE, ALAN (1928). *The House at Pooh Corner*. London: Methuen

MINSKY, MARVIN (1975). 'A framework for representing knowledge'. In Winston (ed.), 211–77

MINSKY, MARVIN & PAPERT, SEYMOUR (1974). *Artificial Intelligence: Condon Lectures*. Eugene: Oregon State System of Higher Education

MISTLER-LACHMAN, JANET (1974). 'Depth of comprehension and sentence memory'. *JVLVB,* 13, 98–106

MISTRÍK, JOSEF (1973). *Exakte Typologie von Texten*. Munich: Sagner

MOHAN, BERNARD (1977). 'Acceptability testing and fuzzy grammar'. In Greenbaum (ed.), 133–48

MORGAN, JERRY (1978). 'Toward a rational model of discourse comprehension'. *TINLAP-2,* 109–114

MOUNIN, GEORGES (1963). *Les problèmes théoriques de la traduction*. Paris: Gallimard

MUIR, JOHN (1969). *How to Keep your Volkswagen Alive: A Manuel of Step-by-Step Procedures for the Compleat Idiot*. Berkeley: Book People

MUKAŘOVSKÝ, JAN (1964). 'Standard language and poetic language'. In Garvin (ed.), 17–30

NEISSER, ULRIC (1967). *Cognitive Psychology*. New York: Appleton-Century-Crofts

NEWELL, ALLAN & SIMON, HERBERT (1972). *Human Problem Solving*. Englewood Cliffs: Prentice-Hall

NICKEL, GERHARD (ed.) (1972). *Reader zur Kontrastiven Linguistik*. Frankfurt: Athenäum

NICKEL, GERHARD (ed.) (1971). *Paper in Contrastive Linguistics*. Cambridge, England: Cambridge UP

NÖTH, WINFRIED (1978). 'The semiotic framework of text linguistics'. In Dressler (ed.), 31–4

NY, JEAN-FRANÇOIS LE (1979). *La sémantique psychologique*. Paris: French UP

NY, JEAN-FRANÇOIS LE & DENHIÈRE, GUY (1980). 'Relative importance of meaningful units in comprehension and recall of narratives by children and adults'. *Poetics*, 9, 147–61

O'CONNELL, DANIEL (1977). 'One of many units: The sentence'. In Rosenberg (ed.), 307–313

OEVERMANN, ULRICH (1970). *Sprache und soziale Herkunft*. Frankfurt: Suhrkamp

OLSON, DAVID & FILBY, NIKOLA (1972). 'On the comprehension of active and passive sentences'. *CogPsy*, 3, 161–81

OOMEN, URSULA (1969). 'Systemtheorie der Texte'. *Folia Linguistica*, 5, 12–34

ORTON, JOE (1967). *Loot*. London: Methuen

ORTONY, ANDREW (1978). 'Remembering, understanding, and representation'. *CogSci*, 2, 53–69

OSBORNE, JOHN (1968). *Time Present and The Hotel in Amsterdam*. London: Faber and Faber

OSBORNE, JOHN (1961*a*). *Luther*. London: Faber and Faber

OSBORNE, JOHN (1961*b*). *The Entertainer*. London: Faber and Faber

OSBORNE, JOHN (1960). *Look Back in Anger*. London: Faber and Faber

OSGOOD, CHARLES (1971). 'Where do sentences come from?' In Steinberg & Jakobovits (eds), 497–529

PADUCEVA, ELENA (1970). 'Anaphoric relations and their manifestations in the text'. *Tenth PICL*, 693–7

PAIVIO, ALLAN (1971). *Imagery and Verbal Processes*. New York: Holt, Rinehart, and Winston

PALEK, BOHUMIL (1968). *Cross-Reference: A Study from Hyper-Syntax*. Prague: Charles UP

PAPERT, SEYMOUR (1980). *Mindstorms: Computers, Children, and Powerful Ideas*. New York: Basic Books

PAVLIDIS, THEODOSIOS (1977). *Structural Pattern Recognition*. Berlin: Springer

PERLMUTTER, DAVID & POSTAL, PAUL (1978). *Some Proposed Laws of Basic Clause Structure*. Yorktown Heights: IBM J. Thomas Watson Research Centre TR

PETÖFI, JÁNOS (1980). 'Einige Grundfragen der pragmatisch-semantischen Interpretation von Texten'. In Ballmer, Thomas & Kindt Walter (eds.), *Zum Thema 'Sprache und Logik': Ergebnisse einer interdisziplinären Diskussion*. Hamburg: Buske, 146–90

PETÖFI, JÁNOS (1978). 'A formal semiotic text theory as an integrated theory of natural languages'. In Dressler (ed.), 35–46

PETÖFI, JÁNOS (1976). 'A frame for FRAMES: A few remarks on the methodology of semantically guided text processing'. In *Proceedings of the Second Annual Meeting of the Berkeley Linguistic Society*. Berkeley: University of California Institute of Human Learning, 319–29

PETÖFI, JÁNOS (1974). 'Towards an empirically motivated grammatical theory of verbal texts'. In Petöfi & Rieser (eds.), 205–275

PETÖFI, JÁNOS (1971). *Transformationsgrammatiken und eine ko-textuelle Texttheorie*. Frankfurt: Athenäum

PETÖFI, JÁNOS & RIESER HANNES (1974). *Probleme der modelltheoretischen Interpretation von Texten*. Hamburg: Buske

PETÖFI, JÁNOS (ed.) (1979). *Text versus Sentence: Basic Questions in Text Linguistics*. Hamburg: Buske

PETÖFI, JÁNOS & FRANCK, DOROTHEA (eds.) (1974). *Presuppositions in Philosophy and Linguistics*. Frankfurt: Athenäum

PETÖFI, JÁNOS & RIESER, HANNES (eds.) (1974). *Studies in Text Grammar*. Dordrecht: Reidel

PETRICK, STANLEY (1965). *A Recognition Procedure for Transformational Grammar*. Cambridge: MIT dissertation

PIKE, KENNETH (1967). *Language in Relation to a Unified Theory of the Structure of Human Behavior*. The Hague: Mouton

PINTER, HAROLD (1960). *The Caretaker and the Dumb Waiter*. New York: Grove

PLETT, HEINRICH (1975). *Textwissenschaft und Textanalyse*. Heidelberg: Quelle und Meyer

PLETT, HEINRICH (ed.) (1977). *Rhetorik: Kritische Positionen zum Stand der Forschung*. Munich: Fink

POLLACK, IRWIN & PICKETT, JAMES (1964). 'Intelligibility of excerpts from fluent speech: Auditory vs. structural content'. *JVLVB*, 3, 79–84

PORTER, BERN (1972). *Found Poems*. New York: Something Else

POSNER, ROLAND (1981). 'Types of dialogue: The functions of commenting'. In Beaugrande (ed.), 381–98

POSNER, ROLAND (1972). *Theorie des Kommentierens*. Frankfurt: Athenäum

POSTAL, PAUL (1969). 'Anaphoric islands'. In *Fifth CLS*, 205–239

PRIESTLEY, JOHN (1950). *An Inspector Calls*. In *The Plays of J.B. Priestley*. New York: Harper & Brothers, 263–323

PRINCE, ELLEN (1978). 'Discourse analysis in the framework of Z.S. Harris'. In Dressler (ed.), 191–211

PROPP, VLADIMIR (1928). *Morfologia Skazki*. Leningrad: Akademia

QUILLIAN, ROSS (1966). *Semantic Memory*. Cambridge: BBN TR AFCRL-66-189

QUINE, WILLARD (1960). *Word and Object*. Cambridge: MIT Press

QUINE, WILLARD (1953). *From a Logical Point of View*. Cambridge: MIT Press

QUIRK, RANDOLPH (1978). 'Focus, scope, and lyrical beginnings'. *LangSty*, 11, 30–39

QUIRK, RANDOLPH, GREENBAUM, SIDNEY, LEECH, GEOFFREY & SVARTVIK, JAN (1972). *A Grammar of Contemporary English*. London: Longman

QUIRK, RANDOLPH & SVARTVIK, JAN (1966). *Investigating Linguistic Acceptability*. The Hague: Mouton

REICHENBACH, HANS (1976). *Laws, Modalities, and Counterfactuals*. Berkeley: University of California Press

REICHENBACH, HANS (1947). *Elements of Symbolic Logic*. London: Macmillan

REICHMAN, RACHAEL (1978). 'Conversational coherency'. *CogSci*, 2, 283–327

RIEGER, CHARLES (1975). 'Conceptual memory and inference'. In Schank et al., 157–288

RIESBECK, CHRISTOPHER (1975). 'Conceptual analysis'. In Schank et al., 83–156

RIESER, HANNES (1978). 'On the development of text grammar'. In Dressler (ed.), 6–20

RIFFATERRE, MICHAEL (1960). 'Stylistic context.' *Word*, 16, 207–218

RIFFATERRE, MICHAEL (1959). 'Criteria for style analysis'. *Word*, 15, 154–74

RINGEN, JON (1975). 'Linguistic facts: A study of the empirical scientific status of transformational grammars'. In Cohen, David & Wirth, Jessica (eds.), *Testing Linguistic Hypotheses*. New York: Wiley, 1–41

ROBINSON, EDWARD ARLINGTON (1914). *Children of the Night*. New York: Scribner

ROGGERO, JACQUES (1968). 'La substitution en anglais'. *Linguistique*, 2, 61–92

ROMPORTL, MILAN ET AL. (1977). *Studies in Linguistic Typology*. Prague: Charles UP

ROSCH, ELEANOR (1973). 'Natural categories'. *CogPsy*, 4, 328–50

ROSCH, ELEANOR & MERVIS, CAROLYN (1975). 'Family resemblances: Studies in the internal structure of categories'. *CogPsy*, 7, 573–605

ROSENBERG, SHELDON (ed.) (1977). *Sentence Production: Developments in Research and Theory*. Hillsdale, N.J.: Erlbaum

ROSS, JOHN (1970). 'Gapping and the order of constituents'. *Tenth PICL*, 841–52

ROTHKOPF, ERNST (1976). 'Writing to teach and reading to learn: A perspective on the psychology of written instruction'. *Yearbook of the National Society for the Study of Education*, 75, 91–129

ROYER, JAMES (1977). 'Remembering: Constructive or reconstructive? In Anderson, Spiro & Montague (eds.), 167–73

RUBIN, ANDEE (1978*a*). *A Theoretical Taxonomy of the Differences between Oral and Written Language*. Cambridge: BBN TR 3731

RUBIN, ANDEE (1978*b*). 'A framework for comparing language experiences, with particular emphasis on the effect of audience on discourse models'. *TINLAP-2*, 133–40

RUMELHART, DAVID (1977*a*). *Introduction to Human Information Processing*. New York: Wiley

RUMELHART, DAVID (1977*b*). 'Understanding and summarizing brief stories'. In LaBerge & Samuels (eds.), 265–303

RUMELHART, DAVID (1975). 'Notes on a schema for stories'. In Bobrow & Collins (eds.), 211–36

RUMELHART, DAVID (1970). 'A multicomponent theory of the perception of briefly exposed visual displays'. *JMathPsy*, 7, 191–218

RUMELHART, DAVID & ORTONY, ANDREW (1977). 'The representation of knowledge in memory'. In Anderson, Spiro & Montague (eds.), 99–135

SACERDOTI, EARL (1977). *A Structure for Plans and Behaviour*. New York: Elsevier

SACKS, HARVEY, SCHEGLOFF, EMMANUEL & JEFFERSON, GAIL (1974). 'A simplest systematics for the organization of turn-taking for conversation'. *Language*, 50, 696–735

SALMOND, ANNE (1974). 'Rituals of encounter among the Maori: Sociolinguistic study of a scene'. In Bauman & Scherzer (eds.), 192–212

SAUSSURE, FERDINAND DE (1916). *Cours de linguistique générale*. Lausanne: Payot

SCHANK, ROGER (1977). 'Rules and topics in conversation'. *CogSci*, 1, 421–41

SCHANK, ROGER (1975). 'The structure of episodes in memory'. In Bobrow & Collins (eds.), 237–72

SCHANK, ROGER & ABELSON, ROBERT (1977). *Scripts, Plans, Goals, and Understanding*. Hillsdale, N.J.: Erlbaum

SCHANK, ROGER, GOLDMAN, NEIL, RIEGER, CHARLES & RIESBECK, CHRISTOPHER (1975). *Conceptual Information Processing*. Amsterdam: North Holland

SCHANK, ROGER & WILENSKY, ROBERT (1977). 'Response to Dresher and Hornstein'. *Cognition*, 5, 133–45

SCHECKER, MICHAEL & WUNDERLI, PETER (eds.) (1975). *Textgrammatik: Beiträge zum Problem der Textualität*. Tübingen: Niemeyer

SCHEGLOFF, EMMANUEL, JEFFERSON, GAIL & SACKS, HARVEY (1977). 'The preference for self-correction in the organization of repair in conversation'. *Language*, 53, 361–82

SCHLESINGER, IZHAK (1977). *Production and Comprehension of Utterances*. Hillsdale, N.J.: Erlbaum

SCHMIDT, CHARLES (1976). 'Understanding human action: Recognizing the plans and motives of other persons'. In Carroll, John S. & Payne, John W. (eds.), *Cognition and Social Behaviour*. Hillsdale, N.J.: Erlbaum, 47–67

SCHMIDT, SIEGFRIED (1981). *Empirical Foundations for the Study of Literature*. In press

SCHMIDT, SIEGFRIED (1979). *Grundzüge der empirischen Literaturwissenschaft*. Brunswick: Vieweg

SCHMIDT, SIEGFRIED (1978). 'Some problems of communicative text theories'. In Dressler (ed.), 47–60

SCHMIDT, SIEGFRIED (1973). *Texttheorie*. Munich: Fink

SCHMIDT, SIEGFRIED (1972). 'Ist "Fiktionalität" eine linguistische oder eine texttheoretische Kategorie?' In Gülich & Raible (eds.), 59–71

SCHMIDT, SIEGFRIED (1971*a*). *Ästhetizität*. Munich: Bayrischer Schulbuchverlag

SCHMIDT SIEGFRIED (1971*b*). 'Text und Bedeutung: Sprachphilosophische Prolegomena zu einer textsemantischen Literaturwissenschaft'. In Schmidt, Siegfried (ed.), *Text, Bedeutung, Ästhetik*. Munich: Bayrischer Schulbuchverlag, 43–79

SCHMIDT, SIEGFRIED (1968). *Bedeutung und Begriff*. Brunswick: Vieweg

SCHNEIDER, PETER (1978). *Organization of Knowledge in a Procedural Semantic Network Formalism*. Toronto: University of Toronto CS-TR 115

SCHWELLER, KENNETH, BREWER, WILLIAM & DAHL, DEBORAH (1976). 'Memory for illocutionary forces and perlocutionary effects of utterances'. *JVLVB*, 15, 325–37

SCRAGG, GREG (1976). 'Semantic nets as memory models'. In Charniak & Wilks (eds.), 101–128

SEARLE, JOHN (1975). 'Indirect speech acts'. In Cole & Morgan (eds.), 59–82

SEARLE, JOHN (1969). *Speech Acts*. London: Cambridge

SEBEOK, THOMAS (ed.) (1960). *Style in Language*. Cambridge: MIT Press

SELFRIDGE, OLIVER & NEISSER, ULRIC (1960). 'Pattern recognition by machine'. *Scientific American*, 203, 60–68

SGALL, PETR, HAJIČOVÁ, EVA & BENEŠOVÁ, EVA (1973). *Topic, Focus, and Generative Semantics*. Kronberg: Scriptor

SHAFFER, PETER (1976). *Equus and Shrivings: Two Plays*. New York: Atheneum

SHAKESPEARE, WILLIAM (1936). *The Complete Works of Shakespeare*, ed. George Lyman Kittredge. Boston: Ginn

SHANNON, CLAUDE (1951). 'Prediction and entropy of printed English'. *Bell System Technical Journal*, 30, 50–64

SHANNON, CLAUDE & WEAVER, WARREN (1949). *The Mathematical Theory of Communication*. Urbana: University of Illinois Press

SIMMONS, ROBERT & CHESTER, DANIEL (1979). *Relating Sentences and Semantic Networks with Clausal Logic NL-40*. Austin: University of Texas CS-TR

SIMON, HERBERT (1979). 'Artificial intelligence research strategies in the light of AI models of scientific discovery'. *Sixth IJCAI*, 1086–94

SINCLAIR, JOHN & COULTHARD, MALCOLM (1975). *Towards an Analysis of Discourse*. London: Oxford

SITTA, HORST & BRINKER, KLAUS (eds) (1973). *Studien zur Texttheorie und zur deutschen Grammatik*. Düsseldorf: Schwann

SKALIČKA, VLADIMIR (1977). 'Kontext-orientierte Typologie'. In Romportl et al., 17–23

SKINNER, BURRHUS (1958). *Verbal Behaviour*. New York: Appleton-Crofts

SMITH, EDWARD (1978). 'Theories of semantic memory'. In Estes, William (ed.), *Handbook of Learning Processes VI*. Hillsdale, N.J.: Erlbaum

SMITH, EDWARD, SHOBEN, EDWARD & RIPS, LANCE (1974). 'Structure and process in semantic memory: A featural model for semantic decisions'. *PsyR*, 81, 214–41

SNOW, CATHERINE & MEIJER, GUUS (1977). 'On the secondary nature of syntactic intuitions'. In Greenbaum (ed.), 163–78

SPARK, MURIEL (1963). *Doctors of Philosophy*. London: Macmillan

SPENCER, NANCY (1973). 'Differences between linguists and non-linguists in intuitions of grammaticality-acceptability'. *Journal of Psycholinguistic Research*, 2, 83–98

SPERLING, GEORGE (1960). 'The information available in brief visual presentations'. *Psychological Monographs*, 74, 1–29

SPILLNER, BERND (1977). 'Das Interesse der Linguistik an Rhetorik'. In Plett (ed.), 93–108

SPILLNER, BERND (1974). *Linguistik und Literaturwissenschaft: Stilforschung, Rhetorik, Textlinguistik*. Stuttgart: Kohlhammer

SPINNER, HELMUT (1977). *Begründung, Kritik und Rationalität*. Brunswick: Vieweg

SPIRO, RAND (1977). 'Remembering information from text: The "state of schema" approach'. In Anderson, Spiro & Montague (eds.), 137–77

SPIRO, RAND, BRUCE, BERTRAM & BREWER, WILLIAM (eds.) (1979). *Theoretical Issues in Reading Comprehension*. Hillsdale, N.J.: Erlbaum

SPITZER, LEO (1948). *Linguistics and Literary History*. Princeton: Princeton UP

SPRUNG, LOTHAR (1964). 'Zur Psychologie des Gedächtnisses I: Über einige Abhängigheitsbeziehungen zwischen Kontexteigenschaften und Reproduktionsleistungen in sinnvollen sprachlichen Texten'. *Zeitschrift für Psychologie,* 169, 35–51

STEGMÜLLER, WOLFGANG (1976). *The Structure and Dynamics of Theories.* New York: Springer

STEGMÜLLER, WOLFGANG (1969). *Probleme und Resultate der Wissenschaftstheorie und analytischen Philosophie I.* Berlin: Springer

STEIN, NANCY & GLENN, CHRISTINE (1979). 'An analysis of story comprehension in elementary school children'. In Freedle (ed.), 53–120

STEIN, NANCY & NEZWORSKI, TERESA (1978). 'The effects of organization and instructional set on story memory'. *DisPro,* 1, 177–93

STEINBERG, DANNY & JAKOBOVITS, LEON (eds.) (1971). *Semantics: An Interdisciplinary Reader in Philosophy, Linguistics, and Psychology.* Cambridge, England: Cambridge UP

STEINITZ, RENATE (1968). *Adverbial-Syntax.* Berlin: Akademie der Wissenschaften

STEMPEL, WOLF-DIETER (ed.) (1971). *Beiträge zur Textlinguistik.* Munich: Fink

STEVENS, ALBERT & RUMELHART, DAVID (1975). 'Errors in reading: Analysis using an augmented transition network model of grammar'. In Norman, Donald & Rumelhart, David, *Explorations in Cognition.* San Francisco: Freeman, 136–55

SUSSMAN, GERALD (1973). *A Computer Model of Skill Acquisition.* Cambridge: MIT dissertation (AI–TR 297)

SWEET, HENRY (1906). *A Primer of Phonetics.* Oxford: Clarendon

TAI, JAMES (1969). *Coordination Reduction.* Bloomington: Indiana University Linguistics Club

TALMY, LEONARD (1978). 'The relation of grammar to cognition: A synopsis'. *TINLAP-2,* 14–24

TATE, GARY (ed.) (1976). *Teaching Composition: Ten Bibliographical Essays.* Fort Worth: Texas Christian UP

TENNYSON, ALFRED (1930). *Poetic Works.* London: Collins

THORNDYKE, PERRY (1977). 'Cognitive structures in comprehension and memory of narrative discourse'. *CogPsy,* 9, 77–110

THORNDYKE, PERRY & YEKOVICH, FRANK (1980). 'A critique of schemata as a theory of human story memory'. *Poetics,* 9, 23–49

THORNE, JAMES (1969). 'Poetry, stylistics, and imaginary grammars'. *JLing,* 5, 147–50

THORNE, JAMES, BRATLEY, PAUL & DEWAR, HAMISH (1968). 'The syntactic analysis of English by machine'. In Michie, Donald (ed.), *Machine Intelligence 3.* Edinburgh: University of Edinburgh Press, 281–309

TULVING, ENDEL (1972). 'Episodic and semantic memory'. In Tulving & Donaldson (eds.), 382–404

TULVING, ENDEL & DONALDSON, WAYNE (eds.) (1972). *The Organization of Memory*. New York: Academic

TWAIN, MARK (1922). *The Adventures of Tom Sawyer*. New York: Harper & Row

TWAIN, MARK (1913). *Roughing It*. New York: Harper and Brothers

TYLER, STEPHEN (1972). 'Context and alternation in Koya kinship terminology'. In Gumperz & Hymes (eds.), 251–69

ULIJN, JAN (1980). 'Foreign language research: recent trends and future prospects'. *Journal of Research on Reading*, 3, 17–37

UNGEHEUER, GEROLD (1969). 'Paraphrase und syntaktische Tiefenstruktur'. *Folia Linguistica*, 3, 178–227

VATER, HEINZ (1975). 'Pro-Formen des Deutschen'. In Schecker & Wunderli (eds.), 20–42

VENDLER, ZENO (1968). *Adjectives and Nominalizations*. The Hague: Mouton

VINAY, JEAN-PAUL & DARBELNET, JEAN (1958). *Stylistique comparée du français et de l'anglais*. Paris: Didier

WALKER, DONALD (ed.) (1978). *Understanding Spoken Language*. Amsterdam: North Holland

WALLACE, WILLIAM (1965). 'Review of the historical, empirical, and theoretical status of the von Restorff phenomenon'. *Psychological Bulletin*, 63, 410–24

WARNING, RAINER (ed.) (1975). *Rezeptionsästhetik*. Munich: Fink

WASON, PETER (1965). 'The contexts of plausible denial'. *JVLVB*, 4, 7–11

WATSON, JOHN BROADUS (1930). *Behaviorism*. Chicago: University of Chicago Press

WEBBER, BONNIE (1978). *A Formal Approach to Discourse Analysis*. Cambridge: BBN TR 3761

WEIL HENRI (1887). *The Order of Words in the Ancient Languages Compared with that of the Modern Languages*. Boston: Ginn

WEIL, HENRI (1844). *De l'ordre des mots dans les langues anciennes comparées aux langues modernes*. Paris: Joubert

WEINRICH, HARALD (1976). *Sprache in Texten*. Stuttgart: Klett

WEINRICH, HARALD (1972). 'Thesen zur Textsortenlinguistik'. In Gülich & Raible (eds.), 161–9

WEINRICH, HARALD (1966). 'Das Zeichen des Jonas: Über das sehr Grosse und das sehr Kleine in der Literatur'. *Merkur*, 20, 737–47

WEINRICH, HARALD (1964). *Tempus: Besprochene und erzählte Welt*. Stuttgart: Kohlhammer

WELTNER, KLAUS (1964). 'Zur empirischen Bestimmung subjektiver Informationswerte von Lehrbuchtexten mit dem Ratetest von

Shannon'. *Grundlagenstudien aus Kybernetik und Geisteswissenschaft*, 5, 3–11

WERTH, PAUL (1976). 'Roman Jakobson's verbal analysis of poetry'. *JLing*, 12, 21–73

WESKER, ARNOLD (1964). *The Wesker Trilogy*. Harmondsworth: Penguin

WHORF, BENJAMIN (1956). *Language, Thought, and Reality*. New York: Wiley

WIDDOWSON, HENRY (1973). *An Applied Linguistic Approach to Discourse Analysis*. Edinburgh: University of Edinburgh dissertation

WIENOLD, GÖTZ (1973). *Die Erlernbarkeit der Sprachen*. Munich: Kösel

WIENOLD, GÖLT (1972). *Semiotik der Literatur*. Frankfurt: Athenäum

WIENOLD, GÖTZ (1971). *Formulierungstheorie*. Frankfurt: Athenäum

WIKBERG, KAY (1978). 'On applications of text linguistics to the analysis and writing of foreign language teaching materials'. In Kohonen & Enkvist (eds.), 143–59

WILDE, OSCAR (1956). *The Importance of Being Earnest*. New York: New York Public Library

WILENSKY, ROBERT (1978*a*). *Understanding Goal-Based Stories*. New Haven: Yale CS–TR 140; now New York; Garland, 1980

WILENSKY, ROBERT (1978*b*). 'Why John married Mary: Understanding stories involving recurring goals'. *CogSci*, 2, 235–66

WILKINS, DAVID (1976). *Notional Syllabuses*. London: Oxford

WILKS, YORICK (1979). 'Making preferences more active'. In Findler (ed.), 239–66

WILKS, YORICK (1977*a*). 'Good and bad arguments for semantic primitives'. *Communication and Cognition*, 10, 181–221

WILKS, YORICK (1977*b*). 'What sort of a taxonomy of causation do we need?' *CogSci*, 1, 235–64

WILKS, YORICK (1972). *Grammar, Meaning, and the Machine Analysis of Language*. London: Routledge

WILSON, ANGUS (1958). *Anglo-Saxon Attitudes*. London: Secker and Warburg

WINOGRAD, TERRY (1979). 'Beyond programming languages'. *CACM*, 22, 391–401

WINOGRAD, TERRY (1976). *Towards a Procedural Analysis of Semantics*. Palo Alto: Stanford AI-TR 292

WINOGRAD, TERRY (1975). 'Frame representation and the declarative-procedural controversy'. In Bobrow & Collins (eds.), 185–210

WINOGRAD, TERRY (1972). *Understanding Natural Languages*. New York: Academic

WINSTON, PATRICK (1977). *Artificial Intelligence*. Reading, Mass.: Addison-Wesley

WINSTON, PATRICK (ed.) (1975). *The Psychology of Computer Vision*. New York: McGraw-Hill

WINSTON, PATRICK & BROWN, RICHARD (eds) (1979). *Artificial Intelligence: An MIT Perspective*. Cambridge: MIT Press

WINTEROWD, ROSS (ed.) (1975). *Contemporary Rhetoric*. New York: Harcourt, Brace, and Jovanovich

WODAK, RUTH (1980). 'Discourse analysis and courtroom interaction'. In Beaugrande (ed.), 369–80

WODAK-LEODOLTER, RUTH (1979). 'Schicht- und geschlechtsspezifische Formen der Selbstdarstellung in einer therapeutischen Gruppe'. In Velde, Marc van de & Vandeweghe, Willy (eds.), *Sprachstruktur, Individuum und Gesellschaft*. Tübingen: Niemeyer, 221–8

WOODS, WILLIAM (1975). 'What's in a link: Foundations for semantic networks'. In Bobrow & Collins (eds.) 35–82

WOODS, WILLIAM (1970). 'Transition network grammars for natural language analysis'. *CACM*, 13, 591–606

WOODS, WILLIAM & BRACHMAN, RONALD (1978). *Research in Natural Language Understanding*. Cambridge: BBN Quarterly Progress Report TR 4, 3963

WOODS, WILLIAM & MAKHOUL, JOHN (1973). 'Mechanical inference problems in continuous speech understanding'. *Third IJCAI*, 200–207

WOODS, WILLIAM, ET AL. (1976). *Speech Understanding Systems: Final Report*. Cambridge: BBN TR 3438

WRIGHT, GEORG VON (1967). 'The logic of action'. In Rescher, Nicholas (ed.), *The Logic of Decision and Action*. Pittsburgh: University of Pittsburgh Press, 121–36

WRIGHT, PATRICIA (1968). 'Sentence retention and transformation theory'. *QJExPsy*, 20, 265–72

WUNDERLICH, DIETER (1971). 'Pragmatik, Sprachsituation, Deixis'. *Literaturwissenschaft und Linguistik*, 1, 153–90

ZADEH, LOTFI (1979). 'Approximate reasoning based on fuzzy logic'. *Sixth IJCAI*, 1004–10

ZADEH, LOTFI (1975). 'Fuzzy logic and approximate reasoning'. *Synthese*, 30, 407–428

ZADEH, LOTFI (1972). 'A fuzzy-set-theoretic interpretation of linguistic hedges'. *Journal of Cybernetics*, 2/3, 4–34

ŽOLKOVSKIJ, ALEXANDER & ŠČEGLOV, JURIJ (1967). 'Strukturnaja poëtika–poroždajuščaja poëtika!' *Voprosy Literatury*, 11, 78–89

Index of names

All numbers cite paragraphs except the superior numbers for chapter notes.

Index of important terms

All numbers refer to paragraphs except the superior numbers for chapter notes. *Italicized* numbers indicate the passages in which the terms are explained. Major notions in our procedural approach are in **bold.**

with a tonic containing iron, quinine, and strychnine. The prosecution introduced testimony that the strychnine in Colonel Swope's tonic was a very small and harmless amount, such as was included in a great many drugs. The defense countered with testimony that the strychnine was "cumulative," the accumulation of a little taken each day.

There was some amusement over Colonel Swope's tonic, because O. H. Gentry, Independence druggist, brought a bottle of it with him to the witness stand. "I suffer from palpitation of the heart; this helps me a lot," said Gentry as he mounted the stand. Then, by way of showing what a harmless little remedy it was, he uncorked the bottle and took a few healthy gulps. Walsh immediately protested that the demonstration was intended to prejudice the jury, and asked that the witness and attorney be censured. Before Walsh could finish his protest the effect on the jury was reversed; for the druggist, after looking wretchedly around the room, called out: "Bring me a glass of water, quick!" The judge hammered for order, and directed the bailiff to "bring some water, quick!"

The prosecution's own witnesses disagreed as to whether the strychnine in Colonel Swope's body was sufficient to have caused death. The experts agreed that Colonel Swope and Chrisman Swope had shown the symptoms of cyanide poisoning, or possibly combined cyanide and strychnine poisoning, but they also said: "You can get ideas but not definite conclusions from symptoms." These confusions and uncertainties led to the first decision which was later reached by the jurors when they retired: to disregard the expert testimony altogether, and see whether they could reach a verdict without it.

The state's case was weakened by the death of the elder Dr. Twyman, before the trial. Dr. Twyman left a full statement of the facts and conversations, but this could not be brought before the jury, as all testimony in Missouri must be received under oath. The nurses, Dr. Stewart, the druggist Brecklein, and the Swopes and the Hydes all testified. Dr. Hyde seemed almost to enjoy the proceedings. When young Tom Swope was testifying about the pieces of capsules in the snow, and the odor which clung to his hand, Dr. Hyde took a piece of paper and wrote: "You may break, you may shatter the vase if you will, but the smell of the cyanide will cling to it still—Apologies to Tom Moore."

Dr. Hyde also proved an impressive witness in his own behalf, as he had stage presence, and a sharp way of giving his answers. He exchanged sarcasm with the attorneys, shut them off with cold courtesy, quibbled with them over fine distinctions and told them they were misusing terms. With all his assurance, however, Dr. Hyde slipped badly at times. His habit of repeatedly saying "I don't remember," and then remembering very distinctly in his own behalf, went against him with the jury. In one place he said he had been using cyanide for eight or ten years. Reed brought him up sharply by the next question: Where had he made purchases of cyanide previous to those at Brecklein's. He could not remember any of his earlier purchases, nor could he say with certainty what he had done with the cyanide that he did buy—he said he bought it to kill "bugs," but had not had time to use it for that purpose. One of the jurors later said it was Dr. Hyde's confused testimony about the cyanide that convicted him.

When the jurors retired they stood eight to four for acquittal. The four proved more persistent than the eight, and after three days a verdict of guilty was brought in, with a recommendation for life imprisonment. The case was then appealed, and the Supreme Court reversed the decision. The high court cited a number of errors in the trial, and argued that the typhoid at the Swopes might well have arisen normally. But the principal reason for the reversal was the fact that there was no unclouded testimony that anyone had died of poisoning—it was never proved that a murder had been committed.

Two more trials were held. One resulted in a mistrial when a juror, a milkman by occupation, became tired of being shut up. He crawled through a transom and escaped. The third trial ended in a hung jury, standing nine to three for acquittal. By that time, seven years had passed, and a quarter of a million dollars had been spent in trying to convict Dr. Hyde. The Swopes, who had provided most of the money, did not wish to spend more, and neither did the state; so the case was dismissed. Dr. Hyde always maintained he was innocent.

After some years at such jobs as truck driving, Dr. Hyde managed to re-establish himself in medical practice, at Lexington, Missouri. There numbers of patients entrusted themselves to his care, with no untoward results. The reporter, A. B. Macdonald, went down to interview him in later years. Dr. Hyde, who had remembered so little at his trial, held Macdonald for half a day with a great exhibition of memory, during which he dramatically recited long passages from Shakespeare and other poets. Mrs. Hyde was his principal support at the trial, but they were divorced a few years later. At the time Macdonald visited him, Dr. Hyde was living in motheaten bachelor quarters connected with his office in Lexington. He lived into his sixties, and died in 1934 of a heart attack which struck him down in a Lexington newspaper office, where he had gone to obtain election returns.

Dr. Hyde's death ended the story behind the most impressive sight in Kansas City: the Swope Memorial. It is a pillared mausoleum, placed high and alone on a timbered hillside in

Swope Park, where it can be viewed across two hundred and fifty acres of lawn. Conversely, from the Memorial the entire sweep of the park can be viewed. The gentle and at times plaintive Colonel Swope was under the impression that he had led a useless existence, in which he had accomplished no real work; but across his Memorial is the Latin inscription which translates: *If you would see his monument, look about you.*

The Memorial was provided from a fund raised to fulfill the colonel's expressed desire that he be buried in the park. Contributions were limited to one dollar so as to make the number of subscribers as large as possible. And nothing in the city ever fitted so well with its surroundings as that pillared mausoleum built for the remains of Thomas H. Swope, who was a good judge of real estate but, in his late years at least, not such a good judge of men.

CHAPTER SIXTEEN

The Lion at Bay

IN THE YEAR 1912, William Rockhill Nelson had grown white-haired and still more corpulent. By this time, he had been publishing the Kansas City *Star* for thirty-two years and had become known throughout the country. The *Star* was a famous newspaper, and Nelson's name more than any other was linked with Kansas City's rise as a strong influence over the developing southwestern section of the country.

Because of an incident which in retrospect seemed something like a tempest in a teapot, Nelson at this stage in his career narrowly escaped spending some time in a Kansas City jail.

The incident grew out of the fact that Nelson did not like lawyers, courts, or court procedure. He thought that court procedure existed principally for the benefit of the attorneys, a very small measure of justice emanating from the legal hocus-pocus involved. A familiar story, often told concerning Nelson, was that he was once summoned for jury duty, and was asked whether there was anything that would prejudice his opinion in the case. "Nothing," he replied, "except my contempt for a man who would try to get justice in a court of law."

His sentiments were more definitely expressed in a letter which he wrote on July 26, 1912, to Theodore Roosevelt, advocating "Free Justice." "As to general policies of government I have two hobbies," wrote Nelson. "My scheme is to drive the money out of the voting booth and out of the courthouse. The government must bear the expense of all elections, and justice must be really—and not merely nominally—free."

Nelson combined a determination to assert his will and have his own way, with a strictly equalitarian philosophy of government. In his letter to Roosevelt, he continued:

> If our form of government is to remain stable, justice must not be virtually for sale as it is today. One of the places where the poor man and the rich man should go arm in arm is the courthouse. But of course they don't. Aside from the advantage which the rich man has in our cumbersome judicial system, and in the personnel of the judges, he has the immense advantage of the ability to hire the best lawyers. The first threat that the rich man makes to the poor man is that he will get the best lawyers in town.
>
> Under such conditions it is absurd to talk of the courts meting out justice. Lawyers are now regarded as officers of the court. They ought to be paid officers; their salary should come from the government, not from private litigants. The state provides the judge and jury. It ought to provide the lawyers. Society would never dream of letting one of the litigants pay the judge. It ought not to permit him to pay another officer of the court—the lawyer.
>
> The private fee system promotes all sorts of incidental evils. It encourages lawyers to make legislation complicated and uncertain. It prevents reform of judicial

procedure. It incites the stirring up of litigation . . . A situation has been produced in which it is impossible to carry out any business transaction whatever without the help of a lawyer . . . The fee system absolutely bars the doing of justice between rich and poor . . . It is my desire in the *Star* to keep hammering on these issues until equality between rich and poor in the selection of officials and the administration of justice shall no longer be a sham.

With Nelson holding such views, his paper often carried news which was unfavorable to the courts, especially where the collection of legal fees was involved. One day the *Star* appeared with the following:

PAY FEES BEFORE ALIMONY

The Lawyers Must Collect First,
Judge Guthrie Decides.
Three Attorneys Awarded $60 in
a Suit for Divorce Which
Never Came to Trial—
Reverses Former
Ruling.

If a woman brings suit for divorce the case cannot be dismissed in the circuit court until the husband has paid her attorney his fee. Judge Guthrie made that ruling yesterday in favor of the divorce lawyers in the suit of Minnie Clevinger against Claude F. Clevinger.

After Mrs. Clevinger filed her suit for divorce, her attorneys filed a motion asking the court to allow her alimony and attorneys' fee. Mr. Clevinger appeared in court with a request signed by his wife that the suit be dismissed, as she wanted neither alimony nor attorney fee.

FEES CLAIMED BY THREE

Her attorneys insisted that they be allowed their fee before the case was dismissed. Judge Guthrie gave them a judgment for $40 against Mr. Clevinger. Then another attorney, making three attorneys in all, came into court and said he also represented Mrs. Clevinger. Judge Guthrie made an order increasing the allowance to the attorneys from $40 to $60.

Mr. Clevinger's attorney insisted that a claim for attorneys' fees in divorce suits was no more binding than suits to collect grocery bills or other claims. Judge Guthrie decided differently. It was an important ruling in favor of the divorce lawyers.

THE LAWYER DECIDED

In a similar proceeding recently the judge told the attorney that the man was not able to pay both the attorney's fee and alimony to his wife.

"Now, which shall I allow," the court asked the lawyer, "the alimony to the woman or the fee to you?"

"Just make the judgment for the fee," the attorney requested, and the order was so made.

This item might have been passed over like others of the same character, except that the judge in question, Judge Joseph A. Guthrie, took strong exception to it, and cited Nelson for contempt of court.

In its original appearance, "PAY FEES BEFORE ALIMONY" was an item on page 4A, half a column long. With the news of his being cited for contempt of court, however, Nelson reprinted "PAY FEES BEFORE ALIMONY" in its entirety on the front page. The next day a reader signing R.L. wrote asking, "Do I understand the *Star* is accused of misrepresenting the facts?" Nelson again carried all of "PAY FEES BEFORE ALIMONY" on the front page, commenting that the article and the citation spoke for themselves.

He also increased the volume of his barrage with stories under such headlines as "COURTS PROMOTE ANARCHY" and "BILL HITS SNITCH LAWYERS." Judge Guthrie grew angrier with each passing day as Nelson's hearing approached, and it was widely reported that William Rockhill Nelson would certainly go to jail.

The press of the country was soon aroused over this attempt to "lock up the lion of American journalism." Colonel Henry Watterson of the Louisville *Courier-Journal* offered to lead one hundred thousand Kentucky riflemen westward into Missouri, if necessary, to rescue him. The New York *Herald* said: "We understand that Mr. Nelson does not like courts and lawyers, but this certainly is no reason to put him in jail." The Fort Scott *Tribune* commented: "It is singular that at this time, when there is such general dissatisfaction with the judicial system, there should occur such a striking example of the abuse of judicial power."

The Philadelphia *North American* defended him at length, and in doing so described his place in history. "Colonel Nelson," said the *North American,* "is closing his seventy-second year, a man of big mind, big achievements and broad sympathies. He is a civic builder. Kansas City owes its remarkable system of parks and boulevards to his inspiration; the Western Gallery of Art is his creation; he has been more potent than any other man in the Southwest, and the *Star,* founded by him and raised to eminence by his ability, is, in character, influence and public service, the foremost of American newspapers. He is the last great editor of the Horace Greeley type . . ."

Nelson's dispute with the court caused Theodore Roosevelt to wire him: "What an extraordinary series of events the courts are perpetrating at present. Apparently the reactionaries have made up their minds that you, and men like you, can be cowed . . . It seems to me like tying down the safety valve to prevent an explosion." In Kansas City, Judge Ralph S. Latshaw took a similar view, declaring: "This is the greatest outrage ever perpetrated by a court of justice . . . It is a case of putting away Caesar so that Rome may have a holiday . . . Mr. Nelson shall not spend a single minute in jail."

However, the sentiment in Kansas City was mixed. Mayor Jost, a member of the Rabbit faction, applauded the court and strongly denounced Nelson. Mayor Jost had been scheduled to address the Young Men's Jefferson Club on the subject: "What I Am Doing, How I Am Doing It, and What I Expect to Do." The *Star* reported: "In the by-paths of his eloquence, in which he got to denouncing the *Star,* the mayor got separated from his subject and did not tell what he was doing, how he was doing it, or what he expected to do."

With his denunciations of Nelson, Mayor Jost drew many more cheers than he could possibly have gained by describing his program. Because of his political position, Nelson was often a target for the city administrations; and undoubtedly there were hundreds in Kansas City who were looking forward with satisfaction to seeing the publisher's great bulk enclosed temporarily in a jail cell.

Nelson's political position was a story in itself, one involving his strong personal traits and the complicated circumstances by which he was surrounded. Back in Indiana, he had been a Democrat, and there he had managed Samuel J. Tilden's campaigns for the Democratic presidential nomination. "As you are the only Democrat in Indiana who is not a candidate for the Presidency, I would like you to manage my campaign," Tilden had wired him. Tilden was the Democratic candidate in 1876, and came so close to winning that many, including Nelson, thought that by a correct count of the votes he had won. When in 1880 the Democratic Convention failed to nominate Tilden a second time, Nelson was deeply chagrined. He renounced his allegiance to the party that year, the same year he came to Kansas City, and he thereafter pursued an independent course in politics.

He retained, however, a peculiar devotion to his presidential favorites. He never forgot Samuel J. Tilden. Upon occasions, Nelson in the *Star* stated without qualification that Tilden had been elected to the Presidency. If a reader wrote in to ask how this conclusion was reached, the *Star* would explain that Tilden was *elected* to the Presidency, but that the electoral commission had thrown out enough votes in Florida and Louisiana to give Hayes the office. Hanging together above Nelson's desk in later years were always pictures of Samuel J. Tilden, Grover Cleveland and Theodore Roosevelt —two Democrats and one Republican.

The circulation of Nelson's newspaper had followed the routes of trade, becoming deeply entrenched in Republican Kansas, where it exerted a direct political influence. Although published in Missouri, the *Star* was (and is) often said to control the politics of the state of Kansas. Nelson always continued to follow an independent political course; frequently he would find that the candidates of both parties were "miserable hacks"; and he would support a progressive in either party. However, as the years passed, his candidates were more often Republicans than Democrats. This was in consonance with the influence he exerted in Kansas.

In Kansas City, Nelson held a kind of initiative and veto power over most civic projects. If these projects received space in the *Star,* they succeeded; if not, they were likely to fail. But on the Missouri side, where the Democrats were in strength, he did not usually elect anyone to office. On the contrary, a recognized method of gaining votes in Missouri was to express opposition to the *Star*.

It was even said that if Nelson had ever supported Senator

James A. Reed, the support would have ruined Reed's career. For Reed, no matter what the other issues might be, usually made his opposition to the *Star* the most spectacular feature of a campaign. Drawing himself up to his full oratorical height, and using rich sarcasm on the word "newspaper," Reed would say: "Down at Eleventh and Grand there is a *newspaper* that calls itself the *Star*. Old Bill Nelson is its mammy, Old Bill Nelson is its pappy, and Old Bill Nelson is its wet nurse. God created the heavens and the earth, and from the ooze of the earth He created the slimy reptiles that crawl the face of the earth, and from the *residue* thereof He created Old Bill Nelson."

Nelson and Reed had been at odds since 1900, when Reed was elected mayor of Kansas City. Exactly how the feud started was never determined for certain. According to some stories, Reed as mayor refused to extend sewage pipes into a piece of Nelson's property. The property was outside the city limits, a fact which Nelson is said to have regarded as a mere technicality. In any case, the two men were completely incompatible. In the course of his feud with Reed, Nelson was drawn toward Reed's legal foe, Frank P. Walsh. The precedent that when Reed was on one side of a case Walsh was engaged on the other operated in this instance; and after a number of actions against the *Star* had been brought through Reed's law office, it followed in the natural course of events that Walsh became Nelson's attorney. So Walsh had the task of defending him when Nelson was haled before the bar of justice on the charge of contempt of court.

Walsh prepared a defense which stated in effect that in the article "PAY FEES BEFORE ALIMONY" the *Star* had made an honest attempt to report the facts, and that in the course of the attempt a mistake or two had been made. As Walsh pointed out, and as Judge Guthrie later said, if Nelson had been willing to plead a mistake he could not have been held in contempt of court, since even lawyers were unable to report cases without making some mistakes. However, Nelson had no intention of granting the court a moral victory, or even of conceding any minor points. Instead he brought one hand down with a resounding whack on his desk, and insisted on pleading that the *Star's* account was "true in substance and fact, true in exact verbiage and true in every line." Walsh revised his defense accordingly, and came into court with it.

When the hearing opened before Judge Guthrie, the courtroom was packed to the railings. The *Star's* reprinting of comments from papers all over the country had given a nation-shaking aspect to the case. Nelson, rather handsome of face despite his bulk, with his white hair and his jowls encased in a huge four-inch collar, sat at the counsel table, a picture of massive defiance. He was mountainous both in size and immobility, and physically one of the most inactive men who ever lived; but his tastes ran strongly to action, and in a grim way he appeared to enjoy the proceedings. As the hearing began, he leaned over and in a hoarse whisper urged his attorneys: "Give 'em hell . . . I don't care what happens . . . If they put me in jail I'll stay there till the ants carry me out through the keyhole."

The part of "PAY FEES BEFORE ALIMONY" to which Judge Guthrie especially objected was that contained under the subhead, "The Lawyer Decided," relating that in a case where a man was not able to pay both his attorney's fee and his alimony the judge had ordered him to pay only the fee. Judge Guthrie held that this was contemptuous toward the court in showing that the woman's rights were disregarded and the lawyer permitted to decide the point.

Walsh led off with the statement that the *Star's* account was "true in substance and fact, true in exact verbiage and true in every line." He then said: "We do not charge that this proceeding with reference to the alimony and the attorney's fee occurred in this court, but we say it occurred someplace else." The *Star's* reporter, in dealing with two different cases, had neglected to state that they occurred in different courtrooms. Walsh was obliged to base his defense on the extremely thin contention that the words "the judge" did not refer to Judge Guthrie, who was named only two lines above.

Reed was in the United States Senate, and had sent his partner to serve as the friend of the court in the proceeding. The partner fairly howled at the nature of the defense. "As though we were children, as though we were babes in the woods and could not interpret the usages of the English tongue . . . It is an insult to the court to come in here with such a specious plea . . . I recommend that the defendant be not fined, but that he be sentenced to the common jail of Jackson County that he may there have an opportunity to reflect upon the course he has voluntarily mapped out for himself and that he has followed."

Judge Guthrie heartily concurred. As soon as the arguments were completed, he began giving his decision, first excoriating Nelson in an eloquent and strongly worded analysis of the case. Walsh's partner, James P. Aylward, had often heard Judge Guthrie give political speeches. It occurred to Aylward that he had never before heard Judge Guthrie speak with such fluency and exactness. Aylward tiptoed across the room, stepped up on the sheriff's dais, peered over the judge's rostrum and saw what he suspected—Judge Guthrie was reading his decision from a manuscript. Aylward then tiptoed back to the counsel table and whispered to Walsh, who interrupted the judge to ask:

"Excuse me, Your Honor, are you reading that decision?"

"I am," replied Judge Guthrie.

Since there had been no recess, no time in which the judge could have written a decision, the conclusion followed that he must have prepared his decision in advance of the hearing. Walsh brought out this point, and was able to say: "Let the record show that at the conclusion of the arguments the judge of this honorable court read his decision, which was prepared in advance."

Judge Guthrie continued with his decision. When he spoke the words which sentenced Nelson to jail, a cheer went up from the courtroom. There was no doubt that Nelson could be freed on a writ of habeas corpus; but because of a technicality which the *Star* said was typical of the legal profession, the writ of habeas corpus could not be issued until after he had been formally sentenced to jail. In the interim it appeared that for at least fifteen or twenty minutes he would actually be in a cell. All arrangements had been made to assure this. A squad of deputy sheriffs was waiting to hustle him out of the courtroom and into the county jail.

Walsh tried to forestall the commitment by asking for time to consult with his client. Judge Guthrie denied this, and spoke the formal order: "The sheriff is hereby commanded to take charge of the body of him, the said William R. Nelson, and commit him into the custody of the marshal of said county, and to the jail thereof."

The squad of deputies advanced on Nelson. At the same time, his attorneys crowded around him so closely that the deputies could not lay hands on him. There ensued a struggle lasting several minutes, during which the deputies attempted to break through the attorneys and seize their prisoner. One deputy twice succeeded in grasping Nelson's arm. The *Star* said that Nelson was "roughly jostled." While holding off the deputies with one hand, Walsh was waving at the judge with the other: "Your Honor, I beg of you . . . This is unprecedented . . . Never before has a defendant been denied time to consult with his counsel." Judge Guthrie said that he had no further jurisdiction, that he washed his hands of the matter, and that he would not differentiate in this case.

Finally, however, Judge Guthrie relented, and granted time for consultation. After several more minutes, a swift messenger arrived from the court of Judge Latshaw with the necessary writ of habeas corpus. Walsh walked out of the courtroom with a free client, and also with something he had not possessed when he entered—a good argument. He had no difficulty in convincing the Missouri Supreme Court that, since Judge Guthrie's decision was prepared in advance, Nelson had been convicted without a hearing. "A person," ruled the high court, "may be guilty of the most atrocious crime, which may be known to hundreds, and he may have proclaimed his guilt from the housetops; nevertheless, he must be accorded the same fair and impartial trial, according to the forms of law, that would be accorded to a king, prince or potentate."

Nelson continued to "hammer away" on the subject of the courts when opportunity arose. Theodore Roosevelt never took any action on Nelson's letter regarding "Free Justice"; but in the course of preparing the ground for his Bull Moose and Progressive party campaign for the Presidency in 1912, Roosevelt had previously come out for applying the initiative, referendum and recall to the courts. Nelson in the *Star* vigorously endorsed this proposal, and the general understanding at first was that any judge, or any judicial decision, might be recalled by a referendum and a majority vote of the people.

Finding himself in stormy political waters over the issue, Roosevelt subsequently had much occasion to explain his statement. He stood by the wording of his speech, but so modified the general understanding of his proposal that it would have applied only to the recall of judicial decisions, with some exceptions. In the modified form, the proposal was included as a plank in the platform of the Progressive party. But Nelson paid little attention to the modifications. Long after the Bull Moose campaign, the *Star* was speaking of "one of the new purposes of politics, which is best expressed in the creed of the Progressive party, to bring the judiciary department of the government into closer relation with the people. The recall of the judiciary, the referendum on decisions (or recall of decisions), the short elective term of judges, and other propositions, are each and all expressions of that purpose."

Concerning modifications and amendments to these proposals, the *Star* merely commented: "The strength of each plan is greater than any reasoned faith that it is scientifically the right plan. Very largely it is the imperfect concrete expression of the perfect abstract understanding that 'something should be done.' "

CHAPTER SEVENTEEN

The Unterrified Moose

DURING THIRTY YEARS of publishing, Nelson had taken a progressive stand on almost every issue, from municipal ownership of public utilities to running water in the farm woman's kitchen, and in fields of art, literature, politics, and commerce. "The city is its streets, the country its roads, the nation its highways of rail and water: everything depends upon accessibility," preached the *Star*. "Education languishes when mud blockades the road; literature must have circulation or be impotent; art cannot ennoble the multitude it cannot reach." The paper was ready to do battle on any of the issues that statement might imply.

To the Kansas editors, Nelson was "the Great Chief," whose publishing courage in the *Star* had made it possible for many smaller newspapers also to take an outspoken and progressive stand. Directly and indirectly, William Allen White thought that Nelson had given color and purpose to the thoughts and aspirations of ten million people living between the Missouri and the Rio Grande. "He and they were dreaming states and building them," wrote White. "Their aspirations were formed and given back in the policies of the *Star*."

There were these thirty years of "city and state building" behind Nelson's progressivism. And he had never lost his "insurgent tendencies," which perhaps were related to egg-throwing in his youth.

The course of national affairs often did not satisfy Nelson. He did not like William Jennings Bryan personally, and so supported William McKinley in 1896 and 1900. But he was lukewarm, at best, toward McKinley's policies. He was against high tariffs, which then were synonymous with "high cost of living" to many in the middle states, and his taste was for dramatic and colorful action.

In 1901, McKinley was assassinated. Theodore Roosevelt entered the White House and instituted liberal policies which completely satisfied Nelson. In 1904, Roosevelt performed the remarkable feat of carrying Missouri, at a time when the Republican party was known as "the mysterious stranger" in the state. He made a number of trips to Missouri, and he and Nelson became fast friends.

In 1908, on Roosevelt's endorsement, Nelson supported William Howard Taft for President. Like other progressives, he was soon disillusioned in Taft, whom he regarded as a bungler, a prisoner of legal phraseology and legalistic thinking—a pleasant and well-intentioned man, but unfitted for the office. Taft had been elected on the promise that the Republicans for the first time would reduce the tariff. The Payne-Aldrich Tariff Act offered so little and so few of the promised reductions that the western congressmen were up in arms. Then Taft defended the Payne-Aldrich Tariff Act. That was in the fall of 1909, and the next election was three years away, but

Nelson knew then that he could never support Taft for re-election.

He determined to support the Democratic nominee in 1912, unless Theodore Roosevelt could be persuaded to run for a third term. The idea of getting Roosevelt to run for a third term seems to have occurred to Nelson as early as to anyone. As the campaign approached, he carried Roosevelt's *African Game Trails* in instalments in the *Star,* and in general did his part to keep Roosevelt's name before the public. Early in 1912, he sponsored a letter signed by the governors of seven states, including those of Missouri and Kansas, inviting Roosevelt to become a candidate. This made a great impression on the country. Then the *Star* polled its 300,000 weekly readers on their presidential favorites. Roosevelt, with 78,000 votes, led five to one over his nearest opponent, Champ Clark, with 15,000 votes; and Taft was in fifth place. Taft was so unsatisfactory to the progressives that there was a clamor for Roosevelt in all parts of the country; but the overwhelming character of his support in the *Star's* poll also reflected Nelson's influence with his readers. The poll figures were announced February 12, 1912, a few days before Roosevelt said he would accept the nomination.

Along with other progressives, Nelson sat grimly through the Republican National Convention, held in Chicago in the summer of 1912. Both of "Nelson's governors" were active in Roosevelt's behalf. Hadley, the first Republican governor of Missouri, was Roosevelt's floor manager. Governor Stubbs of Kansas presented a reason why he should return to Topeka; but William Allen White recorded that Colonel Nelson's flashing eyes and set jaw held him in line, and he remained. The Republican National Committee was in charge of the convention machinery and was calmly seating Taft delegates, in defiance of the popular demand for Roosevelt. The Roosevelt followers went down in defeat and departed in a rage.

As soon as it became apparent that Roosevelt would not get the Republican nomination, Nelson outlined, and the *Star* published, a story predicting the organization of a national Progressive party, with Roosevelt as its candidate. This developed promptly. Nelson accepted the Missouri chairmanship of the Progressive party, the only political office he ever held. He returned to Kansas City and, using a large part of the *Star's* front page, issued a call—"to all voters in Missouri who believe in a new deal and a square deal in politics"—and at his urging, a state convention to choose national delegates was held in Kansas City.

The more ardent Roosevelt followers returned to Chicago a few weeks later, this time for the first national convention of the Progressive party. Theodore Roosevelt, sixty-three years old but still in fine physical condition and fresh from the African game trails, was on hand to accept the nomination. When he was asked how he felt, he grinned a large-toothed grin, waved his hand, and called out: "I'm feeling stronger than a Bull Moose." From then on it was the Bull Moose convention, the Bull Moose party, and the Bull Moose campaign, the only modern presidential race in which there were three major candidates. Roosevelt was duly nominated, and the Bull Moose delegates dispersed for the difficult task of establishing a third party.

A Chicago paper jibed that the Kansas City coterie included no one except Nelson whom the public had ever heard of. Nelson in the *Star* retorted that the Progressive party was a party of the plain people, adding: "The Republican party is out of it; anyone with a lick of sense knows that." He assumed that the real race would be between Theodore Roosevelt and Woodrow Wilson.

Because Nelson was one of the main pillars of Roosevelt's

middle-western support, eastern reporters journeyed westward to see him. They were destined for some surprising interviews. Nelson was Buddha-like in appearance, and Jovian in the range of his emotions. His jowls hung over his collar, and he had a heavy, formidable jaw; but he had a high, handsome forehead and large, expressive, jade-colored eyes. Sometimes he would shake the room with laughter. Again his expressive eyes would open wide with astonishment or with frank cordiality. At times he would chuckle a rumbling chuckle, or he would be immobile, expressionless and imperturbable. Then on occasions his eyes would narrow and flash with anger, and his jaw would set. At such times, one of the reporters remarked, it was a question whether he should be described as "dominant" or "domineering." And there was always that deep, cavernous voice in which he laid down the law for Kansas City and its environs.

The eastern reporters could not avoid the impression that they had visited a mountain, and that the mountain had spoken. "He is more like a volcano than any man I ever met," said a New York writer. "He is even shaped like one, being mountainous in his proportions and also in the way he tapers upward from his vast waist. And the voice which proceeds from the Colonel is Vesuvian: hoarse, deep, rumbling, strong. When he speaks great natural forces seem to stir."

Another eastern writer struck the same vein: "If there is a more defiant, unterrified, eager, enthusiastic Bull Mooser than Colonel Bill anywhere under the flag or the bandanna, it is the Moose himself. When the big-bodied, big-headed, deep-throated Missourian says 'I'm a Bull Mooser,' it is like the crashing reverberation of thunder in the mountains, tangled up with a Kansas cyclone and the booming of the northeast surf. He leaves no doubt upon the point. One will never question that he is a Bull Mooser after he has said it."

In the course of building the Kansas City *Star*, Nelson had built a movement, or a way of thinking, which was casting its shadow even farther than his newspaper. Mark Sullivan once described Nelson as "one of the dozen important personalities of his time," and as "a pioneer in thought and an original source of ideas in public affairs which stood the test of discussion and later came to constitute to a large degree the public opinion of the day."

"The liberal and progressive movement which arose in the Middle West around 1900, and which came to dominate the political and social forces of the period," wrote Sullivan, "centered largely around the Kansas City *Star* and the forces of public opinion which took their leadership from the *Star*. Nelson, through his paper, gave these forces the vehicle for expression which was essential to their existence."

How many of Nelson's opinions came from his readers, and vice versa, might be debated. But many other newspapers rose under similar circumstances without showing similar tendencies. This seemed more clearly a case of a man expressing his own personality and ideas through the avenues which the situation left open; and these avenues happened to be extensive.

From the first the Bull Moosers were moved by a deeply felt idealism. Nelson, for his part, would have nothing less. "Mere smartness will never bring lasting success," he used to say. He organized the Bull Moose campaign, as far as his newspaper was concerned, and he keyed it to the deepest aspirations in the greatest number of people.

The most controversial issue proved to be the plank for "recall of judicial decisions," which Nelson's position on the courts had done much to encourage. If Roosevelt had accepted Nelson's idea for "Free Justice," he would have had a still more lively issue on his hands.* Nelson believed in thorough work, and in tearing up the ground, if necessary.

As Nelson surveyed the national scene in 1912, the significant fact to him was that the last free homestead in the "rain belt" had been pre-empted during the nineties. Before that, he said, life was a fair sort of struggle. All a man needed was a strong body, an ax and a spade; and it was up to him to make good. But with the coming of heavily populated cities, opportunity had been reduced for masses of people, while for others there were rewards that were out of proportion with the service done. The problem, then, was to reorganize industrial conditions on a democratic basis so that equality of opportunity would be preserved, and the rewards of industry would be put on a basis of service to the community.

He was impressed by Jane Addams, the heroine of all the progressives, and by the philosophy which she summed up by referring to "the sheer stupidity of consuming all of life's energies merely to stay alive." He was stirred, too, by the possibility of using the growing surplus of labor for large-scale beautification and improvement projects. "To start up idle factories and give employment to men without jobs," he said, "it must be acknowledged that it does not require the labor of all the people to supply all the needs of the world on the present scale of living. New channels of industry can be opened by the beautification of cities, the improvement of

* In his letter to Roosevelt regarding "Free Justice," quoted in the previous chapter, Nelson made clear that he did not want the proposal brought up immediately, but rather to be considered in the future policies of the Progressive party. Roosevelt replied that he agreed in principle, but that the proposal was so radical he did not know how it would be received. He added that it would be something to fight for later. In general, the courts were a national issue because the period was one of social reform, and a number of progressive measures, including workmen's compensation and income tax laws, had been declared unconstitutional.

country roads, and the enlargement of the expenditures of those who are prosperous."

Nelson's ideas of building, at first applied to the growth of Kansas City, had become fully national in scope. One of the achievements which he most often cited in Theodore Roosevelt's favor was that he "got the canal dug." Actually, the Panama Canal slowed the growth of Kansas City and other railroad centers, by diverting to sea large shipments which otherwise would have crossed the country by rail. But this local factor could not dampen Nelson's ardor for a large-scale building project so exactly to his taste.

Roosevelt was also praised in the words of Professor E. A. Ross of the University of Wisconsin, as a candidate "who thinks in terms of welfare rather than wealth, a man as elemental and uncommercial as Daniel Boone or Davy Crockett, yet withal a scholar, familiar with the ideas of the far-sighted thinkers who have been beseeching people to look at matters from the standpoint of society." In response to the statement that the Bull Moosers did not include many prominent citizens, Nelson pointed out that a long list of well-known writers were in their train—Will Irwin, Emerson Hough, Richard Harding Davis, William Allen White, C. P. Connolly, Hamlin Garland, George Ade and Edna Ferber. "The Progressive party," said the *Star*, "appealed to the men and women who have had the most influence as writers in the last decade—influence because they were identified by sympathy and understanding with the average family, and because they have been thinking along progressive lines."

On October 14, 1912, while speaking in Milwaukee, Theodore Roosevelt was shot by a deranged man. In one of the most dramatic incidents of any campaign, Roosevelt refused to be examined for his wound until after he had finished his speech. The wound proved to be slight, and he recovered in two weeks. Of his first speech after recovering, the *Star* said:

"He came back from the valley of the shadow to make such a speech as this country never has heard in a political campaign. It carried his passion for humanity, the lessons of his long experience in the struggle for human rights, his indomitable courage, his tremendous earnestness; all tinged with the high solemnity of a man who has just been face to face with eternal things."

In italics on the front page, which was as far as the *Star* ever went in emphasis, Nelson carried these excerpts from Roosevelt's speech:

> *There must be bread for all who work; there must be time for play when men and women are young. When they grow old there must be the certainty of life under conditions free from the haunting terrors of utter poverty* * * * *We are for liberty, but we are for the liberty of the oppressed and not the liberty of the oppressor to oppress* * * * *We must not permit the brutal selfishness of arrogance and the brutal selfishness of envy each to run unchecked its evil course* * * * *The doctrine we preach reaches back to the golden rule and the Sermon on the Mount* * * * *We decline to be bound by the empty little cut and dried formulae of a bygone philosophy* * * * *We propose to shackle greedy cunning as we shackle brute force* * * * *We care for deeds and not for words* * * * *We will not consent to make the constitution a fetish for the protection of fossilized wrong* * * * *We are striving to meet the needs of all men and to meet them in such fashion that all alike shall feel bound together in a bond of common brotherhood.*

To the end of the campaign, Nelson held some hope that T. R.'s popularity would overcome the odds against a man running on the ticket of a new and not-fully-organized party. He continued to stress the need for the various proposals in the Progressive party platform, such as prohibition of child labor, pensions for sickness, irregular employment and old age, standards of safety and health, a federal department of labor and the better organization of labor. In a closing editorial headed "FORWARD, MARCH!" the *Star* said: "These are the necessary and inevitable measures in the industrial democracy that is coming. The forces that have made civilization, the irresistible forces of human progress, are behind them. They are bound to win!"

They did not win, but Nelson easily shifted his support to Woodrow Wilson, of whom he had spoken highly even during the campaign. He was proud of his part in the Bull Moose campaign which shook the two-party system to its floor beams; and insisted that if Roosevelt had not drawn off half the Republican vote, Taft might have been re-elected. "If it had not been for Roosevelt," said the *Star*, "Woodrow Wilson would not today be the president-elect, and the progressive program outlined by the incoming president would be an idle dream. Eventually progress would have its way; but the cause of human rights has been advanced years by the compelling personality of Theodore Roosevelt."

Nelson was well past seventy, carrying a hundred pounds or so of excess weight, and may have suspected that the Bull Moose campaign would be his last. He grew retrospective, and seemed to be taking stock of his career. He had his men check back through the years and see how much space the *Star* had devoted to fighting the streetcar and other municipal franchises, which once loomed so large in the news. He was glad to hear that the antifranchise articles measured an impressive total of 2,500 columns. However, he never did sum up his life, in an autobiography or otherwise; and his personal thoughts are known only through the recollections of members of his staff.

He did not have a private office, because he preferred to sit in the big editorial room. He did a tremendous amount of mental labor, and took almost no physical exercise. He seldom wrote anything, in the sense of putting words on paper; but he frequently "outlined" articles for his writers—that is, told them what to write. Then he liked to have these articles read back to him orally, so he could make a few changes if he wished. The writers made a practice of using Nelson's words where they could. He "spoke" in his newspaper; the *Star* during his years was full of Nelson's punchy vernacular. He had a great fondness for such words as "got," "sort" and "miserable."

Nelson would not use halftones (photographs) in the *Star*. He kept artists to convert all photographs, including portraits, into drawings of some artistic merit. In attractive appearance, in thorough coverage of the news, and in clear statement of the facts and issues, his paper has seldom been equaled. "The *Star* is my life," he used to say. This was literally the case, since he cared nothing for social affairs or appearances in public. And since his only daughter was childless, he could not, even if he had wished, have thought of the preservation of his line. His entire life, especially in his later years, was dedicated to the publication of this newspaper.

And yet Nelson was convinced that it would be impossible to preserve the *Star* as he had shaped it. In his will, he simply provided that the *Star* should be sold to the highest bidder. He bequeathed his entire fortune to the completion of a municipal art project which he had started in 1896. At that time he was traveling as a rich American in Europe, during the education of his daughter, and had become interested in acquiring a collection of masterpieces, but had found that even his resources were insufficient for the purpose. The only Rembrandt painting he could find for sale was $50,000. So instead, he had bought a collection of fifty oil copies of masterpieces. These were housed in the Western Gallery of Art. He then decided to devote his fortune to acquiring a collection of authentic pictures. In his will, he provided that the proceeds from the sale of the *Star* and his other property should be placed in a trust fund, the income from which was to be used to buy paintings.

Through 1913 and early 1914 he continued to work long hours at his desk. He spent his last summer in Colorado, visiting vacation places. His eyesight had dimmed until, he said, he could no longer see the mistakes in his own newspaper; and he actually seemed to be growing a little mellow. If he met anyone who read the *Star* he would say: "Well, we're all friends, aren't we?" Through the fall of 1914, he continued to come to the newspaper office, but lacked his usual energy. During the winter of 1914–15, he remained at home, but frequently telephoned suggestions for stories and cartoons.

His physical decline was caused by a gradual stoppage of the liver. Nothing could be done which would permanently improve his condition, but his life could be prolonged by the injection of a salt solution which neutralized the poison. Such injections had been given for a number of weeks, when one day Nelson looked at the doctor and said: "That stuff isn't doing me any good; you're just keeping me alive, aren't you?" The doctor admitted that that was the case, and Nelson, half joking, said: "I thought you were a friend of mine." Then he shook his head and added seriously: "We'll have no more of that."

The injections were discontinued. He failed rapidly and no longer sat up during the day or telephoned the newspaper office. But his last words were an order: "Don't let them prolong my life." He sank into a coma soon afterward and died the following morning, April 13, 1915.

William Allen White said: "He lived largely; he was of giant size . . . When he took a position it was tenable not only the day he took it but ever after. That is genius." Mark Sullivan said: "There are not in any one generation more than twenty such effective foundations of thought." The publisher was buried with all the honors of the town. The presses in Kansas and Missouri and the news wires across the country were stopped in silent tribute, and editorial writers spoke of the end of an era. He was, in the words the Philadelphia *North American* had once used, "the last great editor of the Horace Greeley type."

Nelson's ideas and career would have assumed greater national significance if the Progressive party had lived to carry on his fame. He was boosting for the party up to the time of his death. But the party died a year later, in 1916, when Theodore Roosevelt refused to accept its nomination a second time. The Bull Mooser Harold Ickes, in an article titled "Who Killed the Progressive Party?" did not pretend to answer the question fully. The party died of many blows, and one of the blows was the loss of Nelson.

Besides his part in national affairs, Nelson was closely connected with the development of the Southwest, especially the states of Kansas and Oklahoma. Above all, he was connected with the growth and development of Kansas City, the transformed "capital of cow towns" which now boasted skyscrapers.

In the race of swelling populations and taller skyscrapers, Nelson would have liked to see Kansas City keep pace with

Chicago. That was not possible. Kansas City's stockyards were nearly as large, and it had as many railroad lines with which to start the race; but—the most important thing—Kansas City had no steel, except from scrap. Nevertheless, the eventual Kansas City skyline would be the highest in the Missouri River watershed, which includes one-sixth of the country. At the time of Nelson's death, the height of this skyline was fifteen and sixteen stories, or half the height it later attained. He died in the midst of the period when each new building, to be of importance, had to be taller than the last one built.

The statement that Nelson "found the city in mud and left it in marble" was made when he died. The tribute was then based on the numerous splendid buildings which were in the city, as compared with the frame and dusty brick structures which characterized the city's years as a "capital of cow towns." However, the city's most decorative feature in marble, the William Rockhill Nelson Gallery of Art, was added a number of years after his death, the result of the disposition he made of his wealth.

The *Star* was sold to a bank-financed company formed by his editorial staff. It was thereafter operated under an employee stock-owning plan. The employees paid eleven million dollars, which as a price for a newspaper was second only to the thirteen million paid for the Chicago *Daily News*. The art fund was augmented by the early deaths of Nelson's widow, daughter and son-in-law, all of whom left additional money for the Nelson Gallery. By 1930, the total of the Nelson estates was nearly twenty million dollars, including four million in accumulated income which, under the terms of his will, was available for the purchase of works of art.

Even four million dollars at first seemed a small sum for a municipal art collection. The *Star* recalled that the Huntington Gallery of California had paid $800,000 for Gainsborough's *Blue Boy,* and that the Widener Collection of the National Gallery had paid $500,000 for *The Mill* by Rembrandt. The Nelson trustees reported that for a Rembrandt depicting Aristotle looking at a bust of Homer a London art dealer named Duveen was asking a cool million, in case anybody wanted to buy it and in case he wanted to sell, which he said he didn't.

However, the depression of the thirties forced the sale of many works of art at prices much lower than those commonly mentioned before. The four million dollars bought a collection that probably would have cost ten million in the twenties. J. C. Nichols, Kansas City real-estate man who was one of the Nelson trustees, was glad to be called "the greatest chiseler in art" because of his part in the buying.

With its later additions, the Kansas City collection listed paintings by Titian, Tintoretto, and Veronese; by El Greco, Goya, and Velasquez; by Cézanne, Manet, Van Gogh, and Gauguin; by Breughel the younger, Rembrandt, and Peter Paul Rubens, and by Turner and Gainsborough. It included an unusual collection of Chinese paintings and objects. Among its paintings was *Triumph of Bacchus,* one of the famous trio which old Nicolas Poussin painted for Cardinal Richelieu. The other two, *Triumph of Love* and *Triumph of Flora,* are respectively in the Louvre in Paris and in the Hermitage in Leningrad.

Nelson, as a precaution against the purchase of paintings which might have only current value, provided in his will that his money should be spent only for the works of artists who have been "dead at least thirty years." However, a Friends-of-Art association was formed to buy modern art, and a number of gifts were received, so that the Gallery in fact exhibits the works of both living and dead artists. Among the painters represented are both of Kansas City's noted artists, George Caleb Bingham of Civil War times and Thomas Hart Benton of the present. The Nelson Gallery, opened in 1933, today attracts a quarter of a million visitors a year. It is sometimes referred to as one of the half dozen leading galleries in the country, and in plant it is second to none.

The construction of the Nelson Gallery itself provided a separate story, which developed from Nelson's determination to make use of native stone. The Gallery stands where Nelson's home formerly was located, in the midst of the twenty acres he reserved for his lawn. When Nelson selected that site, he instructed workmen to build his house of the limestone which lies close under the topsoil around Kansas City, and which turns a yellowish color when exposed to the air.

A number of people told him he couldn't use that stone. They said the stone wouldn't hold up, and would crumble in a year or two. Nelson disregarded the warnings, possibly because he was better informed, or perhaps because of his general attitude that if he, William Rockhill Nelson, used anything it would have to hold up. So the native stone was used, and that was the composition of Oak Hall, from which he ruled as the Baron of Brush Creek.

Nelson also undertook to promote the general use of native stone. He built a splendid, arched stone bridge across Brush Creek, as an example to lawmakers of the type of construction they should require, and he campaigned for native stone in his newspaper. The *Star* referred contemptuously to "tin bridges," meaning those of iron and steel. Nelson was envisioning arched stone bridges as the standard means of spanning streams in all parts of the state.

In spite of his successful demonstrations, the native stone

continued to be regarded as cheap building material. Residents chuckled over Nelson's persistence on the subject, and used the stone to build yard and garden walls around their houses. Many of these old yard and garden walls, partly sunken and covered with vines, can still be seen in the vicinity of the Gallery.

The Nelson Gallery is an Ionic structure of only four stories, but is so ample in all its proportions that its cubic interior equals that of the thirty-two-story Power and Light Building, Kansas City's tallest structure. The wide grounds, landscaped with long rows of shrubs and evergreens and flanked by tall trees, so deceive the eye that, from a distance, the Gallery does not appear to be a large building. The first real idea of its size is obtained after entering Kirkwood Hall, where two rows of black marble pillars rise thirty-nine feet above the floor—three feet higher than the similar pillars in the National Gallery at Washington.

At either end of the two rows of black pillars are four giant pillars of a tawny color, called "Missouri Marble," or "Nelson Marble." These were made of native stone, some of which was quarried on the site of the gallery. Several years after Nelson's death, tests showed that the stone would take the high polish of marble. In the Gallery it had its first use as such.

CHAPTER EIGHTEEN

Back to Missouri

THOMAS HART BENTON, the artist, has often been referred to as a grandson or a great-grandson of Senator Benton. Actually, he is a grandnephew of the Senator. The artist's father was Colonel M. E. Benton, a Missouri congressman. In contrast to Senator Benton's large physique and eagle-like bearing, Colonel Benton was short, stumpy and red-bearded. But he had a flow of eloquence, which was very much in the Benton tradition, and a firm allegiance to the Democratic party.

Shortly after the Civil War, Colonel M. E. Benton followed in Senator Benton's footsteps by migrating from Tennessee into Missouri. He stopped in St. Louis long enough to be admitted to the bar, which for a man of some education was then a simple procedure. He continued across the state of Missouri, and set himself up to practice law in the town of Neosho, which was on the fringe of the Ozark Mountains and several counties to the south of Kansas City.

Like others among the Bentons, Colonel Benton was highly individualistic, independent and strong-minded. He sometimes talked furiously to himself, and he had a strange habit of adding, subtracting and dividing long rows of figures. He filled the margins of newspapers and books and the walls of yard buildings with great columns of figures, and obtained some kind of release from this mental exercise. His peculiarities in no way prevented him from seeing exactly the course which society should follow, or from exerting a strong influence over his countrymen. His law office was on the town square, across from the spired brick courthouse. Hill people from the Ozarks as well as flatlanders came to see him. Shaking his red beard and gesturing with upraised arm, he was a fiery speaker at the outdoor political meetings. He became one of the substantial leaders of the town, and served as United States Attorney under Cleveland.

When he was well past forty, Colonel Benton built a mansion on a hill overlooking Neosho, and married a stately Texas girl. They had four children, the first of whom was Thomas Hart Benton, named after the Senator and intended for the same statesmanlike pursuits. Marked out for the boy's reading while he was growing up were bound copies of Senator Benton's extensive literary works, *The Thirty Years View* (two volumes) and *The Abridgement of the Debates of Congress* (fourteen volumes), tomes which historians plough through with difficulty. It always remained Benton's conviction that these weighty works indirectly influenced him toward becoming an artist. Much as he admired his great-uncle, the young Benton did not want to read those books.

There were early indications that the boy tended more toward art than toward law and politics. At the age of seven, he decorated the entire length of the Benton stairwell with a mural freight train, drawing with charcoal on cream-colored wallpaper—a decoration not appreciated by the family. He early showed a preference for "low company," including the town bums and the colored boys he found along the creek banks of the vicinity; and he idly drew pictures of the people and scenes he encountered on his excursions. His father lectured him severely about his "lazy habits," meaning both the loafing with loafers and the picturemaking, and continued to have hopes of getting him to mend his ways. Colonel Benton believed that only lawyers were fitted to hold political power, and that the law was the only suitable profession for a Benton. He was proud of the fact that he himself could read Latin at the age of six, and he went so far as to provide his son with a Latin tutor, whom the young Benton usually managed to avoid.

The Benton house on the hill was a meeting place for famous political figures of the time. Champ Clark and William Jennings Bryan were often guests of the Bentons for several days. Colonel Benton thought this provided his son with an excellent opportunity to learn politics by listening to his elders. Unfortunately for the colonel's point of view, the son chiefly remembered that these great political figures chewed the ends of their cigars and consumed enormous quantities of food. Bryan was the greatest gormandizer of them all; he usually harassed Lucretia, the high-brown cook, by snooping around the kitchen and helping himself, as a preliminary feeding, to everything within reach. One of Benton's earliest recollections is of Bryan at breakfast, engulfing poached eggs set on halves of baked potatoes—half a potato and a poached egg at a bite.

Despite the Southern gentility to which he was born, Benton's boyhood was much like Huckleberry Finn's. The style of living, the activities of the town and his father's political interests, in which every vote counted, had a way of nullifying any social distinctions that might have existed. The Bentons kept two cows. A cow named Bluey had a habit of lying down in fresh manure, and Benton usually spent a half hour cleaning her bag before he could milk her—scarcely a genteel task. He went on midnight possum hunts with a lantern, killed copperhead snakes in the hills, and with other boys of the town sneaked rides on freight trains, from Neosho to a junction two miles out of town.

Political meetings were held at the fairgrounds and resembled a county fair. As soon as a candidate arrived in town, he was placed behind the town band and marched up and down the streets, grasping hands on each side of the line of march. He was then taken to the fairgrounds, and was expected to speak for at least two hours, shouting at the top of his voice in the open air. While he spoke, shooting galleries continued to operate, and the younger generation rode the "spinning jenny," a mule-powered merry-go-round. There were also stands selling pink lemonade. Gypsy fortunetellers and medicine shows took advantage of the political gathering. After the speech, heard by not more than half the crowd, there were barbecues and torchlight parades.

Indians from "The Nations," a strip of land sixteen miles to the west and today a part of Oklahoma, wandered into Neosho. They wore checked shirts, and broad-brimmed, high-crowned hats. On Fourth of July, the Indians dressed in their native costumes and gave powwows for the benefit of the town. There were picnics every year for Union and Confederate veterans, there were old settlers' reunions, and there were band concerts every Saturday night. Benton watched and took part in all the activities. Adults designated him as "M. E.'s son," "M. E." being well known to everyone. Colonel Benton and his family in practice led the most democratic of lives, and the Benton law office was usually filled with seedy, tobacco-spitting old fellows who came there to loaf.

When his son was still a child, in 1896, Colonel Benton was elected to Congress. The son's horizon thereafter was expanded by months in Washington. At the ages of thirteen and fourteen he did some heavy reading in the Library of Congress, and drew pictures depicting the Rhine legends, Beowulf and the Titans of Greek mythology—drawing because it relieved him of the drudgery of studying Latin or history. Neither he nor his father thought of his becoming an artist. The only artists familiar to Colonel Benton were a Washington variety of mincing, bootlicking portrait painters, whom he unhesitatingly referred to as pimps. It did not occur to him that his son could become related by profession to any of these.

However, without exactly knowing the reason, Colonel Benton began to find more and more fault with his son. A suspicion grew in the colonel's mind that his son was "impractical." The young Benton meanwhile sensed that shrewd men among his father's friends could tell at a glance that he would never be a lawyer, and that the friends were feeling sorry for Colonel Benton because his son was "queer." Yet he was perfectly strong and normal in every respect. His dislike grew for the governors, senators, and judges who frequented his father's house, and his preference for "low company" increased. He bought a derby hat, slouched around the pool halls and drugstores of Neosho, and began going with girls. He learned to drink whisky, and to wash it down with salted beer. He became involved in brawls, and twice was hauled into police court for fighting in the streets. He was spoken of as a disgrace to his family.

Beginning in 1904, Colonel Benton's world seemed to collapse around him. First his district developed Republican tendencies, and he was defeated for Congress after serving four terms. Then his son determined to be an artist. The political turn was occasioned by the presence of lead and zinc mines around Joplin, Missouri, and the consequent attraction for industry. The hill people of the district, an independent lot, were already Republican, if only because the flatlanders were Democrats. The arrival of industry and workers from the north tipped the balance in Republican favor.

Young Benton's decision to become an artist was connected with the same industrial development. He had carried a rod and chain for surveyors in laying out the Neosho waterworks, and he obtained a job with a surveying gang working for the lead and zinc mines out of Joplin. He was seventeen years old when he went to Joplin and felt he had attained man's estate. He visited the saloons of the town, including the House of Lords, a place frequented by substantial leaders of the town.

Behind the bar in the House of Lords was a painting of a masked, nude woman, who was lying across a bed and appeared to be dying of a knife wound. In the picture also was a masked man dressed for a costume ball, in the act of stabbing himself. The story behind the picture was that the man had attended a masked ball, had become enamored of the young woman, and had discovered, too late, that the woman was his sister. In his remorse, he had thrust a knife into her, and he was about to commit suicide. Benton was absorbed by the intriguing theme which the picture suggested, and was lost in one of his reveries, when he became aware that a line of men was grinning at him. Several derisive remarks were made. Benton was furiously embarrassed. On the spur of the moment he declared that he was not particularly interested in the naked woman, but was studying the painting because he was an artist and wished to see how it was done. This was the first time he had declared himself to be an artist.

"So you're an artist, eh, Shorty?" said one of the men.

"Yes, by God! I am, and I'm a good one."

The man asked where he was working, and Benton said he was out of work and looking for a job. The man said he might be able to get him on the staff of the Joplin *American.* They walked together down the block to the newspaper office, with a group of others from the saloon following in their wake. To an accompaniment of several winks, the newspaper editor assigned Benton to make a drawing of the druggist across the street. Benton took crayon and paper, and went to the drugstore. He knew nothing technically of drawing. He began with the nose, and sketched in the other features as best he could. The result was a good likeness, a rather effective drawing. To the surprise of his hecklers, Benton was placed on the newspaper staff, at fourteen dollars a week, which was ten dollars more than he was getting for carrying a rod and chain. He worked several months, making drawings of prominent citizens for the Joplin *American,* and he determined to attend an art school and become a big newspaper artist.

Colonel Benton choked with rage and disbelief when he learned of this decision. He and his son were almost completely estranged. A family "compromise" was reached under which Benton enrolled in a military school at Alton, Illinois. He remained at the military school only a few months; and then, taking matters into his own hands, enrolled in the Chicago Art Institute, early in the year 1907.

After a year, he was recognized as the Art Institute's most promising water colorist, and as its boldest in the use of strong colors. He knew there was money at home for his education, and with the help of his mother managed to obtain this. At the age of nineteen, he went to Paris to further his ambition. He held the prevailing belief that an artist *had* to be a genius, and that there was a thin, imaginary line between genius and non-genius. The worst fate of all was to be an almost-but-not-quite genius.

In Paris, Benton studied at Julien's Academy. He felt his eyes grow moist before *Winged Victory* in the Louvre, and he wept at the playing of the cathedral organ in Notre Dame. He also consumed the usual quantities of liquor, and proved attractive to the womenfolk. With his swarthy complexion, heavy black hair, and nervous energy, he was sometimes called "le petit Balzac." He did a great deal of painting, but it seemed to him he did not make much progress toward becoming a genius. There were too many geniuses. The saying in Paris was that one super-genius and two fledglings with money from home to publish a manifesto were enough to start a new school of thought. "I wallowed in every cockeyed ism that came along," Benton admits. "The Quarter was overrun with geniuses, and I was merely a roughneck with a talent for fighting, perhaps, but not for painting as it was cultivated in Paris."

After remaining in Paris for three years, he returned to New York, to face for the first time the task of making his own living. He lived in the old Lincoln Square Arcade Building, at Sixty-fifth and Broadway, where he sojourned with astrologers, muscle builders, prize fighters, artists and cockroaches. He obtained work at the Fox Film Studios in Fort Lee, New Jersey, where he drew seven dollars a day and painted display portraits of Theda Bara and other stars of the time.

It did not occur to him that his work in motion pictures had anything to do with art. "I missed the human dramas that existed side by side with the acted ones," he wrote in his autobiography. Neither did he connect his life in Missouri, Chicago, Paris, or New York with his painting. In looking back later, it seemed to him that the age of fire and steel and soaring skyscrapers, through which he had lived, was the nation's most significant and beautiful attempt to express itself, even though the skyscrapers invariably rose in the midst of poverty;

but none of this occurred to him at the time. "We were studio painters; we painted lifeless cubist and symbolist pictures," he wrote of his circle. "For me, as for all my kind, art was a purity divorced from the common ways of the day. I regarded drawing as an exercise existing apart from the higher abstract values of painting, toward which I had deep hankerings. I still professed to believe, with other young men of my entourage, that no really fine art was representative. I declared that it must convey abstract *principles* to have eternal value. I pretended to see, in those Renaissance masters I loved so much, nothing but geometrical orders."

In 1916, Benton had a row of paintings entered in the Forum Exhibit of American Modernists in New York. The paintings were partly imitative of classical composition and partly "synchromist." Synchromism was a theory of painting in which all form was supposed to be derived from the simple play of color. He did achieve some status as an artist as a result of the exhibition. By the time of America's entry into the first World War, he was nearly thirty years old; and he was making a living, of a sort, from the sale of his paintings.

Benton enlisted in the Navy. He had visions of himself looking out from the deck of a ship, but through a mixup in his papers he was assigned instead to a coal pile at Hampton Roads, Va., where he helped load boats. Shoveling coal was not the form of exercise he most appreciated, so he represented himself as a prize fighter, and obtained an assignment with the Navy athletes. He was allotted training quarters and listed as a Saturday night attraction. He gave a good account of himself in the ring for two or three fights; but then encountered an eighteen-year-old boy who, with superior ring psychology and boxing technique, gave him a terrific beating.

In the course of being helped from the ring, Benton admitted that he was really an artist rather than a prize fighter. On the strength of his statement, some of those who had gathered around helped him to obtain an assignment as an architectural draftsman at the naval base in Norfolk, Virginia.

Since he had had no experience as an architectural draftsman, Benton at first envisioned a quick return to one of the thousands of coal piles that lined Hampton Roads. He determined to avoid this if at all possible. He began making drawings of the naval base for the records of architects. In the course of the work he was forced to notice the details of structures and mechanical contrivances, airplanes, blimps, dredges, and ships. "This was the most important thing that, so far, I had ever done for myself as an artist," he wrote later. "My interests became, in a flash, of an objective nature. The mechanical contrivances and buildings, because they were so interesting in themselves, tore me away from my grooved habits, from my play with colored cubes and classic attenuations, and from my aesthetic drivelings and morbid self-concerns. I left for good the art-for-art's-sake world in which I had hitherto lived. Although my technical habits clung for a while, I abandoned the attitudes which generated them, and opened thereby a way to a world which, though always around me, I had not seen."

The thought struck Benton like a burst of light that it did not make any difference whether he was a "genius" or not. "I had found that it was not necessary to look into myself and my 'genius' to find interesting things," he said. "I had found that these things existed in the world outside myself, and that it made no difference whether I had any 'genius' or not. I was released from the tyranny of the pre-war soul which everybody so assiduously cultivated in the world of art, and which was making it such a precious field of obscurities."

He noticed his companions at the naval base. They were mostly southern boys, eight or ten years younger than himself. They were from the hinterlands of the Carolinas and Tennessee, and from all over the South. "They possessed characteristics which I had known in my childhood companions around Neosho," wrote Benton. "I got along with them easily. I realized that psychologically I was much closer to these boys than I was to the cultivated people of the Chicago, Paris, and New York art worlds. Their egos were not the frigid, touchy sort developed by brooding too much on the importance of self. They were objective. They were interested in things rather than selves. With them my own secret internal animosities, which were always boiling in me against people, ideas, or pretensions, faded away. I felt perfectly natural and at ease for the first time since the old creek-bank days in Missouri."

After the war Benton returned to New York, full of an assurance such as he had not felt since before going to Paris. He proclaimed artistic heresies, and talked about the importance of subject matter in art. He was already vigorously pursuing the line of thought that made him a founder and eventually the leader of the "American Scene" movement in painting. He ridiculed the painters of jumping cubes and cockeyed tables, and of blue bowls and bananas, who read cosmic meaning into their works. He referred to the followers of Alfred Stieglitz as "an intellectually diseased lot, victims of sickly rationalizations, psychic inversions and God-awful self-cultivations." He stirred up fierce controversies, made many enemies and was abused in turn by the purists. But he also attracted followers, and sold paintings.

He felt strong, and sure of himself. He set forth on a gigantic project, which would have been a life work if he had ever completed it, to show the "History of the United States" in sixty-four large mural panels. He read extensively, and drew up a historical progression which would have started with the arrival of the white man, and would have proceeded through the more or less pastoral period before the Civil War, through the war itself, the carpet baggers, the rush for dollars, the vast European immigration, the felling of the forests, the humiliation of the Indian, the slaughter of the buffalo, railroads, saloons, factories, slums, paupers and millionaires, and the mechanical contrivances and complications of the present. Although he did a great deal of other painting, his best energies for seven years were spent on this "History of the United States."

While he was still working on his History, in 1924, he was called back to Missouri by Colonel Benton's last illness. He sat several weeks by his father's bedside, and found that the old animosities which had stirred in him against his father and his father's friends had completely disappeared. Most of his father's last visitors were veterans of the Civil War. As they talked over old times, it occurred to Benton that these old war hawks had experienced more of life than many who had spent years in cultural centers, and that there ran in them a strain of common feeling which he could completely share.

Benton was thirty-five years old. "I cannot honestly say what happened to me while I watched my father die and listened to the voices of his friends," he wrote. "But I know that when, after his death, I went back East I was moved by a great desire to know more of the America I had glimpsed in the suggestive words of his old cronies, who, seeing him at the end of his tether, had tried to jerk him back with reminiscent talk and suggestive anecdote. I was moved by a desire to pick up again the threads of my childhood."

Ten years passed before he returned to Missouri as a resident. During those ten years, Benton made annual excursions across the continent. He visited plantations in the Deep South, ranches in the Far West, steel mills in the East and farms in the Middle West; and he passed many times through the Ozark region of Arkansas and Missouri. He ate in hash houses, slept in country hotels, and attended Holy Roller meetings, country dances, political barbecues, and baptisms. He was half hobo and half high-brow; he had no prejudices against anyone or anyone's way of living; and he was able to share and appreciate the experiences of the different people he met. He was partial to the back country, where old manners persisted, but sketched and drew wherever he went.

The result of these travels was a mountain of material. He had stacks of notebooks containing hundreds of sketches—faces full of character, views of dumpy western towns and cheap dance halls, mountain cabins, and landscapes suggesting the sweep of the country. In addition, Benton had the more formal material which he had gathered for his ambitious "History of the United States." The latter he finally gave up, seeing that no one was going to buy the mural. Before abandoning the project, he had completed sixteen panels. These panels were exhibited year after year at the Architectural League in New York. They caused Benton to be thought of and written about as a muralist, though he had never actually done a mural. He was a muralist with no walls to paint, and was loaded with material that could be used in painting them.

In 1930, his persistent showing of his panels at the Architectural League finally bore fruit. The architect Joseph Urban recommended him with the Mexican, Orozco, as a muralist at the New School for Social Research in New York—a school for adults. The New School had no money with which to pay a muralist, but Benton was so eager to become the muralist he was already supposed to be, that he agreed to do the painting for nothing. The publicity given the murals well repaid him for his work, and led to his being commissioned for a more remunerative mural set, in the Whitney Museum of American Art in New York. In the Whitney Museum murals, *Arts of Life in America,* he showed bronco busting, horseshoe pitching, country dancing, Holy Rollers, mule driving, shooting and the like.

Even after the two New York murals, Benton had yet to reach his best painting stride. That came in 1933 when he was commissioned to do a huge mural of the history of Indiana, for exhibit at the Chicago World Fair. He worked out a historical progression for Indiana, from prairie schooners to the present.

By the time he had finally completed his scheme and had made his clay model, Benton had only sixty-two days left in which to paint the Indiana murals. He worked from dawn until late at night. It was a sort of emotional spree; he was in an exalted state of mind, the color of the world was greatly heightened, and his energies were so strung up that he never seemed to get tired. He felt supremely confident, and as though the sweep of his brushes were beyond error. He made no changes or corrections, and painted steadily until the mural was completed. When he looked it over, he knew he had produced his best work so far. The Indiana mural, twelve feet high and a total of 250 feet long, was exhibited on schedule, and was one of the main points of interest for the millions of visitors during the two years of Chicago's "Century of Progress" world's fair.

With the depression of the thirties and the advent of common misfortunes, a change occurred in the tastes of the country. People were turning from the type of art which for years had emanated mainly from Paris, to an appreciation of paintings which dealt with the plainer aspects of living at home.

Grant Wood of Iowa, John Steuart Curry of Kansas, Thomas Hart Benton of Missouri, and a few other first-rank artists were ready with genuine material suited to the trend. Wood, Curry, and Benton had been working independently; they were not even personally acquainted. The currents of the country, rather than any plan of their own, drew them together in the American Scene movement. Grant Wood produced masterpieces, but his output was small. In range, versatility, fierce energy, and uncompromising realism, and in zest for and conscious understanding of the whole of American life, Benton surpassed the other two. He became the recognized leader of the American Scene, or Regional, movement in painting.

As long as Benton was at work in New York, Missourians thought of him as another painter who had gone the expected way of an artist. When, however, he came out to do the Indiana murals, there were some who thought that if he was to be painting in the Middle West he might well do so in his home state. A bill was passed through the Missouri legislature, offering him $16,000 to decorate the legislators' lounge in the Capitol at Jefferson City, with a mural depicting the social history of the state. At the same time, Benton was offered $3,000 a year to teach at the Kansas City Art Institute. The two events occurring together, in the spring of 1935, resulted in his decision to move to Kansas City.

He spent nearly ten months gathering material for his Missouri murals. He wore a pink shirt to country dances, and played his harmonica all over the state. He attended the night clubs in St. Louis and Kansas City, and the burlesque show which Kansas Citians were calling the "eighth wonder of the world." He sketched rich and poor, famous and obscure. The best-known name in Kansas City was that of the political boss,

Tom Pendergast. Pendergast at first refused to pose for him, so Benton went to W. T. Kemper, Kansas City banker and Democratic national committeeman. Kemper telephoned Pendergast, recalling to his mind the fine Democratic traditions of the Benton family. Pendergast then did agree to pose, although still not of the opinion that his likeness would do him any particular good in the legislative halls. This was one time when Benton's name and his descent from the Senator gave him access to influence which was of some help to him. He also sketched W. T. Kemper, J. C. Nichols, the real-estate man, and lesser lights of the town.

For the Kansas City section of his mural, he showed a background of meat packing, a heifer being led to slaughter, and big carcasses of beef being hung on pegs. Looming in the background also, he placed the Nelson Gallery of Art, the shaft of Kansas City's Liberty Memorial to the dead of the first World War, and the spire of the Power and Light Building, the city's tallest structure; with grain elevators, railroads and the river in the distance. In the middle foreground, gathered around a street bonfire, he showed a group of "gandy dancers," the derelicts of North Main Street; and a group of school children, walking with their teacher toward the Nelson Gallery.

In the foreground, in an armchair of authority and occupying the most prominent place in the mural, he placed Boss Pendergast. Pendergast was seated on a stage where a man was giving a speech, but was shown in a negligent pose, paying very little attention to the speaker's words; which was typical of the political boss, who thought very little of speeches and "resoluting bodies." "They do the resoluting and we get out the vote," he used to say. Shown listening to the speech were likenesses of W. T. Kemper and J. C. Nichols. Although starting with a speech, the scene merged into a night club, with a dancer performing on a stage at the other end of the room.

Another part of the mural showed the booted figures of Frank and Jesse James and their gang, holding up a train. And mingling fiction with fact, the artist showed Huckleberry Finn with his friend Nigger Jim, holding up a big catfish, with the river and the steamboat *Sam Clemens* in the background. Rivers flow all through the fifty feet of mural, both the Missouri and the Mississippi having served as highroads in the state's history. For his strictly historical progression, Benton began with the days of the Santa Fé Trail, with steamboats, pack mules and wagons, trading with the Indians, hunters and hound dogs. He showed early and modern agriculture, a turkey shoot, and border warfare, with uniforms in blue and gray.

For a political meeting, he made a background of the old Pike County Courthouse. Above the speaker's platform he placed a huge poster of Champ Clark, who was long Speaker of the U.S. House of Representatives, and is second only to Senator Benton on the roster of Missouri's great men. On the platform, speaking with his usual gusto, he placed his own father, Colonel Benton; whose peculiar speaking stance, something like a football quarterback, added a great deal to the picture.

While he was doing the painting, Benton left open the door to the lounge, and hundreds came to watch him at work on his scaffolding. Benton, a wiry man with a Groucho Marx mustache, sometimes amused the visitors by showing how fast he could fill in a figure. When he had a brush in his hand and a wall, he felt he couldn't make a mistake. During his lunch periods, he talked to the visitors, and sometimes received help from them. A farmer corrected his treatment of a plow, saying: "The hind part's too short and the handles don't have enough turn in 'em." A Kansas Citian pointed out that Boss Pendergast smoked cigarettes, instead of a cigar as Benton had shown him. Where they didn't interfere with his total design, Benton made all the corrections that were requested. While he was at work, he heard no adverse criticism of the painting.

When the mural was completed, however, a storm broke over him. There were protests concerning his scene showing a pioneer handing a tin cup of whisky to an Osage Indian, and other protests against the scenes depicting a slave auction and a lynching. There were too many mules and hound-dogs to suit some Missourians, who claimed he had pictured Missouri as a shiftless, hound-dog state. One legislator complained that Benton's mural cow was so measly thin that it would never last through the winter, to which the artist replied that any farmer ought to know that a milk cow did not put on fat.

Benton traveled over the state, answering the criticisms. His ultimate purpose was to convince his listeners that beauty, sincerity and honesty of purpose lay in *things as they were and are*. In order to approach this objective, he had to contend with some of the most dearly held attitudes. A heckler at one of his meetings cited the illustrious background of the Bentons, and asked: "Are you proud of your state?" Benton knew he was not "proud" of his state; the word did not fit his conceptions in any respect. So he replied: "I am not proud of it, merely interested." The unexpected reply forced the heckler to throw away a sheaf of questions which were based on the first one. If the matter had to be measured in terms of compliments to the commonwealth, Benton contended that it was no compliment, and in addition showed a lack of mental and moral strength, to be interested only in an idealized, violet-scented version bearing little or no relation to the facts concerning the state.

He did not succeed in persuading everyone to his point of view, but there was much praise as well as criticism of the murals. A number of newspapers said the legislative lounge had become "the most interesting room in Missouri." The Missouri murals probably will stand as the most noteworthy and influential work of Benton's career. The *Star* was among the newspapers which defended the painting, saying, "Benton's dish is beefsteak rather than fudge."

After surviving the major test occasioned by his murals, Benton fell victim of a few remarks that would have been of no consequence, except that they were spread over the country by news-gathering agencies. His ouster from the Kansas City Art Institute, after he had taught there six years, resulted in 1941 from an interview which he gave New York reporters during a trip East for one of his exhibits.

Benton, a little stooped these days and smoking his usual briar pipe, was being perfectly natural and saying what he thought when one of the New York reporters brought up the subject of museums. "Ha!" said the artist, "Museums don't buy enough of my painting in the course of an average year to pay for my boy's music lessons."

"If it were left to me, I wouldn't have any museums," Benton continued. "Who looks at paintings in a museum? I'd rather sell mine to saloons, bawdy houses, Kiwanis and Rotary Clubs, Chambers of Commerce—even women's clubs. People go to saloons, but never to museums, unless they happen to be tourists anxious to 'do' the place and get it over with."

The reporters asked him to elaborate his reasons, and Benton expressed the opinion that turning over living art to museums amounted to "the delivery of the living to those trained professionally as caretakers of the dead." "You've got to have a sort of undertaker's psychology to go into the museum business," he said. "The typical museum is a graveyard run by a pretty boy with delicate curving wrists and a swing in his gait."

When these remarks appeared in the newspapers, they produced various reactions. In New York, Billy Rose offered to exhibit Benton's *Persephone* in his "Diamond Horseshoe" night club, where he later reported forty-three thousand people had seen the painting in the first three weeks. But in Kansas City, at a grim session of the trustees of the Art Institute, the trustees decided not to renew Benton's teaching contract.

The action of the trustees made it impossible ever to know why Benton left the Art Institute without recalling his words. However, the incident did not cause him to leave Kansas City. Although he was free to go wherever he chose, he could not think of another place where he would rather live. He reflected that, in general, pretensions did not fare nearly as well here on the edge of the prairie as they did in some of the more cultivated circles he had known. He knew that a lot of people were wishing him well, and that his work was most closely related to the stream of events in Missouri. He decided that this was where he belonged.

CHAPTER NINETEEN

A Kingdom for a Horse

TOM PENDERGAST, OR "T.J." as he was often designated in Kansas City, was thirty-eight years old in 1910 when he was elected to the city council and succeeded his brother in power. A little later he got into the wholesale liquor business, and bought the Jefferson Hotel. In 1915 he retired from the council and never held public office again. His only political office was his post as president of the Jackson County Democratic Club, which was the machine's official organization.

He ran his political affairs at first from the Jefferson Hotel, and later from a dumpy office, reached by a creaking wooden stairway in a two-story brick building at 1908 Main Street. During his lush years, this little office was called "The Capitol of Missouri"; the real Capitol at Jefferson City was referred to as "Uncle Tom's Cabin."

Until 1916, Pendergast went along under an arrangement made by his brother with the other political boss, Joe Shannon. Pendergast's Goats and Shannon's Rabbits divided the patronage equally, regardless of whose candidate was elected. This limited the factional fighting to the primaries and conventions, and enabled the two factions to join against the Republicans on election days.

Shannon's candidate was mayor from 1912 to 1916, partly because of Shannon's political master stroke in calling attention to the fact that the mayor had been an orphan as a boy. "The Orphan Boy Mayor" was a useful slogan in those campaigns, and in addition the mayor was efficient and well-liked; so Boss Shannon held the top place in its political hierarchy. The wily Shannon, who was something of a character, knew how to appeal to that large majority of people who were not "in politics," who were not identified with either faction, and who merely voted.

In 1916, Pendergast broke with Shannon. Being unable to nominate his own candidate, he threw his support to and elected a Republican mayor. This was the only time Pendergast ever supported a Republican, but it effectively demonstrated his power to do so if he chose. His first ward voted heavily for a Republican mayor, and heavily for a Democratic alderman.

For the next ten years, a seesaw struggle was waged between the Rabbits and Goats. Patchwork arrangements between them were made and broken, and Republicans frequently were helped into office because of the Democratic split.

Then in 1925 Pendergast saw his big chance. The reform element in the community had long been advocating a new city charter which would establish the city-manager form of government. One day Pendergast announced, to the surprise of everyone, that he also favored the city-manager plan. From his study of the proposal, he had concluded that the city-manager plan would tend to freeze in office whoever won the first election; and he thought he could win the first election.

With almost everyone except Shannon supporting the new charter, the city-manager plan was adopted. By the narrowest of margins, Pendergast in 1926 did win the first election. He put five Democrats to four Republicans on the new city council.

Most of the powers of government had been delegated to the city manager, who could be hired and fired only by the city council. For the next thirteen years, the council was controlled by Pendergast and allied Democrats. So the city manager was working for Pendergast to almost the same extent as was the secretary in his own outer office. Rabbi Samuel S. Mayerburg launched a vigorous campaign against the machine in 1932, and the ministerial association and the *Star* joined in the anti-Pendergast crusade. This crusade served to inform the public concerning waste of the taxpayers' money, gambling and other wide-open conditions in the city, and ghost-voting, but in terms of results at the polls it was not successful until after Pendergast's downfall had been brought about through the courts. From 1926 to 1939, the political boss firmly held the reins of power.

Shannon might have been left out of the picture, except for the fact that the victorious Pendergast made him a generous offer: his Rabbits could have one-third of the patronage, and Pendergast would support Shannon himself if he wished to run for Congress. Shannon at first was reluctant to accept assistance from his enemy, and said he would rather take quinine in bulk. Eventually, however, he agreed to run and was elected. During the thirties, Shannon was a popular figure in Congress, where he was known as "Uncle Joe." He was by this time elderly, and weary of the political wars; and he had developed a peculiar habit of devoting most of his speeches to eulogizing Thomas Jefferson, the one topic he had found completely inspiring and non-controversial. Long eulogies of Jefferson by Representative Shannon can be found in the files of the *Congressional Record.*

The agreement with Shannon and his election to Congress welded together the Democratic factions and left Pendergast in full command of the Kansas City scene. He proceeded to win election after election. The majorities, coinciding with the swing against Hoover, kept getting bigger and bigger. Presently, from Jackson County alone, Pendergast could guarantee a fifty-thousand-vote majority for almost any statewide primary candidate; and in special cases he could increase the margin to one hundred thousand votes. In Missouri, fifty to one hundred thousand votes will decide most statewide elections. While it cannot be said that Pendergast ever controlled the state government as he did that of the city, his influence at Jefferson City was certainly immense.

Along with his phenomenal rise in politics, Pendergast had an equally phenomenal rise in business. After prohibition closed his wholesale liquor house, he got into various lines of construction—gravel, sewage pipe and road building—and from that into the sale of ready-mixed concrete. When prohibition was repealed, he reopened his wholesale liquor house, and thereafter sold both liquor and concrete. No one could ever say of Pendergast, as of some political bosses, that he had no visible source of income. The T. J. Pendergast Wholesale Liquor Company was much the largest dispenser of that product; and his truck-mounted cement mixers, mixing the concrete en route to the place of construction, were familiar on the streets.

One of the sights of Kansas City is Brush Creek, paved for more than two miles with an eight-inch concrete floor—the only concrete-floored creek in America, say Kansas Citians. Children of the neighborhood skate and bicycle along the unwet edges of the creek's floor, which runs up to seventy feet wide. A third of a million dollars' worth of Pendergast's concrete went into that floor and its abutments, and there was an anguished outcry from the taxpayers at the time the money was being spent.

However, residents later agreed that the flooring did benefit that part of the city, by speeding the creek's flow, eliminating floods and adding to the attractiveness of the district. Except for the unerring way in which it got all the city's business, Pendergast's Ready-Mixed Concrete Company operated about the same as any other—the concrete was good and the prices were near those paid in other cities. A contractor building a post office during the Hoover administration was told to buy his concrete elsewhere, but reported that he could do better with Pendergast; so Pendergast's concrete went into a Republican post office, a fact which the political boss took pains to impress upon the populace.

Construction of almost any kind was very much in Pendergast's line, and several factors combined in the thirties to create a great deal of business for him. In point of time, the first factor was the raising of the city's constitutional debt limit from 5 to 10 per cent of the tax valuation, and the doubling of the assessed value of property. These moves made possible, for the first time in years, the financing of municipal enterprises at a reasonable rate of interest. Then in 1931 it was discovered that bond issues could be glamorized. Over a period of years, four-fifths of the proposed bond issues had been defeated at the polls; but when these issues were lumped into a "Ten-Year Plan," with ballyhoo concerning the progress the city would make, they were approved by the voters with a large margin to spare.

In this way approval was obtained for a twenty-two-story courthouse, a twenty-nine-story city hall, and a six-million-dollar municipal auditorium. These three structures, in gray Indiana limestone, made Kansas City second to none in public buildings. The county's highway system was improved until it was said to be second only to that of Westchester County in New York. Another project developed Kansas City's thousand-acre municipal airport—in the crook of the Missouri River's elbow, just across from the old steamboat levee—only five minutes by automobile from the business center, and almost as convenient as the railroad station.

As fast as money poured into his hands, Pendergast found means of spending it. He cared nothing for night life and was usually in bed by nine o'clock; but he lived expensively in a $115,000 French Regency house on Ward Parkway in the best part of town. He traveled some, two or three times to Europe with his family, and to political conventions and horse races, keeping a suite at the Waldorf-Astoria in New York when he was in the East. At home, he acquired a stable of race horses in adjacent Platte County, to which, before going to his dumpy political office, he sometimes drove to watch his horses exercise at daybreak. He had a weakness for wagering excessively on his own and other people's horses.

His political expenses also ran high. In the depression of the thirties, as many as six thousand men lined up for his free Christmas dinners, and these dinners were costing Pendergast between $3,000 and $4,000 a year. Among the "gandy dancers" on North Main Street, the sentiment for Pendergast was practically unanimous. In the less prosperous residential districts also, the machine played Santa Claus on a large scale. In one ward, more than a thousand Christmas baskets a year were distributed. New bicycles and go-carts were given as Christmas presents. Carloads of coal were sometimes brought in and distributed free by trucker friends of the machine. Every precinct captain was supposed to have a fund out of which to help destitute families. Much of the money for these activities came from Pendergast's ample purse. Like his brother before him, he handed out money as though it came from an inexhaustible source.

The machine's activities were conspicuous and highly organized. When a family moved into a neighborhood, its first caller was likely to be the precinct captain, offering to help. If the family had trouble getting the water, gas, or electricity turned on, the precinct captain would get them turned on the same day, perhaps within an hour, the machine priding itself on fast as well as sure service. If the voter was given a traffic ticket, the precinct captain would be glad to get this fixed; or if a license was needed for any purpose, he would bring one out from the City Hall. The expression apparently originated in Kansas City, that a politician will do anything in the world for you, except get off your back.

Some unusual services were provided by the machine. If the tires were stolen from a voter's car, and he reported the loss to the political headquarters, he could get the same tires put back on his car during the night. The procedure was to tip off "Fat Willie," who had the tire-stealing concession, that his men had taken the tires from the wrong car. "Fat Willie" would have the tires put back, thus discharging part of his obligation to the machine to which he was indebted for his concession. The machine at the same time was enabled to do a favor for a voter, and the voter was made to feel that he had a kind of free insurance.

The gangster era in Kansas City was similar, though on a smaller scale, to those in Chicago and New York. It developed a little later, and its connection with politics was even more open. In 1929—at the time when justice was closing in on Al Capone—Johnny Lazia was making himself the gang leader of Kansas City. In contrast to the mountainous person of Capone, Lazia was dapper and handsome, and had a master-of-ceremonies personality. He even carried a swagger stick. Gangsters were then enjoying a certain deference, and Lazia cut a large figure in Kansas City before he was finally mowed down by rival gunmen. He first appeared independently and had the votes of his ward in hand before Pendergast recognized him. He then was recognized, and a gangland phase was added to the machine's operations.

Under Lazia's sub-rule of the downtown area, Kansas City became the most wide-open town in America. Kansas Citians still like to tell how it was possible at one place to order a sixty-five-cent highball and have it brought to you by a waitress completely in the nude, or to see four strip-tease acts in the course of a noon lunch costing less than a dollar. This place, with a downtown street entrance and catering to mixed company, became widely known for its extraordinary economy of dress; and similar economy was shown in a number of less conspicuous establishments. Gambling and other usual rackets were widely practiced, and the city acquired at least its full share of dubious characters.

Lazia was in charge of "the rackets," and was justified to the public as a gang leader who was protecting the city from "outside gangsters." When there were kidnapings or bombings, they were called the work of "outside gangsters." Lazia, instead of being hunted, was often at police headquarters directing the search. A federal agent, who came to Kansas City to investigate Lazia's income, reported back to Washington that when he called the Kansas City police department, Lazia answered the telephone. In 1931, Nell Donnelly, Kansas City garment-maker who later married Senator James A. Reed, was kidnaped for ransom. Senator Reed, who was then her attorney, placed little reliance in the police but called in Lazia and told him he had better find her, at once! Taking two carloads of machine-gunners, Lazia did find her; surrounded her kidnapers in a Kansas farmhouse, and aided in her rescue. According to the story, Lazia later spoke disparagingly of her kidnapers as "non-professionals," armed only with a shotgun or two.

Despite the more spectacular activities of the machine and its gangland associates, Kansas City gave the appearance of being a fairly well-operated municipality. Some glaring irregularities were later discovered, such as paying $5,000 a month to a dummy company to "search for water leaks" in the city's mains, and adding to the city payroll several hundred employees whose duties were purely political. Much was said also about City Manager Henry F. McElroy's "country bookkeeping," by which he contrived to hide deficits running into the millions in a budget that on the surface was nearly balanced. Nevertheless, such Kansas City statistics as were available usually compared favorably with those of other cities. The Pendergast-supported administrations accomplished an unusual amount of construction, certainly; and this was paid for with sound, low-interest financing. The tax rate was well below the average; and in tribute to the community's general hardihood, both before and after the disclosures, the city's credit rating was high.

And although ghost-voting was practiced on a considerable scale, often by precinct and ward leaders merely to improve their district's showing, the general belief in Kansas City was that Pendergast always "had the votes." This was substantially demonstrated in 1938 after the political boss had had a falling out with Governor Stark of Missouri. The *Star* revealed that the city's voting lists included between fifty and sixty thousand ghosts—names of persons long dead, and ethereal registrants giving cemeteries, funeral parlors, warehouses and vacant lots as their home addresses. Governor

Stark selected an anti-machine election commission; and all such names, more than fifty thousand of them, were stricken from the registration rolls. A municipal election was then held, in March, 1938, which was conceded to have been reasonably accurate. Yet the machine ticket still won, by a landslide majority of 44,000 votes, which was only 12,000 short of the best the machine had ever done in a municipal poll.

In seeking the explanation of Pendergast's political strength, a start can be made by examining the race question, which exhibits in Kansas City much the same character as elsewhere in the country. All the discriminations familiar to the North and a few from the South apply against the Negroes, who make up approximately eleven per cent of the population. The only place a Negro can get anything to eat in downtown Kansas City is at the stand-up counters in the ten-cent stores. One of these stores has a stand-up counter and a sit-down counter; Negroes are allowed at the former but not at the latter. And looking up a rest room in the downtown area must be quite a problem for colored people, since they seem to be excluded from most of those a person would normally visit.

Kansas City's metropolitan area, stretching over into Kansas, offers a good opportunity to compare attitudes toward the Negro, since abolitionist, border, and Southern territory are all within the reach of a ten-cent bus fare. "Northern people," they say in Independence, speaking of Northern people as though of a distant race, "Northern people don't understand this, but we *like* the Negroes, and the Negroes like us. It's the Northerners who hate the Negroes." There is a good deal of truth in that statement, since a type of race hatred sometimes encountered in the

North, based on total ignorance of the people hated, is seldom found among Southerners. They have a genuine liking for individual Negroes who have been attached to their households or with whom they have otherwise become well acquainted; and in general they seem to have a better understanding of the Negro and his qualities.

On the other hand, the Southerners' liking for the Negro is strictly confined to the Negro in what is conceived to be his proper place. Where public policy is shaped by the Southern tradition, it does not take a form which improves the Negro's lot. In Kansas City, Kansas, where the colored population is seventeen per cent, the Negro schools are excellent; and in Kansas City, Missouri, they are reasonably good; whereas the Negro high school in Independence at one time was found to be offering no courses in foreign languages, none in algebra or geometry, and no third-year English. Not even Lincoln University for Negroes at Jefferson City would accept the credits of the Independence school.

This lack of educational opportunity in Independence, which was repaired by sending the Negro students into Kansas City by bus, might be ascribed to lack of a sufficiently large colored population to support a good high school in Independence. But the gradation in opportunity applies in other respects. In Kansas City, Kansas, colored people are employed in all the public offices, and one of the three county commissioners is sometimes a Negro. In Kansas City, Missouri, a white-collar job for a Negro is a rare political plum, but in Independence there is scarcely ever a thought of such appointments.

The Negro leaders in Kansas City itself have confined themselves to extremely limited objectives, such as "equal access to public buildings," and even these have not been fully realized. When Negroes are admitted to the Music Hall of

Kansas City's Municipal Auditorium they are segregated in special sections. Marian Anderson refused a singing engagement in Kansas City for this reason, and Paul Robeson stopped in the middle of a number to say that he would not have come if he had known segregation would apply. The practice has continued without change under both machine and anti-machine or reform city governments, the claim in both cases being that the public would not stand for a change.

Nevertheless, the Negroes in Kansas City always have had the vote, and during the Pendergast era they felt they had good reason for their choice as between "reform" and "machine" government—the appellations usually used to describe the types of government the city had experienced. In the rank and file, they overwhelmingly preferred the machine.

Their reasons can be gathered from an incident that occurred when a reform administration was in office. A Negro organization was preparing to hold a national convention in Kansas City. They hoped the mayor would appear in person to welcome the delegates, or that he would send someone to welcome them, but they were prepared to be satisfied with a brief welcoming message which could be read to the convention. A committee was appointed to see the mayor and to ask him for some form of official welcome.

Members of the committee were dressed in their best and made a dignified appearance when they called at the mayor's office, but before the effort was over they were a bedraggled lot. They presented their credentials and explained their mission to a not-very-interested desk girl. They were told that the mayor was busy. They waited, then drifted around town and returned, to be put off again. They came back the next day, and the day following. Each time they reached the mayor's office they were told that His Honor was busy. Finally the chairman reported to headquarters that, far from enlisting the services of the mayor, he had not even been able to see him.

The head of the colored organization, a man with a university education and a doctor of laws degree, then tried to see the mayor, and was put off in the same manner. His explanation, that his request might involve nothing more than the use of the mayor's name to welcome a convention, seemed to make no impression on the desk girl; and he was told only that it was against the mayor's policy to "give out statements."

The head of the colored organization knew that there could be no objection to granting his petition, if he could make his request understood. So he wrote a long letter to the mayor. He pointed out that the organization had been holding national conventions for several years, and that mayors of other cities had always greeted the delegates in some way. He informed the mayor that senators and governors had appeared on their programs, and that greetings had been received from Presidents of the United States. An official welcome might seem a small matter, he said, but it was unthinkable that the convention should be held in Kansas City, to the interests of which both he and the mayor were devoted, with no word whatever from the city's chief executive.

To that letter the mayor responded that he had not previously understood what was wanted; and he enclosed a brief note of welcome. Thus the particular request was granted, but not in such a way as to make the Negroes feel they were receiving much consideration from the current municipal government. Similar situations might occur in any city government, if the holder of office does not know the requirements and aspirations of all sections of the population.

But no such distant ineptitude or "benighted non-comprehension" in dealing with the Negroes was ever shown by the efficient political machine. Any Negro, as well as any white person, could go down to the political headquarters, get a place in line, and stand a reasonably good chance of seeing Tom Pendergast. His problem might involve nothing more than a license for a hound-dog, or the rescue of a hound-dog from the city pound; but, if he chose, he could take up the matter with Pendergast himself, a power dwarfing mayors and governors. It was likely that Pendergast would write a few words on a piece of paper, and that this would solve the difficulty.

Receiving a large proportion of the people who called at his office required a great deal of effort on Pendergast's part; but he visibly enjoyed being a political boss, and worked hard at his occupation. He usually opened his office at 6 A.M. In the busiest years, even at that early hour, there would sometimes be two or three hundred people waiting to see him. They necessarily arrived early, to get a place far enough up in the line to reach Pendergast's inner office before noon, since the boss saw no one after that hour. He devoted his afternoons to the intricate task of picking the horses at all the tracks, and to taking care of his business affairs.

But in most cases, a petitioner would get far enough up the line to reach the inner office. There he would find the heavy Mr. Pendergast, with his hat on, seated on the edge of his chair as though about to pounce. He was a perfect type of old time saloon boss; the resemblance remained even though he had shaved his mustache, smoked cigarettes in a holder instead of cigars, and wore a felt hat instead of a derby.

As a petitioner began to grope for words, Pendergast would

poke his head forward with a peculiar gesture that always accompanied the fixing of his eye on a visitor. In a deep baritone voice, he would say: "Well, what's yours?" The petitioner then might get five minutes in which to state his case, if that much time was necessary. More often the problem would be familiar, and before the petitioner had gone far Pendergast would interrupt with: "What you want is this—" If, having succinctly stated the requirement, Pendergast nodded his head and said "I'll do that," or wrote a note directing that something be done, it was as good as done. Even in the midst of extremely loose fiscal affairs, the Pendergast tradition of doing favors and keeping promises held to the last.

When the petitioner's problem was monetary and no job could be given him, Pendergast would reach into a drawer filled with silver and hand him fifty cents. During his career he may have handed out as many fifty-cent pieces as John D. Rockefeller did dimes. Sometimes he gave more, if a family was involved, especially when the caller was a woman—in which case he honored the visitor by the temporary removal of his hat, which he replaced when she left. As soon as a caller turned to go, Pendergast would hunch around in his chair and call out like a barber: "All right, who's next?" and the line outside his door would move up another notch. This went on day after day and year after year.

Even in his later years, Pendergast sometimes had seizures of rage in which he was inclined to resort to his fists; on one such occasion he chased a political rival named Miles Bulger for several blocks up the street. (Pendergast later said he was glad he was unable to catch Bulger, a sentiment which Bulger wholeheartedly shared.) On the whole, however, Pendergast was considered to be good-natured and easy to deal with. He was not averse to compromise, compromise among various elements being his business. He was not interested in policy, except when it threatened to alienate some section of his support; a liberal or a conservative had an equal chance of getting on his ticket if he could attract the votes and would go along on jobs and political favors. He was not even interested in state politics until his growing power forced it on his attention. Such is the checkerboard political nature of Missouri that there are counties that have never gone Democratic beside counties which have never gone Republican; yet when Pendergast first attempted to make state-wide political forecasts the newspaper reporters discovered he was claiming some of the perennially Republican counties. In fifty years of Kansas City politics, he had never taken the trouble to distinguish between these political perennials. Generally speaking, Pendergast was interested in only two things, local Kansas City politics and horse racing, and these absorbed all his time.

Although he always operated on the assumption that "there are more poor people than rich," Pendergast's support was by no means confined to the poor, as a tour around Kansas City even today will quickly disclose. This is recognized by Maurice Milligan, the district attorney who prosecuted Pendergast and sent him to prison. "There's no use talking to these people around here," said Milligan, a little ruefully. "They're all Old Tom's friends."

Perrin D. McElroy, head of the building trades unions and the principal Kansas City figure in the American Federation of Labor, was opposed by the later Pendergast organization when he ran for county chairman and was defeated by vote-juggling methods which were exposed in the *Star*. But of Tom Pendergast, McElroy said: "I think he did as much for labor, and for the poor and underprivileged, as any man I have ever known." The artist G. Van Millet, whose father helped establish Kansas City's first newspaper in 1855, echoed those sentiments. "There's two hundred old women living in this town today because he helped 'em," said Van Millet. "That doesn't mean he was honest," interjected Mrs. Van Millet, to which the artist rejoined: "That's true, but he could have kept the money. I'd hate to tell you how some of these fortunes out here were made." Another good word for Tom Pendergast came from Mayor Roger Sermon of Independence, who said: "All my dealings with Pendergast were very satisfactory. His word was good, and therein lay his strength. There were several times when he helped us out here, and he never asked me to do anything in return."

Gladstone Harvey, an old circus and carnival man with a reputation as a philosopher, stated the case even more strongly. "I believe in machine government," he said. "You could go to them with your troubles and get help. You go to some of these reformers with your troubles, and they want to put you in jail. They've got a Presbyterian idea of heaven: everyone else in jail and them holding the keys." Mr. Harvey conceded that Pendergast had a weakness, for betting on horses—"The wisdom of age did not settle on him"—but he added: "Every man has a weakness, and sometimes it is his weakness that makes him strong." The latter statement required a great deal of explanation; but in the course of a long conversation Mr. Harvey was able to demonstrate that there might be something in what he said.

In his heyday Pendergast could be accounted a friend of down-and-outers, a friend of all minorities and a friend of labor; at least he was so accounted by those who supported him. Although the Kansas City business community leaned Republican, he was not without direct and indirect support there, as a number of prominent figures were Democrats of the original Missouri stock. Also in his political camp was

Senator Reed, who for forty years had the unfailing support of the machine, and who in 1932 was being put forward as a presidential candidate. Pendergast's position as a political boss at that time seemed as secure as the sun.

Whatever large faults must be attributed to him in the course of his fall from that position, or however notorious he was or became, it would be difficult to escape the conclusion that within the scope of his philosophy he was by nature generously disposed. He worked hard at being generous for political reasons, but his role also came naturally to him, as many anecdotes testify.

One such anecdote is told by the painter Thomas Benton. When Benton in 1924 was sitting at his dying father's bedside, a group of his father's political friends came down from Kansas City to see him. They stood around the bed and talked for a while, no one knowing quite what to say, as no one ever does on such occasions; and presently they all left. As they filed out the door, Tom Pendergast hung behind the others and, just before he stepped out the door, pressed into the younger Benton's hands a package which the artist was embarrassed to accept but was given no chance to refuse, and which proved to contain eight hundred dollars. The "boys" had passed the hat, for "a little something that might help along"; and in such cases the Pendergast contribution was never a small one.

Another Kansas City opinion was that of a settlement worker, a slight, selfless woman of excellent reputation. After Pendergast had served his time in prison and had passed on, she confounded a good many people in Kansas City by declaring: "Mr. Pendergast was a fine Christian gentleman." The explanation was that the settlement worker, living in a basement apartment, was interested only in what might be done to assist people in the run-down, low-rent section which, spread out over the side of a hill, could be seen from her sitting room window. When Pendergast was in power, she went to him at different times, and got help; whereas from many whose moral standards were much higher than his, she did not get anything. She overlooked a great deal, and considered the matter strictly from her own single-minded point of view.

However, if Pendergast was open-handed with his friends and with the poor, he was even more open-handed in betting on the horses, and in spending money for everything connected with horses. There was a saying among sporting people that giving Pendergast a tip on a horse was the surest thing in racing. If the horse ran out of the money, Pendergast would take the loss, whereas if it won he would send you part of his winnings in appreciation. As soon as noon halted the stream of his callers, he had lunch sent to his office, and became absorbed in the form sheets and the placing of his bets. He seldom spoke of losses; although occasionally he was like a man trying to stop drinking, pledging himself to make only one or two bets a day, but never keeping within the pledge.

Since he usually could not go to the races, he would have long distance telephone connections established with one or two tracks. Through these connections, he could hear the pounding of the hoofs and the cries of the crowd; and would sit with his ear glued to the receiver, listening to the horses come in. His attorney later described this telephonic method of following the ponies, and said: "All the thrill that can possess any man possessed him then."

For many years the political boss had spent a large part of his income on his pastime, without doing himself serious damage. Then in 1934 his betting assumed phenomenal proportions. A sound tip on a long-shot horse apparently was his undoing. With $10,000 in bets scattered over the country, he won nearly a quarter of a million dollars on a single race. In an effort to repeat that performance, he went in deeper and deeper; and presently was betting two, three or five thousand dollars as casually as he had once bet two dollars. In 1935, as the government figures later showed, he actually wagered two million dollars on the horses, losing six hundred thousand of the sum.

Not even his monopoly of the concrete business, plus the sale of liquor and plus the fact that he evaded the federal tax on most of his income, could cover the new rate of his spending. Consequently he went heavily in debt, pledging the stock in his companies on large loans around Kansas City; and still he was hard pressed to obtain money for the bookmaker who handled his betting in the East. A good many people in Kansas City think that if it had not been for these gambling debts and the necessity for covering them, he would have been satisfied with his more or less legitimate income, and like his brother might have died full of honors. They say that Tom Pendergast literally gave his kingdom for a horse.

The affair which caused Pendergast's downfall stemmed back to 1929, when companies selling fire insurance in Missouri had served notice of intention to increase their rates by 16⅔ per cent. The State Insurance Commissioner refused to permit the increase, so the companies took the matter to court. The court permitted the companies to collect the increased rate, but impounded the amount of the increase in a special fund pending final settlement of the rate case.

Every time anyone paid a fire insurance premium in Missouri, 16⅔ per cent of the amount went into the court's impounded fund. In 1935, there was still no final settlement of the rate case in sight, and the fund had grown to nearly ten million dollars. The money was lying in a bank, like a melon waiting to be carved up. By this time one of Pendergast's least scrupulous men, R. Emmet O'Malley, a former Kansas City alderman, was occupying the office of State Insurance Commissioner.

An out-of-court settlement of the rate case was arranged, releasing the ten million dollars in such a way that the insurance companies received most of the money, but some of it flowed back into the pockets of politicians. As the money was actually divided, the companies received 61 per cent and the policyholders 20 per cent, while 14 per cent went for legal expenses and 5 per cent ($440,000 in cash) flowed to politicians—Pendergast getting the lion's share, $315,000.

The agent for the insurance companies in the transaction was Charles R. Street of Chicago, and his personal affairs soon became involved. In order to pay the politicians, Street had to have cash; and in order to get cash, he had cashed checks which were made out to him by insurance companies. He had done this with no thought of how his personal income tax return would look, if the government found he had been cashing all these checks.

A treasury agent going over some books in connection with an estate came upon an entry showing that on April 8, 1935, Charles R. Street had cashed fourteen insurance company checks totaling more than $100,000. The agent inquired whether Street had paid income tax on these amounts. Street had not paid the tax, nor could he say exactly what he had done with the money.

Street apparently thought at first that if the government knew he had paid the money to Pendergast, it would be awed by the latter's political power, and would not pursue the matter. This illusion caused him to make the original slip. He said he had paid the money to "a man high in Missouri politics, but not an office holder." The description could mean only Pendergast, and Street soon removed any remaining doubt. In a note addressed to the agent, on May 4, 1936, he said: "Leaving for South Dakota. On my return will take a run to Missouri on business anyway—and see what they have to say. Don't think we can do anything at least until the Queen Mary comes in." Pendergast was returning to New York on the Queen Mary, as the agent soon found by checking the passenger list.

After "taking the run to Missouri" Street withdrew everything he had said. He even paid $47,093 in tax on the checks in question, and the government was left without a witness. The government assessed a 50 per cent penalty on his tax, Street appealed from the penalty, and there the matter rested for two years.

Early in 1938, Street conveniently died without having given any further testimony. A month later Pendergast won the "straight" election, after Governor Stark had removed the ghosts from the Kansas City voting lists. Pendergast had double reason to celebrate, and called in reporters for an expansive interview. "Every unkind thing that has been said about our organization has been answered by the men and women who went to the polls," he declared. "We won fairly and squarely with everything against us. It seems that the people here appreciate good government, and we're going to keep right on giving it to them." He then made a statement which was intended to suggest the political doom that would engulf Governor Stark and his followers, but which was really more applicable to Pendergast's own approaching fate: "I now say: Let the river take its course." He was in a good mood for the rest of 1938. He had another big year on the horses, the biggest since 1935, and reportedly for the second time in his life made more than $200,000 on a single race.

Meanwhile, the government finally acquired a witness—A. L. McCormack of St. Louis, who had acted as go-between, and who told almost everything Street could have told. Also, District Attorney Maurice Milligan looked over Pendergast's books, and found such income tax dodges as $50,000 in Ready-Mixed Concrete dividends assigned to his secretary. Milligan estimated that in ten years Pendergast had evaded the tax on at least $1,200,000 in income, including the insurance payment. The government had a great deal of information which was unavailable to the public. Even the *Star's* reporter assigned to Pendergast knew nothing of the case until the day the indictment was announced.

Pendergast was indicted in April, 1939, on two income tax charges. A number of leading penal authorities have pointed out that persons convicted of crimes usually do not think of themselves as criminals; and certainly Pendergast did not think of himself as such. He was taken on Good Friday to be fingerprinted in the United States marshal's office. Someone had offered to help him remove his coat, when he broke down temporarily and cried: "There's nothing the matter with me. They crucified Christ on Good Friday and nailed Him to a cross."

His two appearances in court were brief. The first time he merely pleaded not guilty. Six weeks later he came back to plead guilty, and a short hearing ensued. His attorneys described horse-race betting as a mania which he could not control. Tears streamed down his face as he heard himself described as "a very human man, kind to his family, generous with his friends." The judge in passing sentence paused to say: "I can understand the feeling that has been expressed for him here by his friends; I believe if I had known him I, too, might have been one of his friends; I think he is a man of the character that makes friends." He was sentenced to fifteen months in prison, was fined $10,000, and had agreed to pay $430,000 in back income taxes.

"The bigger the crook the lighter the punishment," chanted other prisoners when he entered Leavenworth penitentiary.

The story was circulated that he amused himself in prison by making gigantic imaginary bets on the horses and reaping super-gigantic imaginary profits. The truth was that after entering the prison he would not even look at a race result, although he read everything else in the papers. He worked a year in the prison library, transcribing medical notes, and then returned to his Ward Parkway home in Kansas City. Under terms of probation, he was prohibited for five years after his release from discussing politics or visiting his political headquarters. He always expected to resume his place as head of the political organization when that period was over; but he died in January, 1945, a few weeks before the probation was to have ended.

CHAPTER TWENTY

Conclusion

THE MOST PROMINENT physical feature of Kansas City is still the two-hundred-foot West Bluff, which staggers the downtown area into two levels. Because nature combined here the perfect meeting-ground for wagons, steamboats, and railroads, the main part of the city was built on the two sides of this fault in the earth's crust. The business district extends westward to the edge of the bluff, which overlooks the stockyards, railroad yards, and the industrial plants. Beyond the yards, twenty or thirty miles of the Kansas and Missouri rivers can be seen twisting in from the distance; and forked hazily between the flow of the rivers is a huge section of the Kansas plain, from which thin clouds drift in summer to join with the curls of smoke that rise from far below in the bottom lands.

Its rugged site, and the conveniences the site paradoxically provided, accounts for one phase of Kansas City's growth. Other aspects are not so readily apparent, for the characteristics particular to the city exist behind a conventional, almost standardized, exterior—like a highly individualistic family in a house that looks the same as every other in the block. From some points, the skyline towering above the Missouri looks much like a replica of Manhattan. The city's per capita distribution of country clubs and beer halls, hotels and hash joints, neon signs and necromancers conforms in every respect to the national pattern.

Yet in the midst of the conformity there remain many reminders of Kansas City's particular past. Plantation-type houses of the Old South are to be seen in the neighborhood. Older people speak familiarly of George Caleb Bingham, and of Jim Lane and the Kansas Red Legs. A landmark is the Coates House, standing decrepitly in a downtown section that used to be Quality Hill. Some people say the biggest thing in the *Star* building still is "Old Bill Nelson's ghost." Occasionally the *Star* contains a reference to Arthur E. Stilwell's belief in "little people," and to his prophetic visions that proved so productive in improving the city's railroad position.

And though it is as middle-western as the Missouri mules and Kansas wheat fields both of which have done much to shape its history, Kansas City has not behaved in a standardized way; it has been full of surprising episodes and contradictions. Whereas the United States as a whole regarded the James boys as cutthroats, this vicinity could not quite forget the hero legends connected with them. In other cities political bosses have come and gone—but here the Pendergast dynasty reigned for fifty years, and is still powerful at this writing. Among its latter-day activities, the city helped push an obscure, and almost humble, native son up to a position from which the White House was only a few further steps. Most of the historic influences of the locality played some part in President Truman's early rise from Jackson County Chairman to the United States Senate; and his background was associated at every stage with the development of this region. One of his grandfathers had a wagon-freighting outfit that operated between Kansas City and San Francisco. His grandparents on both sides were driven off their land under Order No. 11. As a boy Truman saw Frank James and other surviving guerillas striding through the streets during their annual reunions in Independence; and as a youth he worked in the mailing room of the Kansas City *Star*, when Nelson was still in his prime.

The remarkably intense and sometimes violent character of Kansas City's past can well be traced to its geographical position. It stands where the nation's two historic borderlines cross one another. In its early days it was the jumping-off place where the mountain men and Santa Fé traders said good-by to the known and more or less civilized United States; for beyond lay the wild country of the Great American Desert. Kansas City, therefore, was nurtured by the East, but it was literally the place where the West began. It stands squarely, too, on the border between North and South; and because of the decision as to whether newly claimed lands should be slave or free, the countryside was bloody ground even before John Brown came to Ossawatomie. Most of the forces that have disturbed this nation have surged into Kansas City, and very often have met there opposing forces driving in from another quarter. These were the currents of change and conflict that account for much of Kansas City's behavior.

Probably the city today can be described as full grown, and for the time being somewhat quietly disposed toward the march of events. Living influences of the past have dimmed, though they endure in symbols—a legend for Frank James, an art museum for Nelson, a park for Colonel Swope. There are those who mourn the passing of the river boats and regret the end of the day when the cattleman was king and one could stare wide-eyed at a two-gun marshal in the Marble Hall. Others are looking forward to new developments and new movements already gathering force, which will dominate the city on the Missouri bluffs.

Sources and Acknowledgments

THE RECOLLECTIONS OF John C. McCoy, mentioned in several places in the text, originally were published in the Kansas City *Journal,* and are now available in the library which is maintained by the Kansas City Native Sons' Society on the twenty-sixth floor of the City Hall.

Description of Senator Thomas Hart Benton's appearance, dress and demeanor is from several articles which have been published by the *Missouri Historical Review,* and which are indexed in the *Review's* twenty-five-year index. Material was also taken from municipal histories and the biographies of Benton written by W. M. Meigs and Theodore Roosevelt.

The facts concerning Kit Carson and John C. Frémont are mainly from their respective recollections. Carson's autobiography was discovered in 1926. It was published that year in Santa Fe, New Mexico, with Blanche C. Grant as the editor, and in 1935 was published by the Lakeside Press of Chicago, with Milo Milton Quaife as the editor. The local facts interspersed with the movements of Frémont and Carson are from the official histories of Howard and Jackson counties. I also received help from *Kit Carson Days*, by Edwin L. Sabin.

For the origins of Kansas City, I relied on *The History of Kansas City* (1880), by W. H. Miller. Another source was *A Civic History of Kansas City*, by Roy Ellis. I was helped by a number of newspaper features on the city's beginnings and by personal recollections which from time to time have been placed on file in the Kansas City Public Library.

The facts concerning John Brown are from *John Brown after Fifty Years*, by Oswald Garrison Villard, which also contains a good summation of the struggle in Kansas. Most of the facts concerning Quantrill are from *Quantrill and the Border Wars*, by W. E. Connelley. Information concerning the guerilla fighting around Kansas City is from the recollections of John McCorkle and Cole Younger. For surrounding incidents, I consulted the Missouri histories written by Floyd C. Shoemaker and Walter Williams, and by Frederic Arthur Culmer, and I consulted all the books in Culmer's bibliography. The descriptions of the Battle of Baxter Springs and the Battle of Centralia are from newspaper interviews with Frank James, and the recollections of other guerillas. That concerning the Battle of Westport is from *The Battle of Westport*, by Paul Jenkins.

There are two good biographies of George Caleb Bingham, one written by Fern Helen Rusk and the other by Albert Christ-Janer. I received help from these books, but especially relied on Bingham's letters. These letters have been published almost in full by the *Missouri Historical Review* (Volume 32, beginning on pages 3, 165, 340 and 484, and Volume 33, beginning on pages 45, 203, 349 and 499), with good notes by C. B. Rollins. I am indebted to Floyd C. Shoemaker, secretary of the State Historical Society of Missouri at Columbia, for direction to the letters, and to Mrs. Ruth Rollins Westfall of Columbia for permission to quote from them. Bingham's letters were discovered in 1926 by the Rollins family.

The information concerning Frank and Jesse James is largely

from newspaper clippings, a great number of which are collected in *The Crittenden Memoirs,* compiled by H. H. Crittenden. I also received help from *The Rise and Fall of Jesse James,* by Robertus Love. The facts concerning Colonel Kersey Coates are from newspaper features, from *In Memoriam,* by Laura Coates Reed, and from municipal histories describing the city's railroad development. Information concerning Eugene Field, in addition to that provided by Slason Thompson's biography and other standard sources, was obtained from the Kansas City *Globe* for January 1, 1890; from the Kansas City *Post,* for January 2, 1916; from the files of the Kansas City *Times* when Field was its editor, and from the reminiscences carried in Kansas City and St. Louis newspapers at the time of Field's death. For access to the recollections of Field in the Kansas City *Post,* I am indebted to the Kansas State Historical Society of Topeka.

Facts concerning Arthur E. Stilwell are largely from his own recollections, especially a series of articles which was published by the *Saturday Evening Post* in late 1927 and early 1928. The brief sketches of the development of the grain and cattle industries are based on standard historical sources, especially the recollections of Joseph G. McCoy, concerning the beginnings of the cattle trade.

Concerning Nelson, I received help from the two biographies of him, one written in collaboration by the employees of the *Star,* and the other by Icie F. Johnson; from the older members of the *Star's* staff who had worked under Nelson, and who both gave me their recollections and directed me to material taken from the files of the *Star;* from the writings of William Allen White, and from a number of magazine articles which were published in Nelson's time. For direction to the court and newspaper record concerning Nelson's being cited for contempt of court, I am indebted to James P. Aylward, law partner of the late Frank P. Walsh, and to Jerome Walsh, the attorney's son.

All the information about the Pendergasts is from newspaper files, from personal recollections and from current information. The manuscript for this book was completed before the appearance of William M. Reddig's *Tom's Town* and Maurice Milligan's *Inside Story of the Pendergast Machine,* both of which can be highly recommended for a more detailed report on the machine's operations. The description of the trial of Jesse James, Jr., is from the *Star* for October 12, 1898, and subsequent issues following up the story. The facts about Colonel Thomas H. Swope are from newspaper features, concerning him and Swope Park. The information relating to the Swope murder trials is from the testimony given at the trials and before the grand jury, and from the statement left by Dr. G. T. Twyman. I am indebted to James P. Aylward for the use of his transcript of the Swope testimony.

The facts concerning Thomas Hart Benton are from his autobiography, *An Artist in America;* from conversations with him, and from the writings of Thomas Craven, who is Benton's long-time friend and critic, and who is also from Missouri. I was especially helped by an article by Mr. Craven which appeared in *Scribner's Magazine,* for October, 1937.

Index

Books that Live

The Norton imprint on a book means that in the publisher's estimation it is a book not for a single season but for the years.

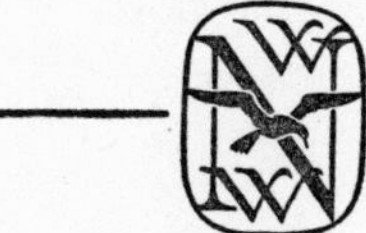

W · W · NORTON & CO · INC ·

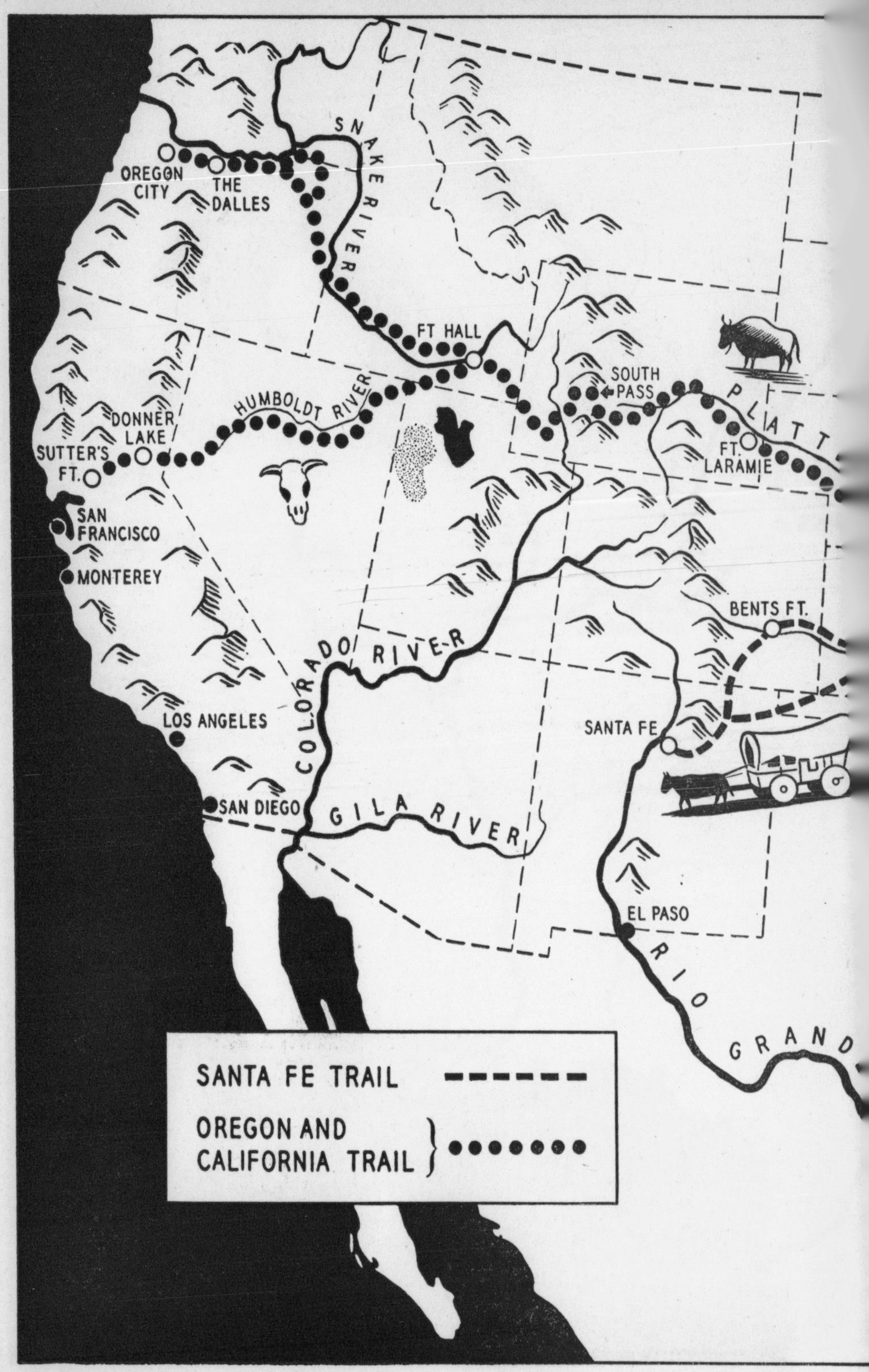

OREGON CITY
THE DALLES
SNAKE RIVER
FT HALL
SOUTH PASS
PLATT
FT. LARAMIE
HUMBOLDT RIVER
DONNER LAKE
SUTTER'S FT.
SAN FRANCISCO
MONTEREY
BENTS FT.
COLORADO RIVER
LOS ANGELES
SANTA FE
SAN DIEGO
GILA RIVER
EL PASO
RIO GRAND
SANTA FE TRAIL
OREGON AND CALIFORNIA TRAIL